F F
ISLAMIC ECONOMICS

Dedicated

to

those noble souls who are tirelessly engaged in the struggle for a world free from exploitation.

Sayyid Abul A'lā Mawdūdī

FIRST PRINCIPLES OF ISLAMIC ECONOMICS

Edited by
Khurshid Ahmad

Translated by
Ahmad Imam Shafaq Hashemi

THE ISLAMIC FOUNDATION

Published by
THE ISLAMIC FOUNDATION,
Markfield Conference Centre,
Ratby Lane, Markfield, Leicestershire
LE67 9SY, United Kingdom
E-mail: publications@islamic-foundation.com
Website: www.islamic-foundation.com

Quran House, PO Box 30611, Nairobi, Kenya

PMB 3193, Kano, Nigeria

Distributed by
KUBE PUBLISHING LTD.
Tel: +44(0)1530 249230, Fax: +44(0)1530 249656
E-mail: info@kubepublishing.com

Cataloguing-in-Publication Data is available
from the British Library

ISBN: 978-0-86037-482-4 *casebound*
ISBN: 978-0-86037-492-3 *paperback*

Typeset by: N.A.Qaddoura
Cover design by: Nasir Cadir

بسم الله الرحمن الرحيم

Contents

Transliteration Table xii
Foreword xiii
Translator's Note xxxvi
Author's Preface xxxviii
Introduction xxxix

PART ONE
THE ISLAMIC CONCEPT OF ECONOMIC WELL-BEING

1. Mankind's Economic Problems and Their Islamic Solutions 3
1.1. The problem of a partial approach 4
1.2. The real issue 7
1.3. The root cause of economic mismanagement 9
1.4. Self-aggrandizement and luxuries 9
1.5. Capital worship 11
1.6. The element of antagonistic competition 12
1.7. Cartels and monopolies 13
1.8. The recipe of communism 15
1.8.1. The super capitalist 15
1.8.2. An exploitative system 15
1.8.3. Slaughter of the self 16
1.9. The fascist solution 17
1.10. The Islamic solution 17
1.10.1. Basic rules 17
1.10.2. Earning money 18
1.10.3. Ownership rights 19
1.10.3.1. Rule for spending money 19
1.10.3.2. Eliminating the capitalist trend 19
1.10.3.3. Circulation of wealth and social security 20
1.11. Points to ponder 22

2. Economic Teachings of the Qur'ān 24

2.1. Fundamental truths 24
2.2. Parameters of permissible and impermissible 25
2.3. Parameters of private ownership 26
2.4. Irrational concept of economic parity 30
2.5. Monasticism or moderation and balance 33
2.6. Distinction between *Ḥalāl* and *Ḥarām* means of livelihood 34
2.7. Forbidden means of livelihood 35
2.8. Prohibition of stinginess and hoarding 38
2.9. Lust for money and greediness 39
2.10. Unchecked spending 39
2.11. Correct way of spending money 41
2.12. Reparation for sinful transgressions 43
2.13. Preconditions for the Divine Acceptability of charity 43
2.14. Charity in the Way of Allah 45
2.15. Collection and distribution of *Zakāh* 48
2.16. One-fifth of revenue from war gains 49
2.17. Disbursement of *Zakāh* funds 50
2.18. Division of inheritance 50
2.19. The will 52
2.20. Rights of those of weaker understanding 52
2.21. Safeguarding public interest in state holdings 53
2.22. Guiding principle about taxation 57
2.23. Salient features of Islamic economics – a resume 57
2.24. Index of source material 60

3. The Differences between Islam and Capitalism 61

3.1. Distinction between lawful and forbidden means of livelihood 61
3.1.1. Bribery and embezzlement 62
3.1.2 Breach of trust and misappropriation of funds, public or private 62
3.1.3. Theft and burglary 63
3.1.4. Mishandling of the orphan's property 63
3.1.5. Fraudulent transactions/disregard of weights and measures 63
3.1.6. Trading in immorality and all means of obscenity and promiscuousness 64
3.1.7. Income generated through the sex trade, brothels, adultery or fornication 64

3.1.8. The production, sale, transportation and marketing of alcoholic beverages 65
3.1.9. Gambling, betting, lottery and all means of income based not on one's labour but on chance 65
3.1.10. Idol-making trading in idols and serving in temples 65
3.1.11. Fortune-telling and soothsaying 66
3.1.12. Usury and all forms of interest-based transactions 66
3.2. The accumulation of wealth 67
3.3. Money is to spend 67
3.4. *Zakāh* 73
3.5. Law of inheritance 76
3.6. War gains and division of the conquered land's revenue 76
3.7. Injunctions about economy and balance 78

4. The Economic Philosophy of Islam 81
4.1. Basic values of the economic philosophy of Islam 81
4.1.1. Social justice 81
4.1.2. Equitable economic system 82
4.1.3. People-friendly political system 82
4.1.4. Equality of opportunity 82
4.2. Eight fundamental principles of the economic philosophy of Islam 83
4.2.1. First principle: General accessibility of the bounties of nature 83
4.2.2. Second principle: The right to make a living 83
4.2.3. Third principle: The right to ownership 83
4.2.4. Fourth principle: The spirit of healthy competition 84
4.2.5. Fifth principle: No artificial way to enforce equality 84
4.2.6. Sixth principle: No 'free economy' 85
4.2.7. Seventh principle: Duties obligatory upon individuals 85
4.2.8. Eighth principle: Duties obligatory upon society 86

5. The Principles and Objectives of Islam's Economic System 87
5.1. Basics of the Islamic economic system 87
5.2. The objectives of Islamic economics 88
5.2.1. Personal freedom 88
5.2.2. Harmony in moral and material progress 89
5.2.3. Promotion of cooperation, harmony and justice 90

5.3. Basic principles of Islam's economic system 91
5.3.1. Parameters of private ownership 91
5.3.2. Equitable distribution of wealth 92
5.3.3. Social obligations 94
5.3.4. *Zakāh* 96
5.3.5. Law of inheritance 97
5.4. Position of labour, capital, and organization 98
5.5. *Zakāh* and social welfare 99
5.6. Interest-free economy 100
5.7. Interrelationship between economic, political and social systems 101

6. Some Principles of Economic Life 103
6.1. Basic values of Islamic society 103
6.2. The Islamic path of moral and economic rejuvenation 105
6.3. The concept of earning and spending 107
6.4. Principles of spending 109
6.5. Principles of moderation and balance 111
6.6. Economic honesty and justice 112
6.7. Distributive justice 113

PART TWO
THE ECONOMIC SYSTEM OF ISLAM: SOME BASIC FEATURES

7. The Question of Land Ownership 119
7.1. The Holy Qur'ān and the question of private ownership 119
7.2. Precedents of the Holy Prophet and his Caliphs 122
7.2.1. First category of land 122
7.2.2. Second category of land 124
7.2.3. Third category of land 126
7.2.4. Fourth category of land 128
7.3. Ownership rights on the basis of settlement 129
7.4. Award of state lands 132
7.5. The *Sharīʿah* perspective on the award of state lands 134
7.6. Feudal estates and Islamic *Sharīʿah* 135
7.7. Respect for ownership rights 136
7.8. Islamic social order and private ownership 138
7.9. The question of delimitation of agricultural land 140
7.10. Sharecropping between landlord and farmer 141
7.11. Principles of property management 142

8. The Question of Interest 144
8.1. Islamic injunctions concerning interest 144
8.1.1 Meaning of *Ribā* 144
8.1.2. *Ribā* of the Days of Ignorance 146
8.1.3. Basic difference between *Ribā* and *Bay*ʿ 146
8.1.4. Rationale for prohibition 148
8.1.5. Strict nature of the ban 149
8.2. Need for interest: a rational reassessment 150
8.2.1. Compensation for elements of risk and sacrifice 150
8.2.2. Compensation for opportunity and grace period 154
8.2.3. Sharing of profit 155
8.2.4. Compensation for time 156
8.2.5. Reasonableness of an interest rate 158
8.2.6. Rationale for varying rates of interest? 160
8.3. 'Economic benefits' of interest? 162
8.4. Need and utility of interest? 164
8.5. Demerits of interest 167
8.6. Economic growth without interest 171
8.6.1. Some misunderstood facts 171
8.6.2. First step towards reform 174
8.6.3. End result of a ban on interest 175
8.7. Availability of loans in an interest-free system 177
8.7.1. For personal needs 177
8.7.2. For commercial purposes 179
8.7.3. For non-productive public sector needs 180
8.7.4. International lending 181
8.7.5. Capital needs of profit-making projects 182
8.8. Islamic modes of banking 184
8.9. Economic and industrial loans from non-Muslim countries 187

9. *Zakāh* in Theory and Practice 189
9.1. Essence of *Zakāh* 189
9.1.1. Meaning 189
9.1.2. Apostolic tradition 189
9.2. *Zakāh*'s place in social life 192
9.3. The Divine Command concerning *Zakāh* 197
9.4. Various categories of *Zakāh* distribution 199
9.4.1. *Al-Fuqarā*' 199
9.4.2. *Al-Masākīn* 200

9.4.3. *Al-'Āmilīn* 200
9.4.4. *Mu'allafat'l-Qulūb* or 'those whose hearts are to be reconciled' 201
9.4.5. *Fī'l-Riqāb* or 'to free those in bondage' 201
9.4.6. *Al-Ghārimīn* or 'those burdened with debt' 201
9.4.7. *Fī-Sabīlillāh* or 'in the Way of Allah' 201
9.4.8. *Ibn al-Sabīl* or 'the Wayfarer' 202
9.5. Basic rules of *Zakāh* 204
9.6. Is any change possible in *Niṣāb* and the rate of *Zakāh*'s deduction? 220
9.7. Company shares and *Zakāh* 222
9.8. *Zakāh's* applicability in *Mushārakah* and *Muḍārabah* 225
9.9. Prescribed minimum limit for *Kunūz* (gold and silver) 226
9.10. The difference between *Zakāh* and tax 228
9.11. Is it permissible to levy income tax over and above *Zakāh*? 229

10. Islam and Social Justice 230
10.1. Falsehood in the garb of truth 230
10.1.1. Deception One: capitalism and secular democracy 230
10.1.2. Deception Two: social justice and communism 231
10.1.3. The modern Muslim's intellectual servility 231
10.2. Social justice in theory and practice 232
10.2.1. Islam alone guarantees social justice 233
10.2.2. Social justice: the goal before Islam 233
10.2.3. Growth and development of the human personality 234
10.2.4. Personal accountability 235
10.2.5. Individual freedom 235
10.2.6. Social institutions and their writ 236
10.3. Failings of capitalism and communism 237
10.4. Communism: the worst form of social oppression 237
10.5. Justice in Islam 239
10.5.1. Parameters of personal freedom 239
10.5.2. Preconditions for the transfer of wealth 240
10.5.3. Restrictions on the use of wealth 241
10.5.4. In service of the society 241
10.5.5. Eradication of injustice 241
10.5.6. Nationalization and public interest 242
10.5.7. Use of the public treasury (*Bayt al-Māl*) 242
10.5.8. The basic issue! 242

11. Issues of Labour, Insurance and Price Control 244
11.1. Labour-related issues and their solutions 244
11.1.1. What has caused the damage? 244
11.1.2. The real need 245
11.1.3. Resolution of problems 246
11.1.4. Agenda for reform 247
11.2. Insurance and measures for reform 252
11.3. The question of price control 255

12. Recodification of the Economic Laws of Islam 258
12.1. The constant and the variables 258
12.2. The need to modernize 260
12.3. Essential prerequisites for modernization of statutes and by-laws 261
12.3.1. First prerequisite 261
12.3.2. Second prerequisite 262
12.3.3. Third prerequisite 264
12.3.4. Fourth prerequisite 265
12.4. General rules of exception 267
12.5. Relaxation in the case of interest 269

Glossary 273
Short Biographies 279
Index 287

Transliteration Table

Arabic Consonants

Initial, unexpressed medial and final:

ء	'	د	d	ض	ḍ	ك	k
ب	b	ذ	dh	ط	ṭ	ل	l
ت	t	ر	r	ظ	ẓ	م	m
ث	th	ز	z	ع	ʿ	ن	n
ج	j	س	s	غ	gh	هـ	h
ح	ḥ	ش	sh	ف	f	و	w
خ	kh	ص	ṣ	ق	q	ي	y

Vowels, diphthongs, etc.

Short:	ـَ	a	ـِ	i	ـُ	u
Long:	ـَا	ā	ـِي	ī	ـُو	ū
Diphthongs:			ـَوْ	aw		
			ـَيْ	ay		

Foreword

The world today is in the grip of a devastating and protracted economic and financial crisis. What began with the collapse of Lehman Brothers in September 2008 has turned into a global catastrophe, shaking the very foundations of the capitalist system. The dominant paradigm of mainstream economics is also being increasingly challenged. If the fall of the Berlin Wall in November 1989 signalled the end of the seventy years' experiment with communism, the crisis that has engulfed the capitalist world has the potential to become an existential threat to capitalism, or at least to its present version of 'Market Fundamentalism', which represents the high watermark of a politico-economic experiment that has endured for over three centuries – a system whose advocates had begun to glibly claim it as 'the final destiny of mankind'.[1] Much seems to have been washed away by the powerful currents of this financial tsunami.

To have some idea of the magnitude and devastating consequences of this unending crisis, it may be worthwhile to reflect for a moment on some aspects of the predicament that has become the fate of humanity today. The leading British economist Roger Bootle describes the current state of the world economy as follows:

> From the events of 2007/9, it seems plain that the financial markets have not worked to promote the common weal, and they have caused, rather than absorbed, chaos and instability. [...] If the system can produce such wealth-destroying success for some, how can it work for our overall benefit? And if the financial markets are like this, then what about the rest of the market system?[2]

By October 2009, within the first years of the advent of the crisis, the International Monetary Fund reported that the global losses in the banking

---

[1] Fukuyama, Francis, *The End of History and the Last Man* (London: Hamilton, 1992).

[2] Bootle, Roger, *The Trouble with Markets: Saving Capitalism from Itself* (London/Boston: Nicholas Berkley Publishing, 2009), p.3.

sector alone were to the tune of $3.6 trillion.[3] From the start of 2008 to the spring of 2009, the crisis knocked $30 trillion off the value of global shares and $11 trillion off the values of homes in the United States. At their worst, these losses amounted to around 75 per cent of world GDP.[4] Philippe Legram observes, 'the collapse was more brutal than during the Great Depression. Within ten months of its peak in April 2008, world industrial production fell by an eighth and stock markets halved in value. In just three months, between November 2008 and February 2009, world trade plunged by a fifth.'[5] The governments and the central banks of the U.S., the U.K., and the Eurozone had to pledge a total of $8,955 billion to hold up the banks: $1,950 billion in liquidity support, $2,525 billion in asset purchases and $4,480 billion in guarantees.[6]

According to a World Bank and IMF Joint Report even though a recovery is underway the impact of the crisis will be lasting and immeasurable.[7] Programmes aimed at poverty reduction around the world will slow down. It is feared that some 20 million people in Sub-Sahara Africa and another 53 million globally will descend into an extreme poverty trap and that those already below the poverty line, some one billion unfortunate human beings, will face a serious erosion of their already miniscule purchasing power. Infant mortality will rise and the availability of safe water, primary education and medical care will nose dive. The conditions of life for the poor of the world will further deteriorate. Even in developed countries, loss of jobs and income are having a heavy toll. Official data show that some 16 million Americans have no jobs and over two million households in the US fear the forced loss of their homes. In the European Union some four million jobs have disappeared, pushing the number of the unemployed to 144 million. While trillions of dollars are being doled out to bailout banks, investment houses, and insurance tycoons, there is little concern for the households that are at the suffering end of this sordid mortgage scandal. The worst part of this obnoxious tale is that the victims, who had no role in driving the world into this crisis, have become the worst sufferers.

Noble Laureate Joseph Stieglitz laments the callous contrast one finds in the U.S. policy to provide massive $700 billion to bailout the banks while 'ignoring

---

[3] Stieglitz, Joseph, *Freefall: Free markets and the Sinking of the Global Economy* (London: Allen Lane, 2010), p.127

[4] Legram, Phillippe, *Aftershock: Reshaping the World Economy after the Crisis* (London: Little Brown, 2010), p.70.

[5] Ibid, p.71.

[6] Ibid, p.71.

[7] *Global Monitoring Report 2010: Achieving the MDGs in the Aftermath of the Global Economic Crisis*, Joint Report of the World Bank and International Monetary Fund.

the millions of homes going into foreclosure'.[8] The U.N. Secretary-General Ban Ki-Moon brings into sharp focus this catastrophic aspect of the crisis, which he rightly describes as a 'moral problem'. He says:

> The ranks of the global unemployed have grown by 34 million, and another 215 million women and men have become working poor. And, for the first time in history, more than one billion people are going hungry worldwide. The moral argument is clear. After all, those least responsible for the global economic meltdown have paid the highest price – in lost jobs, higher costs of living, growing community tensions as families struggle to make ends meet.[9]

Roger Bootle sums up this predicament of mankind in the following words:

> How did we reach the current ghastly position? My answer to this question is a tale of greed, illusion, and self-delusion on a massive scale. It not only reveals the truth about markets and economies, but also shines a torch on the nature of society – and on human nature itself. [10]

However dark, dismal and devastating the costs and consequences are of this global crisis, there is a silver lining on the horizon in the form of serious efforts on the part of an increasing number of intellectuals to revisit the foundations on which the contemporary economic system is built. This crisis has exposed its feet of clay. It does not merely reveal a crisis of the financial system. In fact it has revealed many other dimensions in the forms of a *crisis of economy*, a *crisis of economics*, a *crisis of society* and ultimately a *crisis of civilization*. These crises have become a wake-up call for a number of economists and social thinkers to revisit the fundamentals of their disciplines, to get out of the safe cocoons into which many specialists have retreated, and to explore the root causes of the malaise that afflicts the world economy. It has also prompted people to search for alternatives – some seeking ways out *within* the dominant paradigm of economic thought and economy, and others endeavouring to search for a *new* paradigm – not a mere shift *within* the paradigm but a shift *of* the paradigm. Humanity today stands at a new threshold, seeking fresh avenues to move towards a new world order.

---

[8] Stieglitz, *Freefall*, p.30.

[9] 'Accounting for Success', 21 June 2010, http://www.un.org/sg/articleFull.asp?TID=118&Type=Op-Ed, accessed 21 March 2011.

[10] Bootle, *The Trouble with Markets*, p.4.

Paul Volcker surmises that 'the nature and depth of the financial crisis is forcing us to reconsider some of the basic tenets of financial theory'.[11] Will Hutton, the economic editor of the London *Guardian*, says, 'The financial crisis challenges the assumptions we had about how the world is organized and shows that free market fundamentalism was a huge intellectual mistake.'[12]

Nobel Laureate Paul Krugman raises some fundamental issues about the discipline and practice of economics in a number of articles: 'Few economists saw our current crisis coming, but this predictive failure was the least of the field's problems. More important was the professional blindness to the very possibility of catastrophic failure in a market economy.'[13] Krugman complains of a 'hole in the heart of macro-economics'. He also records the confessions of Allen Greenspan, a key architect of America's policies of economic liberalism, who had to admit in 0ctober 2008 that he was in a state of 'shocked disbelief' because 'the whole intellectual edifice' of global capitalism seemed to have 'collapsed'.

The *Economist* has tried to capture this state of intellectual bewilderment in one of its editorials when it said, 'of all the economic bubbles that have been pricked, few have burst more spectacularly than the reputation of economics itself'.[14] It is being admitted in serious discussions that the 'efficient market hypothesis' has fallen to pieces. George Soros has come up with strong critiques of 'Market Fundamentalism' in all of his recent books and articles. In his book on *Globalization*, he said:

> [H]umans are capable of transcending the pursuit of narrow self-interest. Indeed, they cannot live without some sense of morality. It is market fundamentalism, which holds that the social good is best served by allowing people to pursue their self-interest without any thought for the social good – the two being identical – that is perversion of human nature.[15]

Soros has established at the Central European University in Budapest an 'Initiative for New Economic Thinking' which is sponsoring research on developing new approaches to economics, making the discipline relevant to the

---

[12] Hutton, Will, 'Thanks to the Credit Crunch, All Bets are Off', *The Guardian*, 2 March 2009.

[13] Krungman, Paul, 'How Did Economics Got 1t Wrong', *The New York Times*, 6 September 2009.

[14] Editorial, *The Economist*, July 18th 2009. See also: 'Onwards and Upwards', *The Economist*, 19 December 2009.

[15] Soros, George, *Globalization* (New York: PublicAffairs, 2002), quoted by Joseph E. Stieglitz, 'A Fair Deal for The World', *The New York Review of Books*, 23 May 2002.

current needs of human society and serve the objectives of justice and human well-being.[16]

Edward Conway claims, 'Following its failure to fix the current mess, economics has tumbled into a full-blown existential crisis.' The increasing scepticism about the irrelevance of most of the economic models to the current reality paves the way for search for fresh thoughts and approaches. According to Conway:

> In the future, markets will be less free; there will be more regulation; the state will be more interventionist. Taxes may become more redistributive. But from the ashes of the crisis may come a new understanding of how to run an economy that is both more successful and more stable, than the failed models of the past.[17]

Roger Bootle, among others, has challenged the very concept of *homo economicus* and of market mechanism as the sole arbiter of economic decision-making. He says:

> There is no doubt that *homo economicus* [as the self-interested, rational individual] is a simplifying assumption [in contemporary paradigms of economics] that yields results of analytical value and frequent applicability. But as an attempt at a total description of what drives human beings, there is also no doubt that it is profoundly misleading. There are two problems: the first concerns rationality and the second concerns motivation.[18]

After exposing the hollowness of these oversimplified concepts and the flawed analyses and policies emanating from them Roger Bootle comes to the conclusion that the 'key villain' is 'the subject of economics itself' and emphasizes a pressing need for 'a radical reshaping of the way economics and finance are studied and taught'.[19] He makes a dispassionate plea that:

> Economics must be rooted in an acknowledgment of what it is to be human, both as regards how human beings can be assumed to behave and the values by which their activity should be judged. *Homo economicus* needs to be laid to rest – for good.'[20]

---

[16] Stieglitz, Joseph E. and George Akerlof, 'A New Economics in an Imperfect World', *The Guardian*, 28 October 2009. See also: Andrews, Alex, 'Praying for a Revolution in Economics', *The Guardian*, 11 July 2009.

[17] *The Daily Times*, 31 July 2009.

[18] Bootle, *The Trouble with Markets*, pp.79-80.

[19] Ibid, p.232.

[20] Ibid, p.236.

A similar warning has also come from Anatole Kalatsky, who is also pleading for the birth of a new economics:

> Economics today is a discipline that must either die or undergo a paradigm shift – to make itself both more broad-minded and more modest. It must broaden its horizons to recognize the insights of other social sciences and historical studies and it must return to its roots. [...] Either economics will reform itself quickly or the funeral will be for the discipline as a whole.[21]

Joseph Stieglitz also argues strongly for the reform of economics. He is convinced that some of the major causes for the crisis and injustices and contradictions in the world economy can be traced to the concepts and policy prescriptions of economics as a self-contained discipline, based on a set of assumptions about human nature, economic processes and incentives, market mechanism and the ethos of capitalism that characterizes the modern economy. In his latest work, *Freefall*, he devotes a chapter to 'Reforming Economics' as an essential ingredient to a reconstruction of the economic order. He is of the view that 'as we peel back the layers of "what went wrong" we cannot escape looking at the economics profession'. He is of the firm view that 'if the United States is going to succeed in reforming its economy, it may have to begin by reforming economics'.[22] Stieglitz, after highlighting various key aspects responsible for the failure of the conventional paradigm of economics characterised by self-interest, profit motive, market mechanism, free trade and minimum state intervention, emphasizes the urgent need for a fundamental review of these concepts. He challenges the whole vision of *homo economicus*, the very bedrock of a capitalistic economy. 'Most of us', he surmises, 'would not like to think that we conform to the view of man that underlies prevailing economic models, which is of a calculating rational self-serving, and self-interested individual. There is no room for human empathy, public spiritedness, or altruism.'[23]

He makes a plea for rethinking fundamentals and reformulating key concepts in economics. He also suggests that economists have to be responsive to the needs and aspirations of society. Human longing for a new just order cannot be ignored for long. An effort to rediscover and re-establish the relevance of ethics and morality to economic concepts and policy parameters will have to be an essential part of this exercise. The message of the current crisis is to reconstruct

---

[21] Kalatsky, Anatole, *Capitalism 4.0: The Birth of a New Economy* (London: Bloomsbury, 2010), pp.185-186.

[22] Stiglitz, *Freefall*, p.238.

[23] bid, p. 249

economics to serve the objectives of justice and well-being and not to serve the mere aggrandisement of wealth and power. Stieglitz makes a fervent plea for a new economics and a new society.

Stieglitz's concluding observation deserves serious reflection:

> It is said that a near-death experience forces one to re-evaluate priorities and values. The global economy has just had a near-death experience. The crisis exposed not only flaws in the prevailing economic model but also flaws in our society. Too many people had taken advantage of others. [...] The unrelenting pursuit of profits and the elevation of the pursuit of self-interest may not have created the prosperity that was hoped, but they did help create the moral deficit.[24]

There is a universal urge to develop a more value-based approach to the economic and political problems that beset man and society. The objective should be the establishment of a just and socially responsible world order. This calls for a new approach to life, its challenges and prospects. What is needed is a more integrated and holistic approach to all our problems, keeping in view the moral, social, cultural, spiritual, political, economic and cultural needs and aspirations of mankind. The shift of emphasis from machine to mind, from money to man, from means to ends, represents a qualitative shift in the global human situation. This brings the moral question to the centre of the debate and consequently concerns for justice become the ultimate objective, as against exclusive obsession with material affluence, physical development, and efficiency without reference to equity, as has been the case under the shade of conventional economics and the capitalist economic order.

Robert Fogel, winner of the 1993 Nobel Prize for Economics addresses this issue in his work *The Fourth Great Awakening and the Future of Egalitarianism.* His formulation of the real problem is succinct and perceptive. In his words:

> At the dawn of the new millennium, the critical issues are no longer, whether we can manage business cycles or whether the economy is likely to grow at a satisfactory rate. It is not even whether we can grow without sacrificing the egalitarian advances of the past century. [...] Spiritual (or immaterial) inequity is now as great a problem as material inequity, perhaps even greater.[25]

---

24 Ibid, pp.275, 278.

25 Fogel, Robert, W., *The Fourth Great Awakening and the Future of Egalitarianism,* (Chicago/London: University of Chicago Press, 2000), p.1.

Fogel emphasizes that:

> In a world that our grandchildren will inherit will be materially richer and contain fewer environmental ills. [...] Ethical issues will be at the centre of intellectual life and engagement with those issues will form a large part of the fabric of daily life than is the case today. The democratisation of intellectual life will broaden debate and insinuate spiritual issues more deeply into political life.[26]

The current financial and economic crisis has opened up new vistas for human reflection, dialogue and discourse, research and experimentation, and transformation and reconstruction of a better world. We have wasted too much breath on 'clash of civilizations'. It is time, instead, to give some serious thought to the *crisis of civilization* that has become the predicament of man in the contemporary world. It is a challenge that humans face in all parts of the world. It is time to look into all the resources that are available to mankind in its search for a brighter future.

Muslims constitute one fifth of the human race. There are 1.6 billion Muslims in the world today – some 1.1 billion in 57 independent Muslim states and 500 million in over 100 communities in the rest of the world. While there is a concentration of Muslim populations in countries in Western, Central and South-East Asia and in large parts of Africa, Muslims are a part of the demographic landscape of the entire world. With over 35 million Muslims in Europe and more than seven million in North America, Islam is the second largest religion in Europe and America. Fifty-seven Muslim states straddle over 23 per cent of the land surface of the world. Strategic land, air, and sea routes pass through the Muslim world and there is strong interdependence between the Muslim countries and the rest.

In the main, Muslim countries are resource rich, but they presently lag behind in economic and industrial capabilities. They have huge financial resources, but are weak in the fields of technology, management, and the advanced modes of production. Around 13 per cent of Muslim countries' trade takes place amongst themselves, and 87 per cent with the rest of the world. This shows their strong linkages with the global economy. It may also be noted that while most of the Muslim countries today belong to the group of developing countries, five are in the high human development group, twenty-five in the middle human development group and the rest in the low human development group.

The Muslim world was a global economic power for several centuries, and it was not until the time of the Western Enlightenment that economic

---

[26] Ibid, p.242.

stagnation or decline began to occur; and this lasted for more than 300 years. The re-emergence of the Muslim world as a powerful political and economic force is a recent phenomenon, and a lot of critical thinking is now examining what originally went wrong and how the Muslim world can set its house back in order. The rediscovery of its moral and ideological roots is a critical part of this exercise. The Muslim *Ummah* is passing through a very crucial phase in its history. This is not something new, as its entire history is characterized by challenges and responses. This is inevitable. A message as universal and eternal as Islam can neither avoid crisis nor can it escape phases of depression and renewal, nor, in some cases, even disintegration and reconsolidation. In fact, it is unavoidable in view of the Divine arrangement for humans, which is characterized by the endowment of freedom and discretion. Built into the Islamic scheme are elements that are unchangeable, and, as such, they constitute reference points for the system at all times. Along with these are elements that are flexible and changeable, albeit that these remain within the Divinely-laid ethos of the system.

Today's situation has many similarities with the scenario at the beginning of the twentieth century, notwithstanding some significant differences. By the end of the nineteenth century, the Muslim *Ummah*, which had played a distinguished role as a world power for over a millennium, was then totally overwhelmed by the forces of decay from within and the onslaught of European imperialism from without. The power-equation changed to the utter disadvantage of the Muslim world. It had far-reaching consequences for the entire realm of Muslim civilization. Western imperial powers represented a new civilizational paradigm. The expansionist role of the tutelary powers that vitiated the Muslim civilization's hold on social dynamics defined its predicament: it lost its leading edge in knowledge and technology, its economy went into shambles, and its political power was eclipsed. Even morally, culturally and intellectually it went into a tailspin. The lowest point was the abolition of what was left of the symbolic *khilāfah* in 1924.

This was the context in which a number of Muslim luminaries all over the world addressed themselves to the crucial question of what had gone wrong with the Muslim *Ummah*. Had Islam become irrelevant or was there something wrong with various Muslim approaches to Islam and its role in history? What should be the agenda for making Islam a major influence in the struggle for liberation from the colonial yoke and to reconstruct Muslim society on its own foundations? The purpose of all this effort was to reset the *Ummah* along the road to revival and reconstruction. Jamāl al-Dīn Afghānī, Amīr Shakīb Arsalān, Prince Ḥalīm Pāshā, Sa'īd Nūrsī, Muḥammad Iqbāl, Rashīd Riḍā', Muḥammad

'Abduh, Ḥasan al-Bannā, Abul Kalām Āzād, Sayyid Abul A'lā Mawdūdī, Mālik bin Nabī and a host of other intellectuals and reformers reflected on these questions and came up with positive responses to steer the *Ummah* out of the quagmire it was steeped in.

In this galaxy of thinkers and reformers, Sayyid Mawdūdī occupies a distinct position. At the age of only 17, he took upon his shoulders the task of rebuilding the Muslim *Ummah* in 1920. After 10 years of journalistic encounters, he devoted himself to the uphill task of reconstructing Muslim thought and to establish a movement for socio-political change to pilot the *Ummah*'s march towards a new world order. His aim was to develop a roadmap for the *Ummah*'s revival, something that could also be a blessing for humanity. The publication of *al-Jihād fī al-Islām* (*Law of War and Peace in Islam*) in 1929 was his first major contribution. And thereafter until his death on 22 September 1979, he authored over 140 books and tracts on Islam, covering almost every aspect of its thought and historic experience. His greatest work is a six-volume exegesis of the Qur'an – *Tafhīm al-Qur'ān* – spanning several thousand pages.[27]

Besides his articulation and reconstruction of Islamic thought, Sayyid Mawdūdī developed a critique of the Muslim society, identifying the causes and processes that had led to its decline and decay. He also came up with a powerful critique of the Western civilization, of its worldview, its vision of man, society and economy, and its achievements and failures. He was not oblivious to the positive dimensions of the Western civilization and the ideologies and movements that sprang from its womb. But, at the same time, he was critical of its intellectual confusions, its flawed concepts of man, religion and society, its moral dilemmas, its political and cultural deformities and its economic injustices and exploitations. His thought has influenced three generations of Muslims the world over. His works has been translated in over forty languages. It is small wonder that he is considered as one of the chief architects of the contemporary Islamic resurgence.

Sayyid Mawdūdī was a religious scholar, a social thinker and a political activist. His main contribution, first and foremost, lies in the reconstruction of Islamic thought, drawing on its original sources, yet in a manner that focuses on its relevance to our own times. He presents Islam as a complete way of life. Its message is to change humans from within, to refine and develop them spiritually and morally, and to mobilize these transformed men and women to

---

[27] The English translation of this monumental work is being published by the Islamic Foundation, Leicester under the title *Towards Understanding the Qur'ān*. Ten out of 18 volumes in total have been published at the time of writing.

reconstruct not only their own lives but also human society and civilization in the light of the worldview, values, principles and ideals spelled out in Divine revelation and the model of life and society demonstrated by Allah's prophets in general, and more specifically in the life and teachings of the last Prophet Muhammad (*pbuh*).

Sayyid Mawdūdī has written on almost all aspects of Islamic thought and practice. He has emphasized that Islam is a complete way of life, covering all dimensions of human life and activity. Islam is also a universal religion and the Muslim *Ummah* is a global community. Faith (*Īmān*) is the foundation and defines the true nature of Islam, its culture and civilization. The Muslim *Ummah* is a faith-based community. *Tawḥīd* (the Oneness of God) establishes the unity of the universe, the oneness of humanity, the indivisibility of life and the universality of Islamic laws and values. Islam is not the religion of any particular nation, people, ethnic group, linguistic or territorial entity. Islam does not claim to be a new religion either. It stands for Divine Guidance, provided by the Creator of mankind through all His prophets from the moment life began on the earth. In that sense, Islam has been the religion of all Godly prophets and their followers. Indeed, Muslims believe in all the prophets from Adam through Noah, Abraham, Moses, and Jesus to Muḥammad (peace be upon them all).

Islam literally means 'peace' and 'submission'. It stands for faith in God, as the only object of worship and obedience. It stands for faith in His Prophet as a model and source of guidance. It demands a firm commitment, among its followers, to live in obedience to the Divine Will and guidance. *Sharīʿah* (literally, the Path) is a set of norms, values, and laws that go to make up the landscape of Islamic way of life.

Islam believes in freedom of choice and does not permit any coercion in matters of faith and religion. It spells out a genuinely pluralistic religious and cultural landscape for mankind. It is by free will and dialogue that ideological borders can be crossed. Acceptance of each other, despite differences, is a cardinal principle of Islam. Islam concerns all aspects of human life – faith and worship, spirit and matter, personality and character, individual and society, economy and community, national and international concerns. However, overarching these aspects is its moral approach to life and the universe. The physical and the secular have been brought together under the umbrella of the spiritual and the sacred. It does not exclude the worldly dimension; it does not pit the secular against the sacred. Rather, it integrates all dimensions of life under one moral and spiritual regime. The Islamic approach, therefore, is primarily a moral and ideological approach directed towards all human beings, irrespective of faith, colour, creed, language, or territory. It regards plurality of cultures and religions as genuine and respectable. There is also diversity within the Muslim *Ummah*. Islam does not stand for any artificial unity, forced conformity, or syncretism. It provides an authentic base for coexistence and co-operation.

Another important aspect of the Islamic faith and civilization relates to its emphasis on values, which are absolute and universal, and the identification of certain key institutions, which act as permanent pillars for the system on the one hand, and on the other hand there is a vast area of flexibility, which could cater for the demands of changing times. While its value framework is based on human nature and universal realities, it also acknowledges the need to work out details and develop modalities for the application of this value framework in the context of changing political, economic, and cultural scenarios. While Islam provides an overall regulatory mechanism, it avoids rigid instructions in respect of detailed human formulations. It regards the individual as the cornerstone of society, indeed of all creation. Each individual is personally accountable to God. As such, individuals are not merely cogs in the social machine. Society, state, nation and humanity are all important and each has a specific role to play, yet final accountability rests upon the individual. This ensures the centrality of the individual in the Islamic system. Yet it also relates the individual to the society and its institutions and promotes a balanced network of relations between them.

Islamic morality is based on the concept of fulfilment in life and not the denial of life. It is through moral discipline that all dimensions of human activity become part of virtuous conduct. Personal piety and public morality contribute towards the enrichment of life and the pursuit of personal and social well-being and welfare for all. Wealth is not a dirty word; in fact, wealth creation is a desirable goal, subject only to moral values and social imperatives. A good life (*Ḥayāt al-Ṭayyibah*) is one of the major objectives of human pursuit. Welfare in this world and welfare in the life-to-come are co-dependent, representing two sides of the same coin. It is this spiritualisation of the whole secular realm, and encasement of the entire gamut of worldly life and activities within a moral framework, that enables human beings to seek simultaneously to fulfil their own needs and to create a society wherein the needs of all are also fulfilled. Individual freedom, the right to property and enterprise, the market mechanism, and distributive justice are inalienable parts of the economic framework of Islam. However, there are moral filters at different levels – individual motivation, personal behaviour, social mores and manners, employer–employee conduct, and individual–state relationships that keep the economic processes within a wider framework that ensures equity and welfare in society. The state has a positive role to play, particularly in the nature of supervision, guidance, and essential regularisation; and yet it also has to ensure freedom, economic opportunity, and property rights.

Islam emphasizes a more needs-oriented approach, and is committed to establishing a society in which the basic necessities of life are ensured for all members of the human race, primarily through personal effort, and reward-orientated activity, but to cater for these in an environment in which those who are disadvantaged are helped to live an honourable life and to become active participants in society. While Islam emphasizes wealth creation, its real focus is on moral excellence, spiritual bliss, and the creation of a just and egalitarian society where genuine equality of opportunity exists for all. This is only possible if society provides effective support for the weaker members of the community. This is done both through the institution of the family and through other organs of society and the state. The distinctive contribution of Islam to the economics lies in integrating freedom with responsibility and efficiency with justice. Justice is one the key Islamic values and has been described as one of the objectives for which God raised His prophets.[28] Guidance does not merely relate to man's spiritual relationship with God: it is no less concerned with man's just relationships with all other humans and all that exists in the universe.

This, briefly, is the worldview and vision of man and society through which Mawdūdī's approach to economics and economy can be understood. Mawdūdī was not an economist in the professional sense of the term. Yet his writings on economic issues have led to the development of a distinct approach to the economy, which has come to be described as 'Islamic economics'.

He has not only explained at length the economic teachings of the Qur'ān and the *Sunnah*, but he also tried to define the economic problems of man in the broad context of his total civilizational existence. He has also spelled out in reasonable detail how these problems can be solved through an integrated approach by taking care of moral and material dimensions of economic life simultaneously. His main contribution lies in expounding and explaining the philosophy of Islamic economics in clear terms.

Professor Rodney Wilson, a leading British economist and Director of the Centre for Middle East and Islamic Studies at the University of Durham, says:

> [Mawdūdī's] writings and speeches profoundly influenced a new generation of professional economists in the Indian sub-continent who sought to reconcile Islamic teachings with the ideas and concepts they had acquired through their economic training.... Although Mawdūdī had coined the

[28] The Qur'ān, 57: 25

> term 'Islamic economics' it was really from the 1970s that the subject took on some of the characteristics of an academic discipline.[29]

Dr Muhammad Umer Chapra, Senior Research Advisor at the Islamic Research and Training Institute of the Islamic Development Bank in Jeddah, Saudi Arabia, says:

> In spite of not being a professional economist, Mawdūdī's contribution to Islamic economics was significant. He will go down in history as one of the few great scholars who laid down the foundation for the development of this discipline in modern times. Nearly all those writings in this field in the Indo-Pakistan sub-continent as well as other Muslim countries have been influenced by and owe a debt of gratitude to him.[30]

His main contribution lies in explaining the philosophy of Islamic economics, its methodology and the major contours and institutions of an Islamic economic system as part of the Islamic way of life. He expounds the concept of *homo Islamicus* as against that of the *homo economicus* of conventional economics. It is interesting to recollect that the founders of two major schools of thought in contemporary economics, Adam Smith and Karl Marx were philosophers and not economists *per se*. Yet the classic and the socialist schools owe their origin to the thoughts and contributions of these two great thinkers.[31]

Mawdūdī's writings on economic issues cover five major themes:

First and foremost is Mawdūdī's vision of an economy that is humane, just and efficient, ensuring the fulfilment of needs and the well-being of all members of human society. As such it is the philosophic foundations, the moral values, the social objectives, and principles of socio-economic life that occupy the core of his writings on Islamic economics.

In my humble opinion, this is the most ground-breaking contribution of Mawdūdī. It deserves to be emphasized that it is the vision that constitutes the soul and substance of a discipline. He has not only expounded and developed

---

[29] Wilson, Rodney, 'The Development of Islamic Economics', in Suha Taji-Farouki and Basheer M. Nafi (eds.) *Islamic Thought in the Twentieth Century* (London: I.B.Ttauris, 2004), pp.196-197.

[30] Chapra, M. Umer, 'Mawdūdī's Contribution to Islamic Economics', *The Muslim World*, 94/2, April 2004, pp. 163-180, citation at p.173.

[31] A recent case in point is Elinor Ostrom of Indiana University who received the Nobel Prize for Economics in 2009. She is a professor of political science and is not a professional economist, yet her contributions have far reaching relevance for the discipline.

the vision of an Islamic economy and society with great clarity, but has also discussed in detail how this vision is distinct and different from those visions that inspired conventional economics and its variants. He has also made thought-provoking suggestions as to how economic analysis should have its roots in a holistic vision of economy, society and civilization.

I may submit in all humility that it is the *delinking* of *vision* from *analysis* that lies at the root of the current failure of conventional economics.[32] It is in this context that Mawdūdī has emphasized that there must be an inalienable link between Islam's worldview, value framework and principles of individual and social organisation, and the dynamics of analysis in economic theory and processes of resource mobilisation for the development of economic life and policymaking. The role of religion and moral values in economic analysis and policy formulation is the most distinctive characteristic of the Islamic approach to economics.[33]

Mawdūdī has dwelt on this aspect of economics at length and has shown how the establishment of a humane economy, one that could provide opportunities for the good life to all members of the society, is dependent upon this integrated approach. Economics and morality are inseparable. He has spelled out the implications of this integrated approach for different aspects of economic life and performance.

Secondly, Mawdūdī has highlighted the fact of the close interconnectedness between different aspects of human life and society. Hence he saw the need for an interdisciplinary approach, as against every discipline within the humanities and social sciences being isolated or confined to its own falsely-assumed-to-be-self-contained realm.

---

[32] Heilbroner, Robert, L. and William Milberg, *The Crisis of Vision in Modern Economic Thought* (New York: Cambridge University Press, 1996).

[33] It is interesting to note that an increasing number of ecomists and social thinkers are now emphasizing the need to rediscover the close relationship between economics, religion and ethics. Professor Laurence R. Iannaccone of Chapman University, California, has surveyed some 200 recent articles published in academic journals. His conclusion is citing: 'Nigel Tomes ... once began a paper by observing that "economics is fundamentally atheistic. Religious beliefs, practices, and behavior play no role in the life of homo economicus." I would end mine with a countervailing hope; the economics of religion will eventually bury two myths – that of home economicus as a cold creature with neither need nor capacity for piety, and that of homo religious as a benighted throw back to pre-rational times.' Iannaccone, Laurence R., 'Introduction to the Economies of Religion', *Journal of Economic Literature*, Sept 1998, pp.1465-1496. See also: Roth, Timothy P., *Ethics, Economics and Freedom* (Aldershot/ Sydney: Ashgate, 1999) and Rothschield, Kurt W., *Ethics and Economic Theory* (Hampshire: Edward Elgar, 1993).

Human life is indivisible: each aspect of life influences the others. While specialisation has a genuine role to play, it is unrealistic and highly damaging to divide life into watertight compartments, creating independent worlds for each and every discipline that studies any aspect of human life. The *exclusiveness* with which economics has been developed during the last two centuries has resulted in the emergence of a one-dimensional science, focusing only on self-interest, profit-maximization and competition. Consequently, the pursuit of economic gains became the sole driving force for all human efforts, resulting in a vast array of falsifications, distortions and inequities that characterize our current economic reality. 'Society' has been reduced to 'economy', and 'economy' to the 'market'. What began as an extension of moral philosophy to the realm of material pursuits has been reduced to a calculus of pecuniary gains and losses. The *delinking* of economics from religion and morality was not the end of the tale. Economics was gradually *delinked* from all the other disciplines too, from philosophy, politics, sociology, psychology, history and so on. These linkages have to be restored and strengthened if realistic solutions to human problems are to be worked out. An interdisciplinary approach is a must for this new beginning.

Thirdly, efficiency has become *the* central concern of economists over the years. The efficient allocation of resources is a genuine objective in both economic analysis and policymaking. But in this process of allocation yet another serious *delinking* has taken place – that between *efficiency* and *equity* and *justice*. This has been disastrous for both the economy and society. Mawdūdī, on the other hand, has emphasized that justice must remain the central objective. Efficiency is an essential *means* by which to serve the ends of equity and well-being, but it is *not* an end in itself. This delinking must also be reviewed so that personal interest could be coupled with social responsibility, wealth-creation with useful consumption and production, and economic development with distributive justice and collective well-being. Profit-maximization cannot be the sole objective; it must be tempered with considerations of justice, fair play, security and welfare. The market mechanism is the most suitable process for decision making, but market must operate within the context of well-defined moral, legal and social parameters. Individuals must continue to play a pivotal role, but institutions are equally important, and, in some situations, are even more important. Competition must be the heart of the productive process, but cooperation and compassion have to be equally important forces in fashioning the working of the economy and society. The state cannot and should not be a passive spectator: it has a regulatory and corrective role to play so as to ensure fulfilment of society's goals. Mawdūdī has emphasized that while all stakeholders' must play their respective roles, the state and civil society must have a positive role to ensure that economic development serves the objectives of justice and welfare for all members of the society.

Fourthly, Mawdūdī's distinct contribution lies in demonstrating the relevance of some key Islamic concepts and ideas to the contemporary situations and challenges. He has critically examined the economic ideologies and systems that have held the sway during the last two centuries. He has tried to develop in concrete terms the objectives of economic activity as expounded by Islam and has spelled out the framework and modalities of an Islamic economic system. He has also discussed the possibilities and prospects for the introduction of an Islamic economic system in the contemporary context, first within the Muslim countries, and then possibly as a model for others. In this respect, he has highlighted the need for drawing directly from the Qur'ān and the *Sunnah,* revisiting the contributions made in the *fiqh* literature and developing fresh ideas and approaches by examining the objectives of the *Sharīʿah* and re-codifying its economic injunctions and guidelines.

Finally, Sayyid Mawdūdī has highlighted, in a forceful manner, the principle that money should play an *intermediary* role in the economy and is *not* as an *objective* in itself. The focus of economic effort should always be on the development of the physical economy, i.e. the production of goods and services, their equitable distribution and useful consumption to promote well-being and contentment in society.

A major tragedy of the contemporary capitalist society is an ever-increasing *delinking* between the money economy and the physical economy. Today the economy is awash with money, real and fiduciary, but the concrete processes of value-addition are falling far short of meeting even the essential needs of the global human community. An *autonomous* space has been created for the vicious game of '*money begetting money*', without expanding the real economy. Credit is no longer an instrument for creation of real wealth; it has become as self-sustaining world of its own. There is an explosion of debt at all levels of economy, in households, firms, and states. It is these bubbles that are expanding and multiplying, and not the real flow of goods and services that lead to the fulfilment of human needs and comforts. Islamic economics is a plea to re-establish the *link* between the monetary and physical dimensions of the economy. U.S. President Obama has been forced to admit in one of his recent speeches that 'the world needs less of financial engineering and more of real engineering'. It is an eye-opening situation in the world economy today that daily sale-purchase for foreign exchange is some *fifty* times more than that of the actual international trade in goods and services.[34]

It deserves to be noted here that the main characteristic of Islamic finance is its inalienable link with the real economy and asset-creation. Amongst the factors responsible for current economic crisis are role of *ribā* (interest), *maysir* (speculation) and *gharar* (uncertainty and ambiguity). Islam prohibits all these. A recent IMF Working Paper makes this interesting observation:

> Comparing the performance of Islamic banks to conventional banks globally would suggest that Islamic banks performed better, given the large losses incurred by conventional banks in Europe and the US as a result of the crisis.[35]

Sayyid Mawdūdī's impact on the theory and practice of Islamic economics is visible in at least three directions. Firstly, he not only explained the economic teachings of the Qur'ān and the *Sunnah* with clarity and full command over the subject, but he initiated the process of the development of Islamic economics as an academic discipline. Research into different aspects of economics from an Islamic perspective has progressed during the last 50 years. Many research institutions have been established for this purpose in different parts of the world. Dozens of international conferences have been organized and countless seminars and roundtables have been held to develop different aspects of this nascent yet evolving discipline. Over a hundred universities in the Muslim world and elsewhere have introduced Islamic economics as a teaching discipline. The impact of Mawdūdī's contribution can be seen in all of these pioneering efforts.

Secondly, Sayyid Mawdūdī was not an armchair intellectual. Islam is a message for change and Mawdūdī played a significant role in the emergence and piloting of the global movement for the spiritual and moral transformation of men and women from within and their mobilization for the establishment of a new social order mirroring Islam's ideals, values, and principles. Mawdūdī's key concern has been the establishment of an Islamic order in its entirety. As such,

---

[34] Noam Chomsky says: 'In 1971, 90% of international financial transactions were related to the real economy – trade and long-term investment – and 10 per cent were speculative. By 1990 the percentage was reversed and by 1995 about 95 per cent of the vastly greater sums were speculative, with daily flows regularly exceeding the combined foreign exchange reserves of the seven biggest industrial powers, over 1 trillion a day, and very short term about 80 per cent with round trips of a week or less". Chomsky, Noam, *Profit over People: Neoliberals and Global Order* (New York: Seven Stories Press, 1999), pp.23-24.

[35] Hasan, Maher, and Jemme Dridim, 'The Effects of the Global Crisis on Islamic and Conventional Banks: A Comparative Study', IMF Working Paper, September 2010.

his message has been that Islamic economics cannot be developed in isolation of society's transformation. That is why Islamic economics has three dimensions, which relate to each other and are inseparable: the normative dimension, the positivist or analytical dimension and finally its transformational role to reconstruct and reform economy and society.

He consistently emphasized the need for the reconstruction of the economic life of Muslims, as individuals and at community, societal and state levels to implement an Islamic economic programme in practice. The emergence of the global movements for Islamic finance, banking, and insurance are salient factors to be borne in mind. Other developments relate to establishment of organizations to implement the injunctions relating to *Zakāh, Ṣadaqah* and *Infāq*. These developments represent economic aspects of the contemporary Islamic resurgence. But Mawdūdī has emphasized that these constitute only stepping stones to a process of greater change, i.e. towards the reconstruction of the entire socio-economic-political order.

Finally, Mawdūdī's impact can be seen in respect of areas of policymaking. He has emphasized the need to reformulate the whole spectrum of economic policymaking at all levels, i.e. towards the individual, the firm, the civil society and the state. They must be geared to promote efforts towards the establishment of a just social order. It is instructive to compare the constitutions of Muslim countries that were drafted before Mawdūdī's main period of writing and research and those that have been influenced by the movements for Islamic resurgence. The incorporation of the directive principles of state policy into the constitutions of Pakistan, Iran and Sudan, to give only three examples, clearly show the influence of this new economic thinking based on the socio-economic ideals and imperatives of Islam. As such, Mawdūdī's thought and activism have played an important role in defining the Islamic economic agenda of our times.[36]

[36] Other key influences have been Muḥammad Iqbāl, Ḥasan al-Bannā, Muḥammad Bāqir al-Ṣadr, 'Ali Sharī'atī, Sayyid Quṭb, Necmettin Erbakan, to mention some of the more prominent figures. An idea about the current state of the discipline of Islamic economics in all of its major allied dimensions in philosophy, theory, historiography, research and teaching, as well as developments in the field of policymaking and its institutional and operational advancement can be had from a major research reference, *Encyclopedia of Islamic Economics*, currently being published under the general editorship of Professor Abdelhamid Brahimi and myself. The first volume on *Principles, Definitions and Methodology* (2009), under the editorship of Dr. Nejatullah Siddiqi, and the second volume, *The Islamic Economic System* (2010), under the editorship of Dr. Monzer Kahf, have been published; three more volumes are in preparation at the time of writing.

Mawdūdī's economic writings go back to the 1930s. He penned down scholarly discourses on subjects such as *Sūd* (interest), *Ḍabṭ-i-Wilādat* (birth control), *Zakāh* (poor-due), *Isrāf* (extravagance) and *Qimār* (speculation and gambling). He continued his learned discourses on Islamic economic issues and produced four thought-provoking books – *Sūd* (*Interest*), *Islām Aur Jadīd Ma'āshī Naẓariyāt* (*Islam and Modern Economic Ideologies*), *Mas'ala-i-Milkīyat-i-Zamīn* (*The Question of Land Ownership*), and *Islām aur Ḍabṭ-i-Wilādat* (*Islam and the Issue of Birth Control*). He contributed a series of articles, tracts, booklets and speeches highlighting Islamic perspectives on issues of economic significance. These books and articles will, because of their foundational role in the definition, ethos and scope of Islamic economics, will continue to shape and influence both the development of the discipline and its real-world applications. His ideas on economic issues are prominent in more than a dozen of his books and in hundreds of his speeches and articles. It was in the 1960s that I felt the need to compile a book, which would bring together all of his essential writings on Islamic economics, so as to make his thought available in one volume. This need had gained more urgency because of a national debate in Pakistan on the future shape of the economy in the country, which was caught between the conflicting demands of the emerging capitalist system in the country and its critique from writers of the left. It was in the context of this national debate that Islamic Economics moved into the centre of the political discourse. At the University of Karachi, where I was teaching economics, I took the innovative step of introducing the teaching of Islamic economics in its courses on comparative economic systems. Subsequently, similar steps were taken at other universities in Pakistan. This wider interest prompted me to compile selected writings of Mawdūdī on economic issues into one volume. That is how the original Urdu version of this book *Ma'āshiyāt-i-Islām* came into existence, which was published in 1969. The volume contains, in addition to the author's articles and speeches, excerpts from his monumental exegesis *Tafhīm al-Qur'ān*, as well as relevant portions of his six-volume masterpiece *Rasā'il-wa-Masā'il* (*Questions and Answers on Current Issues*). I also included in this volume an adaptation and synopsis of his writings on the questions of land ownership and interest from his two books *Mas'ala-i-Milkīyat-i-Zamīn* and *Sūd*. Every effort was made at the time to fit these selections with one coherent framework so as to present an integrated discourse throughout the collection. Yet it is important to point out that our efforts to express the matter to suit the scheme of this volume are in no way a proper substitute for the original books themselves, which remain of great importance for detailed study of these subjects.

The book has been divided into two parts. Part One deals with the Islamic philosophy of life and economy. It critically reviews the economic systems currently in practice in the world and provides an in-depth explanation of Islam's standpoint and the principles for the economic dimension of human existence, as laid down in the Qur'ān and the *Sunnah.* This section constitutes the heart of the book and has been a lasting source of guidance to students, scholars, and policymakers. Deriving inspiration from these thoughts and insights, a large galaxy of professional economists has tried to operationalize these ideas into economic instruments. This book has served as a beacon to students of economics to discover and develop a distinctly Islamic approach to economic problems and issues and for the public at large it has served as an inspiration to strive for the establishment of an Islamic economic system as part of an Islamic society and state. Sayyid Mawdūdī has led the way, and now the Muslim economists and business practitioners are engaged in a heroic struggle to develop Islamic economics and to pursue pathways that may lead to the establishment of an Islamizing economy.

Part Two of the book deals with the application of Islam's economic philosophy to certain specific issues and areas of activity. Although it focuses on a few aspects of Islam's economic system, the discussion nonetheless opens up new vistas of research. The articles in Part Two present the Islamic injunctions on some basic economic issues of the day, such as land ownership, interest, *Zakāh* and social justice. They also provide students and scholars of economics with the necessary guidance to study and understand those issues in the light of Islamic injunctions and the fundamental principles of *Sharī'ah.* These articles also show the way towards a creative and innovative approach, instead of merely following the beaten track of unquestioning and blind acceptance of Western economic formulations and models, including its economic theories and precepts. In addition, they give us guidance about the practical limits within which fresh *Ijtihād* or scholarly re-interpretation of the Qur'ān and the *Sunnah* on juridical issues should take place. We need to have a balanced approach towards modern theories and precepts: nothing needs to be rejected outright, but nothing should be blindly followed either. After careful examination and critical scrutiny, we have to determine what is acceptable from an Islamic perspective and what is to be rejected if it violates Islamic norms and values, as reflected in this beautiful proverb:

خُذ مَاصَفَا وَدَع مَاكَدَر

(Take that which is clear and unambiguous and leave that which is muddled and unclear.)

Part Two of the book reflects this constructive and creative approach, and by studying it students of economics can promote the right vision and develop appropriate approaches on issues of economic importance. It can also serve as an inspiration for future study and research.

First Principles of Islamic Economics is an English translation of the original Urdu compilation of 1969, with some new additions. A very important speech of the author, which was given to the Economics Society of the University of Punjab, has been included in this volume. Some other additions have been made in other parts of the book, which add to the usefulness of this English-language edition.

I would like to take this opportunity to express my great appreciation for the meticulous job that has been done by my colleague, Mr Ahmad Imam Shafaq Hashemi, who is a Senior Research Fellow at the Institute of Policy Studies, Islamabad. He deserves our heartiest congratulations for his remarkable translation of the book. It was a difficult task to piece together the material that has been culled from different sources, and written on various occasions, and yet to retain a semblance of continuity and sequence. I tried my best and feel proud that Sayyid Mawdūdī was gracious enough not only to express his satisfaction on the work but to say that even if he had edited this material he could not have been better. I have no hesitation in saying that my work on the Urdu edition of *Maʿāshiyāt-i-Islām* has been taken up with greater dexterity and skill by Shafaq Hashemi, who has rendered the Urdu text into English in a manner that conveys the author's ideas with eloquence and precision. The present format of the book makes for a lucid and pleasant read; I hope that students, scholars, and general readers will find it equally refreshing and helpful in understanding the basics of a discipline of global importance.

Before I conclude I would like to place on record that *First Principles of Islamic Economics* is part of a sixteen-volume project to present in English the essential works of Sayyid Mawdūdī. I have worked on this project for the last five years but due to ill-health, I am now finding it difficult to do justice to this gigantic project. I am happy to note that Dr Anis Ahmad, Vice-Chancellor at Riphah International University, has agreed to serve as the general editor for the series. As part of this project, my worthy colleagues Dr Zafar Ishaq Ansari, Shafaq Hashemi, Tariq Jan and Sayed Akif are working on various volumes that are in the pipeline. I acknowledge with thanks our gratitude to the World of Islam Trust, Islamabad, for sponsoring the project, and the Madina Trust, Peterborough, U.K., and particularly its Chairman, Ziaul Hasan, as well as the Sarwar Jehan Charitable Foundation, Leicester, for their financial support. My thanks are also due to Dr M. Manazir Ahsan, Director General of the Islamic

Foundation, Markfield, Leicestershire, as well as the editorial and administrative assistance of Kube Publishing. May Allah *subḥānahū wa taʿālā* bless this effort with His benign acceptance and give the best of the rewards to all those brothers and sisters who have contributed towards its publication.

Islamabad
13 Rabīʿ al-Thānī 1432
18 March 2011

Khurshid Ahmad

Translator's Note

In the Arabic language, *'Ilm al-Iqtiṣād* is the term for economics. Literally, this means the 'science of economy and balance'. As an academic discipline in the social sciences, we can trace the origin of economics to the last quarter of the eighteenth century. In Islam, however, it has been a subject of prime importance for the last fourteen hundred years. *Zakāh* (mandatory charity) is one of the five pillars of Islam and among the fundamental articles of faith. Because of this, a system has emerged that has determined the fiscal policy of Islam, the parameters of public and private ownership, the relationship between capital, enterprise, the means of production and labour, and the responsibilities of the individual and society to ensure the existence of a welfare state based on the Islamic concept of social justice.

The most revered book after the Book of God has detailed chapters on subjects of economic importance. This is *al-Jāmi' al-Ṣaḥīḥ* by Imām Bukhārī, which is the *magnum opus* of Prophetic Traditions (*Aḥādīth*). There are chapters on finance and accounts, trade and commerce (*al-Buyū'*), leasing (*al-Ijārah*), trusteeship (*al-Wakālah*), debit and credit (*al-Duyūn*), mortgages (*al-Rahn*), endowment (*al-Waqf*), *Zakāh* and *al-'Ushr*, a tax on agricultural produce.

Textbooks define economics as a science that is primarily concerned with the production, distribution and consumption of money, goods and services. However, being welfare-oriented, Islamic economics not only stresses factors concerned with production and issues of supply and demand, but also the ethics related to these factors. It seeks to foster and promote the values necessary for the establishment of a society free from the exploitation of man by man, one that is based on social justice. Because of the importance of Islamic economics for the Islamic state, the society and the individual, both juridically and academically, we can trace the origins of scientific study in this area as early as the first century *Hijrah* (seventh century CE). The founder of the Ḥanafī School, Imām al-A'ẓam Abū Ḥanīfah al-Nu'mān, (80 AH/699 CE–150 AH/767 CE), documented his response to thousands of queries concerning issues of economic and fiscal significance in the light of the Qur'ān and the *Sunnah*. His illustrious student, the author and jurist, Justice Imām Abū Yūsuf (113AH/731CE–182AH/798CE), wrote the monumental *Kitāb al-Kharāj* on Islamic law relating to land revenue, public finance and an Islamic state's fiscal policy.

Subsequently, in the two-volume *Hidāyah*, the tenth-century masterpiece, we see an all-embracing compendium of law dealing, among other subjects, with all the major dimensions of economic activity and behaviour. In this work, the author, Abu'l Ḥasan ʿAlī al-Farghānī (d. 593 AH), explained the juridical and economic aspects of the Islamic *Sharīʿah* in light of the teachings of the Qur'ān and the *Sunnah*. Muḥammad bin Aḥmad bin Rushd, the world-renowned scholar of Muslim Spain (Andalusia), popularly known in the West as Ibn Rushd or Averroes (d. 595 AH), contributed another masterpiece on the subject around 1160 CE with the title, *Bidāyat al-Mujtahid wa Nihāyat al-Muqtaṣid*. After these significant writings, the Muslim world had to wait many centuries to witness further progress and the reflowering of knowledge that followed its phoenix-like rebirth from the ashes of socio-political decay and intellectual decline.

It was the contemporary world's most outstanding Islamic thinker, scholar, reformer and leader of the world Islamic movement, Sayyid Abul Aʿlā Mawdūdī (25th September 1903 CE – 22nd September 1979 CE), who rebuilt the grand edifice of Islamic learning on the foundations laid down by his illustrious predecessors. His multi-dimensional contributions on Islamic thought in various fields include his writings on the *First Principles of Islamic Economics*. This book has been compiled by his worthy disciple and a scholar of world-repute, Professor Khurshid Ahmad, himself a noted figure in Islamic thought and academically trained in the field of economics. Let us hope that the English version of *Maʿāshiyāt-i-Islām* will be greatly beneficial to students, scholars and researchers of economics in general and Islamic economics in particular, which has emerged as a major subject of study both locally and globally.

Islamabad **A.I. Shafaq Hashemi**
19th *Jumādā*-I, 1428 AH
6th June 2007 CE

Author's Preface

This book is a collection of articles that I contributed on different occasions over the last 30 to 35 years. They were published from time to time to explain and elucidate the economic principles and injunctions of Islam and their applicability in the context of today. I have long felt the need to piece them together and compile them in a single volume to provide readers with a complete picture of the economic system of Islam that can also serve as a text and a resource book for students of Islamic Sciences, particularly Economics. Because of my multifarious engagements, however, I was unable to do this until Professor Khurshid Ahmad finally undertook the job. I am grateful to him for the painstaking care with which he has compiled these articles better than I could have done myself. I have reviewed the whole manuscript and made amendments and additions where necessary. I am confident that the book will serve the purpose for which Prof. Khurshid has undertaken this labour of love.

Lahore
14th *Dhū'l Ḥijjah* 1388 AH
3rd March 1969 CE

Abul A'lā

Introduction*

Islam has laid down certain principles and parameters to keep the economic life of mankind firmly based on the twin concepts of justice and fairplay. It seeks to ensure that the entire system of the production of wealth, its use and distribution should function within the limits drawn for the purpose. How should wealth be produced and how should it be circulated? Islam is not much concerned with these issues because the ways and means are continually changing and assuming new shapes and patterns as time passes and civilizations grow and march on. Human needs and circumstances serve as catalysts which determine this change that takes place automatically in response. Islam is principally concerned with the strict observance of its basic principles on a permanent basis, under all circumstances and in all times and climes, irrespective of the shape that the economic affairs of mankind may take.

Islam tells us that the earth and everything it contains have been created by God for mankind. Therefore, it is every human being's birthright to seek his means of living from the land on which he lives. All humans equally share this basic right: nobody can be deprived of this right, nor should anybody enjoy precedence over another in this respect. According to the Islamic *Sharīʿah*, it is unlawful to impose any restriction on a person, class, clan or ethnic group regarding their right to use the means of subsistence or close the doors to certain vocations to them. Similarly, the *Sharīʿah* does not allow any distinction or privilege that results in a particular means of living or source of income becoming the monopoly of a particular class, race or family. Every human being is entitled to work for his share of the means of subsistence made available by Allah *subḥānahū wa taʿālā* on His earth and there must, therefore, be equality of opportunity for all in this respect.

Nature's bounties need no labour or entrepreneurship to be beneficial to mankind; they are humankind's common inheritance. Everyone has the right

* The *Introduction* is based on Sayyid Mawdūdī's talk on the economic system of Islam, which he delivered on Radio Pakistan in Lahore on 2nd March 1948. Because of its relevance to the subject matter, it has been included as the introductory chapter of the book. – Translator.

to make use of them, according to his needs. The water flowing in rivers and streams, the wood available in forests, the wild-growing fruit, fodder and grass, the winged creatures of the skies, the animals of the desert, the fish of the free-flowing rivers or the sea and the mines wide open on the earth's surface – each one of these is nature's free gift. These cannot be monopolized by anyone, nor can any restrictions be imposed to prevent someone making use of them to satisfy his need. However, the government is entitled to levy tax on those who wish to make use of these bounties from God on a commercial scale.

Things that God has created for the benefit of man cannot be kept idle. If you so desire, take advantage of them yourself; otherwise, allow others to put them to their best use. Based on this principle, Islamic Law states that everyone in possession of land given by the government should not let it lie fallow for more than three years. If someone fails to make use of the land for farming, residence or any other purpose for three years, it is deemed to be an abandoned property. If someone else then puts this land to use, no lawsuit is permissible against him. The Islamic government can also cancel ownership of the land and give it to someone else for cultivation or habitation. Anybody who gains anything from the bounties of nature, and through his labour and enterprise makes it worthy of use, is the rightful owner of that property. For example, if a person takes possession of a wasteland that nobody owns the title to, and then starts putting it to some better use, he cannot be dislodged from that land according to the law. According to the *Sharīʿah*, this is how all ownership rights are acquired in the world. In the beginning, when human settlements began to develop on God's earth, everything that belonged to the treasure house of nature was a common legacy. When people started putting what they possessed to use, they eventually became the owners. Their labour, ingenuity and enterprise entitled them to have those things as their exclusive property and to seek compensation from those who subsequently also wished to make use of them. This is the natural basis of all economic transactions of mankind, and ought to remain intact under all circumstances.

The ownership rights available to anyone in this world through lawful means have to be respected at all cost. However, the legality of an ownership claim can be challenged under the terms of the *Sharīʿah*. Any ownership without a legal sanction should be declared null and void; those found to be lawful can neither be taken away by any government or legislature, nor can the lawful rights of their owners be curtailed or enhanced in any way. No system can be introduced in the name of public interest in contravention of the rights guaranteed to individuals by the *Sharīʿah*. In the same way that it is an act of high-handedness to ease the restrictions imposed by the *Sharīʿah* on private ownerships in the name of public interest, it is similarly abominable to circumscribe them further arbitrarily. An Islamic government is obligated to safeguard the legal rights of its citizens, and also to ensure that they truly observe their duties to the State.

Under the Divine Dispensation, there is equity but not necessarily equality in the distribution of His bounties. In His infinite Wisdom, Allah *subḥānahū wa ta'ālā* has elevated some people over others. Beauty of the exterior, mellowness of voice, physical strength, intellectual capability, family background and other similar gifts have not been awarded evenly. It is the same with the means of subsistence. Human instinct, itself a Divine creation, demands that humans should not have parity in their earnings. From the *Sharī'ah* perspective, all measures that are taken to impose an artificial economic parity on the people are, therefore, wrong both in approach and objective. The equality that Islam stands for is not in the amount earned for living on, but in the opportunity to struggle for a better living. Islam aims at purging society of those legal and conventional hurdles which restrict mankind's ability to struggle for economic benefits according to their own capacity and qualifications. It also removes those distinctions and privileges which seek to turn the inherited good fortune of a certain class, race or family into permanent lawful prerogatives. Both of these factors tend to replace the natural disparity forcefully with a system of artificial disparity. By eliminating these factors, Islam thus aims at bringing society's economic order back to its natural position, where every individual enjoys an equal opportunity to make efforts to improve his lot.

However, Islam totally disagrees with those who want to force people to be equal in their means for their struggle and its outcomes because this seeks to turn natural inequality into an artificial equality. A system can only be closer to nature if individuals are free to join in the economic race from the starting point of their birth as set for them by the Almighty. Whoever comes with a car is free to drive it and those who have with them only the assets of their two legs have the right to full use of them. But the one who is born lame cannot lag behind either and should have the opportunity to use his only leg to his best advantage. A society's legal set-up must not allow the owner of the car to monopolize his opportunity, making it difficult for the lame to own a car. It must also not force every member to begin his race from one and the same point, making it binding on all of them to run together. Justice demands that everyone should be free to undertake his own struggle in his own way. Anyone who is able to own a car by his efforts must not be deprived of this opportunity, and if someone loses the car he received at his birth or becomes lame due to his own negligence must also be free to bear the consequences of his acts.

Islam not only aims to keep this economic competition and race open and free from unwarranted encumbrances, it also encourages those in the race to cooperate and be sympathetic to each other instead of being apathetic or antagonistic. Through its moral values and precepts, it inspires people, on the one hand, to be steadfast in their support for their fellow humans who are ill-provided and backward and, on the other, it calls on society to have a fully-fledged system and mechanism to guarantee this support for the less privileged and handicapped. Those who are not able to take part in the economic struggle are guaranteed to have their needs provided for by this institution. Proper help is also ensured for those people whom circumstances have pushed out of the race or whose progress has been halted so that they can rise once again and continue their struggle with honour and dignity; while necessary help is also available to those who may need it to join the race. Keeping these lofty objectives in view, Islam levies an annual 2.5 percent compulsory deduction of *Zakāh* on the capital accumulated during a calendar year and the revenue generated annually through trade and commerce. *Zakāh* is also levied on agricultural produce at the rate of ten and five percent per annum, and on various other items at different rates. (For complete details, please see Chapter 9.) *Zakāh* is thus a system of social insurance and public welfare, which means that nobody can ever remain deprived of the basic necessities of life in a Muslim society. No workhand can ever be so helpless that he must agree to serve on terms dictated by the mill-owner or landlord, and no-one can ever suffer because of his failure to qualify for participation in the struggle for survival.

Islam seeks to establish a balance between the individual and society so that the individual may retain his personal freedom on the one hand and, on the other, his freedom is not detrimental to the interests of society, but is more beneficial instead. It does not approve of any political or economic set-up that compels an individual to submerge himself totally into society and leaves no room for his personal freedom, which is so essential for the proper growth and development of his personality. The natural outcome of placing the entire means of a country's production under public ownership is that every individual is turned into a slave of the party in power. It will be difficult, or rather impossible, for people under such a system to retain and sustain their individuality. Socio-political and economic freedoms are essential for private enterprise to flourish. If we do not intend to cripple humanity absolutely, we must allow a person enough space in our social set-up that he is able to earn a livelihood independently, to retain freedom of conscience and to let his intellectual and moral faculties grow and prosper according to his aptitude and leanings. No 'ration' that is issued by the authorities for subsistence, however plentiful, can ever be pleasant and nourishing until the key to that 'ration' is in the hands of the person himself. A bird in a cage, though adequately fed, may grow fat but will never be fit to fly unless it is set free.

Just as Islam disapproves of all totalitarian dictatorships, it also does not commend a system that gives unfettered freedom to individuals in the socio-economic milieu of a nation, letting them do whatever they like in pursuance of their personal ambitions and interests regardless of the danger caused to the society and the nation. The middle road that Islam follows between these two extremes makes it incumbent upon the individual, on the one hand, to remain within his well-defined limits and always be mindful of his responsibilities towards society; and on the other hand, it allows him freedom to conduct his own affairs within the prescribed limits. It may be out of place to give full details of the restrictions and responsibilities here; a brief resume may, however, be worthwhile.

Let us first look at the question of earning a living. The minutest details of the *lawful* and the *prohibited* provided by the Islamic *Sharī'ah* about the means of livelihood are hard to find in any legal code anywhere in the world. It singles out and declares *Ḥarām* (prohibited) all those means that encourage the individual to earn his living by harming others' interests or damaging the society's cause either morally or materially. Islam has thus totally banned the production and sale of wine and all intoxicants, as well as every form of obscenity and undignified profession, such as music, dance, gambling, betting, the lottery, interest-based transactions, speculation, fraudulent deals, hoarding of essential goods to increase their market value and every deal which is against public interest. The deeper you go into the economic laws of Islam, the more evident it becomes why all shady deals and unhealthy practices have been declared *Ḥarām*. These are the means that people use under the capitalist system of our times to amass wealth and to become men of millions. The *Sharī'ah* has declared all such means *ultra vires*, but has given complete freedom to every individual to earn his living in a manner that may be beneficial in real terms, not only for himself but also for his society.

Islam affirms the ownership right of man on wealth that he earns through *Ḥalāl* (lawful) means. But this right is also not unlimited. He is only allowed to spend lawfully from that which he has earned through lawful means. Islam thus lays down a system of checks and balances, so that a believer, though free to live a clean and comfortable life, cannot indulge in unwarranted luxuries or squander his wealth at will. He is not authorized to live a life of pomp and show simply to masquerade as an elite member of a privileged class. There are certain categories of overspending which are strictly forbidden in Islam. An Islamic government can legally ban people's indulgence in unwarranted expenditure and displays of wealth.

There is no restriction on a person's saving from his legitimate earnings. He can also reinvest his savings to generate more money in a lawful manner. In both of these cases, however, the Islamic *Sharīʿah* has certain restrictions in place. A man has to pay *Zakāh* on his savings and is only allowed to invest in a lawful business. Everyone is permitted to start an enterprise through lawful means, or to make a joint venture with another person and lend him his capital, land, tools or other means on a profit and loss-sharing basis. It is also acceptable if, working within the prescribed limits, one becomes a billionaire. The profit thus earned will in fact be treated as a blessing of Allah *subḥānahū wa taʿālā*. In the interests of society, however, Islam obliges the individual to fulfil the following two preconditions: (i) he must pay *Zakāh* on his business commodities and *ʿUshr* on his agricultural produce; and (ii) he must act justly towards those who are his partners in business, his employees and workers. If he fails in these areas, the Islamic State can force him to fulfil his obligations.

The wealth that is gathered by a person through lawful means and saved after paying the mandatory dues should not simply lie to accumulate for long. Through the law of inheritance, Islam lets it pass on to the legal heirs for a larger circulation, one generation after the other. The trend that is set by the Islamic Law is quite different in this respect from other legal systems around the world. According to other legal codes, once the wealth is accumulated, it is allowed to continue growing from one generation to another. In contrast, Islam makes it binding on every Muslim that the assets gathered during his lifetime must be divided immediately following his death among the next of kin in a manner laid down by the *Sharīʿah*. Should the deceased have no near relatives alive, the legacy passes on to more distant relations and, in the absence of anybody even distantly related, the Islamic state becomes the legal heir. It is thus impossible under the Islamic legal system for any sort of feudalism or capitalist cartels and monopolies to prosper and flourish. The mandatory charity of *Zakāh* and *ʿUshr* along with other social obligations are sufficient to discourage the accumulation of wealth. The Islamic Law of Inheritance goes a step further and places a lasting curb on the possibilities of the rich growing richer in an Islamic social order.

PART ONE

THE ISLAMIC CONCEPT OF ECONOMIC WELL-BEING

1 Mankind's Economic Problems and their Islamic Solutions*

The importance that is now being given so pronouncedly to the economic problems of nations and states around the world is greater than ever before. I have used the phrase 'so pronouncedly' because the economic aspect of life has always been of great importance to mankind, and as such has always attracted the attention of individuals, groups, communities and countries across the globe. However, what has focussed this attention today is the arrival of specialized institutions and more and more books with high-sounding jargon and terms dedicated to Economics as a discipline, accompanied by a growing complexity in the processes of production and supply, as well as access to the basic amenities of life. Because of this, so much debate, dialogue and scholarly research is being carried out today on economic issues that every other issue of human life has now been relegated to the background. Strangely enough, however, the phenomenon that has become the focus of attention all over the world is becoming more and more complicated and enigmatic, rather than getting resolved or better understood. The common man has become so overawed by the high-sounding jargon and terminologies of this social science and the scholarly hair-splitting by economic wizards that he seems to lose all hope of any prospect of improving his lot, in the same way that a patient thinks his condition is hopeless on hearing some quaint Latin synonym for his disease from the physician's mouth. Nevertheless, when viewed in a more simple and natural way, shorn of its technical trappings and academic bombasts, the economic issue becomes easier to understand and, without much difficulty, we can discover the merits and demerits of various measures that have been taken by the world to resolve it. There then remains no difficulty in finding out the correct and more natural approach to the solution of this issue.

---

* This talk was delivered by the author on 30th October 1941 at Stratchy Hall, Aligarh Muslim University, at the special invitation of the university's Association of Islamic History and Civilization. – Translator.

1.1. The problem of a partial approach

In addition to the confusion caused by the bamboozling terminologies and jargon, the economic issue of mankind has become more complicated because it has been removed from the main body of the greater issue[1] facing them as humans and moral beings, and attempts have been made to handle it in isolation as an independent question. This approach has gradually led to the economic question being viewed as the main issue in the whole of life. This is a mistake even greater than ignoring other issues of human life, as a result of which the confusion has become even worse. The paradox can be better understood if we take as an example the case of a specialist physician trying to treat his patient's infected liver by focusing his entire attention on the diseased organ without caring to check at the same time its role, functions and impact on other parts of the anatomy. Similarly, one can easily understand the effectiveness, or otherwise, of attempting to solve all the problems of human health by treating just one infected limb. The economic problem is just one of a host of complex issues facing human beings, and any attempt to resolve it independent of the multifarious other issues of human life, in the narrow context of economics alone, is bound to result in nothing but chaos, confusion and desperation.

Specialization may be a blessing in certain cases, but it has generally led today to an unfortunate tendency to compartmentalize life and an inability to take a holistic approach towards the issues facing mankind. It has actually added to the complexity of these issues. The human being today has been reduced to a plaything in the hands of the one-eyed experts of different sciences, arts and crafts. For a leading physicist, the mysteries of the universe can be resolved only through physics; while one who specializes in psychology seeks to formulate his entire philosophy of life on the strength of his perceptions and experiments in his own field. To somebody who is focused exclusively on the gender dimension,

---

[1] As will be evident from the ensuing pages, the greatest issue facing man in his life is how to acquit himself well of the responsibilities lying heavily upon his shoulders as deputy to his Lord and His vicegerant on earth. These responsibilities devolve on him as an individual member of a family, of a society and as a citizen of a state. The multi-dimensional nature of his obligations has been catagorized broadly as *Ḥuqūq Allāh* (rights of Allah) and *Ḥuqūq al-'Ibād* (rights of His subjects). Whatever one has by way of the life-span given to him, health, physical strength, intellectual faculties and personal assets and resources are gifts from the All-Merciful. He is not the master but the custodian of each and everything he has been blessed with and will have to account for it on the Day of Reckoning: ('Then, on that Day, you will be called to account for all the bounties you enjoyed.') ثُمَّ لَتُسْـَٔلُنَّ يَوْمَئِذٍ عَنِ ٱلنَّعِيمِ (*al-Takāthur*, 102: 8). This is the biggest challenge before man and the greatest issue for which he is required to carefully plan his multifaceted life and satisfy himself, before anybody else, that he has acquitted himself well to the best of his capabilities and has no dues to settle either of the Lord or His subjects.– Translator.

human life would appear to revolve entirely around the issue of sex. In the same way, those devoted to economics would like to assure humanity that its sole problem is how to earn a living, and everything else is only a peripheral matter. The fact remains, however, that all of these are some of the various facets of human life. Each one has its own place and role and is part of the same single whole. The corporeal frame of man is governed by the laws of nature, and as such he is the subject of physics. And yet he consists not just of his body, which could be handled entirely under the laws of physics in order to resolve his problems. He is also a living being on whom the biological laws apply and is therefore part of the subject matter of biology. But he is not simply a biological substance, governed entirely under the terms of biology or zoology, as he needs food, clothing and shelter to survive. Hence, economics covers an important part of his social existence; but he is not merely a social animal whose life can be confined to the domain of his basic needs of food, clothing and shelter. Mankind is compelled to rely on procreation for continuing the species, and for this there is an instinctive attraction towards sex. As a result, sexology and genealogy assume a significance for life, but he is not simply a breeder intended exclusively to propagate his progeny. He is endowed with a psyche as well, and is thus gifted with powers of perception, discernment, feelings, emotions and ambitions. Viewed from this backdrop, psychology would appear to encompass a major part of life. But the psyche is just a little part of the whole self and, therefore, the entire scheme of life cannot be laid out on the basis of psychology alone. Man is also a social being with a civilizational legacy that impels him to live with his fellow humans, and as such many aspects of life are governed by the rules of sociology. But even this is just one aspect of a human's multifaceted life, making it impossible for sociologists to work out a comprehensive plan for life. A human being is also a rational being, and has an urge for logic and reasoning beyond the realms of feelings and emotions. From this perspective, logic occupies an important place in life. However, a man is not reason reincarnate, able to lead his entire life on the basis of logic and reasoning alone. He is also a moral and spiritual being who has within himself the instinctive capability to distinguish between good and bad, and an unending urge to peer into realities beyond the realm of the known and visible facts. Morality and spirituality are thus two other vital facets of a human being's personality; but no one is simply a personification of these two segments, so that they could base the entire scheme of their life on the twin foundations of morality and spirituality.

In fact, a human being is a happy blend of all of these and much more at the same time. In addition to the various facets of personality mentioned above, there is yet another equally important aspect: a human is also part of the cosmic order's grand scheme of things. A code of conduct for life must also, therefore, be necessary in order to determine mankind's position in that order and how one must discharge his responsibilities as a component. Man must also identify his goal in life and reflect on how to achieve that goal. These are in fact the two fundamental issues facing a human being, and a philosophy of life emerges from these, which then leads all the sciences concerning mankind and the universe to offer the relevant data that eventually help to develop a plan of action in the grand scheme of things.

Evidently, a person who desires to understand any issue of life should not concentrate simply on that area, or to look at the whole spectrum of life with a definite bias in favour of that particular issue. For a clear perception and understanding, one has to look at each issue in the broader context of the whole of life and without a blurred vision. Similarly, if someone notices a tilt somewhere in the harmony and balance of life and is keen to remove that tilt and restore the balance, it is more risky for him to tackle that problem piecemeal and focus his attention entirely on one piece, rather than attempting to treat the malaise in a holistic manner. The correct way to reform is to focus on the entire spectrum of life, without any bias or tilt, comprehensively keeping in view each minutest detail and then pinpointing the afflicted part and the actual nature of the disease.

The difficulty that is being faced in achieving a correct diagnosis and treatment of the economic problem is a result of this partial approach. There are those who believe that it is a problem that only concerns economics. There are others who tend to overstress the significance of this aspect, and believe it is the very problem of life; while yet others hold that the life's basic philosophy, manners and morals, indeed the entire social set-up, need to be remodeled on the foundations of economics. The fact remains, however, that overstressing the importance of economics ignores the fundamental difference that is there between a man's goal in life and that of the cattle, whose sole objective in life is nothing more than feeding on lush green grass and keeping their stomachs full. It is this goal that determines the cattle's actions in the pastures and meadows of the world. The pre-eminence of the economic approach in the realms of morality, spirituality, logic, sociology, psychology and other human sciences is bound, therefore, to create a great imbalance, because economics offers no basis for those facets of human life except when spirituality and morality are allowed to degenerate into materialism and self-aggrandizement, when the power of reason turns into the power of the palate, when the entire realm of the social sciences recedes into commercialism and psychology starts to treat man merely as a 'social animal'.

1.2. The real issue

Mankind's economic problem, viewed simplistically and keeping aside linguistic and technical nuances, would appear to be no more than a question of how best to acquire the basic necessities of life, while at the same time trying to maintain the pace of socio-economic progress and ensuring that every member of society has the opportunity to make the best use of his qualifications and potential.

In ancient times, the question of subsistence was as easy to solve for mankind as it was for other living beings. There was no dearth of the means of subsistence on God's earth. Every creature could have what it sought to its heart's content. Whoever desired to seek his livelihood could have plenty. He had to pay nobody for it, nor was he dependent on anyone for his living. Humans, like all other creatures, were free to earn their living from nature's bounties, whether in the abundantly growing fruit or the freely roaming wild animals and game-birds. The products of nature were sufficient for their needs for clothing, and the vast expanse of the earth with all its treasures was available to provide them with shelter as and when they desired.

However, Allah *subḥānahū wa taʿālā* had not created man to continue living like other creatures forever. He had bestowed within him the instincts and inclinations that soon compelled him to give up lone and isolated living, adopt a social life and produce for himself through his own ingenuity and enterprise means of livelihood better than those gifted by nature. Nature itself had induced within mankind the trends and tendencies that served as an impetus for living as a community. These trends and tendencies included a natural instinct in men for a sustained relationship with women, the dependence of children on parents for their upkeep and sustenance for a longer time, man's undying interest in his offspring and his love for blood relations. Similarly, man's impatience to go beyond nature's own products to produce his own food through agriculture, to rely no more on leaves and foliage to cover his body but to prepare his own clothes through industry and skill, to build a house of his own instead of living contentedly in caves and grottoes and to invent tools and implements of stone, wood and iron instead of continuing to subsist on his physical strength for the necessities of life – all of these were ingrained within his instinct and naturally forced him to become more and more civilized. Hence, humanity's march on the road to civilization was in accordance with the dictates of his own nature, as much as it was desired and predestined by his Lord, the Creator.

With the birth of civilization, it became inevitable:

- that human needs should rise and interdependence take over self-sufficiency, with each individual becoming dependent on the other to satisfy some of his requirements and others requiring his assistance for the fulfillment of some of their needs;

- that there should take place an exchange of the daily necessities of life, and for this there should gradually emerge a medium of exchange;
- that there would be more and more tools for the production and transportation of the necessities of life so that man may continue benefiting from the new means and resources available to him; and
- that man should have the satisfaction of owning the things he has acquired through his labour, the tools and implements of his use, the piece of land he has selected for his residence and the place where he works, and that he could thereafter transfer whatever is in his possession to his next of kin and those closer to him than others.

The growth and development of various vocations, businesses and trade, varying rates of commodities, the emergence of currency as a standard mode of exchange, the rise of international trade, imports and exports, an increasing use of tools and means of production and the phenomena of ownership rights and the right of inheritance were thus part of a natural process in the civilizational progress of mankind. There was nothing sinful in all of this to lead to a call for penance.

As human civilization advanced, it further became inevitable that:

- due to natural difference in human capabilities and potential, some would earn more than they actually needed, some just according to their needs and others would make even less than their basic requirements;
- there would be those inheriting good fortune and others starting their struggle for survival with little or no means;
- every human society would have those incapable of earning their own livelihood, like the underaged, the old, the sick and the disabled; and
- there should be those who employed and those others who served, thereby creating avenues for the growth of free enterprise, trade, commerce and agriculture, as well as different kinds of vocations, employment and jobs.

All of these in themselves are natural phenomena and normal manifestations of human civilization, and as such there is nothing wrong or sinful about them. The ills that subsequently cropped up due to various factors of civilizational malaise caused many to curse, out of sheer ignorance, private enterprise, money, machines, the natural disparity between humans and often the civilization itself. This is actually a wrong diagnosis and a faulty prescription. Every attempt to check the process of civilizational development that takes place in keeping with the demands of human nature, and to curb its various forms and manifestations, is only a sign of ignorance and could lead to more damage and devastation than progress and prosperity. The real economic challenge facing man is not how to check the onward march of civilization, or to change its natural manifestations, but how to eliminate social injustice and tyranny while maintaining the natural rate of progress; how to accomplish nature's design that every creature should get what it needs for its subsistence; and how to remove the hurdles that cause the energies and potential of the majority of mankind to go to waste because they lack the necessary wherewithal to flourish.

1.3. The root cause of economic mismanagement

Let us now examine the factors that are actually responsible for economic troubles to discover what exactly is the nature of this malaise?

The starting point of economic problems is selfishness that transgresses the boundaries of moderation. This ugly trait grows and develops with the active support of a corrupt social and political environment until it eventually pollutes the entire economic system and poisons other walks of life as well. I have stated that there is nothing integrally wrong with private ownership or with some people enjoying a better position in life than others. If the intrinsic goodness of human character were given the opportunity to play a full part and there was a political system in place externally to enforce the rule of law and social justice effectively, then there would have been no room for any corruption. The factor that is primarily responsible for the malaise, however, was the degeneration of those people blessed with a better economic position into selfishness, greed, stinginess, dishonesty, short-sightedness and self-righteousness. The devil within prompted them to believe that the correct and logical use of the means of sustenance available to them that went beyond their actual needs and of which they enjoyed full control was, first of all, to spend it on their own personal comfort, luxuries, enjoyment and self-aggrandizement; and then to exploit it to grab more and more economic resources and, given the opportunity, to perpetuate their supremacy as despots and demi-gods.

1.4. Self-aggrandizement and luxuries

As a natural corollary of the first devilish trend, the rich refused to accept the rights of those in the community who were deprived of their due share of the national wealth or who could get much less than they actually needed. The affluent class thought it logical to let the under-privileged suffer and go from bad to worse. They were too myopic to see how this attitude forced so many in the community to turn criminal, remain illiterate, degenerate morally, suffer physically and mentally and lack the ability to play their role in the society's proper growth and development, thus causing greater damage to the social set-up of which they themselves were a part. These misguided people did not remain content with this, but continued to boost their ever-growing demands far beyond their actual requirements and diverted a major portion of the community's human and material resources to serve their ends. The human capital that could very well have been used in the service of civilization and culture was utilized instead to satisfy their lust and personal egos. They saw fornication as a need for which they recruited a class of professionals, like pimps and prostitutes. They believed they needed music, and thus came into being a whole host of groups and bands of dancers, singers, vocalists, instrumentalists and those engaged in producing musical instruments. Their craving for recreation knew no bounds, and hence there emerged a variety of performers, actors, mimics, painters, sculptors, storytellers, etc. Sport was equally important for them, for which they engaged hundreds of men to trap the animals. They were fond of boozing too, and therefore wished to 'enjoy' the pleasure of drunkenness, creating an army of men and women who were involved in the business of producing and serving them wine, opium, cocaine and other intoxicants. In short, these devil's disciples were not content with callously allowing a large segment of society to suffer morally, spiritually and physically. Criminally, they even went on to divert a good part of humanity from the course of better and useful vocations so that they could indulge in futile, mean and harmful pastimes that led to humanity's doom and destruction. Not only did they thus waste the human capital, but they also misused the material capital. These unfortunate people felt the need for villas, mansions, castles, gardens, amusement parks, clubs and opera houses, as well as acres of land and impressive structures just to get buried in. This is how those pieces of land, the construction material and the human labour, which could have sufficed for the housing needs and economic benefit of a large segment of society's homeless people, were lost to provide shelter and a burial place for every spendthrift. They also saw a need for attractive jewelry, gorgeous costumes, sophisticated implements and household wares, decorative artifacts, luxury coaches and so on. Their doors and galleries required costly curtains, their walls precious paintings, their floors expensive carpets and their lap-dogs cushions of velvet and collars of gold. This is how so much material and enterprise, which could have been used to serve the human needs for clothing and food, was instead consumed in satisfying the whims of a few self-willed aristocrats.

1.5. Capital worship

This was the outcome of just one aspect of the misguided trend of indulging in luxuries and self-aggrandizement. The consequences of the other aspects were even more horrifying. It is obviously wrong for a person to use the resources he has accumulated beyond his needs to grab more resources and economic clout. The resources that were created by the Almighty are intended to fulfill the subsistence needs and essential requirements of all His creatures. If by some chance you have been able to gather more than you need, it simply means that the share that belonged to somebody else has reached you by default. Why should you then try to amass it? Why don't you look at the many people around you who are unable or have failed in their efforts to get what they need from the means of subsistence, or have received much less than they require? This kind of soul-searching will convince you that it is the shares from these people's bounties of life that have somehow reached you. If they cannot get what should have belonged to them, why don't you step forward and pass on to them what was their due? Instead of following this right course, if you exploit the resources at your command in order to multiply them further, your work will be counter-productive, because you will go on exceeding your limits and your riches will serve no purpose other than satisfying your lust for wealth. The amount of time, energy and potential that you spend in satisfying your genuine needs is being utilized rightly, in a reasonable and correct way. But once you overstep your limits in your quest for wealth, you have degenerated into an economic animal or a money-making machine. You then become oblivious to the fact that there are much better uses for your time, energy and intellectual and physical faculties than in simply amassing wealth. The exploitative trend that is so glamorized by the devil to his disciples is, therefore, totally wrong rationally, logically and according to all the dictates of human instinct, and the measures evolved on the basis of this trend are so abominable and their consequences so horrific that nobody can realize their full extent.

Economic resources in excess of one's needs can be used in one of the following two ways in order to grab more resources:

- their advancement on interest-based loans;
- their investment in commercial and industrial enterprises.

These two methods, though somewhat different from each other, jointly lead to the division of the society into two classes: (i) the moneyed class of a small group of privileged people, who own more than they need and use their riches to grow even richer; and (ii) the larger segment of the society who have little, just enough for their needs or may have nothing at all. This kind of situation is bound to give rise to class-conflicts and confrontation in society. This is how the system of economic management that nature has based on the principles of exchange and equity lapses into a system of antagonistic competition.

1.6. The element of antagonistic competition

With the rise of such an unhealthy race, which in Islamic Economics is called *Muḥārabah* or antagonistic competition, the number of 'haves' in society continually decreases while the 'have-nots' multiply by leaps and bounds. This is due to the fact that, in this kind of competition, the more affluent absorb the resources of even the less privileged and push them into the category of the 'have-nots'. The resources of the land thus continue to accumulate in the hands of fewer and fewer people, while the larger section of the population goes on sliding downward and becoming more and more dependent on the affluent class.

Beginning on a small scale, antagonistic competition has gradually moved on through countries and communities until it eventually encompasses the entire world. Generally speaking, when a country generates a surplus of revenue, it invests it in productive uses, and thus more and more consumer items start rolling out of its factories. But there soon comes a saturation point, when the production level rises over the consumption level and, as is natural in this eventuality, the inability of the low-income groups to buy the products which they may need, but cannot afford, results in the dumping of surplus products and a build up of the rich classes' money in ventures that are rendered unproductive. A portion of the money they invested thus becomes irretrievable and turns into loans payable by the industrial sector of a country. This is the case of just one cycle, and from this analogy we may guess how much amount of money will go on turning into unproductive loans in many other sectors and cycles if it is allowed to be reinvested in profitable ventures that have the sole purpose of letting the affluent class make more money without paying attention to equitable distribution or raising the purchasing power and standard of living of society's less-privileged members. The surplus products are often taken out of the country to foreign markets, where they gradually create the same situation due to the similar, inequitable distribution of wealth and the disparity of income between the various classes. This leads to a vicious circle where the rich become richer and national wealth accumulates in the hands of a chosen few in each country and community.

The trend of antagonistic competition thus crosses national boundaries to globalize an exploitative economic system. It gives rise to global competition and takes the following shapes:

- Every country tries to produce more and more at less and less cost in order to sell its products in world markets and get the maximum profit. To achieve this, they keep the wages of the labourers very low. The common man in the producing country thus gets too small a share in any venture to meet even the basic necessities of life.
- Each country imposes restrictions on the entry of goods from other countries into its territory and into less-developed countries under its sphere of influence. It also checks the outflow of its raw materials in order to prevent any other country from making use of them to its advantage. This gives rise to international feuds that often lead to wars.
- Thirdly, the countries that are unable to check the machinations of the forces of economic exploitation fall prey to their exploitative thrust. Economic pirates not only try to sell their surplus to these countries, but the capital that they cannot absorb themselves in profitable ventures is taken to these countries to bring back better dividends. This eventually transfers the same problem to the countries at the receiving end. The capital invested cannot be retrieved in full and a major portion of the income generated is reinvested yet again in more profitable ventures, causing the developing countries to groan under the ever-increasing burden of the capitalist nations' loans. The time eventually comes when these countries are unable to repay their debts, even if they sell themselves out. This vicious circle, if not properly checked, means the entire world is doomed to go bankrupt, with no market left to consume the overflow of capital.

1.7. Cartels and monopolies

The element of global antagonistic competition has given rise to a small group of exploitative people that includes bankers, brokers and the heads of industrial and commercial cartels and monopolies. This group has so dominated the world's economic resources that the whole of humanity today appears to be helpless before it. It has now become virtually impossible for an entrepreneur to start a venture independently, using only his own physical and intellectual strength, and gainfully utilize his share of the resources available on God's earth. There is not much breathing space freely available today for small entrepreneurs, traders, artisans, farmers and so on to make a niche for themselves on the world stage. Each of them is helpless, forced to live as bondsmen, serfs or servants of the global economic giants. These giants squeeze all of the potential out of their minds and bodies, as well as using up their time, in return for the bare minimum level of sustenance, enough only for them to make ends meet. This is why the human being today is reduced to no better than an economic animal. Only the few lucky ones have the opportunity now, in the midst of their back-breaking struggle for economic survival, to do something for their moral, intellectual and spiritual sustenance, to devote a little time to something nobler than the demands of the belly and to let those God-given facets of their personalities that seek objectives higher and sublimer than the quest for living to flourish. In fact, the economic struggle has become so tough in the contemporary satanic system that all of life's other issues have been rendered almost meaningless and futile.

To the misfortune of humanity, this satanic economic order has also adversely affected the world's moral outlook, its political systems and legal codes. The guardians of morality and ethics are busy from East to West preaching the need to save for the future. People are made to believe that it is both foolish and unethical to spend whatever one earns, and that every bread winner must save from his income to deposit money in banks, buy an insurance policy or invest in shares. An element that is so damaging for humanity is thus being projected as most beneficial and a sign of prudence. As for political control in the world, this is evidently in the tight grip of a system which is the means of the exploitation and economic subjugation of people. The world's legal order is being governed by the same exploitative system. According to these laws, individuals are practically free to carry on their economic struggle as they deem fit, regardless of their community's interests. Rarely is anyone bothered to check which means of earning money is legally and ethically permissible, and which is prohibited. Those who toil hard to make a living through lawful means and those who grow rich using both fair means and foul are all equal in the eyes of the law. A person is free to produce liquor, set up brothels or sex shops, produce pornographic material in an audio-visual form or print, spread vulgarity through articles or sex-exploiting movies, establish interest-based ventures and gambling dens and promote speculation, betting, lottery and other similar means of making easy money. In short, a person may do anything that suits his agenda, and the law will be there not only to facilitate his project, but also to protect his rights. The wealth that he gathers is then allowed to remain accumulated even after his death. The *Rule of Primogeniture*, the practice of adoption and the joint family system have been devised with the same end in mind: one black cobra replacing another to guard the chest that holds the treasure. If no young cobra is left behind by the one dying, then the rule of adoption is used to help and the treasure finds a new custodian, instead of allowing it to pass on to the community for a wider circulation.

These are the reasons why humanity is faced today with a massive challenge to arrange a means of subsistence for every individual on God's earth, to let each and every individual have the opportunity for progress according to their qualifications and abilities and to allow their personalities to develop and grow freely.

1.8. The recipe of communism

Communism came up with a unique solution to the economic issue. This recipe was to transfer the means of the production of wealth from private to public ownership, and also to assign to the community (with the Communist Party as its sole representative) the responsibility for its distribution. On the face of it, this appears to be a reasonable solution. But the more that one reflects on its practical side, the more its drawbacks are revealed and one is forced to admit that the result of this prescription is bound to be as deadly as that which it sought to replace.

1.8.1. *The super capitalist*

An additional problem with this system is that, even if making use of the means of production and the distribution of produced goods is entrusted theoretically to the community, it will still have to be carried out practically by a small group of managers who form the *Executive.* Although initially elected by the community, this group will have all the resources of the land at its disposal, while the people will be at the receiving end. The entire population will thus be left at the mercy of this all-powerful coterie of managers, or rather exploiters. Who would have the courage to go against their wishes, to challenge their authority in the country or to organize a peaceful struggle that could replace them through a popular ballot? The reality is that anyone who earns the displeasure of the ruling elites under this kind of dispensation foregoes their very right to exist. The workers have no courage to go on strike against their mill-owner to uphold their rights. They have no option to choose a workplace for themselves, as there is but one sole mill-owner for the whole country, who also rules the land. It is not possible to seek popular support and sympathy even for a good cause if this is contrary to the wishes of the Party. The natural outcome of communist rule is therefore the emergence of one Super Capitalist out of the ashes of many large and small ones in the country and the rise of a single mill-owner and feudal lord, who is simultaneously the Czar as well as the capital baron.

1.8.2. *An exploitative system*

An absolute power like this is bound to corrupt its power absolutely. It will be hard for the ruler to refrain from tyranny and oppression, particularly because he has no faith or sense of being answerable to any Supreme Being. Hypothetically speaking, even if we presume that a group of ruling elites would not go beyond certain limits in their use of the absolute power at their command and would continue to fulfill the demands of justice and fairplay, there is no avenue under such a totalitarian dispensation for the natural growth and development of the personalities of individuals. What the human personality needs most for its proper growth is freedom and the means to use that freedom according to its discretion for the further development of its hidden potential. The communist system offers no room for this. The resources of the land are entirely out of the individual's reach and are concentrated in the hands of the executive authority, which then uses them according to its own plan and in furtherance of the rulers' interests. Individuals who wish to benefit from the state's resources are left with no option but to follow the plan drawn up by those in power and actually to surrender themselves to the dictates of the ruling elites, who mould them according to their own scheme of things. This kind of social order places virtually every individual in society at the disposal of a few persons, as if they were no better than inanimate raw material. Under this so-called *Dictatorship of the Proletariat*, a small band of the most powerful men in the land are free to put the enormous human material at their disposal to whatever plan and use they choose, in exactly the same way that shoes are moulded from leather and tools are wrought from raw iron.

1.8.3. *Slaughter of the self*

The drawbacks of the communist system are so terrible for human civilization that, even if it succeeds in the judicious distribution of the basic needs of life, its disadvantages are going to be far more meaningful than the benefits. The natural growth and development of human civilization depends entirely on the availability of equal opportunity to each and every person, helping them to develop the distinct faculties and potential with which they are born. This is how everyone can play his due role in life's joint venture. This natural growth cannot be achieved in an environment where there is regimented planning to 'tame' humans. A group of humans, however intelligent, well-meaning and well-qualified, cannot be so knowledgeable and *omniscient* that they can correctly assess the intrinsic qualities and inborn faculties of countless millions of their fellow humans, and then chart out for each of them a perfect course for their growth and development. Such a group of 'master-planners' is liable to make mistakes due to the limitations of their knowledge, while also failing to serve their own group interest due to their lop-sided approach. A ruthless regimentation of this type will be a death-blow to human civilization's diversity and will turn a society into a lifeless monotony; it will put an end to the natural growth of civilization and giving rise to an artificial and sham evolutionary process, eventually leading to the freezing of human potential and a severe mental and moral degeneration. A human being is after all not a sapling or grass grown in a garden that a gardener may trim and prune to suit his design. Every individual has his own personality and likes to grow and develop as demanded by his nature. If you try to deprive a person of his freedom by force, he will grow not as you have planned, but will instead either rebel or slowly whither away.

Communism's fundamental mistake is that it takes the economic issue as the core factor in human life. It lacks insight into the problems that face human beings and thus the capacity to resolve these from a correct perspective. Its attitude towards all of the issues of life is lopsided. Its approach towards metaphysics, morality, history, the social and physical sciences and everything within the sphere of human knowledge and learning is economy-centred and, because of this one-sided approach, the entire balance of life is disturbed. It therefore does not offer a correct or natural solution to the economic problems of man.

1.9. The fascist solution

Fascism and national socialism also claim to offer a solution. This solution aims at retaining the individual's right over his economic resources, but keeping this right subservient to the national interest and under the state's tight control. Practically speaking, the consequences of this approach do not appear to be greatly different from those of communism. Like the communist agenda, the fascist solution also demands that the individual lose himself in the melting pot of the group, leaving no room for his personality to develop and grow freely. Moreover, the fascist state that keeps this right of the individual under tight control is as oppressive, tyrannical and autocratic as communist rule. It needs a strong, coercive state power to keep all the resources of the land under its thumb and make them serve its agenda. The population of a state that has such coercive power at its disposal can only be a helpless entity, reduced to the level of serfs by its rulers.

1.10. The Islamic solution

Now, let us examine the solution that Islam offers for the economic problems of man.

1.10.1. *Basic rules*

Among the rules that Islam follows for all issues of human life, the first is to retain those principles that are natural and, in case of deviation, turn a person back to the natural course. The second precept on which all the social reforms of

Islam are based is to place a heavy emphasis on the reformation of conduct and mentality in order to strike at the root of what is wrong in the human psyche, instead of remaining content with the external precautions of introducing a few rules and regulations into society's social set-up. The third basic rule, which may be found everywhere in the legal code of Islam, is that the state's coercive power and the force of law should only be used as and when it is deemed essential.

In the light of these three basic rules, Islam seeks to eliminate the unnatural ways that man has followed in economic affairs, and to do this it relies more on reforming conduct and less on recourse to state intervention. Islam acknowledges that man should be free in his struggle to earn a living, that he should enjoy the ownership right of whatever he earns through his hard labour and that there must be a difference and diversity among humans in line with the variations in their qualifications and capabilities, to the extent to which these conform to the demands of nature. However, it also imposes restrictions on people to help restrain them from transgressing the natural limits of justice and fairplay and straying into the domains of tyranny and injustice.

1.10.2. *Earning money*

Let us first look at the question of earning money. Islam acknowledges a man's right to earn a living in this world, according to his aptitude, qualifications and capabilities. It does not, however, permit him to use anti-social or corrupt means to earn this living. It makes a distinction between the *Ḥarām* and *Ḥalāl* (forbidden and lawful) means of earning money, and declares every anti-social means to be *Ḥarām*, which it highlights in greater detail. According to the *Sharīʿah*'s legal code, wine and all intoxicants are not only *Ḥarām* in themselves, but their production, sale, purchase and storage are also unlawful. The *Sharīʿah* disapproves of professions like the sex trade, music, dance, etc. as a means of livelihood. It similarly declares unlawful gaining economic resources used for one person's profits at the expense of others. It has therefore proclaimed as *Ḥarām* means of livelihood such as bribery, theft, gambling, speculation, betting, all fraudulent deals, hoarding, monopolies and cartels. Islam has also prohibited all forms of business transactions that lead to litigations, or where the profit and loss depends entirely on chance and sheer good luck, as well as those businesses in which the rights of the two parties remain undefined. If you study the mercantile law of Islam deeply, you will notice that most of the sources of income by which people become millionaires and billionaires today have been forbidden by Islam, and there are severe legal restrictions in these areas. The economic resources which Islam declares lawful make it difficult for an entrepreneur to mint money for himself, if he abides honestly by its parameters.

1.10.3. *Ownership rights*

Islam also acknowledges an individual's right to own whatever he may have obtained though lawful means. It does not leave him free to use it as he will, however, but imposes certain restrictions on this. These are the following three ways that it considers suitable for putting an earned income to use: (i) by spending; (ii) by investing in profitable ventures; or (iii) by saving. The restrictions imposed by Islam on each of these three modes of utilizing a person's income are explained below:

1.10.3.1. RULES FOR SPENDING MONEY

It is unlawful in Islam to spend one's income in a manner that may be ethically damaging or socially injurious: You cannot squander your hard-earned money in gambling; you cannot indulge in drinking wine or any other intoxicant; you are forbidden from using your legitimate financial resources in wasteful expenditures and unproductive pastimes, like music, dance and similar extravaganza. This is why it is forbidden to wear a dress made of silk fabric, to use silver and gold ornaments and utensils or to decorate a wall with photographs and replicas of human figures. In short, Islam has shut all the doors through which a man could waste the best part of his earning on self-aggrandizement. The ways that are permitted by Islam for spending money are mainly those by which one may afford a decent living of a reasonable standard. Whatever one thus saves must be spent on a good cause, in projects of charity and public welfare, and also to help the socially deprived and underprivileged who may have been unable to get enough of the bounties of life to satisfy their legitimate needs. The best use of money, according to Islam, is to spend one's earnings in a reasonable manner on one's lawful requirements, and let the amount that is saved be used to support those in need. This is the quality that Islam rates as the noblest in social conduct and a model of a true Muslim's behaviour. A society governed by the social norms of Islam will always treat those noble souls who earn to spend according to Islam's precepts as role models, rather than those who accumulate wealth or use their earnings simply to earn even more.

1.10.3.2. ELIMINATING THE CAPITALIST TREND

Practically speaking, the human weakness for money and luxuries can never be completely overcome by mere sermonizing or abstract moral precepts. No matter how many exhortations they are given, many people will continue to indulge in extravagance and the quest to make more money. Islam has, therefore, imposed certain legal restrictions on the use of the wealth that is saved after spending on one's lawful needs. It has totally prohibited all interest-based transactions. If you lend your money to someone as a loan, or as a means to help him generate an income, you should only get back from him the amount of capital you gave. Islam has thus broken the backbone of the oppressive capitalist system. It has blunted the sharp edges of the tools through which a capitalist goes on multiplying his wealth and grabbing economic resources from others. On the other hand, it permits an entrepreneur to use his surplus money in his personal business, trade, industry, a joint venture or in an equity participation on a profit and loss sharing basis. It uses different means to check the accumulation of wealth in a few hands in excess of their personal needs.

1.10.3.3. CIRCULATION OF WEALTH AND SOCIAL SECURITY

As stated earlier, Islam does not approve of people amassing their surplus wealth. By demanding its followers to spend whatever they earn in satisfying their needs, investing in business or lending to others to help them satisfy their needs, it keeps the capital in circulation. However, if one manages to save and pool a surplus out of his earnings, then two and a half percent of the total amount saved will be compulsorily deducted annually as mandatory charity or *Zakāh* to be used according to a well-devised plan of social welfare. The funds so generated will be deposited in the public treasury (*Bayt al-Māl*). The *Bayt al-Māl* will thus be a guaranteed source of help for all those in need of support. The Islamic system of *Zakāh* is actually the best-known institution of social insurance in human society to date. It also prevents the evils that crop up due to the absence of an institutionalized mechanism for social assistance and security.

The main factor responsible for inducing people in a capitalist system to accumulate wealth and reinvest it in profit-making ventures, which results in the need for life insurance, etc., is that every individual in a capitalist milieu is dependent entirely on his personal resources. If someone does not save for his old age, he is likely to die of hunger and want. If someone dies under that system without leaving behind enough for his family, his dependents will be left high and dry, with no one even able to give him alms. In the case of illness, with nothing saved for the 'rainy days', a person may have nobody to take care of him. He can expect no support from anywhere in the event of contingencies like a fire destroying his house, a loss in business or other similar eventualities. The reason that the working class in a capitalist system are compelled to accept the terms and conditions imposed by their masters, and serve them as their bondsmen, is this same element of dependence and helplessness. Poor workers know that, if they refuse to accept the terms offered and do not work for their petty and insufficient wages, they would go without food, clothing and shelter. Because of this accursed system, today there are millions of people begging for food on the one hand, and on the other, surplus products piled up in factories and tons of wheat being dumped into the sea. This is because, under the capitalist dispensation, there is no provision for making additional economic resources available to the needy. Capitalism does not bother to generate the purchasing power to enable the 'have nots' to secure their needs without having to beg for them. If everyone is able to buy the things he needs, this will lead to an overall progress in industry, trade, agriculture, arts and crafts.

The Islamic system of *Zakāh* and *Bayt al-Māl* (public treasury) provides such a benevolent mechanism. The *Bayt al-Māl* is an infallible institution of social security for support in times of need. People do not have to care for tomorrow. As and when the need arises, they may go to the *Bayt al-Māl* and get their due. Is there ever any need for bank deposits or life insurance policies if such a mechanism is in place? Under the benevolent umbrella of the Islamic system, one may die in peace, leaving behind any dependents safe in the knowledge that the public treasury will automatically take care of them when they depart. One can always seek the help of *Bayt al-Māl* in the case of disease, old age or natural disasters. There is no heartless capitalist who will ever force someone to work on his terms and conditions. This is an institutionalized arrangement that enables a person to be free of the lurking fear of going without food, clothing and shelter. It helps every member of the society who is either incapable of producing capital or is producing less than he needs to support himself and his dependents. This means that a balance is maintained between the production and consumption of goods and services, and there is no need to roam around the world shifting the weight of your bankruptcy to everyone else, and perhaps even further beyond to other planets.

Another measure that Islam has in place, in addition to *Zakāh*, to broaden the basis of wealth is through its law of inheritance. All of the legal systems of the world, other than the Islamic *Sharī'ah*, seek to allow the wealth that someone has gathered to continue accumulating even after his death. On the contrary, Islam does not permit the wealth to be kept hoarded. Once the owner dies, his assets are divided and distributed according to predetermined shares. Islam declares that the deceased's sons, daughters, wives, parents, brothers and sisters are his heirs, among whom the legacy must be distributed in accordance with the Islamic Law of Inheritance. In the absence of near relatives, efforts are made to find out those who are distantly related for the distribution of the legacy as determined by the law. In the case of a person with no close or distant relatives, any adopted son is not considered to be his legal heir, and the community as a whole then becomes the lawful inheritor, and the wealth that is left behind is deposited in the *Bayt al-Māl*. The Islamic *Sharīʿah* has thus ensured that, even if somebody piles up riches worth billions of rupees, this should be split into small fragments within two to three generations following his death and its concentration should gradually give way to dispersal and a wider circulation.

1.11. Points to ponder

Let us reflect on the economic system that I have tried to present here using some broad outlines. Does this not completely eliminate the drawbacks of private ownership that surface in Muslim society, simply due to ignorance of Islamic teachings? If this is so, then why should we use the communist, fascist or nationalist-socialist models and follow artificial means of economic management, which rather than removing one wrong actually create so many others? I have not explained the entire economic system of Islam. It is not possible to discuss in detail here the ways and means that Islam allows to manage land, settle business disputes and provide capital for trade and industry. I similarly cannot expand on how Islam has removed restrictions of the tax on the inland transportation of trade goods and duties on imports and exports in order to facilitate the free exchange of consumer goods. The paucity of time and space also does not permit me to elaborate on how benign the economic system of Islam is, as it reduces to the minimum possible limit an Islamic state's expenditure on civil and military services and government administration, and totally withdraws stamp duty from the courts of law. It thus removes a great economic burden from the community's shoulders. Instead of consuming the revenue generated through taxes in heavy, unproductive expenditure, it spends the capital on schemes of public welfare for society's betterment as a whole. The opportunities thus offered for the prosperity and well-being of people living in a model welfare state make the Islamic economic system a great boon and blessing for mankind. If viewed dispassionately and examined incisively, setting aside the biases, prejudices and narrow-mindedness inherited from the past and overcoming the trend to be overawed by everything new because of the predominance of non-Islamic systems in the world, I am confident that every right-thinking and clear-headed person will admit that the Islamic economic system is the best and most-suited to solve humanity's economic problems. However, one would be grossly mistaken if one thinks that this system can function independently of the whole body of Islamic beliefs, moral values and social norms. The economic system of Islam is closely interlinked with its political, judicial, legal, civil and social systems, while these are all based on its moral code. Even the moral code is not self-sustaining, but depends entirely on faith in the Lord, the All-Knowing and All-Seeing, to Whom each is answerable for all that he does. One similarly has to have a firm faith in the life Hereafter, in the accountability of the Day of Reckoning and in the fact that whatever he knows of the Islamic teachings and code of conduct, of which the economic system of Islam is also a part, is based entirely on the Divine Guidance preserved by the Qur'ān and the *Sunnah* of the Holy Prophet (*pbuh*). One must take on this whole system of belief and conduct, the Islamic way of life in its totality, because the economic system of Islam cannot function in isolation even for a day and no benefit can be drawn from a lifeless experiment.

2 Economic Teachings of the Qur'ān

2.1. Fundamental truths

The most basic fact about human economy, which the Holy Qur'ān emphatically and repeatedly seeks to bring home to us, is that all the means and resources on which mankind's survival depends have been raised by Allah *subḥānahū wa ta'ālā*. It is He Who has created and established them on the laws of nature so that they have become beneficial to man. It is He Who has granted human beings the opportunity and authority to make use of these resources as they please:

هُوَ ٱلَّذِى جَعَلَ لَكُمُ ٱلْأَرْضَ ذَلُولًا فَٱمْشُوا۟ فِى مَنَاكِبِهَا وَكُلُوا۟ مِن رِّزْقِهِۦ ۖ وَإِلَيْهِ ٱلنُّشُورُ ﴿١٥﴾

('He it is Who made the earth subservient to you. So traverse in its tracks and partake of the sustenance He has provided. To Him will you be resurrected.')

(*al-Mulk*, 67: 15)

وَهُوَ ٱلَّذِى مَدَّ ٱلْأَرْضَ وَجَعَلَ فِيهَا رَوَٰسِىَ وَأَنْهَـٰرًا ۖ وَمِن كُلِّ ٱلثَّمَرَٰتِ جَعَلَ فِيهَا زَوْجَيْنِ ٱثْنَيْنِ ۖ يُغْشِى
ٱلَّيْلَ ٱلنَّهَارَ ۚ إِنَّ فِى ذَٰلِكَ لَـَٔايَـٰتٍ لِّقَوْمٍ يَتَفَكَّرُونَ ﴿٣﴾

('He it is Who has stretched out the earth and has placed in it firm mountains and has caused the rivers to flow. He has made every fruit in pairs, two and two, and He it is Who causes the night to cover the day. Surely there are signs in these for those who reflect.')

(*al-Ra'd*, 13: 3)

هُوَ ٱلَّذِى خَلَقَ لَكُم مَّا فِى ٱلْأَرْضِ جَمِيعًا ... ﴿٢٩﴾

('It is He Who has created for you all things that are on earth.')

(*al-Baqarah*, 2: 29)

اللَّهُ الَّذِي خَلَقَ السَّمَاوَاتِ وَالْأَرْضَ وَأَنزَلَ مِنَ السَّمَاءِ مَاءً فَأَخْرَجَ بِهِ مِنَ الثَّمَرَاتِ رِزْقًا لَّكُمْ ۖ وَسَخَّرَ
لَكُمُ الْفُلْكَ لِتَجْرِيَ فِي الْبَحْرِ بِأَمْرِهِ ۖ وَسَخَّرَ لَكُمُ الْأَنْهَارَ ﴿٣٢﴾ وَسَخَّرَ لَكُمُ الشَّمْسَ وَالْقَمَرَ دَائِبَيْنِ ۖ
وَسَخَّرَ لَكُمُ اللَّيْلَ وَالنَّهَارَ ﴿٣٣﴾ وَآتَاكُم مِّن كُلِّ مَا سَأَلْتُمُوهُ ۚ وَإِن تَعُدُّوا نِعْمَتَ اللَّهِ لَا تُحْصُوهَا ۗ إِنَّ الْإِنسَانَ
لَظَلُومٌ كَفَّارٌ ﴿٣٤﴾

('It is Allah Who created the heavens and the earth, Who sent down water from the heaven and thereby brought forth a variety of fruits as your sustenance, Who subjected for you the ships that they may sail in the sea by His command, Who subjected for you the rivers, Who subjected for you the sun and the moon and both of them are constant on their courses, Who subjected for you the night and the day, and Who gave you all that you asked Him for. Were you to count the favours of Allah you shall never be able to encompass them. Verily man is highly unjust, exceedingly ungrateful.')

(*Ibrāhīm*, 14: 32-34)

وَلَقَدْ مَكَّنَّاكُمْ فِي الْأَرْضِ وَجَعَلْنَا لَكُمْ فِيهَا مَعَايِشَ ۗ ... ﴿١٠﴾

('We assuredly established you in the earth and arranged for your livelihood in it.')

(*al-A'rāf*, 7: 10)

أَفَرَأَيْتُم مَّا تَحْرُثُونَ ﴿٦٣﴾ أَأَنتُمْ تَزْرَعُونَهُ أَمْ نَحْنُ الزَّارِعُونَ ﴿٦٤﴾

('Have you considered the seeds you till? Is it you or We Who make them grow.')

(*al-Wāqi'ah*, 56: 63,64)

2.2 Parameters of permissible and impermissible

On the basis of these facts, the Holy Qur'ān lays down the principle that man is not free to harness and make use of these resources, nor is he authorized to set his own parameters on the permissible and the impermissible, the lawful and the forbidden. It is entirely the Prerogative of Allah *subḥanahū wa ta'ālā* to define such limits.

The Qur'ān rejects the plea of the Midianites, an ancient Arab people, that they should be free to earn and spend the way they liked because they thought they had absolute right over the bounties of nature:

قَالُوا يَا شُعَيْبُ أَصَلَاتُكَ تَأْمُرُكَ أَن نَّتْرُكَ مَا يَعْبُدُ آبَاؤُنَا أَوْ أَن نَّفْعَلَ فِي أَمْوَالِنَا مَا نَشَاءُ ۖ ... ﴿٨٧﴾

('They replied: 'O Shu'ayb! Does your Prayer enjoin upon you that we should forsake the deities whom our forefathers worshipped, or that we should give up using our wealth as we please?")

(*Hūd*, 11: 87)

The Qur'ān decries as 'falsehood' the idea that a man may himself pronounce something *Ḥarām* (forbidden) and some other thing *Ḥalāl* (lawful).

وَلَا تَقُولُوا۟ لِمَا تَصِفُ أَلْسِنَتُكُمُ ٱلْكَذِبَ هَٰذَا حَلَٰلٌ وَهَٰذَا حَرَامٌ ... ﴿١١٦﴾

('And do not utter falsehood by letting your tongues declare: 'This is lawful' and 'That is unlawful.')

(*al-Naḥl*, 16: 116)

It attributes this authority only to Allah *subḥānahū wa taʿālā* and to His Messenger as His Deputy:

... يَأْمُرُهُم بِٱلْمَعْرُوفِ وَيَنْهَىٰهُمْ عَنِ ٱلْمُنكَرِ وَيُحِلُّ لَهُمُ ٱلطَّيِّبَٰتِ وَيُحَرِّمُ عَلَيْهِمُ ٱلْخَبَٰٓئِثَ وَيَضَعُ عَنْهُمْ إِصْرَهُمْ وَٱلْأَغْلَٰلَ ٱلَّتِى كَانَتْ عَلَيْهِمْ ... ﴿١٥٧﴾

('He enjoins upon them what is good and forbids them what is evil. He makes the clean things lawful to them and prohibits all corrupt things and removes from them their burdens and the shackles that were upon them.')

(*al-Aʿrāf*, 7: 157)

2.3. Parameters of private ownership

The Holy Qur'ān reaffirms the individual's ownership right under the Supreme Ownership of Allah *subḥānahū wa taʿālā* and within the parameters set by Him:

يَٰٓأَيُّهَا ٱلَّذِينَ ءَامَنُوا۟ لَا تَأْكُلُوٓا۟ أَمْوَٰلَكُم بَيْنَكُم بِٱلْبَٰطِلِ إِلَّآ أَن تَكُونَ تِجَٰرَةً عَن تَرَاضٍ مِّنكُمْ ... ﴿٢٩﴾

('Believers! Do not devour one another's possessions wrongfully; rather, let there be trading by mutual consent.')

(*al-Nisā'*, 4: 29)

... وَأَحَلَّ ٱللَّهُ ٱلْبَيْعَ وَحَرَّمَ ٱلرِّبَوٰا۟ ... ﴿٢٧٥﴾

('... even though Allah has made buying and selling lawful, and interest unlawful.')

(*al-Baqarah*, 2: 275)

... وَإِن تُبْتُمْ فَلَكُمْ رُءُوسُ أَمْوَٰلِكُمْ لَا تَظْلِمُونَ وَلَا تُظْلَمُونَ ﴿٢٧٩﴾

('If you repent even now, you have the right of the return of your capital; neither will you do wrong nor will you be wronged.')

(*al-Baqarah*, 2: 279)

يَٰٓأَيُّهَا ٱلَّذِينَ ءَامَنُوٓا۟ إِذَا تَدَايَنتُم بِدَيْنٍ إِلَىٰٓ أَجَلٍ مُّسَمًّى فَٱكْتُبُوهُ ۚ وَلْيَكْتُب بَّيْنَكُمْ كَاتِبٌۢ بِٱلْعَدْلِ ۚ ... ﴿٢٨٢﴾

('Believers! Whenever you contract a debt from one another for a known term, commit it to writing. Let a scribe write it down between you justly.')

(*al-Baqarah*, 2: 282)

وَإِن كُنتُمْ عَلَىٰ سَفَرٍ وَلَمْ تَجِدُوا۟ كَاتِبًا فَرِهَٰنٌ مَّقْبُوضَةٌ ۖ ... ﴿٢٨٣﴾

('And if you are on a journey and do not find a scribe to write the document then resort to taking pledges in hand!')

(*al-Baqarah*, 2: 283)

لِّلرِّجَالِ نَصِيبٌ مِّمَّا تَرَكَ ٱلْوَٰلِدَانِ وَٱلْأَقْرَبُونَ وَلِلنِّسَآءِ نَصِيبٌ مِّمَّا تَرَكَ ٱلْوَٰلِدَانِ وَٱلْأَقْرَبُونَ مِمَّا قَلَّ مِنْهُ
أَوْ كَثُرَ ۚ نَصِيبًا مَّفْرُوضًا ﴿٧﴾

('Just as there is a share for men in what their parents and kinsfolk leave behind, so there is a share for women in what their parents and kinsfolk leave behind – be it little or much – a share ordained (by Allah).')

(*al-Nisā'*, 4: 7)

يَٰٓأَيُّهَا ٱلَّذِينَ ءَامَنُوا۟ لَا تَدْخُلُوا۟ بُيُوتًا غَيْرَ بُيُوتِكُمْ حَتَّىٰ تَسْتَأْنِسُوا۟ وَتُسَلِّمُوا۟ عَلَىٰٓ أَهْلِهَا ۚ ... ﴿٢٧﴾

('Believers! Enter not houses other than your own houses until you have obtained the permission of the inmates of those houses and have greeted them with peace.')

(*al-Nūr*, 24: 27)

أَوَلَمْ يَرَوْا۟ أَنَّا خَلَقْنَا لَهُم مِّمَّا عَمِلَتْ أَيْدِينَآ أَنْعَٰمًا فَهُمْ لَهَا مَٰلِكُونَ ﴿٧١﴾

('Do they not see Our handiwork: We created for them cattle which they own.')

(*Yā Sīn*, 36: 71)

وَٱلسَّارِقُ وَٱلسَّارِقَةُ فَٱقْطَعُوٓا۟ أَيْدِيَهُمَا جَزَآءًۢ بِمَا كَسَبَا نَكَٰلًا مِّنَ ٱللَّهِ ۗ ... ﴿٣٨﴾

('As for the thief – male or female – cut off the hands of both. This is a recompense for what they have done, and an exemplary punishment from Allah.')

(*al-Māʾidah*, 5: 38)

...كُلُواْ مِن ثَمَرِهِۦٓ إِذَآ أَثْمَرَ وَءَاتُواْ حَقَّهُۥ يَوْمَ حَصَادِهِۦ...

('Eat of their fruits when they come to fruition and pay His due on the day of harvesting.')

(*al-Anʿām*, 6: 141)

خُذْ مِنْ أَمْوَٰلِهِمْ صَدَقَةً تُطَهِّرُهُمْ وَتُزَكِّيهِم بِهَا وَصَلِّ عَلَيْهِمْ...

('Take alms out of their riches and thereby cleanse them and bring about their growth (in righteousness), and pray for them.')

(*al-Tawbah*, 9: 103)

وَءَاتُواْ ٱلْيَتَٰمَىٰٓ أَمْوَٰلَهُمْ وَلَا تَتَبَدَّلُواْ ٱلْخَبِيثَ بِٱلطَّيِّبِ وَلَا تَأْكُلُوٓاْ أَمْوَٰلَهُمْ إِلَىٰٓ أَمْوَٰلِكُمْ...

('Give orphans their property, and do not exchange the bad for the good, and do not eat up their property by mixing it with your own.')

(*al-Nisāʾ*, 4: 2)

وَءَاتُواْ ٱلنِّسَآءَ صَدُقَٰتِهِنَّ نِحْلَةً...

('Give women their bridal-due in good cheer (considering it a duty).')

(*al-Nisāʾ*, 4: 4)

وَإِنْ أَرَدتُّمُ ٱسْتِبْدَالَ زَوْجٍ مَّكَانَ زَوْجٍ وَءَاتَيْتُمْ إِحْدَىٰهُنَّ قِنطَارًا فَلَا تَأْخُذُواْ مِنْهُ شَيْـًٔا...

('And if ye decide to dispense with a wife in order to take another, do not take away anything of what you might have given the first one, even if you had given her a heap of gold.')

(*al-Nisāʾ*, 4: 20)

مَّثَلُ ٱلَّذِينَ يُنفِقُونَ أَمْوَٰلَهُمْ فِى سَبِيلِ ٱللَّهِ كَمَثَلِ حَبَّةٍ أَنۢبَتَتْ سَبْعَ سَنَابِلَ فِى كُلِّ سُنۢبُلَةٍ مِّاْئَةُ حَبَّةٍ...

('The example of those who spend their wealth in the Way of Allah is like that of a grain of corn that sprouts seven ears, and in every ear there are a hundred grains.')

(*al-Baqarah*, 2: 261)

... وَتُجَٰهِدُونَ فِي سَبِيلِ ٱللَّهِ بِأَمْوَٰلِكُمْ وَأَنفُسِكُمْ ... ﴿١١﴾

('... and strive in the Way of Allah with your possessions and your lives.')

(*al-Ṣaff*, 61: 11)

وَفِيٓ أَمْوَٰلِهِمْ حَقٌّ لِّلسَّآئِلِ وَٱلْمَحْرُومِ ﴿١٩﴾

('... and in their wealth there was a rightful share for him who would ask and for the destitute.')

(*al-Dhāriyāt*, 51: 19)

Private ownership is thus shown to be essential in order to carry out the Divine injunctions mentioned above. The blueprint for the economy that the Book of God presents is entirely based on the individual's right to own. According to this blueprint, no distinction has been made between consumer goods and the means of production that could restrict private ownership of the former and make the latter public property. It similarly treats earned income and unearned income, in which no personal labour is involved, equally. For example, whatever someone inherits from his parents, children, wife, husband, brother and sister is not an income earned through his labour. The income that a recipient of *Zakāh* gets has no element of his labour. The blueprint also leaves no impression that this is an interim arrangement until the ultimate goal of public ownership is finally reached, after eliminating all forms of private ownership. If this goal been part of the Qur'ānic scheme, it would have been clearly stated and the Almighty would have given detailed instructions and guidelines regarding this.

Just because the Qur'ān has stated a universal truth: إِنَّ ٱلْأَرْضَ لِلَّهِ (... 'The earth is Allah's') (*al-A'rāf*, 7: 128), does not inevitably lead to a conclusion negating private ownership. The Qur'ān has also proclaimed: لِّلَّهِ مَا فِى ٱلسَّمَٰوَٰتِ وَمَا فِى ٱلْأَرْضِ ('All that is in the heavens and the earth belongs to Allah.') (*al-Baqarah*, 2: 284). Is it correct to deduce from this that there is nothing in the heavens and the earth which can become an individual's property, but must instead be a national asset? If Divine Ownership is taken to negate human proprietorship, the same principle will equally negate public ownership as well.

Similarly, it is incorrect to deduce from *Āyah* 10 of *Sūrah Ḥā. Mīm. al-Sajdah* (41:10) – وَقَدَّرَ فِيهَآ أَقْوَٰتَهَا فِىٓ أَرْبَعَةِ أَيَّامٍ سَوَآءً لِّلسَّآئِلِينَ ('... and provided it with sustenance in proportion to the needs of all who seek (sustenance). All this was done in four days.') – that the Holy Qur'ān seeks to distribute the earth's food resources equally among all human beings, and that this equality can only be achieved through public ownership. The Qur'ānic text in no way supports this interpretation. Firstly, the clause سَوَآءً لِّلسَّآئِلِينَ ('in proportion to the needs of all who seek (sustenance)') does not mean 'in equal proportion', in the sense that every human being must have an equal share of the means of production. This is something which is naturally and logically neither feasible nor possible. Secondly, there is no justification for restricting the connotation of 'all who seek' to include humans only. The Holy Qur'ān uses a broad-based expression to cover all species of living being. Hence, if the above *Āyah* is taken to imply the equal sharing by human beings of the ownership of the means of production, how can we exclude from this privilege so many of God's creatures who are equally in need of sustenance? Similarly, we cannot deduce from the Qur'ānic injunctions about helping the weaker sections of society that Islam seeks to establish a system of public ownership in the land. All these injunctions clearly state that those who are well off must generously share their wealth with their poor relatives, orphans, the indigent and those in need, and they should not do this to show off their spirit of generosity, but purely for the sake of Allah's Pleasure. The generosity desired from the rich for the needy actually supplements the state's obligation to them. The only feasible method of carrying this out, therefore, is a judicious system of public-private ownership.

The Holy Qur'ān does not prevent something being taken into public control, if so needed, rather than letting it continue under private management. However, the total negation of private ownership and the promotion of state control as an ideology and a system is contrary to the Qur'ānic scheme for human economy. The political system that the Book of God recommends for human society does not leave the option for any 'Party' to decide whether something should be taken away from private into public ownership. This decision rests entirely with the Shūrā Council, elected through the exercise of the people's[1] free will.

2.4. Irrational concept of economic parity

It is an established fact that parity is not naturally possible among humans or other creatures either in their income, or in their means of sustenance. The Qur'ān tells us that this 'disparity' is part of the Divine Dispensation on earth and is according to the Lord's Infinite Wisdom. However, this does not include the artificial imbalance of human society that is willfully created by different civilizational systems. We do not find anywhere in Allah *subḥānahū wa ta'ālā's* entire scheme of things the idea that His natural disparity ought to be leveled out and a system established in which all human beings are brought on a par with each other in their economic resources:

[1] For more details concerning the political system of Islam, please consult my book *Khilāfat-wa-Mulūkiyat* (The Caliphate and Kingship), Chapter 1. – Author.

وَهُوَ ٱلَّذِى جَعَلَكُمْ خَلَٰٓئِفَ ٱلْأَرْضِ وَرَفَعَ بَعْضَكُمْ فَوْقَ بَعْضٍ دَرَجَٰتٍ لِّيَبْلُوَكُمْ فِى مَآ ءَاتَىٰكُمْ ... ﴿١٦٥﴾

('For He it is Who has appointed you vicegerent over the earth, and has exalted some of you over others in rank that He may try you in what He has bestowed upon you.')

(*al-An'ām*, 6: 165)

ٱنظُرْ كَيْفَ فَضَّلْنَا بَعْضَهُمْ عَلَىٰ بَعْضٍ ۚ وَلَلْءَاخِرَةُ أَكْبَرُ دَرَجَٰتٍ وَأَكْبَرُ تَفْضِيلًا ﴿٢١﴾

('See how We have exalted some above others; in this world, and in the Life to Come they will have higher ranks and greater degrees of excellence over others.')

(*Banī Isrā'īl*, 17: 21)

أَهُمْ يَقْسِمُونَ رَحْمَتَ رَبِّكَ ۚ نَحْنُ قَسَمْنَا بَيْنَهُم مَّعِيشَتَهُمْ فِى ٱلْحَيَوٰةِ ٱلدُّنْيَا ۚ وَرَفَعْنَا بَعْضَهُمْ فَوْقَ بَعْضٍ دَرَجَٰتٍ
لِّيَتَّخِذَ بَعْضُهُم بَعْضًا سُخْرِيًّا ۗ وَرَحْمَتُ رَبِّكَ خَيْرٌ مِّمَّا يَجْمَعُونَ ﴿٣٢﴾

('Is it they who distribute the Mercy of your Lord? It is We who have distributed their livelihood among them in the life of this world, and have raised some above others in rank that some of them may harness others to their service. Your Lord's Mercy is better than all the treasures that they hoard.')

(*al-Zukhruf*, 43: 32)

إِنَّ رَبَّكَ يَبْسُطُ ٱلرِّزْقَ لِمَن يَشَآءُ وَيَقْدِرُ ۚ إِنَّهُۥ كَانَ بِعِبَادِهِۦ خَبِيرًۢا بَصِيرًا ﴿٣٠﴾

('Certainly Your Lord makes plentiful the provision of whomsoever He wills and straitens it for whomsoever He wills. He is well-aware and is fully observant.')

(*Banī Isrā'īl*, 17: 30)

قُلْ إِنَّ رَبِّى يَبْسُطُ ٱلرِّزْقَ لِمَن يَشَآءُ مِنْ عِبَادِهِۦ وَيَقْدِرُ لَهُۥ ۚ ... ﴿٣٩﴾

('Say, (O Prophet) "Verily my Lord grants provision abundantly to whomsoever He pleases and straitens it for whomsoever He pleases".')

(*Saba'*, 34: 39)

لَهُۥ مَقَالِيدُ ٱلسَّمَٰوَٰتِ وَٱلْأَرْضِ ۖ يَبْسُطُ ٱلرِّزْقَ لِمَن يَشَآءُ وَيَقْدِرُ ۚ إِنَّهُۥ بِكُلِّ شَىْءٍ عَلِيمٌ ﴿١٢﴾

('His are the keys of the heavens and the earth. He enlarges and straitens the sustenance of whomsoever He pleases. Surely He has knowledge of everything.').

(*al-Shūrā*, 42: 12)

The Qur'ān guides us to dispassionately accept this natural disparity and not to feel jealous or spiteful concerning the precedence that God has given one over another:

وَلَا تَتَمَنَّوْا۟ مَا فَضَّلَ ٱللَّهُ بِهِۦ بَعْضَكُمْ عَلَىٰ بَعْضٍ ۚ لِّلرِّجَالِ نَصِيبٌ مِّمَّا ٱكْتَسَبُوا۟ ۖ وَلِلنِّسَآءِ نَصِيبٌ مِّمَّا ٱكْتَسَبْنَ ۚ
وَسْـَٔلُوا۟ ٱللَّهَ مِن فَضْلِهِۦٓ ۗ إِنَّ ٱللَّهَ كَانَ بِكُلِّ شَىْءٍ عَلِيمًا ﴿٣٢﴾

('Do not covet what Allah has conferred more abundantly on some of you than others. Men shall have a share according to what they have earned, and women shall have a share according to what they have earned. Do ask Allah for His bounty. Allah has full knowledge of every thing.'[2])

(*al-Nisā'*, 4: 32)

There are some who have misinterpreted the following two *Āyāt* from the Holy Qur'ān to argue that the Almighty would like parity in sustenance between His people:

وَٱللَّهُ فَضَّلَ بَعْضَكُمْ عَلَىٰ بَعْضٍ فِى ٱلرِّزْقِ ۚ فَمَا ٱلَّذِينَ فُضِّلُوا۟ بِرَآدِّى رِزْقِهِمْ عَلَىٰ مَا مَلَكَتْ أَيْمَٰنُهُمْ فَهُمْ فِيهِ
سَوَآءٌ ۚ أَفَبِنِعْمَةِ ٱللَّهِ يَجْحَدُونَ ﴿٧١﴾

(Allah has favoured some of you with more worldly provisions than others. Then those who are more favoured do not give away their provisions to their slaves lest they become equal sharers in it. Do they, then, deny that favour of Allah?'[3])

(*al-Naḥl*, 16: 71)

---

[2] Men and women have gifts from God – some greater than others. They may seem unequal, but we are assured that Providence has allotted them through a scheme so that people receive what they earn. If this does not appear clear in our sight, let us remember that we do not have a full knowledge, but God does have. We must not be jealous if other people have more than we – in wealth, position, strength, honour, talent or happiness. Things may be equalized in aggregate, or in the long run, or equated to needs and merit on a scale which we cannot know. If we want more, instead of being jealous or covetous, we should pray to God and place our needs before Him. Although He knows all and has no need of our prayer, our prayer may yet reveal to us our shortcomings and enable us to deserve more of God's bounty or to make ourselves fit for it. (*The Holy Qur'ān: Translation and Commentary* by Abdullah Yusuf Ali, n. 542, p.189) – Editor.

[3] This verse has been grossly misinterpreted in recent times. According to some people, the true purpose of the verse is to tell those who have been granted ample worldly provisions to return them to their servants and slaves, so as to make them equal sharers of these provisions. It is contended that, if they fail to do so, they will be guilty of denying these people God's favour. The fact of the matter is that the context in which this verse occurs renders any discussion of economic matters quite irrelevant. The discourse is actually devoted to emphasizing God's unity and refuting polytheism. The preceding verses are directed to this subject and the discussion continues on these lines. It would be quite out

ضَرَبَ لَكُم مَّثَلًا مِّنْ أَنفُسِكُمْ ۖ هَل لَّكُم مِّن مَّا مَلَكَتْ أَيْمَـٰنُكُم مِّن شُرَكَآءَ فِى مَا رَزَقْنَـٰكُمْ فَأَنتُمْ فِيهِ
سَوَآءٌ تَخَافُونَهُمْ كَخِيفَتِكُمْ أَنفُسَكُمْ ۚ كَذَٰلِكَ نُفَصِّلُ ٱلْـَٔايَـٰتِ لِقَوْمٍ يَعْقِلُونَ ﴿٢٨﴾

('He sets forth for you a parable from your own lives. Do you have among your slaves some who share with you the sustenance that We have bestowed on you so that you become equals in it, all being alike, and then you would hold them in fear as you fear each other? Thus do We make plain the Signs for those who use reason.')

(*al-Rūm*, 30: 28)

Both the wordings of these *Āyāt* and their syntax have nothing to suggest a condemnation of economic disparity among humans and a need to bring them on a par with each other in terms of income and expenditure. In fact, this basic reality of the human situation is cited by Allah *subḥānahū wa taʿālā* in an entirely different context as an argument against pantheism. The Almighty asks how a man with good sense can make created things partners with God, when he himself is not willing to share the gifts the Lord has given to him with those inferior to him in society.

2.5. Monasticism or moderation and balance

The Holy Qur'ān repeatedly stresses the fact that the Lord has created the bounties of this world for the benefit of His servants. It is neither His Desire nor His Design that man should abstain from these gifts of God and live a life of denial as a hermit. However, what is required of us is to differentiate between the pure and the profane, the permissible and the prohibited, and to remain within the limits of *Ḥalāl* and *Ṭayyib* (lawful and pure) while making use of the means available to us and not cross the boundaries of temperance and moderation:

هُوَ ٱلَّذِى خَلَقَ لَكُم مَّا فِى ٱلْأَرْضِ جَمِيعًا ... ﴿٢٩﴾

('It is He Who created for you all that is on earth.')

(*al-Baqarah*, 2: 29)

---

of place if an economic principle were suddenly enunciated at this point in the midst of a discussion of a quite separate subject matter. If one bears in mind the correct context of the verse, it can easily be appreciated that this verse is saying something quite different. People are first being reminded here of an actual fact of life. They are told that they do not share their wealth – even though it has been bestowed upon them by God – with their slaves and servants. In view of this, how can they justify associating God's helpless servants with Him in giving thanks for the favour that has been conferred upon them by God alone? How can they consider these creatures of God equal to Him in respect of both rights and authority? ('*Towards Understanding the Qur'ān*'. Abridged version of *Tafhīm al-Qur'ān* by Sayyid Abul Aʿlā Mawdūdī, trans. & ed. Zafar Ishaq Ansari, n.20, p.563).

قُلْ مَنْ حَرَّمَ زِينَةَ ٱللَّهِ ٱلَّتِىٓ أَخْرَجَ لِعِبَادِهِۦ وَٱلطَّيِّبَٰتِ مِنَ ٱلرِّزْقِ ۚ ... ﴿٣٢﴾

('Say: (O Muhammad): "who has forbidden the adornment which Allah has brought forth for His creatures or the good things from among the means of sustenance?"')

(*al-A'rāf*, 7: 32)

يَٰٓأَيُّهَا ٱلَّذِينَ ءَامَنُوا۟ لَا تُحَرِّمُوا۟ طَيِّبَٰتِ مَآ أَحَلَّ ٱللَّهُ لَكُمْ وَلَا تَعْتَدُوٓا۟ ۚ إِنَّ ٱللَّهَ لَا يُحِبُّ ٱلْمُعْتَدِينَ ﴿٨٧﴾ وَكُلُوا۟
مِمَّا رَزَقَكُمُ ٱللَّهُ حَلَٰلًا طَيِّبًا ۚ وَٱتَّقُوا۟ ٱللَّهَ ٱلَّذِىٓ أَنتُم بِهِۦ مُؤْمِنُونَ ﴿٨٨﴾

('Believers! Do not hold as unlawful the good things which Allah has made lawful to you, and do not exceed the bounds of right. Allah does not love those who transgress the bounds of right, and partake of the lawful, good things which Allah has provided you as sustenance, and refrain from disobeying Allah in Whom you believe.')

(*al-Mā'idah*, 5: 87-88)

يَٰٓأَيُّهَا ٱلنَّاسُ كُلُوا۟ مِمَّا فِى ٱلْأَرْضِ حَلَٰلًا طَيِّبًا وَلَا تَتَّبِعُوا۟ خُطُوَٰتِ ٱلشَّيْطَٰنِ ۚ إِنَّهُۥ لَكُمْ عَدُوٌّ مُّبِينٌ ﴿١٦٨﴾

('O people! Eat of the lawful and pure things in the earth and follow not the footsteps of Satan. For surely he is your open enemy.')

(*al-Baqarah*, 2: 168)

يَٰبَنِىٓ ءَادَمَ خُذُوا۟ زِينَتَكُمْ عِندَ كُلِّ مَسْجِدٍ وَكُلُوا۟ وَٱشْرَبُوا۟ وَلَا تُسْرِفُوٓا۟ ۚ إِنَّهُۥ لَا يُحِبُّ ٱلْمُسْرِفِينَ ﴿٣١﴾

('Children of Adam! Take your adornment at every time of Prayer, and eat and drink without going to excesses. For Allah does not like those who go to excess.')

(*al-A'rāf*, 7: 31)

... وَرَهْبَانِيَّةً ٱبْتَدَعُوهَا مَا كَتَبْنَٰهَا عَلَيْهِمْ إِلَّا ٱبْتِغَآءَ رِضْوَٰنِ ٱللَّهِ فَمَا رَعَوْهَا حَقَّ رِعَايَتِهَا ... ﴿٢٧﴾

('As for monasticism, it is they who invented it; We did not prescribe it for them. They themselves invented it in pursuit of Allah's good pleasure, and then they did not observe it as it ought to have been observed.')

(*al-Ḥadīd*, 57: 27)

2.6. Distinction between *ḥalāl* and *ḥarām* means of livelihood

To achieve this moderation and balance, the Qur'ān has in place a rule that income has to be generated and earned strictly through lawful (*Ḥalāl*) means, and all prohibited (*Ḥarām*) means have to be avoided:

يَٰٓأَيُّهَا ٱلَّذِينَ ءَامَنُوا۟ لَا تَأْكُلُوٓا۟ أَمْوَٰلَكُم بَيْنَكُم بِٱلْبَٰطِلِ إِلَّآ أَن تَكُونَ تِجَٰرَةً عَن تَرَاضٍ مِّنكُمْ ۚ
وَلَا تَقْتُلُوٓا۟ أَنفُسَكُمْ ۚ إِنَّ ٱللَّهَ كَانَ بِكُمْ رَحِيمًا ﴿٢٩﴾

('Believers! Do not devour one another's possessions wrongfully; rather, let there be trading by mutual consent, and do not kill yourselves. Surely Allah is ever Compassionate to you.')

(*al-Nisā'*, 4: 29)

2.7. Forbidden means of livelihood

Details regarding the wrong means of living, which the Islamic *Sharī'ah* has disapproved of, are available in the Prophetic Traditions (*Aḥādīth*) and are duly elaborated by Muslim jurists (*Fuqahā'*) in their books. Some of these that are explained in the Holy Qur'ān are as follows:

وَلَا تَأْكُلُوٓا۟ أَمْوَٰلَكُم بَيْنَكُم بِٱلْبَٰطِلِ وَتُدْلُوا۟ بِهَآ إِلَى ٱلْحُكَّامِ لِتَأْكُلُوا۟ فَرِيقًا مِّنْ أَمْوَٰلِ ٱلنَّاسِ
بِٱلْإِثْمِ وَأَنتُمْ تَعْلَمُونَ ﴿١٨٨﴾

('Do not usurp one another's possessions by false means, nor proffer your possessions to the authorities so that you may sinfully and knowingly usurp a portion of another's possessions.')

(*al-Baqarah*, 2: 188)

... فَإِنْ أَمِنَ بَعْضُكُم بَعْضًا فَلْيُؤَدِّ ٱلَّذِى ٱؤْتُمِنَ أَمَٰنَتَهُۥ وَلْيَتَّقِ ٱللَّهَ رَبَّهُۥ ... ﴿٢٨٣﴾

('But if any of you trusts another, let him who is trusted, fulfill the trust and fear Allah, his Lord.')

(*al-Baqarah*, 2: 283)

...وَمَن يَغْلُلْ يَأْتِ بِمَا غَلَّ يَوْمَ ٱلْقِيَٰمَةِ ۚ ثُمَّ تُوَفَّىٰ كُلُّ نَفْسٍ مَّا كَسَبَتْ وَهُمْ لَا يُظْلَمُونَ ﴿١٦١﴾

('... and whoever defrauds shall bring with him the fruits of his fraud on the Day of Resurrection, when every human being shall be paid in full what he has earned, and shall not be wronged.')

(*Āl 'Imrān*, 3: 161)

وَٱلسَّارِقُ وَٱلسَّارِقَةُ فَٱقْطَعُوٓا۟ أَيْدِيَهُمَا جَزَآءًۢ بِمَا كَسَبَا نَكَٰلًا مِّنَ ٱللَّهِ ۗ وَٱللَّهُ عَزِيزٌ حَكِيمٌ ﴿٣٨﴾

('As for the thief – male or female – cut off the hands of both. This is a recompense for what they have done, and an exemplary punishment from Allah. Allah is All-Mighty, All-Wise.')

(*al-Mā'idah*, 5: 38)

إِنَّمَا جَزَٰٓؤُاْ ٱلَّذِينَ يُحَارِبُونَ ٱللَّهَ وَرَسُولَهُۥ وَيَسۡعَوۡنَ فِي ٱلۡأَرۡضِ فَسَادًا أَن يُقَتَّلُوٓاْ أَوۡ يُصَلَّبُوٓاْ أَوۡ تُقَطَّعَ أَيۡدِيهِمۡ وَأَرۡجُلُهُم
مِّنۡ خِلَٰفٍ أَوۡ يُنفَوۡاْ مِنَ ٱلۡأَرۡضِۚ ... ﴿٣٣﴾

(‘Those who wage war against Allah and His Messenger, and go about the earth spreading mischief – indeed their recompense is that they either be done to death, or be crucified, or have their hands and feet be cut off from the opposite sides or they be banished from the land.’)

(*al-Mā’idah*, 5: 33)

إِنَّ ٱلَّذِينَ يَأۡكُلُونَ أَمۡوَٰلَ ٱلۡيَتَٰمَىٰ ظُلۡمًا إِنَّمَا يَأۡكُلُونَ فِي بُطُونِهِمۡ نَارٗاۖ ... ﴿١٠﴾

(‘Behold, those who wrongfully devour the properties of orphans only fill their bellies with fire.’)

(*al-Nisā’*, 4: 10)

وَمِنَ ٱلنَّاسِ مَن يَشۡتَرِي لَهۡوَ ٱلۡحَدِيثِ لِيُضِلَّ عَن سَبِيلِ ٱللَّهِ بِغَيۡرِ عِلۡمٖ وَيَتَّخِذَهَا هُزُوًاۚ أُوْلَٰٓئِكَ لَهُمۡ عَذَابٞ مُّهِينٞ ﴿٦﴾

(‘There are some human beings who purchase an enchanting diversion in order to lead people away from the way of Allah without having any knowledge, who hold the call to the Way of Allah to ridicule. A humiliating chastisement awaits them.’)

(*Luqmān*, 31: 6)

... وَلَا تُكۡرِهُواْ فَتَيَٰتِكُمۡ عَلَى ٱلۡبِغَآءِ إِنۡ أَرَدۡنَ تَحَصُّنٗا لِّتَبۡتَغُواْ عَرَضَ ٱلۡحَيَوٰةِ ٱلدُّنۡيَاۚ ... ﴿٣٣﴾

(‘And do not compel your slave-girls to prostitution for the sake of the benefits of worldly life.’)

(*al-Nūr*, 24: 33)

وَلَا تَقۡرَبُواْ ٱلزِّنَىٰٓۖ إِنَّهُۥ كَانَ فَٰحِشَةٗ وَسَآءَ سَبِيلٗا ﴿٣٢﴾

(‘Do not even approach fornication for it is an outrageous act, and an evil way.’)

(*Banī Isrā’īl*, 17: 32)

ٱلزَّانِيَةُ وَٱلزَّانِي فَٱجۡلِدُواْ كُلَّ وَٰحِدٖ مِّنۡهُمَا مِاْئَةَ جَلۡدَةٖۖ ... ﴿٢﴾

(‘Those who fornicate – whether female or male – flog each one of them with a hundred lashes.’)

(*al-Nūr*, 24: 2)

يَٰٓأَيُّهَا ٱلَّذِينَ ءَامَنُوٓاْ إِنَّمَا ٱلْخَمْرُ وَٱلْمَيْسِرُ وَٱلْأَنصَابُ وَٱلْأَزْلَٰمُ رِجْسٌ مِّنْ عَمَلِ ٱلشَّيْطَٰنِ فَٱجْتَنِبُوهُ
لَعَلَّكُمْ تُفْلِحُونَ ٩٠

('Believers! Intoxicants, games of chance, idolatrous sacrifices at altars, and divining arrows are all abominations, the handiwork of Satan. So turn wholly away from it that you may attain true success.')

(*al-Mā'idah*, 5: 90)

... وَأَحَلَّ ٱللَّهُ ٱلْبَيْعَ وَحَرَّمَ ٱلرِّبَوٰاْ ... ٢٧٥

('... Allah has made buying and selling lawful, and interest unlawful.')

(*al-Baqarah*, 2: 275)

يَٰٓأَيُّهَا ٱلَّذِينَ ءَامَنُواْ ٱتَّقُواْ ٱللَّهَ وَذَرُواْ مَا بَقِيَ مِنَ ٱلرِّبَوٰٓاْ إِن كُنتُم مُّؤْمِنِينَ ٢٧٨ فَإِن لَّمْ تَفْعَلُواْ فَأْذَنُواْ بِحَرْبٍ مِّنَ ٱللَّهِ
وَرَسُولِهِۦ وَإِن تُبْتُمْ فَلَكُمْ رُءُوسُ أَمْوَٰلِكُمْ لَا تَظْلِمُونَ وَلَا تُظْلَمُونَ ٢٧٩ وَإِن كَانَ ذُو عُسْرَةٍ فَنَظِرَةٌ إِلَىٰ مَيْسَرَةٍ
وَأَن تَصَدَّقُواْ خَيْرٌ لَّكُمْ إِن كُنتُمْ تَعْلَمُونَ ٢٨٠

('Believers! Have fear of Allah and give up all outstanding interest if you do truly believe. But if you fail to do so, then be warned of war from Allah and His Messenger. If you repent even now, you have the right of the return of your capital; neither will you do wrong nor will you be wronged. But if the debtor is in straightened circumstance, let him have respite until the time of ease; and whatever you remit by way of charity is better for you, if only you know'.)

(*al-Baqarah*, 2: 278-280)

In the light of these *Āyāt*, the forbidden means of earning may be summed up as follows:

- Grabbing other people's property without their consent or without paying them compensation, or occupying it with the owner's consent and after paying compensation, but through deceitful means or fraud.
- Bribery.
- Extortion.
- Dishonesty in private and public funds.
- Burglary, robbery and theft.
- Abuse or misappropriation of an orphan's property.
- Abuse of weights and measures.
- Trading in anything that spreads obscenity and indecency.
- Music and dance as a profession.

- Income generated through prostitution and the sex trade.
- The liquor industry, its trade, marketing and transportation.
- Betting and all those means through which one person's wealth is transferred to another simply by chance or a stroke of fate.
- Idol-making, selling idols or services rendered in idol-houses.
- The professions of fortune-tellers and sooth-sayers.
- Usury and all forms of interest-based transactions, whether the rate of interest is large or small, and whether it has been imposed on personal loans, or commercial, industrial and agricultural credits.

2.8. Prohibition of stinginess and hoarding

While forbidding all these wrong means of earning a livelihood, the Holy Qur'ān at the same time strongly condemns the accumulation of wealth, even if it is earned through lawful means. It rejects miserliness as an evil:

وَيْلٌ لِّكُلِّ هُمَزَةٍ لُّمَزَةٍ ۝ ٱلَّذِى جَمَعَ مَالًا وَعَدَّدَهُۥ ۝ يَحْسَبُ أَنَّ مَالَهُۥٓ أَخْلَدَهُۥ ۝ كَلَّا ۖ لَيُنۢبَذَنَّ فِى ٱلْحُطَمَةِ ۝

('Woe to every fault-finding backbiter; Who amasses wealth and counts it over and again, He thinks that his wealth will immortalize him forever! Nay, he shall be thrown into the Crusher.')

(*al-Humazah*, 104: 1-4)

...وَٱلَّذِينَ يَكْنِزُونَ ٱلذَّهَبَ وَٱلْفِضَّةَ وَلَا يُنفِقُونَهَا فِى سَبِيلِ ٱللَّهِ فَبَشِّرْهُم بِعَذَابٍ أَلِيمٍ ۝

('And there are those who amass gold and silver and do not spend it in the Way of Allah. Announce to them the tiding of a painful chastisement.')

(*al-Tawbah*, 9: 34)

...وَمَن يُوقَ شُحَّ نَفْسِهِۦ فَأُو۟لَٰٓئِكَ هُمُ ٱلْمُفْلِحُونَ ۝

('And whoever remains safe from his own greediness, it is such that will prosper.')

(*al-Taghābun*, 64: 16)

وَلَا يَحْسَبَنَّ ٱلَّذِينَ يَبْخَلُونَ بِمَآ ءَاتَىٰهُمُ ٱللَّهُ مِن فَضْلِهِۦ هُوَ خَيْرًا لَّهُم ۖ بَلْ هُوَ شَرٌّ لَّهُمْ ۖ سَيُطَوَّقُونَ مَا بَخِلُوا۟ بِهِۦ يَوْمَ ٱلْقِيَٰمَةِ ۗ وَلِلَّهِ مِيرَٰثُ ٱلسَّمَٰوَٰتِ وَٱلْأَرْضِ ۗ وَٱللَّهُ بِمَا تَعْمَلُونَ خَبِيرٌ ۝

('Those who are niggardly about what Allah has granted them out of His bounty think that niggardliness is good for them; rather, it is bad for them. What they were niggardly about will turn into a halter round their necks on the Day of Resurrection. To Allah belongs the inheritance of the heavens and the earth. Allah is well aware of what you do.')

(*Āl 'Imrān*, 3: 180)

2.9. Lust for money and greediness

The Qur'ān also condemns a lust for power and wealth, the craving to pile up more and more worldly riches and taking pride in affluence and abundance. It tells us that these are among the greatest causes of mankind going astray and eventually facing his doom:

أَلْهَىٰكُمُ ٱلتَّكَاثُرُ ۝١ حَتَّىٰ زُرْتُمُ ٱلْمَقَابِرَ ۝٢ كَلَّا سَوْفَ تَعْلَمُونَ ۝٣

('The craving for ever-greater worldly gains and to excel others in that regard keeps you occupied, until you reach your graves. Nay, you will soon come to know.')

(*al-Takāthur*, 102: 1-3)

وَكَمْ أَهْلَكْنَا مِن قَرْيَةٍ بَطِرَتْ مَعِيشَتَهَا ۖ فَتِلْكَ مَسَٰكِنُهُمْ لَمْ تُسْكَن مِّنۢ بَعْدِهِمْ إِلَّا قَلِيلًا ۖ وَكُنَّا نَحْنُ ٱلْوَٰرِثِينَ ۝٥٨

('And how many a town did We destroy whose inhabitants exulted on account of their affluence. These are their dwellings in which very few dwelt after them. Eventually it is We who inherited them.')

(*al-Qaṣaṣ* 28: 58)

وَمَآ أَرْسَلْنَا فِى قَرْيَةٍ مِّن نَّذِيرٍ إِلَّا قَالَ مُتْرَفُوهَآ إِنَّا بِمَآ أُرْسِلْتُم بِهِۦ كَٰفِرُونَ ۝٣٤ وَقَالُوا۟ نَحْنُ أَكْثَرُ أَمْوَٰلًا
وَأَوْلَٰدًا وَمَا نَحْنُ بِمُعَذَّبِينَ ۝٣٥

('We never sent a warner to any town but its wealthy ones said: "We disbelieve in the Message you have brought." They always said: "We have more wealth and children than you have, and we shall not be chastised".')

(*Saba'*, 34: 34-35)

2.10. Unchecked spending

The Qur'ān similarly condemns in strong terms anyone who squanders away the wealth he earned through lawful means in unlawful ventures, or who consumes it by living lavishly and with luxuries, as though he has no right use or purpose for his riches other than raising his living standards higher and higher:

... وَلَا تُسْرِفُوٓا۟ ۚ إِنَّهُۥ لَا يُحِبُّ ٱلْمُسْرِفِينَ ۝١٤١

('... and do not exceed the proper limits, for He does not love those who exceed the proper limits.')

(*al-An'ām*, 6: 141)

وَءَاتِ ذَا ٱلْقُرْبَىٰ حَقَّهُۥ وَٱلْمِسْكِينَ وَٱبْنَ ٱلسَّبِيلِ وَلَا تُبَذِّرْ تَبْذِيرًا ﴿٢٦﴾ إِنَّ ٱلْمُبَذِّرِينَ كَانُوٓاْ إِخْوَٰنَ ٱلشَّيَٰطِينِ ۖ وَكَانَ ٱلشَّيْطَٰنُ لِرَبِّهِۦ كَفُورًا ﴿٢٧﴾

('Give to the near of kin his due, and also to the needy and the wayfarer. Do not squander your wealth wastefully, for those who squander wastefully are Satan's brothers, and Satan is ever ungrateful to his Lord')

(*Banī Isrā'īl*, 17: 26-27)

... وَكُلُواْ وَٱشْرَبُواْ وَلَا تُسْرِفُوٓاْ ۚ إِنَّهُۥ لَا يُحِبُّ ٱلْمُسْرِفِينَ ﴿٣١﴾

('... and eat and drink without going to excesses. For Allah does not like those who go to excess.')

(*al-A'rāf*, 7: 31)

The best course for man, according to the Holy Qur'ān, is to follow the middle road in his spending. He himself, the members of his family and his dependents have a right to his wealth, and he must not be niggardly in discharging his obligations towards them. However, this does not mean that he should spend lavishly on them, but must remain mindful of his other social and religious obligations:

وَلَا تَجْعَلْ يَدَكَ مَغْلُولَةً إِلَىٰ عُنُقِكَ وَلَا تَبْسُطْهَا كُلَّ ٱلْبَسْطِ فَتَقْعُدَ مَلُومًا مَّحْسُورًا ﴿٢٩﴾

('Do not keep your hand fastened to your neck nor outspread it, altogether outspread, for you will be left sitting rebuked, destitute.')

(*Banī Isrā'īl*, 17: 29)

وَٱلَّذِينَ إِذَآ أَنفَقُواْ لَمْ يُسْرِفُواْ وَلَمْ يَقْتُرُواْ وَكَانَ بَيْنَ ذَٰلِكَ قَوَامًا ﴿٦٧﴾

('(The true servants of the Merciful One are) those who are neither extravagant nor niggardly in their spending but keep the golden mean between the two.')

(*al-Furqān*, 25: 67)

وَٱبْتَغِ فِيمَآ ءَاتَىٰكَ ٱللَّهُ ٱلدَّارَ ٱلْءَاخِرَةَ ۖ وَلَا تَنسَ نَصِيبَكَ مِنَ ٱلدُّنْيَا ۖ وَأَحْسِن كَمَآ أَحْسَنَ ٱللَّهُ إِلَيْكَ ۖ وَلَا تَبْغِ ٱلْفَسَادَ فِى ٱلْأَرْضِ ۖ إِنَّ ٱللَّهَ لَا يُحِبُّ ٱلْمُفْسِدِينَ ﴿٧٧﴾

('Seek by means of the wealth that Allah has granted you the Abode of the Hereafter, but forget not your share in this world and do good, as Allah has been good to you and do not strive to create mischief in the land, for Allah loves not those who create mischief.')

(*al-Qaṣaṣ*, 28: 77)

2.11. Correct way of spending money

The Book of God tells us that the money one saves, after that which is spent judiciously on one's personal needs, should be used in the following manner:

...وَيَسْـَٔلُونَكَ مَاذَا يُنفِقُونَ قُلِ ٱلْعَفْوَ... ﴿٢١٩﴾

('They ask: 'What should we spend in the Way of Allah?' Say: 'Whatsoever you can spare.'')

(*al-Baqarah*, 2: 219)

لَّيْسَ ٱلْبِرَّ أَن تُوَلُّوا۟ وُجُوهَكُمْ قِبَلَ ٱلْمَشْرِقِ وَٱلْمَغْرِبِ وَلَـٰكِنَّ ٱلْبِرَّ مَنْ ءَامَنَ بِٱللَّهِ وَٱلْيَوْمِ ٱلْـَٔاخِرِ وَٱلْمَلَـٰٓئِكَةِ
وَٱلْكِتَـٰبِ وَٱلنَّبِيِّـۧنَ وَءَاتَى ٱلْمَالَ عَلَىٰ حُبِّهِۦ ذَوِى ٱلْقُرْبَىٰ وَٱلْيَتَـٰمَىٰ وَٱلْمَسَـٰكِينَ وَٱبْنَ ٱلسَّبِيلِ
وَٱلسَّآئِلِينَ وَفِى ٱلرِّقَابِ ... ﴿١٧٧﴾

('Righteousness does not consist in turning your faces towards the east or towards the west; true righteousness consists in believing in Allah and the Last Day, the angels, the Book and the Prophets, and in giving away one's property in love of Him to one's kinsmen, the orphans, the poor and the wayfarer, and to those who ask for help and in freeing the necks of slaves.')

(*al-Baqarah*, 2: 177)

لَن تَنَالُوا۟ ٱلْبِرَّ حَتَّىٰ تُنفِقُوا۟ مِمَّا تُحِبُّونَ ۚ وَمَا تُنفِقُوا۟ مِن شَىْءٍ فَإِنَّ ٱللَّهَ بِهِۦ عَلِيمٌ ﴿٩٢﴾

('You shall not attain righteousness until you spend (for the sake of Allah) out of what you love. Allah knows whatever you spend.')

(*Āl ʿImrān*, 3: 92)

وَٱعْبُدُوا۟ ٱللَّهَ وَلَا تُشْرِكُوا۟ بِهِۦ شَيْـًٔا ۖ وَبِٱلْوَٰلِدَيْنِ إِحْسَـٰنًا وَبِذِى ٱلْقُرْبَىٰ وَٱلْيَتَـٰمَىٰ وَٱلْمَسَـٰكِينِ وَٱلْجَارِ ذِى
ٱلْقُرْبَىٰ وَٱلْجَارِ ٱلْجُنُبِ وَٱلصَّاحِبِ بِٱلْجَنۢبِ وَٱبْنِ ٱلسَّبِيلِ وَمَا مَلَكَتْ أَيْمَـٰنُكُمْ ۗ إِنَّ ٱللَّهَ لَا يُحِبُّ مَن كَانَ
مُخْتَالًا فَخُورًا ﴿٣٦﴾ ٱلَّذِينَ يَبْخَلُونَ وَيَأْمُرُونَ ٱلنَّاسَ بِٱلْبُخْلِ وَيَكْتُمُونَ مَآ ءَاتَىٰهُمُ ٱللَّهُ مِن فَضْلِهِۦ ۗ وَأَعْتَدْنَا
لِلْكَـٰفِرِينَ عَذَابًا مُّهِينًا ﴿٣٧﴾ وَٱلَّذِينَ يُنفِقُونَ أَمْوَٰلَهُمْ رِئَآءَ ٱلنَّاسِ وَلَا يُؤْمِنُونَ بِٱللَّهِ وَلَا بِٱلْيَوْمِ ٱلْـَٔاخِرِ ... ﴿٣٨﴾

('Serve Allah and ascribe no partners to Him. Do good to your parents, to near of kin, to orphans, and to the needy, and to the neighbour who is of kin, and to the neighbour who is a stranger, and to the companion by your side, and to the wayfarer, and to those whom your right hands possess. Allah does not love the arrogant, and the boastful, who are niggardly and bid others to be niggardly and conceal the bounty which Allah has bestowed upon them. We have kept in readiness a humiliating chastisement for such deniers (of Allah's bounty). Allah does not love those who spend out of their wealth to make a show of it to people when in fact they neither believe in Allah nor in the Last Day..')

(*al-Nisā'*, 4: 36-38)

لِلْفُقَرَآءِ ٱلَّذِينَ أُحْصِرُوا۟ فِى سَبِيلِ ٱللَّهِ لَا يَسْتَطِيعُونَ ضَرْبًا فِى ٱلْأَرْضِ يَحْسَبُهُمُ ٱلْجَاهِلُ أَغْنِيَآءَ مِنَ ٱلتَّعَفُّفِ تَعْرِفُهُم
بِسِيمَٰهُمْ لَا يَسْـَٔلُونَ ٱلنَّاسَ إِلْحَافًا ۗ وَمَا تُنفِقُوا۟ مِنْ خَيْرٍ فَإِنَّ ٱللَّهَ بِهِۦ عَلِيمٌ ﴿٢٧٣﴾

('Those needy ones who are wholly wrapped up in the cause of Allah, and who are hindered from moving about the earth in search of their livelihood, especially deserve help. He who is unaware of their circumstances supposes them to be wealthy because of their dignified bearing, but you will know them by their countenance, although they do not go about begging of people with importunity. Whatever wealth you spend on helping them, Allah will know of it.')

(*al-Baqarah*, 2: 273)

وَيُطْعِمُونَ ٱلطَّعَامَ عَلَىٰ حُبِّهِۦ مِسْكِينًا وَيَتِيمًا وَأَسِيرًا ﴿٨﴾ إِنَّمَا نُطْعِمُكُمْ لِوَجْهِ ٱللَّهِ لَا نُرِيدُ مِنكُمْ جَزَآءً وَلَا شُكُورًا ﴿٩﴾

('Those who, for the love of Him, feed the needy and the orphan, and the captive, (saying): 'We feed you only for Allah's sake, we do not seek of you any recompense or thanks".')

(*al-Dahr*, 76: 8-9)

وَٱلَّذِينَ فِىٓ أَمْوَٰلِهِمْ حَقٌّ مَّعْلُومٌ ﴿٢٤﴾ لِّلسَّآئِلِ وَٱلْمَحْرُومِ ﴿٢٥﴾

('... and those in whose wealth there is a known right for those that ask and those that are dispossessed.')

(*al-Ma'ārij*, 70: 24-25)

... وَٱلَّذِينَ يَبْتَغُونَ ٱلْكِتَٰبَ مِمَّا مَلَكَتْ أَيْمَٰنُكُمْ فَكَاتِبُوهُمْ إِنْ عَلِمْتُمْ فِيهِمْ خَيْرًا ۖ وَءَاتُوهُم مِّن مَّالِ ٱللَّهِ
ٱلَّذِىٓ ءَاتَىٰكُمْ ۚ ... ﴿٣٣﴾

('And write out a deed of manumission for such of your slaves that desire their freedom in lieu of payment – if you see any good in them – and give them out of the wealth that Allah has given you.')

(*al-Nūr*, 24: 33)

وَأَنفِقُوا۟ فِى سَبِيلِ ٱللَّهِ وَلَا تُلْقُوا۟ بِأَيْدِيكُمْ إِلَى ٱلتَّهْلُكَةِ ۛ وَأَحْسِنُوٓا۟ ۛ إِنَّ ٱللَّهَ يُحِبُّ ٱلْمُحْسِنِينَ ﴿١٩٥﴾

('Spend in the Way of Allah and do not cast yourselves into destruction with your own hands; and do good, for Allah loves those who do good.')

(*al-Baqarah*, 2: 195)

2.12. Reparation for sinful transgressions

In addition to these general and voluntary means of spending in the Way of Allah, the Qur'ān has also prescribed penalties as reparation for sinful transgressions. For example, a person who violates an oath that was sworn in earnest is required to obey the following:

...فَكَفَّٰرَتُهُۥٓ إِطْعَامُ عَشَرَةِ مَسَٰكِينَ مِنْ أَوْسَطِ مَا تُطْعِمُونَ أَهْلِيكُمْ أَوْ كِسْوَتُهُمْ أَوْ تَحْرِيرُ رَقَبَةٍ ۖ فَمَن لَّمْ يَجِدْ
فَصِيَامُ ثَلَٰثَةِ أَيَّامٍ ۚ... ﴿٨٩﴾

('The expiation (for breaking such oaths) is either to feed ten needy persons with more or les the same food as you are wont to give to your families, or to clothe them, or to set free from bondage the neck of one man; and he who does not find the means shall fast for three days.')

(*al-Mā'idah*, 5: 89)

Similarly, if a married man indulges in *Ẓihār* (the pre-Islamic form of divorce consisting of the words of repudiation, such as telling his wife that she was to him like the back of his mother) and then seeks to take her back and enjoy conjugal rights, he has to pay a certain penalty:

وَٱلَّذِينَ يُظَٰهِرُونَ مِن نِّسَآئِهِمْ ثُمَّ يَعُودُونَ لِمَا قَالُوا۟ فَتَحْرِيرُ رَقَبَةٍ مِّن قَبْلِ أَن يَتَمَآسَّا ۚ ذَٰلِكُمْ تُوعَظُونَ بِهِۦ ۚ
وَٱللَّهُ بِمَا تَعْمَلُونَ خَبِيرٌ ﴿٣﴾ فَمَن لَّمْ يَجِدْ فَصِيَامُ شَهْرَيْنِ مُتَتَابِعَيْنِ مِن قَبْلِ أَن يَتَمَآسَّا ۖ فَمَن لَّمْ يَسْتَطِعْ فَإِطْعَامُ
سِتِّينَ مِسْكِينًا ۚ... ﴿٤﴾

('Those who declare their wives to be their mothers and thereafter go back on what they have said shall free a slave before they may touch each other. That is what you are exhorted to do. Allah is fully aware of all your deeds. And he who does not find a slave (to free) shall fast for two months consecutively before they may touch each other, and he who is unable to do so shall feed sixty needy people.')

(*al-Mujādalah*, 58: 3-4)

Similar penalties are imposed in case of certain shortcomings during the *Ḥajj* (*al-Baqarah*, 196; *al-Mā'idah*, 95) or in *Ṣawm* (Ramaḍān Fast) (*al-Baqarah*, 184).

2.13. Preconditions for the Divine Acceptability of charity

However, these forms of spending in the Way of the Lord are worthy of His Acceptance only if there is no element of selfishness or self-promotion in them;

if no attempt is made to make others feel obliged; and as long as the recipient is not subjected to mental or physical torture. Whatever is spent in the Way of the Lord must be from the best that one has and not the worst; and any philanthropy must be inspired by the sole motive of pleasing Allah *subḥānahū wa ta'ālā* and no other consideration:

وَٱلَّذِينَ يُنفِقُونَ أَمْوَٰلَهُمْ رِئَآءَ ٱلنَّاسِ وَلَا يُؤْمِنُونَ بِٱللَّهِ وَلَا بِٱلْيَوْمِ ٱلْآخِرِ...۞

('Allah does not love those who spend out of their wealth to make a show of it to people when in fact they neither believe in Allah nor in the Last Day.')

(*al-Nisā'*, 4: 38)

يَٰٓأَيُّهَا ٱلَّذِينَ ءَامَنُوا۟ لَا تُبْطِلُوا۟ صَدَقَٰتِكُم بِٱلْمَنِّ وَٱلْأَذَىٰ كَٱلَّذِى يُنفِقُ مَالَهُۥ رِئَآءَ ٱلنَّاسِ وَلَا يُؤْمِنُ بِٱللَّهِ وَٱلْيَوْمِ ٱلْآخِرِ...۞

('Believers! Do not nullify your acts of charity by stressing your benevolence and causing hurt as does he who spends his wealth only to be seen by people and does not believe in Allah and the Last Day.')

(*al-Baqarah*, 2: 264)

ٱلَّذِينَ يُنفِقُونَ أَمْوَٰلَهُمْ فِى سَبِيلِ ٱللَّهِ ثُمَّ لَا يُتْبِعُونَ مَآ أَنفَقُوا۟ مَنًّا وَلَآ أَذًى لَّهُمْ أَجْرُهُمْ عِندَ رَبِّهِمْ وَلَا خَوْفٌ عَلَيْهِمْ وَلَا هُمْ يَحْزَنُونَ ۞ قَوْلٌ مَّعْرُوفٌ وَمَغْفِرَةٌ خَيْرٌ مِّن صَدَقَةٍ يَتْبَعُهَآ أَذًى وَٱللَّهُ غَنِىٌّ حَلِيمٌ ۞

('Those who spend their wealth in the Way of Allah and do not follow up their spending by stressing their benevolence and causing hurt, will find their reward secure with their Lord. They have no cause for fear and grief. To speak a kind word and to forgive people's faults is better than charity followed by hurt. Allah is All-Sufficient, All-Forbearing.')

(*al-Baqarah*, 2: 262-263)

يَٰٓأَيُّهَا ٱلَّذِينَ ءَامَنُوٓا۟ أَنفِقُوا۟ مِن طَيِّبَٰتِ مَا كَسَبْتُمْ وَمِمَّآ أَخْرَجْنَا لَكُم مِّنَ ٱلْأَرْضِ وَلَا تَيَمَّمُوا۟ ٱلْخَبِيثَ مِنْهُ تُنفِقُونَ وَلَسْتُم بِـَٔاخِذِيهِ إِلَّآ أَن تُغْمِضُوا۟ فِيهِ وَٱعْلَمُوٓا۟ أَنَّ ٱللَّهَ غَنِىٌّ حَمِيدٌ ۞

('Believers! Spend (in the Way of Allah) out of the good things you have earned and out of what We have produced for you from the earth, and choose not for your spending the bad things such as you yourselves would not accept or accept only by overlooking its defects. Allah is All-Munificent, Most Praiseworthy.')

(*al-Baqarah*, 2: 267)

إِن تُبْدُوا۟ ٱلصَّدَقَـٰتِ فَنِعِمَّا هِىَ ۖ وَإِن تُخْفُوهَا وَتُؤْتُوهَا ٱلْفُقَرَآءَ فَهُوَ خَيْرٌ لَّكُمْ ۚ وَيُكَفِّرُ عَنكُم مِّن سَيِّـَٔاتِكُمْ ۗ
وَٱللَّهُ بِمَا تَعْمَلُونَ خَبِيرٌ ﴿٢٧١﴾

('If you dispense your charity publicly, it is well; but if you conceal it and pay it to the needy in secret, it will be even better for you.This will atone for several of your misdeeds. Allah is well aware of all that you do.')

(*al-Baqarah*, 2: 271)

2.14. Charity in the Way of Allah

Charity in the Way of Allah *subḥānahū wa ta'ālā* is to spend one's wealth in His Cause. This is what the Holy Qur'ān describes sometimes as '*Infāq fī sabīlillāh*' (spending in the Way of Allah), at some places as '*Ṣadaqah*' (charity) and elsewhere as '*Zakāh*' (Mandatory Charity). Therefore, *Zakāh* is not just an act of charity and almsgiving, but one of the five pillars of Islam – the other four being *Īmān* (Faith), *Ṣalāh* (Mandatory Prayer), *Ṣawm* (Fast) and *Ḥajj* (Pilgrimage to the House of God). *Ṣalāh* and *Zakāh* are mentioned side by side at thirty-seven different places in the Holy Qur'ān, and it has been emphatically stressed that these principles are among the fundamentals of Islam on which our salvation in this world and the Hereafter depends. The Qur'ān tells us that *Zakāh* has been a pillar of Islam since the earliest times:

وَجَعَلْنَـٰهُمْ أَئِمَّةً يَهْدُونَ بِأَمْرِنَا وَأَوْحَيْنَآ إِلَيْهِمْ فِعْلَ ٱلْخَيْرَٰتِ وَإِقَامَ ٱلصَّلَوٰةِ وَإِيتَآءَ ٱلزَّكَوٰةِ ۖ وَكَانُوا۟ لَنَا عَـٰبِدِينَ ﴿٧٣﴾

('And We made them into leaders to guide people in accordance with Our Command, and We inspired them to good works, and to establish Prayers and to give *Zakāh*. They worshipped Us alone.')

(*al-Anbiyā'*, 21: 73)

وَمَآ أُمِرُوٓا۟ إِلَّا لِيَعْبُدُوا۟ ٱللَّهَ مُخْلِصِينَ لَهُ ٱلدِّينَ حُنَفَآءَ وَيُقِيمُوا۟ ٱلصَّلَوٰةَ وَيُؤْتُوا۟ ٱلزَّكَوٰةَ ۚ وَذَٰلِكَ دِينُ ٱلْقَيِّمَةِ ﴿٥﴾

('Yet all that they had been commanded was that they serve Allah, with utter sincerity, devoting themselves exclusively to Him, and that they establish Prayer and pay *Zakāh*. That is the Right Faith.')

(*al-Bayyinah*, 98: 5)

وَٱذْكُرْ فِى ٱلْكِتَـٰبِ إِسْمَـٰعِيلَ ۚ إِنَّهُۥ كَانَ صَادِقَ ٱلْوَعْدِ وَكَانَ رَسُولًا نَّبِيًّا ﴿٥٤﴾ وَكَانَ يَأْمُرُ أَهْلَهُۥ بِٱلصَّلَوٰةِ
وَٱلزَّكَوٰةِ وَكَانَ عِندَ رَبِّهِۦ مَرْضِيًّا ﴿٥٥﴾

('And recite in the Book the account of Ishmael! He was ever true to his promise, and was a Messenger, a Prophet. He enjoined his household to observe Prayer and to give *Zakāh* (purifying alms); and his Lord was well pleased with him.')

(*Maryam*, 19: 54-55)

وَإِذْ أَخَذْنَا مِيثَٰقَ بَنِىٓ إِسْرَٰٓءِيلَ لَا تَعْبُدُونَ إِلَّا ٱللَّهَ وَبِٱلْوَٰلِدَيْنِ إِحْسَانًا وَذِى ٱلْقُرْبَىٰ وَٱلْيَتَٰمَىٰ وَٱلْمَسَٰكِينِ
وَقُولُوا۟ لِلنَّاسِ حُسْنًا وَأَقِيمُوا۟ ٱلصَّلَوٰةَ وَءَاتُوا۟ ٱلزَّكَوٰةَ ... ﴿٨٣﴾

('And recall when We made a covenant with the Children of Israel: 'You shall serve none but Allah and do good to parents, kinsmen, orphans and the needy; you shall speak kindly to people, and establish Prayer and give *Zakāh* (Purifying Alms).')

(*al-Baqarah*, 2: 83)

قَالَ إِنِّى عَبْدُ ٱللَّهِ ءَاتَىٰنِىَ ٱلْكِتَٰبَ وَجَعَلَنِى نَبِيًّا ﴿٣٠﴾ وَجَعَلَنِى مُبَارَكًا أَيْنَ مَا كُنتُ وَأَوْصَٰنِى بِٱلصَّلَوٰةِ
وَٱلزَّكَوٰةِ مَا دُمْتُ حَيًّا ﴿٣١﴾

('The child cried out: 'Verily I am Allah's servant. He has granted me the Book and has made me a Prophet and has blessed me wherever I might be and has enjoined upon me Prayer and *Zakāh* (purifying alms) as long as I live".')

(*Maryam*, 19: 30-31)

This hallowed tradition of Islam continues, and *Zakāh* remains an essential element of Religion and an Article of Faith for the Muslims, along with *Ṣalāh* and other fundamentals of Islam:

... مِّلَّةَ أَبِيكُمْ إِبْرَٰهِيمَ ۚ هُوَ سَمَّىٰكُمُ ٱلْمُسْلِمِينَ مِن قَبْلُ وَفِى هَٰذَا لِيَكُونَ ٱلرَّسُولُ شَهِيدًا عَلَيْكُمْ وَتَكُونُوا۟ شُهَدَآءَ
عَلَى ٱلنَّاسِ ۚ فَأَقِيمُوا۟ ٱلصَّلَوٰةَ وَءَاتُوا۟ ٱلزَّكَوٰةَ وَٱعْتَصِمُوا۟ بِٱللَّهِ ... ﴿٧٨﴾

('Keep the faith of your father Abraham. Allah named you Muslim earlier and even in this (Book), that the Messenger may be a witness over you, and that you may be witnesses over all mankind. So establish Prayer, and pay *Zakāh,* and hold fast to Allah.')

(*al-Ḥajj*, 22: 78)

ذَٰلِكَ ٱلْكِتَٰبُ لَا رَيْبَ ۛ فِيهِ ۛ هُدًى لِّلْمُتَّقِينَ ﴿٢﴾ ٱلَّذِينَ يُؤْمِنُونَ بِٱلْغَيْبِ وَيُقِيمُونَ ٱلصَّلَوٰةَ
وَمِمَّا رَزَقْنَٰهُمْ يُنفِقُونَ ﴿٣﴾

('This is the Book of Allah, there is no doubt in it; it is a guidance for the pious, for those who believe in the existence of that which is beyond the reach of perception, who establish Prayer and spend out of what We have provided them.')

(*al-Baqarah*, 2: 2-3)

إِنَّمَا ٱلْمُؤْمِنُونَ ٱلَّذِينَ إِذَا ذُكِرَ ٱللَّهُ وَجِلَتْ قُلُوبُهُمْ ... ﴿٢﴾ ٱلَّذِينَ يُقِيمُونَ ٱلصَّلَوٰةَ وَمِمَّا رَزَقْنَٰهُمْ يُنفِقُونَ ﴿٣﴾
أُو۟لَٰٓئِكَ هُمُ ٱلْمُؤْمِنُونَ حَقًّا ... ﴿٤﴾

('The true believers are those who, when Allah's name is mentioned, their hearts quake, – who establish Prayer and spend out of what We have provided them. Such indeed are true believers.')

(*al-Anfāl*, 8: 2-4)

إِنَّمَا وَلِيُّكُمُ ٱللَّهُ وَرَسُولُهُۥ وَٱلَّذِينَ ءَامَنُوا۟ ٱلَّذِينَ يُقِيمُونَ ٱلصَّلَوٰةَ وَيُؤْتُونَ ٱلزَّكَوٰةَ وَهُمْ رَٰكِعُونَ ﴿٥٥﴾

('Only Allah, His Messenger, and those who believe and who establish Prayer, pay *Zakāh*, and bow down (before Allah) are your allies.')

(*al-Mā'idah*, 5: 55)

فَإِن تَابُوا۟ وَأَقَامُوا۟ ٱلصَّلَوٰةَ وَءَاتَوُا۟ ٱلزَّكَوٰةَ فَإِخْوَٰنُكُمْ فِى ٱلدِّينِ ... ﴿١١﴾

('But if they repent and establish Prayers and give *Zakāh* they are your brethren in faith.')

(*al-Tawbah*, 9: 11)

Zakāh is not only designed for the welfare of society. It is equally beneficial for the spiritual advancement of the one who pays *Zakāh*, for the improvement of his social conduct and for his success in this world and salvation in the Hereafter. It is not a tax, but an act of worship, as is *Ṣalāh*. It is an integral part of the Plan of Action that the Qur'ān provides for the reformation of the human self:

خُذْ مِنْ أَمْوَٰلِهِمْ صَدَقَةً تُطَهِّرُهُمْ وَتُزَكِّيهِم بِهَا وَصَلِّ عَلَيْهِمْ إِنَّ صَلَوٰتَكَ سَكَنٌ لَّهُمْ ... ﴿١٠٣﴾

('(O Prophet)! Take alms out of their riches and thereby cleanse them and bring about their growth (in righteousness), and pray for them. Indeed your prayer is a source of tranquility for them.')

(*al-Tawbah*, 9: 103)

لَن تَنَالُوا۟ ٱلْبِرَّ حَتَّىٰ تُنفِقُوا۟ مِمَّا تُحِبُّونَ وَمَا تُنفِقُوا۟ مِن شَىْءٍ فَإِنَّ ٱللَّهَ بِهِۦ عَلِيمٌ ﴿٩٢﴾

('You shall not attain righteousness until you spend (for the sake of Allah) out of what you love. Allah knows whatever you spend.')

(*Āl 'Imrān*, 3: 92)

فَٱتَّقُواْ ٱللَّهَ مَا ٱسْتَطَعْتُمْ وَٱسْمَعُواْ وَأَطِيعُواْ وَأَنفِقُواْ خَيْرًا لِّأَنفُسِكُمْ وَمَن يُوقَ شُحَّ نَفْسِهِۦ فَأُوْلَٰٓئِكَ هُمُ ٱلْمُفْلِحُونَ ﴿١٦﴾

('So hold Allah in awe as much as you can, and listen and obey, and be charitable. This is for your own good. And whoever remains safe from his own greediness, it is such that will prosper.')

(*al-Taghābun*, 64: 16)

2.15. Collection and distribution of *Zakāh*

Through its injunctions and guidance, the Holy Qur'ān infused into people a spirit of voluntary spending for a good cause. Furthermore, the Holy Prophet (*pbuh*) was enjoined to prescribe a minimum limit for the mandatory spending and the Islamic State was assigned the duty of arranging collection and distribution of *Zakāh* officially. The Divine Command in this respect was:

خُذْ مِنْ أَمْوَٰلِهِمْ صَدَقَةً تُطَهِّرُهُمْ وَتُزَكِّيهِم بِهَا … ﴿١٠٣﴾

('Take alms out of their riches and thereby cleanse them and bring about their growth (in righteousness).')

(*al-Tawbah*, 9: 103)

The word "*Ṣadaqah*" (charity or alms) in this *Āyah* indicates that, in addition to the normal charity and alms (*Ṣadaqāt*) voluntarily offered by the people, a certain amount needed to be made mandatory and determined by the Holy Prophet himself. Following this injunction, the Prophet of God fixed a minimum limit for the deduction of *Zakāh* on various kinds of *Zakāhable* assets. These deductions are to be made at the prescribed rates, as follows:

- 2½ percent per annum on the wealth possessed in the form of gold, silver and other cash;
- 10 percent per annum on agricultural produce from rain-fed lands;
- 5 percent per annum on agricultural produce from irrigated lands;
- 20 percent per annum on minerals in private ownership and on buried treasure;
- A deduction to be made, at different rates, on flocks intended for breeding or sale, like sheep, goats, cows, camels, etc. (For details, books of jurisprudence may be consulted.)

The *Niṣāb* (various rates of *Zakāh* deduction) was determined by the Holy Prophet (*pbuh*) in pursuance of Allah's Command in the same way that he fixed the number of *Raka'āt* (bending of the body from the upright position, followed by two *Sajdah* (prostrations)) for the five regular Prayers. Both are obligatory for Muslims as mandatory acts of worship. Therefore, the Qur'ān makes it obligatory for an Islamic State, as part of its fundamental objectives, to establish the systems of *Ṣalāh* and *Zakāh*:

ٱلَّذِينَ إِن مَّكَّنَّٰهُمْ فِى ٱلْأَرْضِ أَقَامُوا۟ ٱلصَّلَوٰةَ وَءَاتَوُا۟ ٱلزَّكَوٰةَ وَأَمَرُوا۟ بِٱلْمَعْرُوفِ وَنَهَوْا۟ عَنِ ٱلْمُنكَرِ ۗ وَلِلَّهِ
عَٰقِبَةُ ٱلْأُمُورِ ﴿٤١﴾

('Those who, were We to bestow authority on them in the land, will establish Prayers, render *Zakāh*, enjoin good, and forbid evil. The end of all matters rests with Allah.')

(*al-Ḥajj*, 22: 41)

وَأَقِيمُوا۟ ٱلصَّلَوٰةَ وَءَاتُوا۟ ٱلزَّكَوٰةَ وَأَطِيعُوا۟ ٱلرَّسُولَ لَعَلَّكُمْ تُرْحَمُونَ ﴿٥٦﴾

('Establish Prayer and pay *Zakāh* and obey the Messenger so that mercy may be shown to you.')

(*al-Nūr*, 24: 56)

As is evident from the *Āyāt* above, the system of collection and disbursement of *Zakāh* are among the basic charters of the duties of an Islamic government. In the absence of an Islamic government, or when such a government is negligent, it remains obligatory for the Muslims as a community to ensure observance of *Zakāh*. Just as the performance of the regular Prayer is not dependent on an Islamic state's formal arrangements, the payment and collection of *Zakāh* similarly remain mandatory for Muslims individually and as a community. If there is no official arrangement for the collection and distribution of *Zakāh*, then every Muslim who is in possession of the prescribed amount of wealth is duty-bound to make his regular payment of *Zakāh*.

2.16. One-fifth of revenue from war gains

In addition to the funds generated through *Zakāh*, the Qur'ān levies a certain amount on the revenue from *Amwāl al-Ghanīmah* (War Gains). The Qur'ānic injunctions prescribe that the spoils of war must not be misappropriated by the soldiers as war booty. It is obligatory for them to surrender whatever they collect after a war to their Supreme Commander (or the State), who in turn will divide what is collected into five parts, with four to be distributed in equal shares to the soldiers engaged in the battle and the fifth to go to the Islamic State's Public Treasury (*Bayt al-Māl*):

وَٱعْلَمُوٓا۟ أَنَّمَا غَنِمْتُم مِّن شَىْءٍ فَأَنَّ لِلَّهِ خُمُسَهُۥ وَلِلرَّسُولِ وَلِذِى ٱلْقُرْبَىٰ وَٱلْيَتَـٰمَىٰ وَٱلْمَسَـٰكِينِ وَٱبْنِ ٱلسَّبِيلِ ... ﴿٤١﴾

('Know that one-fifth of the spoils that you obtain belongs to Allah and to the Messenger and to the near of kin, to the orphans and the needy, and the wayfarer.')

(*al-Anfāl*, 8: 41)

2.17. Disbursement of *Zakāh* funds

According to the Holy Qur'ān, the revenue thus generated from *Zakāh* and *Amwāl al-Ghanīmah* is not part of the public exchequer, which is mandated to provide facilities and essential services to the people, including those who pay *Zakāh*. The Book of God has prescribed the following for the use of the *Zakāh* money:

إِنَّمَا ٱلصَّدَقَـٰتُ لِلْفُقَرَآءِ وَٱلْمَسَـٰكِينِ وَٱلْعَـٰمِلِينَ عَلَيْهَا وَٱلْمُؤَلَّفَةِ قُلُوبُهُمْ وَفِى ٱلرِّقَابِ وَٱلْغَـٰرِمِينَ وَفِى سَبِيلِ ٱللَّهِ وَٱبْنِ ٱلسَّبِيلِ ۖ فَرِيضَةً مِّنَ ٱللَّهِ ۗ وَٱللَّهُ عَلِيمٌ حَكِيمٌ ﴿٦٠﴾

('The alms are meant only for the poor and the needy and those who are in charge thereof, those whose hearts are to be reconciled,[4] and to free those in bondage,[5] and to help those burdened with debt, and for expenditure in the Way of Allah and for the wayfarer. This is an obligation from Allah. Allah is All-Knowing, All-Wise.')

(*al-Tawbah*, 9: 60)

2.18. Division of inheritance

According to the Islamic Law of Inheritance, whatever a man or woman leaves behind in their belongings at the time of their death must be distributed according to the prescribed proportions between their parents, children and wife or husband. In the absence of parents and children, their brothers and sisters or others from their mother or father's side will get their share of the inheritance. Details of the 'Law' concerning this are available in *Sūrah* 4, *al-Nisā'*, *Āyāt* 7 to 12 and *Āyah* 176.

---

[4] During the days of the Holy Prophet (*pbuh*), the *Zakāh* funds were spent on the following three categories of people in order to win their hearts in favour of Islam: (i) those hostile to Islam and Muslims; (ii) those averse to letting their kinfolk join the new Religion; and (iii) those who had newly embraced Islam (al-Jaṣṣāṣ, vol.III, p.152). – Author.

[5] This category includes those Muslims who may fall into the hands of enemy forces or non-Muslims captured during the war, as well as the slaves that were kept in bondage in pre-Islamic days. The funds from *Zakāh* can be used to seek their release by helping them pay their ransom. – Author.

The guiding principle of the Holy Qur'ān in this context is that the wealth gathered during a person's lifetime should simply not be allowed to accumulate, but must be spread after his death among his close relations. This principle is contrary to the practice of *primogeniture*, the joint family holding, etc., which essentially aim at keeping the wealth concentrated in one place, even after the death of its owner.

The Qur'ān similarly rejects an artificial relationship created through adoption. It lays down that those who will inherit from the deceased are actually related to them through blood, and no stranger can claim the right of inheritance because they have been 'adopted' as a son or daughter:

...وَمَا جَعَلَ أَزْوَٰجَكُمُ ٱلَّٰٓـِٔى تُظَٰهِرُونَ مِنْهُنَّ أُمَّهَٰتِكُمْ ۚ وَمَا جَعَلَ أَدْعِيَآءَكُمْ أَبْنَآءَكُمْ ۚ ذَٰلِكُمْ قَوْلُكُم بِأَفْوَٰهِكُمْ... ﴿٤﴾

('... Nor has He made your wives, whom you compare to your mothers' backs (to divorce them), your true mothers; nor has He made those whom you adopt as sons your own sons. These are only words that you utter with your mouths.')

(*al-Aḥzāb*, 33: 4)

...وَأُو۟لُوا۟ ٱلْأَرْحَامِ بَعْضُهُمْ أَوْلَىٰ بِبَعْضٍ فِى كِتَٰبِ ٱللَّهِ... ﴿٦﴾

('According to the Book of Allah, blood relatives have greater claim over each other than the rest of the believers.')

(*al-Aḥzāb*, 33: 6)

Having safeguarded the rights of the deceased's actual heirs, the Holy Qur'ān goes on to direct them to be big-hearted and not to turn anyone away, even if he is distantly related to the deceased, if he is there at the time of the distribution of the inheritance, and also to give him something of their own free will:

وَإِذَا حَضَرَ ٱلْقِسْمَةَ أُو۟لُوا۟ ٱلْقُرْبَىٰ وَٱلْيَتَٰمَىٰ وَٱلْمَسَٰكِينُ فَٱرْزُقُوهُم مِّنْهُ وَقُولُوا۟ لَهُمْ قَوْلًا مَّعْرُوفًا ﴿٨﴾ وَلْيَخْشَ ٱلَّذِينَ لَوْ تَرَكُوا۟ مِنْ خَلْفِهِمْ ذُرِّيَّةً ضِعَٰفًا خَافُوا۟ عَلَيْهِمْ فَلْيَتَّقُوا۟ ٱللَّهَ وَلْيَقُولُوا۟ قَوْلًا سَدِيدًا ﴿٩﴾

('And if other near of kin, orphans and needy are present at the time of division of inheritance give them something of it and speak to them kindly. And those who would have been fearful on account of their helpless offspring they may have behind them, let them fear Allah and say what is right.')

(*al-Nisā'*, 4: 8-9)

2.19. The Will

As well as providing us with the Law of Inheritance, the Holy Qur'ān also directs us to leave behind a will concerning our legacy:

كُتِبَ عَلَيْكُمْ إِذَا حَضَرَ أَحَدَكُمُ ٱلْمَوْتُ إِن تَرَكَ خَيْرًا ٱلْوَصِيَّةُ لِلْوَٰلِدَيْنِ وَٱلْأَقْرَبِينَ بِٱلْمَعْرُوفِ حَقًّا عَلَى ٱلْمُتَّقِينَ ﴿١٨٠﴾

('It is prescribed that when death approaches, those of you who leave behind property shall bequeath equitably to parents and kinsmen. This is an obligation on the God-fearing.')

(*al-Baqarah*, 2: 180)

According to this injunction, it is obligatory for a person to impress upon his legal heirs the need for them to take care of his parents after his death. He should also advise them to give something from his legacy to those of his relatives whom he considers deserving, though they may have no claim to it according to the Law of Inheritance. Additionally, if somebody is leaving behind a considerable amount of wealth, he can bequeath a certain portion of it for the public welfare, as the import of the *Āyah* is clear that a will is not restricted to include only the parents and kinsmen.

The Islamic Law of Will and Inheritance confirms that the Qur'ānic scheme in respect of personal property is that its two-thirds must be distributed according to the Law of Inheritance, and one-third may be left to the dying person's discretion, which he can bequeath through his will as he deems fit. However, he is bound by the Law to bequeath it in a lawful manner, which means that (i) the objective for which the will has been made must be lawful, and (ii) it should not entail depriving his lawful heirs.[6]

2.20. Rights of those of weaker understanding

The Qur'ān enjoins that the property must not be handed over to those of weaker understanding, lest they fail to safeguard their own interests properly. It directs that, in this case, the property should be entrusted to their guardians, the Magistrate or the Judge, and its custody should be transferred only after ensuring that such persons are capable of handling it properly themselves:

---

[6] Elaborating on the Law of Will, the Holy Prophet (*pbuh*) imposed the following conditions: (i) one can only use his discretionary powers concerning his will to the extent of one-third of his property; (ii) no extra amount can be bequeathed to a legally eligible heir over and above his predetermined share without the explicit consent of the other lawful inheritors; (iii) no will is lawful according to which a legally eligible heir is deprived of his inheritance, or if his share is reduced. – Author.

وَلَا تُؤْتُوا۟ ٱلسُّفَهَآءَ أَمْوَٰلَكُمُ ٱلَّتِى جَعَلَ ٱللَّهُ لَكُمْ قِيَـٰمًا وَٱرْزُقُوهُمْ فِيهَا وَٱكْسُوهُمْ وَقُولُوا۟ لَهُمْ قَوْلًا مَّعْرُوفًا ۝ وَٱبْتَلُوا۟ ٱلْيَتَـٰمَىٰ حَتَّىٰٓ إِذَا بَلَغُوا۟ ٱلنِّكَاحَ فَإِنْ ءَانَسْتُم مِّنْهُمْ رُشْدًا فَٱدْفَعُوٓا۟ إِلَيْهِمْ أَمْوَٰلَهُمْ ۖ وَلَا تَأْكُلُوهَآ إِسْرَافًا وَبِدَارًا أَن يَكْبَرُوا۟ ۚ وَمَن كَانَ غَنِيًّا فَلْيَسْتَعْفِفْ ۖ وَمَن كَانَ فَقِيرًا فَلْيَأْكُلْ بِٱلْمَعْرُوفِ ۚ فَإِذَا دَفَعْتُمْ إِلَيْهِمْ أَمْوَٰلَهُمْ فَأَشْهِدُوا۟ عَلَيْهِمْ ۚ وَكَفَىٰ بِٱللَّهِ حَسِيبًا ۝

('Do not entrust your properties – which Allah has made a means of support for you – to the weak of understanding, but maintain and clothe them out of it, and say to them a kind word of advice. Test the orphans until they reach the age of marriage, and then if you find them mature of mind hand over to them their property, and do not eat it up by either spending extravagantly or in haste, fearing that they would grow up (and claim it). If the guardian of the orphan is rich let him partake of it in a fair measure. When you hand over their property to them let there be witnesses on their behalf. Allah is sufficient to take account (of your deeds).')

(*al-Nisā'*, 4: 5-6)

The above *Āyāt* also bring home another subtle point that although a property belongs to those who are its legal owners, it does not concern them alone, but the community's collective interests are also involved in such matters. This is why the Qur'ān, instead of saying أَمْوَٰلَهُمْ (their property), describes it as أَمْوَٰلَكُمْ (your property) and makes it incumbent upon society to look after the interests of its weaker elements.

2.21. Safeguarding public interest in state holdings

Regarding state holdings, public funds and government revenue, the Holy Qur'ān directs that these should not be used in the interest of a particular class of moneyed people, but in the public interest as well and with a special stress on the betterment and welfare of the poorer sections of the society:

مَّآ أَفَآءَ ٱللَّهُ عَلَىٰ رَسُولِهِۦ مِنْ أَهْلِ ٱلْقُرَىٰ فَلِلَّهِ وَلِلرَّسُولِ وَلِذِى ٱلْقُرْبَىٰ وَٱلْيَتَـٰمَىٰ وَٱلْمَسَـٰكِينِ وَٱبْنِ ٱلسَّبِيلِ كَىْ لَا يَكُونَ دُولَةًۢ بَيْنَ ٱلْأَغْنِيَآءِ مِنكُمْ ۚ وَمَآ ءَاتَىٰكُمُ ٱلرَّسُولُ فَخُذُوهُ وَمَا نَهَىٰكُمْ عَنْهُ فَٱنتَهُوا۟ ۚ وَٱتَّقُوا۟ ٱللَّهَ ۖ إِنَّ ٱللَّهَ شَدِيدُ ٱلْعِقَابِ ۝ لِلْفُقَرَآءِ ٱلْمُهَـٰجِرِينَ ٱلَّذِينَ أُخْرِجُوا۟ مِن دِيَـٰرِهِمْ وَأَمْوَٰلِهِمْ يَبْتَغُونَ فَضْلًا مِّنَ ٱللَّهِ وَرِضْوَٰنًا وَيَنصُرُونَ ٱللَّهَ وَرَسُولَهُۥٓ ۚ أُو۟لَـٰٓئِكَ هُمُ ٱلصَّـٰدِقُونَ ۝ وَٱلَّذِينَ تَبَوَّءُو ٱلدَّارَ وَٱلْإِيمَـٰنَ مِن قَبْلِهِمْ يُحِبُّونَ مَنْ هَاجَرَ إِلَيْهِمْ وَلَا يَجِدُونَ فِى صُدُورِهِمْ حَاجَةً مِّمَّآ أُوتُوا۟ وَيُؤْثِرُونَ عَلَىٰٓ أَنفُسِهِمْ وَلَوْ كَانَ بِهِمْ خَصَاصَةٌ ۚ وَمَن يُوقَ شُحَّ نَفْسِهِۦ فَأُو۟لَـٰٓئِكَ هُمُ ٱلْمُفْلِحُونَ ۝ وَٱلَّذِينَ جَآءُو مِنۢ بَعْدِهِمْ يَقُولُونَ رَبَّنَا ٱغْفِرْ لَنَا وَلِإِخْوَٰنِنَا ٱلَّذِينَ سَبَقُونَا بِٱلْإِيمَـٰنِ وَلَا تَجْعَلْ فِى قُلُوبِنَا غِلًّا لِّلَّذِينَ ءَامَنُوا۟ رَبَّنَآ إِنَّكَ رَءُوفٌ رَّحِيمٌ ۝

('Whatever (from the possessions of the towns-people) Allah has bestowed on His Messenger belongs to Allah, and to the Messenger, and to his kinsfolk, and to the orphans, and to the needy, and to the wayfarer so that it may not merely circulate between the rich among you.[7] So accept whatever the Messenger gives you, and refrain from whatever he forbids you. And fear Allah, verily Allah is Most Stern in retribution. It also belongs to the poor Emigrants who have been driven out of their homes and their possessions, those who seek Allah's favour and good pleasure and help Allah and His Messenger. Such are the truthful ones. It also belongs to those who were already settled in this abode[8] (of *Hijrah*) having come to faith before the

---

[7] In his explanatory note in *Tafhīm al-Qur'ān,* Sayyid Mawdūdī described this as one of the most important *Āyāt* of the Holy Qur'ān juridically. The *Āyah* enunciates the basic principle of the economic policy of an Islamic state and society, that is: the wealth is to be allowed free circulation *so that it may not merely circulate between the rich* and the poor are left to become poorer and the rich richer. This is not just a policy statement of the Book of God, but has duly been backed up by some very effective practical measures. These measures include: a total ban on interest-based transactions, enforcement of *Zakāh,* levy of one-fifth on war gains, encouragement of voluntary acts of charity and public welfare (*Ṣadaqāt*), imposition of different kinds of penalties as reparation of sinful transgressions, the Law of Will and Inheritance, prohitition of hoarding and stinginess, and condemnation of unchecked spending on luxuries and personal comforts. All these measures are intended to allow free flow of capital from the rich in society to the larger sections in the best interest of the poor and the indigent. It has been impressed on the affluent ones that their affluence makes them in no way superior to others and that the voluntary or mandatory charity that they are required to offer is no tax imposed on them by the state but the poor man's right which they are duty-bound by the Lord to discharge and for which the poor owe them no compliment. The qualities of generosity and benevolence thus become the outstanding features of the Islamic community. According to the rule laid down for *Amwāl al-Fay'* (public funds), which form major portion of the govt's revenue, a part of it will have to be spent on schemes of public welfare and to support the common man and those in need. Another aspect which must also be kept in mind is that funds raised from *Zakāh* and *Fay'* are the two principal sources of revenue for an Islamic state. Of these, the first one is meant exclusively for the amelioration of the poorer sections' lot. The revenue under *Fay'* is generated through various sources of income, including *jizyah,* or the capital tax levied on *Ahl al-Dhimmah* (the non-Muslim subjects of an Islamic state who enjoy the gurarantee (*Dhimmah*) of state's protection in lieu of their undertaking to live as its peaceful citizens and not as combatants – hence also called (*Dhimmīs*) and in return of this guarantee are required to pay a nominal token tax, much less than *Zakāh,* levied exclusively on Muslim subjects, and *Kharāj,* or the land tax. A major portion of the revenue thus generated is spent again on the welfare needs of the poor and the less affluent. It thus becomes quite clear that the special feature of the economic policy of an Islamic state and government is to regulate its income and expenditure in such a way that the moneyed and influential people may not have the monopoly on the state's sources of income, and capital is allowed to flow freely instead of accumulating among the rich or flying from the poor to the moneyed. (*Tafhīm al-Qur'ān,* vol.5, n.14, p.393) – Translation & adaptation – Translator.

[8] The injunctions determine, in the lands won in battle, the rights of Allah and His Messenger (the Islamic cause and the State), the Kinsmen of the Holy Prophet (*pbuh*) (because of their dedication to the Islamic Mission that spares them no time to earn their living), the

orphans, the needy, the wayfarer, the Muslim Emigrants to the State of Madinah (*Muhājirīn*), their local Helpers (*Anṣār*) and the future generations of the Islamic community. The Second Caliph Ḥaḍrat 'Umar decided accordingly the dispensation of the immense lands that became part of the flourishing Islamic Caliphate of his time following the conquests of Iraq, Syria and Egypt. His era was marked by unprecedented territorial expansion and political, economic and military strength of the Islamic state. This, however, gave rise to a major juridical debate among prominent leaders of public opinions, the eminent Companions of the Holy Prophet (*pbuh*). They demanded the *Amīr al-Mu'minīn* to distribute the lands of the conquered territory exactly according to the formula adopted by the Prophet at Khaybar. As the debate went on, the Caliph expressed his stand in the matter in decisive terms:

... فَمَا لِمَنْ جَاءَ بَعْدَكُم مِنَ الْمُسلِمِين؟ وَاَخَافُ اِنْ قَسمتُهُ اَن تُفَاسِدُوا بَيْنَكُم فِي الْمِيَاه ...

('What will then be left for the Muslims that come after you? I am afraid, if I distribute these lands, you will (soon) start fighting among yourselves over water.')

(Narrated by Abū 'Ubayd)

... لَوْلَا آخِرُ النَّاسِ مَا فُتِحَتْ قَرْيَةٌ اِلاَّ قَسَمْتُهَا كَمَا قَسَمَ رَسُولُ الله صَلَّى اللهُ عَلَيهِ وَسَلَّم خَيبَرَ

('Had there been none to follow (after present generation of Muslims), I would have distributed the lands conquered exactly the way the Prophet of Allah (*pbuh*) did at Khaybar)

(*al-Jāmi' al-Ṣaḥīḥ* of Imām Bukhārī, *Muwaṭṭa'* of Imām Mālik and Abū 'Ubayd)

... لَا، هٰذَا عَيْنُ الْمَالِ، وَلٰكِنِّى اَحبِسَهُ فِيمَا يَجْرِى عَلَيهِم وَ عَلَى الْمُسْلِمِين

('... No, this is real estate. I will hold it safe in the best interest of those fighting in the Way of Allah and the Muslims in general.')

(Narrated by Abū 'Ubayd)

There were, however, many dissenting voices and the Caliph decided to refer the matter to the *Majlis al-Shūrā* (Parliament) in a bid to arrive at a consensus. Luminaries like Ḥaḍrat 'Uthmān, Ḥaḍrat 'Alī, Ḥaḍrat Ṭalḥah, Ḥaḍrat 'Abd Allāh bin 'Umar and many others supported the Caliph's stand. The consensus, nonetheless, was not reached and the issue became the burning one across the Islamic Caliphate. Finally, Ḥaḍrat 'Umar rose to settle it once for all. He recited the injunctions contained in *Āyāt* 7 to 10 of *Sūrah al-Ḥashr* to reaffirm his standpoint. He stressed that the *Āyāt* had so decided in order to let the Muslim community as a whole and their generations to follow remain beneficiaries of the bounties Allah *subḥānahū wa ta'ālā* had bestowed on the Islamic state through victories in battlefield and also to prevent their concentration within a few hands.

In the light of this ruling by the Second Caliph, the status of the conquered lands has been determined once for all as public property (*Amwāl al-Fay'*). The broad outlines in this context may be summed up as follows:

- Proprietory rights of conquered lands would revert to the Islamic State.
- Farming rights would continue to be exercised by those who tilled the land at the time of conquest. They would, however, be required to pay a certain amount as land tax, the way they did to the erstwhile governments (with varying rates).

(arrival of the) *Muhājirūn* (Emigrants). They love those who have migrated to them and do not covet what has been given them; they even prefer them above themselves though poverty be their own lot. And whosoever are preserved from their own greed, such are the ones that will prosper. (And it also belongs to) those who came after them, and who pray:[9] 'Lord,

---

- The original farmers would be entitled to sell these rights to whomsoever they liked, and also to pass these on as legacy to their heirs from generation to generation.

All the four major schools of Islamic jurisprudence, thus, agree on the status of conquered lands being state property (*Fay'*). There are, however, slight variations in specifics as briefly noted below:

- The *Ḥanafīyah* (followers of Imām al-A'ẓam Abū Ḥanīfah) authorize the state either to take in its custody one-fifth of the land as public property and allow the rest to be distributed among the soldiers who won the battle, or to let it remain in possession of its former owners after levying *Jizyah* and *Kharāj* (the capital and land tax).
- The *Mālikīyah* (followers of Imām Mālik's school) are of the view that the conquered lands automatically become the Muslim community's trust following victory in battle; the Islamic state may or may not make a formal announcement in that respect. According to them, the buildings and constructed property of the enemy's land also revert to the Muslims as trust property, on which the Islamic government can charge no rent.
- The *Shāfi'īyah* (followers of Imām Shāfi'ī) consider all movable property of the conquered land as part of *ghanīmah* (war gains) and the immovable ones as *Fay'* (public property).
- The *Ḥanābilah* (those belonging to the school of Imām Aḥmad bin Ḥanbal) agree with the Ḥanafīyah in so far as the state's discretion is concerned to retain a part of these lands as public property and distribute the rest among the soldiers. They subscribe, however, to the *Mālikīyah*'s views regarding buildings and constructed property, allowing the state no authority to impose rent on these. (*Tafhīm al-Qur'ān*, vol.5, n.20, pp.397-402) – Translation and adaptation – Translator.

[9] *Āyah* 10 of the *Sūrah* tells us that the the conquered lands are not for distribution exclusively among the Muslims present at the time of conquest. These equally belong to the future generations of Muslims to follow. It simultaneously contains an important lesson and message for the Islamic community that nothing should ever cause any ill will and rancour in a Muslim's heart against his fellow Muslim and they should better seek forgiveness of the Lord for those who have preceded them in faith and speak no ill against them either. It has thus been impressed upon the Muslims, individually and collectively, that the nation of Islam has been bound together in the bond of faith and so long as their faith is strong and impregnable, this bond will remain strong, which would bring each member of the community close to the other as brother and part of the same fraternity. This has so aptly been illustrated by the following Tradition narrated by Ḥaḍrat Anas. The Holy Preophet (*pbuh*) informed his assembly of Companions for three consecutive days that the next person to join them there was one of the *ahl al-jannah* (destined for Heaven) and each day it happened to be the same person from Anṣār (the Helpers from Madinah). This was such a big news that each one of the Companions present became curious to know about the good deeds of that particular

forgive us and our brethren who have preceded us in faith, and do not put in our hearts any rancour towards those who believe. Lord, You are the Most Tender, the Most Compassionate".')

(*al-Ḥashr*, 59: 7-10)

2.22. Guiding principle about taxation

The fundamental principle laid down by the Book of God concerning the Islamic State's taxation policy is that the burden of taxes should fall on the shoulders of those who own wealth in excess of their needs, and this should also cover that part of their fortune which they have saved after fulfilling their needs:

...وَيَسْـَٔلُونَكَ مَاذَا يُنفِقُونَ قُلِ ٱلْعَفْوَ... ﴿٢١٩﴾

('They ask: "What should we spend in the Way of Allah?" Say: "Whatever you can spare".')

(*al-Baqarah*, 2: 219)

2.23. Salient features of Islamic economics – a resume

To sum up what has been explained in the preceding sections, below is a summary of the basic principles that are contained in the 22-point Qur'ānic scheme for the economic well-being of humankind:

- The Qur'ānic scheme aims at introducing economic justice into society in such a manner as to check, on the one hand, all forms of economic imbalance and exploitation and, on the other, to promote the growth and development of moral values. The Qur'ān does not seek to create a social set-up where no one can contribute to the good of another and all the welfare needs of the people are assigned to a collective mechanism be-

---

Companion. They informed him of the great tidings from the Holy Prophet and asked him what he thought entitled him have an extraordinary honour. The man from the Anṣār said that so far as his *'Ibādah* (worship) of the Lord is concerned, they should know better as he was just like them in that respect. There was, however, one thing that might have merited him that honour and it was:

لاَ أَجِدُ فِى نَفسِى غِلاً لِأَحَدٍ مِنَ الـمُسلِمِينَ وَلاَ أَحسُدُهُ على خَيرٍ أَعطَاهُ الله تَعَالى إِيَّاه

('I find no rancour in my heart towards any fellow Muslim; nor do I feel spiteful against him for any goodness, done to him by Allah *subḥānahū wa ta'ālā*.)

(Nasā'ī, narrated by Anas; see also *Tafhīm al-Qur'ān*, vol.5, n.21, pp.403-409)

– Translation and adaptation – Translator.

cause, under this kind of dispensation, the growth and development of mankind's moral conduct is hardly possible. On the contrary, it promotes a social order in which individuals are encouraged to deal with each other voluntarily and selflessly in a spirit of magnanimity, sympathy and generosity, as a result of which an atmosphere of love and understanding develops among them. For this purpose, the Qur'ān relies chiefly on infusing the spirit of Faith in people, and on measures to make them better human beings through education and training. To back this up, it also makes use of some compulsory steps that are essentially required for the collective well-being of society (Points: 2.8. to 2.13. and 2.15. to 2.19.).

- Under the Qur'ānic scheme for human welfare, the economic and moral values are not kept apart, but are integrated into a harmonious whole, and instead of resolving economic problems from an economic perspective alone, they are resolved with relation to the social order, the grand edifice of which has been raised by Islam on the foundations of a God-fearing concept of this cosmic system and a moral philosophy of life (Points: 2.1., 2.2., 2.4. and 2.5.).
- Under this scheme, all of the economic means and resources of the earth are treated as blessings for the human race from the Almighty, a fact that demands that no personal, group or national monopoly over the God-gifted resources of nature is encouraged, and that humanity is provided with more and more free means and opportunities to make use of them and earn its living (Point: 2.5.).
- Under this Qur'ānic scheme, individuals have been given the right of private ownership, although this is not unlimited. While laying down necessary restrictions on the rights of private ownership in the interest of other members of society, the Qur'ān also establishes the personal holdings of an individual and the rights of his relatives, neighbours, friends, the needy and deserving and the community as a whole. Some of these rights can be compulsorily enforced, while some others are to be discharged by individuals themselves, for which provisions have been made to train them mentally and morally (Points: 2.3., 2.5., 2.7. to 2.15., 2.17., 2.19. and 2.20.).
- The natural way of managing the community's economic system according to this scheme is to encourage and promote individuals' free enterprise. However, this freedom is not unchecked or unlimited, but has been circumscribed by certain limits in the best interests of individuals themselves and their social, moral and economic well-being (Points: 2.6., 2.15. and 2.22.).

- The Qur'ānic scheme acknowledges both men and women as rightful owners of the wealth they earn, inherit or acquire through lawful means, and no gender distinction is allowed that would prevent either from making use of their wealth. Both men and women have been granted equal rights to exercise control over their property (Points: 2.3., 2.4. to 2.18.).
- In order to maintain an economic balance, the people have been exhorted, on the one hand, to make proper use of the resources they have been gifted by the Almighty, instead of resorting to stinginess or hermit-like renunciation; and, on the other, they are strictly forbidden to indulge in extravagance, uncalled-for spending and luxuries (Points: 2.5., 2.8. to 2.10.).
- In the interests of economic justice, there is an arrangement in this scheme to check the unwarranted flow of wealth in one particular direction, and also to prevent the unproductive accumulation of wealth in certain hands, even though it has been earned through lawful means. At the same time, it seeks to ensure a wider circulation and better use of wealth, and to facilitate the maximum benefit that can be attained from the state's resources by the poorer sections of the society, who may be deprived of their normal share for one reason or another (Points: 2.6. to 2.10., 2.12., 2.13., 2.15., 2.17. to 2.19. and 2.21.).
- The Qur'ānic scheme does not depend entirely on the intervention of the state or the law to establish economic justice in a society. It does make the state responsible for certain essential measures in this respect, but then goes on to implement its remaining measures through the intellectual and moral training of individuals and by reforming the society as a whole, in order to achieve the objective of socio-economic justice without disturbing the logical demands of free enterprise (Points: 2.5. to 2.22.).
- By eliminating the causes of class conflicts, the scheme generates within the various segments of the society a spirit of cooperation and fellowship, instead of unhealthy competition and rivalry (Points: 2.4., 2.6. to 2.9., 2.12., 2.15. to 2.17., 2.21. and 2.22.).

The way in which the Qur'ānic scheme and principles for a society's economic well-being were practically enforced during the golden era of *Sayyidinā* Rasūl Allah (*pbuh*) and his Rightly-Guided Caliphs (*al-Khulafā' al-Rāshidūn*) has provided us with a wealth of information in the form of rulings and precedents. Those who are interested in greater detail can revert to the pristine source of knowledge about the Islamic *Sharī'ah*, available in the books of Prophetic Traditions, *Sīrah*, Islamic Jurisprudence and Islamic History.

2.24. Index of Source Material

1-	The Holy Qur'ān			
2-	al-Bayḍāwī	*Anwār al-Tanzīl*	Muṣṭafā al-Bābī al-Ḥalabī, Cairo.	(1330 AH/ 1912 CE).
3-	al-Ālūsī	*Rūḥ al-Maʿānī*	Idārah al-Ṭibāʿah al-Munīrīyah, Cairo.	(1345 AH).
4-	al-Jaṣṣāṣ	*Aḥkām al-Qur'ān*	al-Maṭbaʿah al-Bahīyah, Cairo.	(1347 AH).
5-	Ibn al-ʿArabī	*Aḥkām al-Qur'ān*	Maṭbaʿah al-Saʿādah, Cairo.	(1331 AH).
6-	Ibn Jarīr	*Jāmiʿ al-Bayān*	al-Maṭbaʿah al-Amīrīyah, Cairo.	(1328 AH).
7-	Ibn al-Kathīr	*Tafsīr al-Qur'ān al-ʿAẓīm*	Maṭbaʿah Muṣṭafā Muḥammad, Cairo.	(1947 CE).
8-	al-Zamakhsharī	*al-Kashshāf*	al- Maṭbaʿah al-Bahīyah, Cairo.	(1343 AH).
9-	Imām al-Bukhārī	*al-Jāmiʿ al-Ṣaḥīḥ*		
10-	Imām Muslim	*al-Jāmiʿ al-Ṣaḥīḥ*		
11-	Imām al-Tirmidhī	*al-Sunan*		
12-	Abū Dāwūd	*al-Sunan*		
13-	al-Nasā'ī	*al-Sunan*		
14-	al-Shawkānī	*Nayl al-Awṭār*	Muṣṭafā al-Bābī, Cairo.	(1347 AH).
15-	Ibn ʿAbd al-Barr	*al-Istīʿāb*	Dā'irah al-Maʿārif, Hyderabad (Deccan).	(1337 AH).
16-	Ibn Manẓūr	*Lisān al-ʿArab*	Beirut.	(1956 CE).

3 The Differences between Islam and Capitalism

The middle of the road policy for a society's economic well-being that Islam adopts is unique and rewarding in so many ways, especially when viewed against the backdrop of the extremist ideologies of socialism and capitalism. To give this policy a practical shape, Islam raises the grand edifice of its economic scheme on the twin foundations of law and morality. Through its moral teachings, it mentally prepares the society and each of its members to subscribe to this scheme voluntarily; while by the force of its legal code it imposes restrictions that compulsorily keep them within the ambit of that scheme. These moral principles and legal regulations are the basic ingredients and mainstays of the Islamic economic system. In order to grasp its tone and tenor fully, it is essential to examine it in more detail.

3.1. Distinction between lawful and forbidden means of livelihood

The first thing to note is that Islam does not give free license to its followers to earn a living or to conduct their economic activities as they choose. Instead, it lays down distinct criteria of what is *Ḥalāl* (lawful) and *Ḥarām* (forbidden) for all economic activities, both public and private, in the best interests of society. This distinguishing feature of Islam's economic system is based on the guiding principle that all means of production and earning wealth are unlawful where one person's gain is another's loss, and that every economic activity is lawful which permits the equitable distribution of dividends among the persons involved. This universal principle of Islam has been enunciated by the Holy Qur'ān thus:

يَٰٓأَيُّهَا ٱلَّذِينَ ءَامَنُوا۟ لَا تَأْكُلُوٓا۟ أَمْوَٰلَكُم بَيْنَكُم بِٱلْبَٰطِلِ إِلَّآ أَن تَكُونَ تِجَٰرَةً عَن تَرَاضٍ مِّنكُمْ ۚ
وَلَا تَقْتُلُوٓا۟ أَنفُسَكُمْ ۚ إِنَّ ٱللَّهَ كَانَ بِكُمْ رَحِيمًا ﴿٢٩﴾ وَمَن يَفْعَلْ ذَٰلِكَ عُدْوَٰنًا وَظُلْمًا فَسَوْفَ نُصْلِيهِ نَارًا ۚ وَكَانَ
ذَٰلِكَ عَلَى ٱللَّهِ يَسِيرًا ﴿٣٠﴾

('Believers! Do not devour one another's possessions wrongfully; rather, let there be trading by mutual consent, and do not kill yourselves. Surely Allah is ever Compassionate to you. And whoever does this by way of transgression and injustice We shall surely cast him into the Fire; that indeed is quite easy for Allah.')

(*al-Nisā'*, 4: 29-30)

This injunction to '*let there be trading by mutual consent*' involves the exchange of goods and services on a substitutional basis. By making it conditional on 'mutual consent', every form of transaction is rejected as unlawful where there is an element of coercion, deception, fraud or trickery, which may make the deal undesirable for if discovered by the other party. To stress this point further, it goes on: 'do not kill (or destroy) yourselves'. The *Āyah* can be interpreted in either of two ways, and both interpretations are applicable here: (i) 'Do not try to financially eliminate and destroy each other'; or (ii) 'Do not indulge in self-destruction'. According to the Holy Qur'ān, anybody who does something that is damaging to others for his own personal gains is in fact guilty of manslaughter, and thus leads the way to his own eventual doom.

In addition to the above fundamental injunction, the Qur'ān has declared unlawful in different places the following means of money making:

3.1.1. *Bribery and embezzlement*

وَلَا تَأْكُلُوٓا۟ أَمْوَٰلَكُم بَيْنَكُم بِٱلْبَٰطِلِ وَتُدْلُوا۟ بِهَآ إِلَى ٱلْحُكَّامِ لِتَأْكُلُوا۟ فَرِيقًا مِّنْ أَمْوَٰلِ ٱلنَّاسِ بِٱلْإِثْمِ
وَأَنتُمْ تَعْلَمُونَ ﴿١٨٨﴾

('And do not usurp one another's possessions by false means, nor proffer your possessions to the authorities so that you may sinfully and knowingly usurp a portion of another's possessions.')

(*al-Baqarah*, 2: 188)

3.1.2. *Breach of trust and misappropriation of funds, public or private*

وَإِن كُنتُمْ عَلَىٰ سَفَرٍ وَلَمْ تَجِدُوا۟ كَاتِبًا فَرِهَٰنٌ مَّقْبُوضَةٌ ۖ فَإِنْ أَمِنَ بَعْضُكُم بَعْضًا فَلْيُؤَدِّ ٱلَّذِى ٱؤْتُمِنَ أَمَٰنَتَهُۥ
وَلْيَتَّقِ ٱللَّهَ رَبَّهُۥ ۗ وَلَا تَكْتُمُوا۟ ٱلشَّهَٰدَةَ ۚ وَمَن يَكْتُمْهَا فَإِنَّهُۥٓ ءَاثِمٌ قَلْبُهُۥ ۗ وَٱللَّهُ بِمَا تَعْمَلُونَ عَلِيمٌ ﴿٢٨٣﴾

('And if you are on a journey and do not find a scribe to write the document then resort to taking pledges in hand. But if any of you trusts another, let him who is trusted, fulfill the trust and fear Allah, his Lord. And do not conceal what you have witnessed, for whoever conceals it, his heart is sinful. Allah has full knowledge of all that you do.')

(*al-Baqarah*, 2: 283)

وَمَا كَانَ لِنَبِيٍّ أَن يَغُلَّ ۚ وَمَن يَغْلُلْ يَأْتِ بِمَا غَلَّ يَوْمَ ٱلْقِيَـٰمَةِ ۚ ثُمَّ تُوَفَّىٰ كُلُّ نَفْسٍ مَّا كَسَبَتْ وَهُمْ لَا يُظْلَمُونَ ﴿١٦١﴾

('It is not for a Prophet to defraud; and whoever defrauds shall bring with him the fruits of his fraud on the Day of Resurrection, when every human being shall be paid in full what he has earned, and shall not be wronged.')

(*Āl 'Imrān*, 3: 161)

3.1.3. *Theft and burglary*

وَٱلسَّارِقُ وَٱلسَّارِقَةُ فَٱقْطَعُوٓا۟ أَيْدِيَهُمَا جَزَآءًۢ بِمَا كَسَبَا نَكَـٰلًا مِّنَ ٱللَّهِ ۗ وَٱللَّهُ عَزِيزٌ حَكِيمٌ ﴿٣٨﴾

('As for the thief – male or female – cut off the hands of both. This is a recompense for what they have done, and an exemplary punishment from Allah. Allah is All-Mighty, All-Wise.')

(*al-Mā'idah*, 5: 38)

3.1.4. *Mishandling of the orphan's property*

إِنَّ ٱلَّذِينَ يَأْكُلُونَ أَمْوَٰلَ ٱلْيَتَـٰمَىٰ ظُلْمًا إِنَّمَا يَأْكُلُونَ فِى بُطُونِهِمْ نَارًا ۖ وَسَيَصْلَوْنَ سَعِيرًا ﴿١٠﴾

('Behold, those who wrongfully devour the properties of orphans only fill their bellies with fire. Soon they will burn in the Blazing Flame.')

(*al-Nisā'*, 4: 10)

3.1.5. *Fraudulent transactions/disregard of weights and measures*

وَيْلٌ لِّلْمُطَفِّفِينَ ﴿١﴾ ٱلَّذِينَ إِذَا ٱكْتَالُوا۟ عَلَى ٱلنَّاسِ يَسْتَوْفُونَ ﴿٢﴾ وَإِذَا كَالُوهُمْ أَو وَّزَنُوهُمْ يُخْسِرُونَ ﴿٣﴾

('Woe to the stinters,[1] those who, when they take from others by measure, take their full share; but who, when they measure or weigh for others, give less than their due.')

(*al-Muṭaffifīn*, 83: 1-3)

---

[1] The Qur'ānic term *Muṭaffifīn* is derived from the infinitive *Ṭaṭfīf*. *Ṭafīf*, adjective from the same root, means deficient, small, slight. *Ṭaṭfīf* as term denotes pilferage in weights and measures. The trader, who indulges in this fraudulent act, slyly deprives the buyer of his right to get his money's worth. He does not take away in lump sum from the goods sold, but does it in small measures to remain unchecked by his customer and the law enforcers. The Book of God has condemned in strongest terms social evils like embezzlement in weights and measures and frauds of all kinds. *Āyah* 152 of *Sūrah Āl 'Imrān* says: '… and give full measures and weight with justice.' The believers have been commanded: 'Give full measure when you measure, and weigh with even scales. That is fair and better in consequence.' (*Banī Isrā'īl*, 17: 35). The commandement in *Sūrah al-Raḥmān* (55) is unique in its import: '.. and He raised up the heaven and has set a balance that you may not transgress in the balance, but weigh things equitably and skimp not in the balance.' (7-9). According to the author,

3.1.6. *Trading in immorality and all means of obscenity and promiscuousness*

إِنَّ ٱلَّذِينَ يُحِبُّونَ أَن تَشِيعَ ٱلْفَـٰحِشَةُ فِى ٱلَّذِينَ ءَامَنُوا۟ لَهُمْ عَذَابٌ أَلِيمٌ فِى ٱلدُّنْيَا وَٱلْـَٔاخِرَةِ ۚ وَٱللَّهُ يَعْلَمُ
وَأَنتُمْ لَا تَعْلَمُونَ ﴿١٩﴾

('Verily those who love that indecency should spread among the believers deserve a painful chastisement in the world and the Hereafter. Allah knows, but you do not know.')

(*al-Nūr*, 24: 19)

3.1.7. *Income generated through the sex trade, brothels, adultery or fornication*

ٱلزَّانِيَةُ وَٱلزَّانِى فَٱجْلِدُوا۟ كُلَّ وَٰحِدٍ مِّنْهُمَا مِا۟ئَةَ جَلْدَةٍ ۖ وَلَا تَأْخُذْكُم بِهِمَا رَأْفَةٌ فِى دِينِ ٱللَّهِ إِن كُنتُمْ تُؤْمِنُونَ
بِٱللَّهِ وَٱلْيَوْمِ ٱلْـَٔاخِرِ ۖ وَلْيَشْهَدْ عَذَابَهُمَا طَآئِفَةٌ مِّنَ ٱلْمُؤْمِنِينَ ﴿٢﴾

('Those who fornicate – whether female or male – flog each one of them with a hundred lashes. And let not tenderness for them deter you from what pertains to Allah's religion, if you do truly believe in Allah and the Last Day; and let a party of believers witness their punishment.')

(*al-Nūr*, 24: 2)

وَلْيَسْتَعْفِفِ ٱلَّذِينَ لَا يَجِدُونَ نِكَاحًا حَتَّىٰ يُغْنِيَهُمُ ٱللَّهُ مِن فَضْلِهِۦ ۗ وَٱلَّذِينَ يَبْتَغُونَ ٱلْكِتَـٰبَ مِمَّا مَلَكَتْ
أَيْمَـٰنُكُمْ فَكَاتِبُوهُمْ إِنْ عَلِمْتُمْ فِيهِمْ خَيْرًا ۖ وَءَاتُوهُم مِّن مَّالِ ٱللَّهِ ٱلَّذِىٓ ءَاتَىٰكُمْ ۚ وَلَا تُكْرِهُوا۟ فَتَيَـٰتِكُمْ عَلَى ٱلْبِغَآءِ
إِنْ أَرَدْنَ تَحَصُّنًا لِّتَبْتَغُوا۟ عَرَضَ ٱلْحَيَوٰةِ ٱلدُّنْيَا ۚ وَمَن يُكْرِههُّنَّ فَإِنَّ ٱللَّهَ مِنۢ بَعْدِ إِكْرَٰهِهِنَّ غَفُورٌ رَّحِيمٌ ﴿٣٣﴾

('Let those who cannot afford to marry keep themselves chaste until Allah enriches them out of His Bounty. And write out a deed of manumission for such of your slaves that desire their freedom in lieu of payment – if you see any good in them – and give them out of the wealth that Allah has given

---

all Qur'ānic commentators have interpreted the word *mīzān* (balance) used in these *Āyāt*, as signifying justice and the words '.. *set a balance*' as meaning that God has made justice embrace the entire universe. The thrust of the statement is that since man lives in a balanced universe, the entire system of which is based on justice, he too should adhere to justice. For if he acts unjustly within the sphere in which he has been granted choice, it will be discordant with the very grain of the universe and the Divine scheme of things drawn for it.

The Midyanites, or the people of the Prophet Shuʿayb were punished by the *Blast* that left them lifeless in their homes because they had refused to heed to the warnings and exhortations of Ḥaḍrat Shuʿayb: 'My people! Give full measure and weight with justice, do not diminish the goods of others, and do not go about creating corruption in the land.' (*Hūd*, 11: 85). (*Tafhīm al-Qur'ān*, vol.6, n.1-2, pp.280-281). – Trans. and Adaptation – Translator.

you.[2] And do not compel your slave-girls to prostitutions for the sake of the benefits of worldly life the while they desire to remain chaste. And if anyone compels them to prostitution, Allah will be Most Pardoning, Much Merciful (to them) after their subjection to such compulsion.')

(*al-Nūr*, 24: 33)

3.1.8. *The production, sale, transportation and marketing of alcoholic beverages*

يَـٰٓأَيُّهَا ٱلَّذِينَ ءَامَنُوٓاْ إِنَّمَا ٱلْخَمْرُ وَٱلْمَيْسِرُ وَٱلْأَنصَابُ وَٱلْأَزْلَـٰمُ رِجْسٌ مِّنْ عَمَلِ ٱلشَّيْطَـٰنِ فَٱجْتَنِبُوهُ لَعَلَّكُمْ تُفْلِحُونَ ﴿٩٠﴾

('Believers! Intoxicants, games of chance, idolatrous sacrifices at altars, and divining arrows are all abominations, the handiwork of Satan. So turn wholly away from it that you may attain to true success.')

(*al-Mā'idah*, 5: 90)

3.1.9. *Gambling, betting, lottery and all means of income based not on one's labour but on chance*

يَـٰٓأَيُّهَا ٱلَّذِينَ ءَامَنُوٓاْ إِنَّمَا ٱلْخَمْرُ وَٱلْمَيْسِرُ وَٱلْأَنصَابُ وَٱلْأَزْلَـٰمُ رِجْسٌ مِّنْ عَمَلِ ٱلشَّيْطَـٰنِ فَٱجْتَنِبُوهُ لَعَلَّكُمْ تُفْلِحُونَ ﴿٩٠﴾

('Believers! Intoxicants, games of chance, idolatrous sacrifices at altars, and divining arrows are all abominations, the handiwork of Satan. So turn wholly away from it that you may attain to true success.')

(*al-Mā'idah*, 5: 90)

3.1.10. *Idol-making, trading in idols and serving in temples*

يَـٰٓأَيُّهَا ٱلَّذِينَ ءَامَنُوٓاْ إِنَّمَا ٱلْخَمْرُ وَٱلْمَيْسِرُ وَٱلْأَنصَابُ وَٱلْأَزْلَـٰمُ رِجْسٌ مِّنْ عَمَلِ ٱلشَّيْطَـٰنِ فَٱجْتَنِبُوهُ لَعَلَّكُمْ تُفْلِحُونَ ﴿٩٠﴾

('Believers! Intoxicants, games of chance, idolatrous sacrifices at altars, and divining arrows are all abominations, the handiwork of Satan. So turn wholly away from it that you may attain to true success.')

(*al-Mā'idah*, 5: 90)

---

[2] The masters are directed to remit at least a part of the amount which the slaves are required to pay according to the manumission agreement. Muslims in general are also directed that they should generously help those who ask them for the money required for their manumission. A part of the *Zakāh* in the Public Treasury should be spent on assisting slaves who have entered into manumission agreements so that they might become free ('*Towards Understanding the Qur'ān*'. Abridged version of *Tafhīm*, Translation: Zafar Ishaq Ansari, n.29, p.738).

3.1.11. *Fortune-telling and soothsaying*

يَـٰٓأَيُّهَا ٱلَّذِينَ ءَامَنُوٓا۟ إِنَّمَا ٱلْخَمْرُ وَٱلْمَيْسِرُ وَٱلْأَنصَابُ وَٱلْأَزْلَـٰمُ رِجْسٌ مِّنْ عَمَلِ ٱلشَّيْطَـٰنِ فَٱجْتَنِبُوهُ
لَعَلَّكُمْ تُفْلِحُونَ ۝٩٠

('Believers! Intoxicants, games of chance, idolatrous sacrifices at altars, and divining arrows are all abominations, the handiwork of Satan. So turn wholly away from it that you may attain to true success.')

(*al-Mā'idah*, 5: 90)

3.1.12. *Usury and all forms of interest-based transactions*

ٱلَّذِينَ يَأْكُلُونَ ٱلرِّبَوٰا۟ لَا يَقُومُونَ إِلَّا كَمَا يَقُومُ ٱلَّذِى يَتَخَبَّطُهُ ٱلشَّيْطَـٰنُ مِنَ ٱلْمَسِّ ۚ ذَٰلِكَ بِأَنَّهُمْ قَالُوٓا۟ إِنَّمَا ٱلْبَيْعُ
مِثْلُ ٱلرِّبَوٰا۟ ۗ وَأَحَلَّ ٱللَّهُ ٱلْبَيْعَ وَحَرَّمَ ٱلرِّبَوٰا۟ ۚ فَمَن جَآءَهُۥ مَوْعِظَةٌ مِّن رَّبِّهِۦ فَٱنتَهَىٰ فَلَهُۥ مَا سَلَفَ وَأَمْرُهُۥٓ إِلَى ٱللَّهِ ۖ وَمَنْ
عَادَ فَأُو۟لَـٰٓئِكَ أَصْحَـٰبُ ٱلنَّارِ ۖ هُمْ فِيهَا خَـٰلِدُونَ ۝٢٧٥ يَمْحَقُ ٱللَّهُ ٱلرِّبَوٰا۟ وَيُرْبِى ٱلصَّدَقَـٰتِ ۗ وَٱللَّهُ لَا يُحِبُّ كُلَّ
كَفَّارٍ أَثِيمٍ ۝٢٧٦

('As for those who devour interest, they behave as the one whom Satan has confounded with his touch. Seized in this state they say: "Buying and selling is but a kind of interest", even though Allah has made buying and selling lawful, and interest unlawful. Hence, he who receives this admonition from his Lord, and then gives up (dealing in interest), may keep his previous gains, and it will be for Allah to judge him. As for those who revert to it, they are the people of the Fire, and in it shall they abide. Allah deprives interest of all blessing, whereas He blesses charity with growth. Allah loves none who is ungrateful and persists in sin.')

(*al-Baqarah*, 2: 275-276)

يَـٰٓأَيُّهَا ٱلَّذِينَ ءَامَنُوا۟ ٱتَّقُوا۟ ٱللَّهَ وَذَرُوا۟ مَا بَقِىَ مِنَ ٱلرِّبَوٰٓا۟ إِن كُنتُم مُّؤْمِنِينَ ۝٢٧٨ فَإِن لَّمْ تَفْعَلُوا۟ فَأْذَنُوا۟ بِحَرْبٍ مِّنَ ٱللَّهِ
وَرَسُولِهِۦ ۖ وَإِن تُبْتُمْ فَلَكُمْ رُءُوسُ أَمْوَٰلِكُمْ لَا تَظْلِمُونَ وَلَا تُظْلَمُونَ ۝٢٧٩

('Believers! Have fear of Allah and give up all outstanding interest if you do truly believe. But if you fail to do so, then be warned of war from Allah and His Messenger. If you repent even now, you have the right of the return of your capital; neither will you do wrong nor will you be wronged.')

(*al-Baqarah*, 2: 278-279)

يَـٰٓأَيُّهَا ٱلَّذِينَ ءَامَنُوا۟ لَا تَأْكُلُوا۟ ٱلرِّبَوٰٓا۟ أَضْعَـٰفًا مُّضَـٰعَفَةً ۖ وَٱتَّقُوا۟ ٱللَّهَ لَعَلَّكُمْ تُفْلِحُونَ ۝١٣٠

('Believers! Do not devour interest, doubled and redoubled, and be mindful of Allah so that you may attain true success.')

(*Āl 'Imrān*, 3: 130)

3.2. The accumulation of wealth

The second injunction regarding the conduct of economic activities is that wealth produced through lawful means must not be allowed to accumulate, because its circulation is thus checked and the balance is lost in the distribution of wealth. A person who is given to amassing wealth does not afflict only himself with a grievous wrongdoing, he is actually guilty of committing a serious crime against the society as a whole and thereby ultimately harming himself. This is why the Book of God is so opposed to the traits of selfishness, stinginess and greed:

وَلَا يَحْسَبَنَّ ٱلَّذِينَ يَبْخَلُونَ بِمَآ ءَاتَىٰهُمُ ٱللَّهُ مِن فَضْلِهِۦ هُوَ خَيْرًا لَّهُم ۖ بَلْ هُوَ شَرٌّ لَّهُمْ ۖ سَيُطَوَّقُونَ مَا بَخِلُوا۟ بِهِۦ يَوْمَ ٱلْقِيَـٰمَةِ ۗ وَلِلَّهِ مِيرَٰثُ ٱلسَّمَـٰوَٰتِ وَٱلْأَرْضِ ۗ وَٱللَّهُ بِمَا تَعْمَلُونَ خَبِيرٌ ﴿١٨٠﴾

('Those who are niggardly about what Allah has granted them out of His bounty think that niggardliness is good for them; rather, it is bad for them. What they were niggardly about will turn into a halter round their necks on the Day of Resurrection. To Allah belongs the inheritance of the heavens and the earth. Allah is well aware of what you do.')

(*Āl 'Imrān*, 3: 180).

...وَٱلَّذِينَ يَكْنِزُونَ ٱلذَّهَبَ وَٱلْفِضَّةَ وَلَا يُنفِقُونَهَا فِى سَبِيلِ ٱللَّهِ فَبَشِّرْهُم بِعَذَابٍ أَلِيمٍ ﴿٣٤﴾

('And there are those who amass gold and silver and do not spend it in the Way of Allah. Announce to them the tidings of a painful chastisement.')

(*al-Tawbah*, 9: 34)

This injunction cuts at the very roots of capitalism. To amass savings and then use them to produce more wealth is the basis of capitalism. Islam, on the other hand, does not encourage a person to pile up wealth in excess of his needs.

3.3. Money is to spend

Instead of stockpiling, Islam guides us to spend the money we have earned through lawful means. However, this does not imply that Islam seeks to promote profligacy and extravagant living. The command to spend is conditional on some checks and balances, and the biggest check of all is that the wealth has to be spent '*fī Sabīlillāh*,' i.e. 'in the Way of Allah'. Whatever one saves after meeting his needs will have to be utilized in welfare schemes for the society. Allah *subḥānahū wa ta'ālā* says:

...وَيَسْـَٔلُونَكَ مَاذَا يُنفِقُونَ قُلِ ٱلْعَفْوَ ۗ... ﴿٢١٩﴾

('They ask: "What should we spend in the Way of Allah?" Say: "Whatever you can spare".')

(*al-Baqarah*, 2: 219)

...وَبِٱلْوَٰلِدَيْنِ إِحْسَٰنًا وَبِذِى ٱلْقُرْبَىٰ وَٱلْيَتَٰمَىٰ وَٱلْمَسَٰكِينِ وَٱلْجَارِ ذِى ٱلْقُرْبَىٰ وَٱلْجَارِ ٱلْجُنُبِ وَٱلصَّاحِبِ
بِٱلْجَنۢبِ وَٱبْنِ ٱلسَّبِيلِ وَمَا مَلَكَتْ أَيْمَٰنُكُمْ ۗ ... ﴿٣٦﴾

('Do good to parents, to near of kin, to orphans and to the needy, and to the neighbour who is of kin and to the neighbour who is a stranger and to the companion by your side, and to the wayfarer and to those whom your right hands possess.')

(*al-Nisā'*, 4: 36)

وَفِىٓ أَمْوَٰلِهِمْ حَقٌّ لِّلسَّآئِلِ وَٱلْمَحْرُومِ ﴿١٩﴾

('And in their wealth there was a rightful share for him who would ask and for the destitute.'[3])

(*al-Dhāriyāt*, 51: 19)

In this, Islam's approach totally differs from that of capitalism. A capitalist thinks that he would go bankrupt by spending, but become wealthier by stockpiling his riches. Islam, on the other hand, guides us to spend our wealth as this would further bless whatever we have and, instead of diminishing, our wealth would actually increase and multiply further:

ٱلشَّيْطَٰنُ يَعِدُكُمُ ٱلْفَقْرَ وَيَأْمُرُكُم بِٱلْفَحْشَآءِ ۖ وَٱللَّهُ يَعِدُكُم مَّغْفِرَةً مِّنْهُ وَفَضْلًا ۗ وَٱللَّهُ وَٰسِعٌ عَلِيمٌ ﴿٢٦٨﴾

('Satan frightens you with poverty and bids you to commit indecency whereas Allah promises you His forgiveness and bounty. Allah is Munificent, All-Knowing.').

(*al-Baqarah*, 2: 268)

---

[3] This describes how the believers are and ought to be in their behaviours and attitudes. As stated in *Āyāt* 15-18, before attaining the ultimate reward of paradise, they are not only God-fearing, doing good works, spending their nights in communion with the Lord and with little sleep to relax their mortal frame, performing pre-dawn Prayer and seeking His forgiveness, but when it comes to help their fellow humans, they are ever ready to spend on them from whatever Allah *subḥānahū wa ta'ālā* bestowed on them, and this not as an act of benevolence to let the needy feel obliged to them but taking it as an obligation in the context of the poor men's due in their wealth. Thus, the Qur'ān impresses upon us that the behaviour of a believer and true *Muttaqī* (God-fearing) should be such that he should be cognizant of his duty towards the Lord, on the one hand and on the other, must realize that whatever has been bestowed upon him by the All-Merciful, whether little or much, does not simply belong to him and his family alone and that the needy too have a rightful claim on his wealth. (*Tafhīm al-Qur'ān*, vol.5, n.17, pp.139-140) – Translator.

A capitalist's viewpoint is that whatever he spends is consumed and finished. Islam tells us that, instead of losing, we actually gain and the advantages of what we spend for a good cause eventually revert to us:

...وَمَا تُنفِقُوا۟ مِنْ خَيْرٍ فَلِأَنفُسِكُمْ ۚ وَمَا تُنفِقُونَ إِلَّا ٱبْتِغَآءَ وَجْهِ ٱللَّهِ ۚ وَمَا تُنفِقُوا۟ مِنْ خَيْرٍ يُوَفَّ إِلَيْكُمْ
وَأَنتُمْ لَا تُظْلَمُونَ ﴿٢٧٢﴾

('Whatever wealth you spend in charity is to your own benefit for you spend merely to please Allah. So, whatever you spend in charity will be repaid to you in full and you shall not be wronged.')

(*al-Baqarah*, 2: 272)

إِنَّ ٱلَّذِينَ يَتْلُونَ كِتَٰبَ ٱللَّهِ وَأَقَامُوا۟ ٱلصَّلَوٰةَ وَأَنفَقُوا۟ مِمَّا رَزَقْنَٰهُمْ سِرًّا وَعَلَانِيَةً يَرْجُونَ تِجَٰرَةً لَّن تَبُورَ ﴿٢٩﴾
لِيُوَفِّيَهُمْ أُجُورَهُمْ وَيَزِيدَهُم مِّن فَضْلِهِۦٓ ۚ إِنَّهُۥ غَفُورٌ شَكُورٌ ﴿٣٠﴾

('Surely those who recite the Book of Allah and establish Prayer and spend, privately and publicly, out of what We have provided them, look forward to a trade that shall suffer no loss; (a trade in which they have invested their all) so that Allah may pay them their wages in full and may add to them out of His Bounty. He is Most Forgiving, Most Appreciative.')

(*Fāṭir*, 35: 29-30)

A capitalist believes that, by accumulating wealth and then reinvesting it in interest-based schemes, he is multiplying his money. But Islam tells us that, instead of multiplying, the wealth diminishes because of the interest and the best way to increase our wealth is its utilization in a good cause:

يَمْحَقُ ٱللَّهُ ٱلرِّبَوٰا۟ وَيُرْبِى ٱلصَّدَقَٰتِ ۗ ... ﴿٢٧٦﴾

('Allah deprives interest of all blessing, where as he blesses charity with growth.')

(*al-Baqarah*, 2: 276)

وَمَآ ءَاتَيْتُم مِّن رِّبًا لِّيَرْبُوَا۟ فِىٓ أَمْوَٰلِ ٱلنَّاسِ فَلَا يَرْبُوا۟ عِندَ ٱللَّهِ ۖ وَمَآ ءَاتَيْتُم مِّن زَكَوٰةٍ تُرِيدُونَ وَجْهَ ٱللَّهِ فَأُو۟لَٰٓئِكَ
هُمُ ٱلْمُضْعِفُونَ ﴿٣٩﴾

('Whatever you pay as interest so that it may increase the wealth of people does not increase in the sight of Allah. As for the *Zakāh* that you give, seeking with it Allah's good pleasure, that is multiplied manifold.')

(*al-Rūm*, 30: 39)

This is an absolutely new theory and is diametrically opposed to the capitalist viewpoint. The ideas that, instead of going to waste, wealth actually rises by spending and the dividends from the amount spent return to us with added benefits, and also that interest causes greater loss rather than helping our amount to multiply, are standpoints which sound strange on the surface. One would tend to think that these concepts only apply to the Day of Judgment and the reward of the Hereafter. It is undoubtedly true that they do relate to the reward of the Day of Judgment, and that must be the cherished goal for every Muslim. But viewed from a purely mundane perspective, the concepts can equally be applied as firm economic foundations for life in this world. The stockpiling of wealth and its reinvestment on interest to amass more wealth eventually leads to its accumulation in a few hands. There is thus a gradual erosion of the common man's purchasing power; a recession takes over the local trade, industry and agriculture; the economic life of a nation is jeopardized; and even the capitalist cartels and monopolies are left with no avenues to invest their accumulated income in to generate more wealth.[4] By contrast, the money spent in the Way of Allah and for *Zakāh* and *Ṣadaqāt* leads to its wider circulation. Each and every member of society is thus enabled to satisfy their basic needs: the people's purchasing power increases; industries flourish; agriculture prospers; trade grows; and everyone in the community gets what he needs for survival and sustenance. It is true that the phenomenon missing in this set-up is that of the high-profile business tycoons and privileged moneyed classes with millions and billions stockpiled in banks at home and abroad. If one wishes to compare the blessings of this Islamic economic approach with the ugly face of capitalism, one can look at the current economic situation of the United States[5] where, due to the interest-based economic system, the scales of equitable wealth distribution stand imbalanced and a recession in the trade and industry sectors has brought the economic life of US citizens to the verge of collapse.[6] In a remarkable contrast to this situation, observe the early Islamic era when the Islamic economic system held sway. Because of the blessings of

[4] There is a reference to the same factor in the Prophetic Tradition narrated by Ibn Mājah, Bayhaqī and Imām Aḥmad, wherein *Sayyidinā* Rasūl Allāh says, 'Usury and interest, howsoever massive they may appear quantitatively, eventually get reduced in worth.' – Author.

[5] This refers to the devastating spell of recession that prevailed in the United States at the time of writing this book. – Translator.

[6] This is, in fact, a recurring phenomenon the capitalist West has experienced time and again. Had it not been for the billions and bullions of the oil-rich Gulf States, available to the US and the West for extortion and exploitation, the whole West would have been bankrupt. Even today as we review this book, the US and EU countries are facing worst economic crisis and every US citizen is the world's most indebted person. – Translator.

the Islamic system, the economic prosperity of the Nation of Islam within a few years reached a level where it was difficult to find anyone who could receive *Zakāh*. The people used to search for those in need, but they invariably encountered people who had themselves attained the status of *Zakāh* payer. As one compares the two situations, it becomes crystal clear how Allah *subḥānahū wa taʿālā 'deprives interest of all blessing'* and *'blesses charity with growth'*.

The mindset produced by the Islamic economic system is totally different from that created by capitalism. No capitalist would ever think of lending his money free of interest. He remains content simply to impose the fixed amount of interest on the loans he advances and then to retrieve forcibly both the principal amount and interest thereon. He even goes to the extent of confiscating and taking control of the borrower's property, including his household effects and clothes. Islam, on the other hand, enjoins the lender not only to help the needy in giving a loan, but also tells him to be more generous and conscientious when demanding the loan amount back. If the debtor is destitute and unable to repay, it even exhorts the lender to forego their principal amount:

وَإِن كَانَ ذُو عُسْرَةٍ فَنَظِرَةٌ إِلَىٰ مَيْسَرَةٍ ۚ وَأَن تَصَدَّقُوا خَيْرٌ لَّكُمْ ۖ إِن كُنتُمْ تَعْلَمُونَ ﴿٢٨٠﴾

('But if the debtor is in straitened circumstance, let him have respite until the time of ease; and whatever you remit by way of charity is better for you, if only you know.')

(*al-Baqarah*, 2: 280)

The capitalist concept of a 'cooperative movement' is that you first need to pay into a 'cooperative society' to become a member. You will then be eligible to get a loan from it at the 'specially' reduced rates of interest. However, if you have no money, you can expect no 'cooperation' from the 'cooperative'. In contrast, Islam's concept of cooperation is totally different. It enjoins those who are well-off to come forward and extend loans on favourable terms to those who are in need and, instead of getting a 'special' rates of interest on the principal amount, they are encouraged to facilitate the debtor to repay his loan; this is not meant to be a gesture of benevolence towards him, but purely for the sake of Allah's pleasure. The disbursement categories of *Zakāh*, therefore, include that of '*wa'l-Ghārimīn*', i.e. the debtors who are hard-pressed under the liability of their loans.

The capitalist spends his money on good causes in order to boost his image, because the best he can expect from his charity is promotion of his name and public acknowledgement. Islam, on the other hand, forbids such glory seeking and an exhibitionist approach. It tells us that we should have no worldly dividend in view for anything that we spend in public or in private. Our goal must invariably be the ultimate gain of the Hereafter. This is what should motivate our spending, viewing it as an investment flourishing and bearing fruit all through this worldly life to the life beyond. In a beautiful parable, the Qur'ān discredits false acts of 'charity' that are only done to be seen by men:

يَٰٓأَيُّهَا ٱلَّذِينَ ءَامَنُوا۟ لَا تُبْطِلُوا۟ صَدَقَٰتِكُم بِٱلْمَنِّ وَٱلْأَذَىٰ كَٱلَّذِى يُنفِقُ مَالَهُۥ رِئَآءَ ٱلنَّاسِ وَلَا يُؤْمِنُ بِٱللَّهِ وَٱلْيَوْمِ
ٱلْءَاخِرِ ۖ فَمَثَلُهُۥ كَمَثَلِ صَفْوَانٍ عَلَيْهِ تُرَابٌ فَأَصَابَهُۥ وَابِلٌ فَتَرَكَهُۥ صَلْدًا ۖ لَّا يَقْدِرُونَ عَلَىٰ شَىْءٍ مِّمَّا كَسَبُوا۟ ۗ وَٱللَّهُ
لَا يَهْدِى ٱلْقَوْمَ ٱلْكَٰفِرِينَ ﴿٢٦٤﴾ وَمَثَلُ ٱلَّذِينَ يُنفِقُونَ أَمْوَٰلَهُمُ ٱبْتِغَآءَ مَرْضَاتِ ٱللَّهِ وَتَثْبِيتًا مِّنْ أَنفُسِهِمْ كَمَثَلِ
جَنَّةٍۭ بِرَبْوَةٍ أَصَابَهَا وَابِلٌ فَـَٔاتَتْ أُكُلَهَا ضِعْفَيْنِ فَإِن لَّمْ يُصِبْهَا وَابِلٌ فَطَلٌّ ۗ وَٱللَّهُ بِمَا تَعْمَلُونَ بَصِيرٌ ﴿٢٦٥﴾

('Believers! Do not nullify your acts of charity by stressing your benevolence and causing hurt as does he who spends his wealth only to be seen by people and does not believe in Allah and the Last Day. The example of his spending is that of a rock with a thin coating of earth upon it: when a heavy rain smites it, the earth is washed away, leaving the rock bare; such people derive no gain from their acts of charity. Allah does not set the deniers of the Truth on the Right Way. The example of those who spend their wealth single-mindedly to please Allah is that of a garden on a high ground. If a heavy rain smites it, it brings forth its fruits twofold, and if there is no heavy rain, even a light shower suffices it. Allah sees all that you do.')

(*al-Baqarah*, 2: 264-265)

إِن تُبْدُوا۟ ٱلصَّدَقَٰتِ فَنِعِمَّا هِىَ ۖ وَإِن تُخْفُوهَا وَتُؤْتُوهَا ٱلْفُقَرَآءَ فَهُوَ خَيْرٌ لَّكُمْ ۚ وَيُكَفِّرُ عَنكُم مِّن سَيِّـَٔاتِكُمْ ۗ
وَٱللَّهُ بِمَا تَعْمَلُونَ خَبِيرٌ ﴿٢٧١﴾

('If you dispense your charity publicly, it is well; but if you conceal it and pay it to the needy in secret, it will be even better for you. This will atone for several of your misdeeds. Allah is well aware of all that you do.')

(*al-Baqarah*, 2: 271)

The capitalist, if he is inspired at all to perform an act of charity, generally does it quite reluctantly, giving away the most undesirable part of his possession; whoever he honours with his favours is thus made to feel encumbered under the weight of his 'generosity'. On the contrary, Islam teaches its followers to give the best they have in their charity, and the charity is not allowed to harm the recipient's sense of dignity:

يَٰٓأَيُّهَا ٱلَّذِينَ ءَامَنُوٓا۟ أَنفِقُوا۟ مِن طَيِّبَٰتِ مَا كَسَبْتُمْ وَمِمَّآ أَخْرَجْنَا لَكُم مِّنَ ٱلْأَرْضِ ۖ وَلَا تَيَمَّمُوا۟ ٱلْخَبِيثَ مِنْهُ
تُنفِقُونَ وَلَسْتُم بِـَٔاخِذِيهِ إِلَّآ أَن تُغْمِضُوا۟ فِيهِ ۚ وَٱعْلَمُوٓا۟ أَنَّ ٱللَّهَ غَنِىٌّ حَمِيدٌ ﴿٢٦٧﴾

('Believers! Spend (in the Way of Allah) out of the good things you have earned and out of what We have produced for you from the earth, and choose not for your spending the bad things such as you yourselves would not accept or accept only by overlooking its defects. Know well that Allah is All-Munificent, Most Praiseworthy.')

(*al-Baqarah*, 2: 267)

يَٰٓأَيُّهَا ٱلَّذِينَ ءَامَنُوا۟ لَا تُبْطِلُوا۟ صَدَقَٰتِكُم بِٱلْمَنِّ وَٱلْأَذَىٰ كَٱلَّذِى يُنفِقُ مَالَهُۥ رِئَآءَ ٱلنَّاسِ وَلَا يُؤْمِنُ بِٱللَّهِ وَٱلْيَوْمِ
ٱلْءَاخِرِ ۖ فَمَثَلُهُۥ كَمَثَلِ صَفْوَانٍ عَلَيْهِ تُرَابٌ فَأَصَابَهُۥ وَابِلٌ فَتَرَكَهُۥ صَلْدًا ۖ لَّا يَقْدِرُونَ عَلَىٰ شَىْءٍ مِّمَّا كَسَبُوا۟ ۗ وَٱللَّهُ
لَا يَهْدِى ٱلْقَوْمَ ٱلْكَٰفِرِينَ ﴿٢٦٤﴾

('Believers! Do not nullify your acts of charity by stressing your benevolence and causing hurt as does he who spends his wealth only to be seen by people and does not believe in Allah and the Last Day. The example of his spending is that of a rock with a thin coating of earth upon it: when a heavy rain smites it, the earth is washed away, leaving the rock bare; such people derive no gain from their acts of charity. Allah does not set the deniers of the Truth on the Right Way.')

(*al-Baqarah*, 2: 264)

وَيُطْعِمُونَ ٱلطَّعَامَ عَلَىٰ حُبِّهِۦ مِسْكِينًا وَيَتِيمًا وَأَسِيرًا ﴿٨﴾ إِنَّمَا نُطْعِمُكُمْ لِوَجْهِ ٱللَّهِ لَا نُرِيدُ مِنكُمْ جَزَآءً وَلَا شُكُورًا ﴿٩﴾

('Those who, for the love of Him, feed the needy, and the orphan, and the captive, (saying): "We feed you only for Allah's sake; we do not seek of you any recompense or thanks".')

(*al-Dahr*, 76: 8-9)

The big difference between these two mind-sets from a moral point of view is quite obvious. Even when we look at them from a purely economic standpoint, it becomes crystal clear which of the two divergent theories of gain and loss is sounder in terms of its far-reaching social impact and economic benefits. This is the reason why Islam is so averse to all interest-based transactions and usury in all forms – both ancient and modern.

3.4. *Zakāh*

As explained earlier, the Islamic approach to the economic issues of mankind is that wealth is like life-blood and must not simply be allowed to accumulate and clog the economic arteries of the state. What Islam seeks from those members of the society who succeed in acquiring a better position and wealth by virtue of their competence or good fortune is to spend their money generously in schemes of public welfare, so that these benefits filter down to the lowest strata of the society, to those who have not been so lucky as these people. With this end in view, the Islamic system generates, on the one hand, a spirit of magnanimity and genuine cooperation through its most effective means – its grand moral teachings, persuasions and exhortations – in order to inspire the people to develop the inclination to shun the lust for money and enjoy using it generously for the public good. On the other hand, Islam makes it obligatory for every member who has money to contribute a prescribed amount for the welfare and uplift of society. This is what the *Sharīʿah* terms *Zakāh.*

Zakāh occupies a pivotal position in the Islamic economic system. It has therefore been designated as one of the five pillars of Islam's grand edifice. It is second only to *Ṣalāh* (regular Prayer) in importance. A person is allowed to spend his wealth, even that earned through lawful means, only when he has paid the prescribed amount of *Zakāh* admissible on his earnings:

خُذْ مِنْ أَمْوَٰلِهِمْ صَدَقَةً تُطَهِّرُهُمْ وَتُزَكِّيهِم بِهَا ... ﴿١٠٣﴾

('Take alms out of their riches and thereby cleanse them and bring about their growth (in righteousness)...')

(*al-Tawbah*, 9: 103)

According to the concluding part of this *Āyah*, the money gathered by the rich person needs to be purified, and it cannot become pure until a certain amount has been given in charity in the Way of Allah. The question raised is, what is 'the Way of Allah?', for God is neither in need of our money, nor does the money given in alms reach Him. Briefly described, '*Sabīlillāh*' or the 'Way of Allah' is the cause of public good. Islam enjoins us to strive for the socio-economic uplift of the down-trodden and to contribute to works of public welfare for the general benefit of the society as a whole:

إِنَّمَا ٱلصَّدَقَٰتُ لِلْفُقَرَآءِ وَٱلْمَسَٰكِينِ وَٱلْعَٰمِلِينَ عَلَيْهَا وَٱلْمُؤَلَّفَةِ قُلُوبُهُمْ وَفِى ٱلرِّقَابِ وَٱلْغَٰرِمِينَ وَفِى سَبِيلِ
ٱللَّهِ وَٱبْنِ ٱلسَّبِيلِ ۖ فَرِيضَةً مِّنَ ٱللَّهِ ۗ وَٱللَّهُ عَلِيمٌ حَكِيمٌ ﴿٦٠﴾

('The alms are meant for the poor and the needy and those who are in charge thereof, those whose hearts are to be reconciled, and to free those in bondage, and to help those burdened with debt, and for expenditure in the Way of Allah and for the wayfarer. This is an obligation from Allah. Allah is All-Knowing, All-Wise.')

(*al-Tawbah*, 9: 60)

The institution of *Zakāh* is the Muslim community's version of the 'Cooperative Society'. It is their 'Insurance Company' and their 'Provident Fund'. It is a subsidy for the unemployed. It is the scheme of social security for widows, orphans, the handicapped and all those without the means to sustain themselves. *Zakāh* ensures that no member of a Muslim society should remain unprovided for and, to top it all, it takes away any worries concerning a person's future. The pure and simple principle of the blessed system of *Zakāh* is: '*Help others if you are in a position to do so today, to let others help you if you are in need of it tomorrow.*' *Zakāh* is the cornerstone of the Islamic economic system. It liberates man from his economic problems, so that he does not have to worry what might happen to him and his family if he gets indigent or dies; or, in the case of illness, incapacitation, destruction of house and property by fire, floods or earthquakes, bankruptcy and other natural or man-made disasters, who might stand by his side to provide him with relief; or, if he runs out of money while travelling, who might come to his rescue. *Zakāh* takes away all such fears. All one is required to do is to pay a prescribed amount from one's money, property and livestock in hand into a charity annually, and they are thus insured by the Divine Insurance System. The amount one contributes is from what he does not need and serves to help those who have a greater need for it. He gets back dividends in a multiplied form as and when either he or his children and family are in need of assistance.

Here again, Islam and capitalism stand in sharp contrast to each other in their fundamental principles and methodologies. Capitalism demands that money be saved and invested, and to multiply these savings interest is charged in order to divert the capital flow to the capitalist's own pool. Islam, on the contrary, enjoins that the free flow of capital must not be checked in the first place and, in case of a clogging, any blocked capital should be released through the channels of *Zakāh* to let the dry land get the much-needed water covering every inch of the ground, the high and the low, the plains and the deserts, so that it blooms with a myriad of flowers and foliage. In the capitalist system, the exchange of wealth is restrained, while in Islam it is unchecked. To get benefits from the capitalist pool, you need to have a certain amount of your own deposit there or you cannot receive even a droplet. Compared to this, the Islamic reservoir is always full to the brim for all thirsty people to quench their thirst. The principle being followed here is that those in possession of wealth (resources) in excess of their requirements should deposit their surplus in the reservoir, and those in need should come forward and fill their buckets. By their nature and temperament, these are evidently two different models of economy that are diametrically opposed to each other, and no sane person could ever think of bringing the two together under a single economic system.

3.5. Law of inheritance

The wealth that a person has after satisfying his personal needs, contributing to noble causes and payment of *Zakāh*, is distributed through the law of inheritance. The philosophy governing the Islamic Law of Inheritance is that property and wealth, whether they are small or large, should not be monopolised by one or two of the deceased's descendants, but should be distributed according to an elaborate, pre-determined system among their heirs and relatives, both distant and close. In the case of a person with no legal heir or relative, the law does not permit the adoption of another as a 'son' in order to transfer the wealth to him. Instead, the Islamic State's *Bayt al-Māl* (Public Treasury) is empowered to take care of the deceased's property so that it can be used in the public interest.[7] Islam's law of inheritance is unique and has no parallel in any economic system anywhere in the world. All other systems of economy tend to allow wealth to remain accumulated in the hands of one person, or a limited number of persons, even after the death of its owner. The law of '*primogeniture*' and the concept of the joint family system are based on this objective. Islam, on the other hand, disapproves of the very idea of cartels and monopolies, and encourages a wider circulation of wealth in the interests of public welfare and social security for every member of the society.

3.6. War gains and division of a conquered land's revenue

The same philosophy with the same intention governs Islam's approach to war gains and the revenue from a conquered land. The material gains of war are to be divided into five equal parts. Of these, four are to be distributed among the fighting forces and the fifth is to be kept in *Bayt al-Māl* for the general good:

وَٱعْلَمُوٓاْ أَنَّمَا غَنِمْتُم مِّن شَىْءٍ فَأَنَّ لِلَّهِ خُمُسَهُۥ وَلِلرَّسُولِ وَلِذِى ٱلْقُرْبَىٰ وَٱلْيَتَـٰمَىٰ وَٱلْمَسَـٰكِينِ وَٱبْنِ ٱلسَّبِيلِ ... ﴿٤١﴾

('Know that one-fifth of the spoils that you obtain belongs to Allah and to the Messenger and to the near of kin, to the orphans and the needy, and the wayfarer…')

(*al-Anfāl*, 8: 41)

---

[7] If a person with no legal heir so desires, he can bequeath through his will a certain portion of his property as an endowment for a welfare project of his choice, or donate a part of it in the name of his 'adopted son'. Two-thirds of his wealth will, however, go to the state's treasury after his death. – Translator.

Assigning the fifth part to Allah and His Apostle involves allocating it for the social objectives of public welfare, which the Islamic State has the responsibility for safeguarding as decreed by God and His Apostle (*pbuh*). Initially, a part of this was also earmarked for close relatives of the Holy Prophet (*pbuh*), as they had no share in the funds related to *Zakāh.* Later on, however, it was diverted to the first head of social objectives and public welfare.

The fifth part thus belongs exclusively to the three remaining categories, '*the orphans, the needy and the wayfarer*'. The community's orphan children top this list and their proper upbringing, education and care has been made the state's responsibility. The 'needy' include the poor and indigent, widows, the handicapped, the sick and those who are incapacitated. The moral teachings of Islam also show that the State should take due care of the 'wayfarer' and his exigencies. They have been included in the list of those eligible for help and succour from the Islamic State's welfare funds of *Zakāh, Ṣadaqāt* and war gains. The importance attached by the Divine Law to this category has been instrumental in the promotion of travel to distant lands by those seeking knowledge, scholars, traders and explorers.

The lands and property, both moveable and immovable, that come under the custody of the Islamic government as a result of war are placed under the exclusive jurisdiction of the state:

مَّآ أَفَآءَ ٱللَّهُ عَلَىٰ رَسُولِهِۦ مِنْ أَهْلِ ٱلْقُرَىٰ فَلِلَّهِ وَلِلرَّسُولِ وَلِذِى ٱلْقُرْبَىٰ وَٱلْيَتَـٰمَىٰ وَٱلْمَسَـٰكِينِ وَٱبْنِ ٱلسَّبِيلِ كَىْ
لَا يَكُونَ دُولَةًۢ بَيْنَ ٱلْأَغْنِيَآءِ مِنكُمْ ۚ وَمَآ ءَاتَىٰكُمُ ٱلرَّسُولُ فَخُذُوهُ وَمَا نَهَىٰكُمْ عَنْهُ فَٱنتَهُوا۟ ۚ وَٱتَّقُوا۟ ٱللَّهَ ۖ إِنَّ ٱللَّهَ
شَدِيدُ ٱلْعِقَابِ ﴿٧﴾ لِلْفُقَرَآءِ ٱلْمُهَـٰجِرِينَ ٱلَّذِينَ أُخْرِجُوا۟ مِن دِيَـٰرِهِمْ وَأَمْوَٰلِهِمْ يَبْتَغُونَ فَضْلًا مِّنَ ٱللَّهِ وَرِضْوَٰنًا
وَيَنصُرُونَ ٱللَّهَ وَرَسُولَهُۥٓ ۚ أُو۟لَـٰٓئِكَ هُمُ ٱلصَّـٰدِقُونَ ﴿٨﴾ وَٱلَّذِينَ تَبَوَّءُو ٱلدَّارَ وَٱلْإِيمَـٰنَ مِن قَبْلِهِمْ يُحِبُّونَ مَنْ
هَاجَرَ إِلَيْهِمْ وَلَا يَجِدُونَ فِى صُدُورِهِمْ حَاجَةً مِّمَّآ أُوتُوا۟ وَيُؤْثِرُونَ عَلَىٰٓ أَنفُسِهِمْ وَلَوْ كَانَ بِهِمْ خَصَاصَةٌ ۚ وَمَن يُوقَ
شُحَّ نَفْسِهِۦ فَأُو۟لَـٰٓئِكَ هُمُ ٱلْمُفْلِحُونَ ﴿٩﴾ وَٱلَّذِينَ جَآءُو مِنۢ بَعْدِهِمْ يَقُولُونَ رَبَّنَا ٱغْفِرْ لَنَا وَلِإِخْوَٰنِنَا ٱلَّذِينَ سَبَقُونَا
بِٱلْإِيمَـٰنِ وَلَا تَجْعَلْ فِى قُلُوبِنَا غِلًّا لِّلَّذِينَ ءَامَنُوا۟ رَبَّنَآ إِنَّكَ رَءُوفٌ رَّحِيمٌ ﴿١٠﴾

('Whatever (from the possessions of the towns-people) Allah has bestowed on His Messenger belongs to Allah, and to the Messenger, and to his kinsfolk, and to the orphans, and to the needy, and to the wayfarer so that it may not merely circulate between the rich among you. So accept whatever the Messenger gives you, and refrain from whatever he forbids you. And fear Allah, verily Allah is Most Stern in retribution. It also belongs to the poor Emigrants who have been driven out of their homes and their possessions, those who seek Allah's favour and good pleasure and help Allah and His Messenger. Such are the truthful ones. It also belongs to those who were

> already settled in this abode (of *Hijrah*) having come to faith before the (arrival of the) *Muhājirūn* (Emigrants). They love those who have migrated to them and do not covet what has been given them; they even prefer them above themselves though poverty be their own lot. And whosoever are preserved from their own greed, such are the ones that will prosper. (And it also belongs to) those who came after them, and who pray: "Lord, forgive us and our brethren who have preceded us in faith, and do not put in our hearts any rancour towards those who believe. Lord, You are the Most Tender, the Most Compassionate".')
>
> (*al-Ḥashr*, 59: 7-10)

These *Āyāt* provide details not only of the headings under which public funds are to be spent, they also underscore in unequivocal terms the objective that governs the use of public funds and indeed the entire economic system of Islam. This objective is: كَيۡ لَا يَكُونَ دُولَةَۢ بَيۡنَ ٱلۡأَغۡنِيَآءِ مِنكُمۡ ('so that it (the wealth) may not merely circulate between the rich among you'). This brief statement made by the Holy Qur'ān so aphoristically forms the foundation stone of the Islamic economic system (as discussed earlier).

3.7. Injunctions about economy and balance

Islam has arranged, on the one hand, to let the wealth circulate among everyone in the community, so that the have-nots are shareholders in the affluence of those with money, as discussed above; and on the other hand, it enjoins every Muslim to observe economy and balance in his spending so that no individual can unbalance the economic scale by their intemperance in making use of his income. The comprehensive Qur'ānic approach in this context is as follows:

> وَلَا تَجۡعَلۡ يَدَكَ مَغۡلُولَةً إِلَىٰ عُنُقِكَ وَلَا تَبۡسُطۡهَا كُلَّ ٱلۡبَسۡطِ فَتَقۡعُدَ مَلُومٗا مَّحۡسُورًا ٢٩
>
> ('Do not keep your hand fastened to your neck nor outspread it, altogether outspread, for you will be left sitting rebuked, destitute.'[8])
>
> (*al-Banī Isrā'īl*, 17: 29)

> وَٱلَّذِينَ إِذَآ أَنفَقُواْ لَمۡ يُسۡرِفُواْ وَلَمۡ يَقۡتُرُواْ وَكَانَ بَيۡنَ ذَٰلِكَ قَوَامٗا ٦٧
>
> ('[The true servants of the Merciful One are] those who are neither extravagant nor niggardly in their spending but keep the golden mean between the two.')
>
> (*al-Furqān*, 25: 67)

[8] 'To keep one's hand fastened to one's neck' is an Arabic idiom that denotes miserliness, and 'to outspread it, altogether outspread' denotes extravagance. – Author.

This precept makes it incumbent on every member of the Muslim community to live within his means. He is forbidden to let his expenditure exceed his income, thus compelling him to stretch his hands out to others in order to sustain his extravagance, use unfair means to grab the wealth of others or become indebted to others to help finance his unending needs and, by consuming his resources in clearing his debt, eventually join the ranks of the destitute. He has also been warned against becoming stingy and withholding money, even when his resources permit him to spend or to release a lesser amount than is needed for a certain purpose. To live within one's means does not imply that one should focus entirely on oneself and his own comforts and luxuries while using his resources judiciously, forgetting everyone else such as relatives, friends and neighbours who may be in greater need of help. Such selfish living is treated as an extravagance in Islam:

وَءَاتِ ذَا ٱلْقُرْبَىٰ حَقَّهُۥ وَٱلْمِسْكِينَ وَٱبْنَ ٱلسَّبِيلِ وَلَا تُبَذِّرْ تَبْذِيرًا ﴿٢٦﴾ إِنَّ ٱلْمُبَذِّرِينَ كَانُوٓا۟ إِخْوَٰنَ ٱلشَّيَٰطِينِ ۖ
وَكَانَ ٱلشَّيْطَٰنُ لِرَبِّهِۦ كَفُورًا ﴿٢٧﴾

('Give to the near of kin his due, and also to the needy and the wayfarer. Do not squander your wealth wastefully. For those who squander wastefully are Satan's brothers, and Satan is ever ungrateful to his Lord.')

(*Banī Isrā'īl*, 17: 26-27)

Islam offers not only moral precepts, but has also laid down rules and regulations to check the extreme forms of both niggardliness and extravagance. It has taken measures to forestall any imbalance in the equitable distribution of wealth. It has banned gambling, forbidden intoxicants, adultery, fornication and the sex trade and declared unlawful all such pastimes that cause people to waste time, money and precious human and material resources. Islam does not allow the natural human instinct for music and entertainment to lapse into vulgarity, the loss of moral and spiritual values and economic indiscipline and extravagance. The human taste for aesthetics is also encouraged to abide by the dictates of certain social norms and values. The instructions contained in the Prophetic Traditions about costly dress, ornaments and jewelries, gold and silver wares and sculptures are motivated by a greater interest in public welfare, in addition to other considerations. The wealth, of which one is a custodian (because the ultimate ownership belongs to the Lord, the Provider and Sustainer), has to be spent in such a way that it fulfills not just one's own requirements, but also the essential needs of so many of one's less affluent brothers and sisters. To squander one's riches merely on decorating one's immortal frame or home is not aesthetics, but a heartless act of gross cruelty, perversity and selfishness of the worst kind. In short, the lifestyle that Islam guides humanity to adopt through its moral and legal instructions is one of simple living, which does not let the sphere of human needs and desires expand beyond the limits of a decent and affordable standard. It makes it easier for everyone to live within their means, without becoming indebted to others because of intemperance. If someone has more than he needs for a modest living, he should feel encouraged to shed off the extra load of his wealth to serve his fellow humans in society who may be in greater need of it.

4 The Economic Philosophy of Islam

An attempt has been made in this Chapter to provide answers to the following important question, often asked regarding the economic system of Islam:

> Does Islam have a distinct economic philosophy of its own?

NOTABLE FEATURES OF THE ECONOMIC PHILOSOPHY OF ISLAM[1]

It is imperative for an economic philosophy to be capable of grappling with the economic issues facing a particular country and the people and offering necessary solutions. Secondly, it should conform to the moral attitudes and socio-cultural norms and traditions of that country. No country or nation can afford to adopt an economic system that has no relevance with its moral philosophy and the normal way of life.

4.1. Basic values of the economic philosophy of Islam

At the outset, let me pinpoint first the values which are essentially needed for a viable, forward looking, and dynamic economic philosophy. The basic values of the economic philosophy of Islam are as follows:

4.1.1. *Social justice*

The exact connotation of social justice is that our social system should have complete balance between the rights and obligations of individuals and the society. One can be sure of the rights the society guarantees to an individual and those he owes to the society. Both these sets of rights and obligations should be very well defined and safeguarded. The economic exploits of an individual should be in no way detrimental to the interests of the society. The individual should feel convinced that his welfare lies in the welfare of the society and there is no conflict of interests between the two. This is possible only when he has been guaranteed about his own rights in the society, while the society is geared

[1] Based on Sayyid Mawdūdī's speech delivered at a specially convened moot of The Economic Society of the University of the Punjab, Lahore, 9 February, 1951. – Translator.

up to secure these for him as it finds this the best way to ensure its own uplift and welfare.

4.1.2. *Equitable economic system*

The second essential value of Islam's economic philosophy, which is no less important than the first, is that every individual should have equal opportunity for his moral, social, and material growth. In other words, it means that the society should be capable of offering the necessary avenues to its members to protect and promote their God-given potential to their best advantage and at the same time achieve nobility of character and moral excellence. On the contrary, an economic system, which may ensure plenty of food to eat, luxury buildings to live in, and all amenities of life at doorstep but no moral values and nobility of character, can hardly be called rich and prosperous. A society like this is, in fact, morally backward, socially impoverished, and economically exploitative.

4.4.3. *People-friendly political system*

This is the third value that requires an economic system to be based on a democratic polity. The system should be such as to prevent the society from adopting an anti-people and undemocratic political order, where individuals are denied of their basic rights and freedoms. It should, instead, be a system that may support the people and get support from them. It should be a system that may foster and promote a polity which is people friendly, where individuals enjoy freedom of thought and expression and are guaranteed avenues of collective struggle for their rights and a better future.

4.1.4. *Equality of opportunity*

According to the fourth basic value of the economic philosophy of Islam, it seeks growth of an economic system that should provide proper avenues of material progress to each and every member of the society. It should be a system that facilitates the use of every advanced means for the society's moral and material progress and community development, the means which the society may be free to adopt without bartering away its principles and harming the process of all-round progress and development. It should ensure sustainability and further strengthening of those principles even at the peak of the material and technological progress of the society and the state.

While keeping in mind all these four values integral to Islam's dynamic economic philosophy when we critically examine the economic philosophies of the present and the past, we find that none of them comes up to that level.

The only conclusion that we are led to draw is that neither the socialist nor the capitalist or the liberal philosophies of economy can be termed as panacea for the economic ills and fit for the society's healthy and multi-dimensional growth. All our unbiased and scientific appraisals and analysis lead us to conclude that the economic philosophy of Islam is unique in every respect and it alone ensures a society's multidimensional progress.

4.2. Eight fundamental principles of the economic philosophy of Islam

There are eight fundamental principles of the economic philosophy of Islam. Due to paucity of time, I am restrained not to go into detail and would restrict myself to discussing only their essential aspects.

4.2.1. *First principle: General accessibility of the bounties of nature*

This means that every individual is free to make proper use of the gifts of nature. These bounties include air, light, heat, water, minerals, and the biological and botanical treasures of the earth. Allah *subḥānahū wa taʿāla* has endowed the earth with these gifts for man and hence Islam permits no check on their proper and legitimate use. This is the cardinal principle of the economic philosophy of Islam. The Islamic *Sharīʿah* makes it clear that every gift of nature, other than those prohibited by the Lord Himself, must be accessible to all; everyone is entitled to put it to use provided no other person has already invested his labour and capital to harness that.

4.2.2. *Second principle: The right to make a living*

Every member of the society must have the avenue open for him to seek his livelihood in a lawful manner, unhindered by any restriction or obstruction. In case of such restrictions or obstructions being there, the society is duty-bound to remove them. Every field of economic activity must be open to all with no particular family, group of individuals, or class being permitted to enjoy a monopoly of any field.

4.2.3. *Third principle: The right to ownership*

A person investing his labour to acquire a gift of nature and putting it to suitable use must be entitled to its proprietary rights. For example, if someone gets a few litres of water from a river and recycles it for use, he should be free to benefit from his labour and even earn a few bucks by selling it. According to *Sharīʿah* law, if a person acquires a piece of waste land, which is not anyone's property, and erects a boundary wall for setting up some enterprise, he becomes its lawful owner, provided he is not a land-grabber nor does he leave that piece of land unutilized. In case he fails to put it to productive use for a period of three years, the state can claim it back. So long as the land remains in use, no one is entitled to interfere. In the event of the entrepreneur's death or abandoning his venture, it will pass on according to the *Sharīʿah* law of inheritance to his next of kin and legal heirs, like parents, brothers, sisters, etc. The *Sharīʿah* does not allow the wealth to accumulate within one hand or circulate only among a selected few.

4.2.4. *Fourth principle: The spirit of healthy competition*

According to this principle, Islam does not curb the natural urge for competition, but allows no artificial way to win that competition or facilitate one against the other for this purpose. As is well known, Allah *subḥānahū wa taʿāla* has made no two persons equal physically, intellectually, or materially. Some of them are better off than others in respect of health; some more knowledgeable and learned; while some have more wealth than others. One may be weak physically but intellectually very strong; one may have a poor or no eyesight, but rich in memory and retention power. Human potentials vary from person to person and this variance is natural. Similarly, there is no equal division of wealth and income. Islam is not averse to this natural phenomenon. It, however, strongly prohibits every artificial way to boost one's economic capability and for this it has framed laws, rules, and regulations. The *Sharīʿah* laws prevent unnatural accumulation of wealth or monopoly of a single person, family, or class on the economic resources of the state. For example, if a person is born lame, the other with both legs intact, while the third getting a car to ride, Islam would like to ensure each one of them the right to begin his life struggle from that particular starting point without disturbing the natural dispensation. It would like to see the lame reap the harvest of his labour and acquire the capability to ride a car. It would not mind similarly if the one born with the golden spoon in his mouth loses his car due to his incompetence.

4.2.5. *Fifth principle: No artificial way to enforce equality*

Islam favours the equality enforced by nature, but prohibits all artificial ways to achieve that. It would like every individual to enjoy equality of opportunity and rise in a field of his choice to the best of his capability. It does not permit any attempt to create undesirable hurdles in the way of an individual's forward march. It is unlawful in Islam to obstruct a person capable of running fast because others cannot keep pace with him or to tie the one unfit to move fast with someone fit in the name of bringing each to an equal level.

4.2.6. *Sixth principle: No 'free economy'*

While allowing freedom of opportunity for every individual, the economic system of Islam does not permit an unfettered economic pursuit for progress, which in today's parlance is called 'free economy'. The restrictions imposed by Islam on economic freedom may be summed up thus:

i. The lawful and unlawful means have been very elaborately defined for ownership and earning income. The details found in the *Sharīʿah* law regarding the *Ḥalāl* and *Ḥarām* economic means can be found nowhere else in any divine or man-made legal system. Islam clearly tells us what is lawful and what unlawful in fields of trade, industry, agriculture, and other wealth generating resources. Today the world is groaning under the impact of social injustice and economic disparity due mainly to the fact that most of the means declared unlawful by Islam is lawful elsewhere. The *Sharīʿah* has attached more importance to the social, moral, economic, cultural and civilizational health of the society than an unchecked economic exploitation of the resources of wealth regardless of fair or foul means.

ii. No person is permitted to spend in an unfair manner the resources he owns. Islam allows him to lead a clean and healthy life but forbids indulgence in luxuries and extravagance. It legally forbids certain expenditure and trains the individual to use his means in such a way that he may not give in to pomp and show. It inspires the society to discourage accumulation of wealth and let the excess reach the poor and the needy. *Zakāh* and *ʿUshr* have been levied on the amount of money saved and the agricultural produce beyond one's need. If one wishes to invest his saved income in a business, Islam identifies the lawful and the unlawful ways of doing that. It has absolutely forbidden interest and prevented the use of extra money for investment in interest-based ventures. The moment a person leaves this world, his lawfully acquired wealth is not allowed to stagnate or transferred to a single person but to be distributed among his legal heirs according to the prescribed proportion. Even if he leaves only a metre of cloth and has ten heirs, each one of them gets a piece of it in the prescribed measure.

4.2.7. *Seventh principle: Duties obligatory for individuals*

Just as Islam has made it imperative for the society to take care of the collective uplift, it does not leave the individual unchecked. The way an individual can rightly claim the society to guarantee him certain rights, the society too has some well-defined obligations for him to observe. *Zakāh* is an obligatory duty he has to discharge and pay a certain prescribed amount on his annual saving, for which an elaborate system has been devised. While *Zakāh* is levied @ 2½% on the amount of money saved, he has to pay *ʿUshr* at 10 or 5% of his agricultural produce. Whether it is trade, industry, agriculture, livestock, arts and crafts, Islam has left no field of economic activity without levying *Zakāh*. It has simultaneously determined the mode of its disbursement and those to benefit from this extraordinary public welfare undertaking. No human ingenuity has ever evolved a system of *social insurance*, like *Zakāh* and *ʿUshr*, that can guarantee such an extensive provision of succor and sustenance to such a vast variety of the deserving and the needy.

4.2.8. *Eighth principle: Duties obligatory for the society*

Islam has similarly prescribed certain obligations that the society owes towards individuals. Firstly, it seeks the society to create conditions that may allow every individual member to enjoy equal rights. No one is left without the basic amenities of life, such as food, clothing, shelter, facilities of medical care, and education. Secondly, Islam would like the society to ensure necessary treatment and assistance in emergencies and natural calamities, like accidents, floods, epidemics, earthquakes and cases of individual sufferings. Thirdly, Islam seeks to encourage the society to be sympathetic and not apathetic towards its members, who may be temporarily out of job, ill, or incapable of earning their living. An Islamic society is not a society indifferent to its individual members and their essential needs.

These are the eight fundamental principles which lay the foundations of the economic philosophy of Islam. One may note how much fundamental these principles are for the achievement of the four values mentioned in the beginning. They offer the most appropriate and practical bases for the blossoming of those values. Of these, the first value of social justice is adequately sustained and developed by these principles. The second value concerning an equitable economic system has similarly been provided moral support to create an environment of sympathy, generosity, love, cooperation, and fellow-feeling in the society. These principles also help in promoting a democratic polity based on the Islamic fundamental of social justice, as also does the fourth value of material advancement. Through these principles society is saved from the evils of a lopsided economic growth and its dire consequences, as are evident in the socialist and capitalist economies.(Biweekly *Kausar*, Lahore, 21st-25th February, 1951).

5 The Principles and Objectives of Islam's Economic System

The chapter is intended to offer answers to the following crucial questions often raised regarding Islam's Economic System:[1]

- Does Islam offer an economic system, and if so, what is the blueprint of that system? What is the position of land, labour, capital and organization in this blueprint?
- Can the funds of *Zakāh* and *Ṣadaqāt* (mandatory and normal charity) be used for social welfare?
- Can we successfully introduce an interest-free economy?
- What is the interrelationship of the economic, political, social and religious systems in Islam?

Each of these questions merits a detailed discussion worthy of a book. The occasion, however, does not permit a lengthy discourse and, therefore, only brief answers are offered in the following paragraphs.

5.1. Basics of the Islamic economic system

There are two parts of the first question. The one is whether Islam offers an economic system and if so what is its blueprint? Its second part is: what is the position of land, labour, capital and organization in that blueprint? The answer to the first part is that Islam has definitely provided an economic system. This, however, does not mean that it has prepared a blueprint with the minutest details for all times to come, in which everything has been predetermined regarding the economic issues of mankind. What this actually means is that Islam has provided to us the basic principles and determined the essential parameters, according to which we can always prepare a system capable of satisfying our economic needs in all times and climes. The approach followed

[1] Based on Sayyid Mawdūdī's address at the seminar held in the Administration Department of the University of the Punjab, Lahore, 17 December, 1965 – Translator.

by Islam, as evident from a careful study of the Holy Qur'ān and the Traditions of the Holy Prophet (*pbuh*) , is that it establishes the four corners and then tells us that we can raise the edifice of a particular aspect of our life on the basis of those well-defined parameters. We are not permitted to transgress the pre-determined limits, but are free therein to work out details as demanded by our circumstances, requirements, and experience. From the sphere of personal life to each and every realm of human civilization and culture, this is how Islam has offered guidance to mankind. This is the course followed for our economic system as well. Islam has given us broad outlines and principles and set the four corners of the proposed structure to enable us give concrete shape to an economic system of our own. One may very well see how our leading jurists had during their time formulated in detail statutes, by-laws, rules, and regulations concerning the economic system of Islam. These are available in our books of jurisprudence and serve as an invaluable treasure house of knowledge on the subject. In fact, these detailed chapters on Islam's economic system occupy a unique position as the pioneering work of scholarship in the field of economics and precursor to similar attempts that mankind was to subsequently witness in the world. Out of this treasury of knowledge we can borrow verbatim details that satisfy the needs of the time and evolve our own strategy for the new issues facing us today in light of the paradigms and parameters available to us. Whatever rules and regulations we frame are required, however, to be based essentially on the principles provided to us by the Qur'ān and the *Sunnah* and to remain within their well-defined borderlines.

5.2. The objectives of Islamic economics

Having explained what we mean when we say that Islam has its own economic system, I now proceed to discuss at length the principles and rules that Islam has given us in the realm of economics. Before I start, let me first explain the most important objectives in this system, because we otherwise cannot properly understand those principles or apply them to our contemporary situation and needs, nor can we frame, using the deductive method, detailed laws, rules and regulations in their true spirit.

5.2.1. *Personal freedom*

The prime factor for Islam in respect of the economy is safeguarding personal freedom and imposing only as much restriction as is necessary for the collective well-being of a society. Islam attaches a great importance to human freedom. The reason for this is quite simple: every individual in Islam is accountable before the Lord for the deeds in his personal capacity. This is not a collective accountability. It is therefore essential to let each person have more and more avenues for the development and growth of his personality, according to his options and discretion, and to allow him the freedom of choice to do as he desires. This is why Islam attaches great importance to the individual's moral, political and economic freedom. One can imagine how free a person who is dependent on someone else, an institution or a government for his subsistence can be, if at all, to act according to his own views, if he is even free to hold them. Islam has therefore given us principles for an economic system which guarantee an individual's freedom to earn their daily bread. There are also restrictions, but only to the extent that they are necessary for a society's progress and prosperity. This is why Islam seeks to establish a political system that guarantees active participation of the people and a government of their choice: a government answerable to the people, which they can change as and when they deem this is in the interests of the nation and the state; a government that is run in consultation with the people and representatives of their trust, where the people may enjoy complete freedom of criticism and expression; and a government whose powers should not be unlimited, but circumscribed by the parameters set by the Qur'ān and the *Sunnah* as the supreme law of the land.

Furthermore, the basic human rights of the people are also guaranteed by Islam. These rights are not the gift of any state authority or world body, but have been decreed by Allah *subḥānahū wa taʿālā* Himself and nobody is authorized to violate or deny them to His subjects. All of these measures have been taken by Islam to ensure that an individual maintains his freedom, and they prevent the possibility of a repressive regime taking over the land and restraining proper growth and development of someone's personality.

5.2.2. *Harmony in moral and material progress*

The second objective of Islam's economic system is to guarantee the harmonious growth of human personality both morally and materially. Islam lays a special stress on the moral growth and development of man. For this, it is incumbent on a society to provide the individual with ample opportunities to help him choose to do good deeds. It seeks to create an environment that is conducive for the blossoming of noble human traits and moral virtues like magnanimity, cooperation, compassion, tolerance, etc. Because of this, Islam does not depend entirely on the strong arm of law to establish social justice in the land. It assigns greater importance in this context to *Īmān* (Faith), *ʿIbādāt* (Prayers and other solemn acts of worship), education and moral upbringing in order to reform a person from within, to modify his taste and temperament, to change his way of thinking and to create within him a strong moral urge to stand upright and steadfast in all circumstances. If and when these measures fall short of producing the desired results, the Muslim society should be morally strong enough to force the individual purely through social pressure to abide by its norms and values. In case social pressure also falls short of producing a change, Islam then uses the strong arm of law as a last resort to establish justice. According to the Islamic standpoint, every social system is wrong that relies mainly on force to establish the rule of law and justice and which renders the individual incapable of doing good of his own free will.

5.2.3. *Promotion of cooperation, harmony and justice*

The third important objective of the economic system of Islam is the promotion and sustainability of a society's unity and cohesion. Islam is the torchbearer of human unity and brotherhood, and is opposed to division and disharmony. Therefore, it does not encourage a society's division on the basis of class, clan and ethnic or linguistic considerations. The classes that naturally emerge under a particular social set-up are led to live in an environment of mutual cooperation, compassion and trust, rather than an atmosphere of hatred and conflict. When one examines the texture of human society analytically, one discovers that it is composed of two types of classes. There is the category of classes that seek to promote a coercive political, social and economic system artificially, and then perpetuate their supremacy over other segments of society unlawfully. Racialist ideologies, such as Brahmanism and Zionism, or systems of landed aristocracy and financial imperialism, such as feudalism and the Western capitalist system, have been instrumental in producing and promoting this type of class. Islam itself does not create or patronize any such exploitative or anti-human system, nor would it ever allow such a system to sustain itself and prosper. In fact, Islam eliminates every anti-human social order through its reformatory and legal measures. The second category of classes consists of those which automatically develop due to the diversity of human qualifications, capabilities and circumstances, and undergoes change naturally. Islam does not forcibly eliminate this category, nor does it permit the members of these classes to fight among themselves. On the contrary, it creates an atmosphere of amity and cooperation among them through its moral, political, social and economic structures. It makes people helpful and compassionate to one another and, by providing an equality of opportunities to all, it creates an environment in which they freely intermix and gradually lose their separate identities to make a uniform whole naturally.

5.3. Basic principles of Islam's economic system

Once you keep these three objectives in mind, you are in a better position to understand the fundamentals of the economic system of Islam in their true perspective. Let me now briefly explain some of the major principles of this system.

5.3.1. *Parameters of private ownership*

Islam reaffirms a person's right to own property, subject to certain conditions. It makes no distinction in this regard between the means of production and consumer goods, or between earned and unearned income. While granting people the right to own property, however, Islam circumscribes this right with certain limits. Islam does not approve of treating the means of production and consumer goods differently and excluding the former from the ambit of personal ownership. From the Islamic perspective, just as a person is authorized to have his own wardrobe, kitchenware and furniture, so he is entitled to own land, machines and factories. Similarly, as everybody can own the wealth he earns through his labour, he can also own the wealth left behind by his father, mother, wife or husband. He can also be a shareholder in an income earned on the principle of *Muḍārabah* or *Mushārakah* through the capital he has invested on which somebody may have laboured to produce dividends. Islam thus does not differentiate between one type of ownership and another, whether it is the ownership of the means of productions or that of consumer goods, or whether it is earned or unearned income.

The difference that Islam makes between the various types of wealth is on whether they are earned or produced through fair means or foul, and whether it has been used in a right or wrong manner. The blueprint that Islam has prepared for the entire spectrum of mankind's economic life has been formed in such a manner that it leaves a person free, within certain limits, to earn his living. As explained earlier, human freedom is of prime importance to Islam, which builds the entire edifice of the community's growth and development on the cornerstone of this freedom. To grant a person the right of personal ownership of his economic means and resources is therefore essential for preserving this freedom. To deprive a person of this right and impose public ownership on all the resources of the land would naturally mean denying him his personal freedom, because under this kind of dispensation every individual automatically becomes a servant of the state machinery that controls its economic resources through its administration.

5.3.2. *Equitable distribution of wealth*

Another basic principle of Islam's economic system is that it aims at an equitable, but not necessarily equal, distribution of wealth. It does not seek an absolutely equal distribution of the means of living for every human being. Anybody studying the Qur'ān will notice that such an equality does not exist anywhere in the whole of the universe. The very concept of parity is contrary to the dictates of nature. Has each one of us been granted the same level of health? Do all of us enjoy the same amount of intelligence? Do all of us have equally strong memories? Is every individual on a par with others in beauty, physical strength and intellectual prowess? Is everyone born under similar circumstances and in the same environment, and does each enjoy the same opportunities and avenues for progress and prosperity? If there is no equality anywhere in any of these matters, how logical is a claim for equality in the means of production or distribution of wealth? Practically speaking, such equality is not remotely feasible, and any attempt to enforce this through artificial means is bound to fail. Islam, therefore, does not seek an equal distribution of economic resources and economic gains. Instead, it places a stress on their equitable distribution and prescribes certain rules for this in order to achieve equity and justice. These rules may be summed up as follows.

The first rule in this context is that Islam has distinctly classified the means of the production of wealth into the two broad categories of lawful (*Ḥalāl*) and forbidden (*Ḥarām*). On the one hand, it gives the individual the freedom to struggle for his economic well-being and to own what he earns; and on the other, this freedom is subjected to the provisos of *Ḥalāl* and *Ḥarām*. According to this rule, every person is free to earn his living through lawful means in a way that is convenient to him, and to earn as much as he can. He is also the lawful owner of all that he has earned. Nobody has the right to put a curb on his ownership or to deprive him either totally or partially of what he has earned. Of course, he is not authorized to secure even a farthing through unlawful or forbidden means. He is not simply unauthorized to make this kind of earning, but the law will forcibly stop him from any such attempt. He cannot be the owner of anything earned unlawfully and will also be liable for punishment according to the nature of the crime committed. This punishment may range from an imprisonment to a fine or even confiscation of his property. Steps will also be taken to prevent him from committing such crimes again.

The means of wealth production that are declared *Ḥarām* by the Islamic *Sharīʿah* are as follows: dishonesty in public accounts, bribery, distortion, misappropriation of public funds, theft and burglary, irregularity in weights and measures, trading in obscene and immoral items, prostitution and sex trade, production and sale of wine and other intoxicants, usury and all interest-based transactions, gambling, betting, speculation, all sale and purchase deals based on fraud or coercion and those causing bad blood or corruption, or which may be contrary to the demands of justice and public interest. The *Sharīʿah* has banned all these means. Islam also prohibits hoarding, monopolies and cartels that deprive the common man of the opportunity to make use of their wealth and the means of its production against the dictates of reason and fairplay.

Apart from these, anything that is earned through lawful means is the legal income of a man. He is entitled to make use of this wealth himself, or to transfer it to others by gift or donation. He may also use it to earn more wealth or leave it behind for his heirs. There is no restriction on this legal income that could prevent it from earning more wealth at any stage. If a person becomes a billionaire lawfully, Islam does not obstruct him. He is free to make as much headway economically as he can, so long as he does not cross the prescribed limits. Frankly speaking, it is not easy under an Islamic dispensation to make millions, if one strictly follows the lawful means. Except for God's grace, it needs extraordinary efforts and acumen to multiply one's wealth in a lawful manner. However, Islam does not tie anybody's hands to prevent him from seeking 'Allah's Blessings' through the means He approves because unwarranted hurdles and checks leave no incentive for someone to put in more labour.

The wealth thus lawfully earned has been subjected to certain restrictions on its use, which are summed up in the following paragraphs.

The first use of one's wealth is to spend it on oneself. Islam puts such restrictions on this use to prevent a person's conduct from becoming harmful for the individual and for the society. He is forbidden to spend it on liquor, and so he cannot drink. He cannot indulge in fornication and illicit sexual relations. He cannot squander it in gambling. He can follow no immoral or ethically wrong course of personal conduct. He is not authorized to have gold or silverware for his own use, nor can he indulge in ostentatious living to show off his riches.

Another way to use one's personal wealth is to withhold a part of it from spending and keep it safe in one's coffers. Islam does not support this approach. It would like the flow of wealth to continue uninterrupted in a lawful manner. It therefore levies *Zakāh* on the amount saved to allow a portion of this to reach the less privileged and be diverted to schemes of public welfare. The acts that are disapproved of by the Book of God include the hoarding of wealth, which has been forcefully condemned. We have been warned that those who amass gold and silver and do not spend it in the Way of Allah will face a '*a painful chastisement on a Day when they shall be heated up in the Fire of Hell, and their foreheads and their sides and their backs shall be branded with it, (and they shall be told): "This is the treasure which you hoarded for yourselves. Taste, then, the punishment for what you have hoarded".'* (*al-Tawbah*, 9: 34-35). The reason for this penalty is that Allah *subḥānahū wa taʿālā* has produced the treasures of the heavens and the earth for the benefit of mankind. Therefore, nobody is authorized to lock this in his golden chests. The message given to us is this: 'Earn as much as you can through lawful means; spend it on your personal needs; and then whatever you save bring it in circulation in whatever manner possible to you legally.'

Hoarding, for which the Islamic Economics uses the term '*Iḥtikār*', is thus strictly prohibited in Islam. *Iḥtikār* means to purposely hold back consumer goods to create a scarcity in their supply, thereby causing the prices to soar. The principle that Islam has laid down for business and commerce sanctions no such unhealthy practice. If you have a commodity for sale and there is a demand for it in the market, you have no right to hold it back. Creating a scarcity of items for daily use simply to earn a little extra money turns a trader into a bandit, and Islam totally disapproves of this.

Monopolies and cartels are also disallowed by Islam for the same reason. In the Islamic scheme of things, the public good occupies the highest position, and monopolies and cartels prevent the general public from making use of the available economic resources. Islam has therefore made it unlawful for certain means and opportunities of earning a living to be declared the exclusive domain of a particular class of people, family or household, making it difficult for others to enter that sector. There is only room for that kind of monopoly which is inevitable for the collective good of a society. Otherwise, Islam seeks to keep the field of economic activities open to everyone who wants to try his luck and make use of an opportunity to his advantage.

If someone wants to invest his savings to earn more money, he can do so only through the channels permitted by Islam for earning a livelihood. No forbidden means can ever be used for this purpose, as mentioned earlier.

5.3.3. *Social obligations*

Islam thus superimposes the right of the society on private ownership, and safeguards this right in various ways. The Holy Qur'ān lays a special emphasis on the rights of the kindred, which means that, in addition to an individual's own rights on his income, his relatives also have their right to his earnings. Each and every member of the society who earns more than he actually needs is duty-bound to do his best to help those among his relations who have less than they need to satisfy their day-to-day requirements. When every family sincerely tries to fulfil its obligations towards those families in the community who are lacking, there is bound to be an overall economic improvement in the society as a whole, leaving behind hardly any household in need of external support. The rights of one's mother, father and close relatives, therefore, occupy the highest position in the list that the Holy Qur'ān has offered us in respect of *Ḥuqūq al-ʿIbād* (Rights of Men or Human Rights).

Islam similarly acknowledges a neighbour's rights to one's income. This simply means that it seeks to establish a society that is self-sufficient and requires no outside help to sustain itself economically. Islam would like to see every street and locality peopled by God-fearing men who know that to live also means to let others live with honour and dignity, and that the needs of one person are the responsibility of everyone else around him.

After putting the onus on the two responsibilities above, Islam then makes every affluent person responsible for providing the best assistance he can to those who may approach him or may be in need of it:

وَفِيٓ أَمۡوَٰلِهِمۡ حَقّٞ لِّلسَّآئِلِ وَٱلۡمَحۡرُومِ ١٩

> (And in their wealth there was a rightful share for him who would ask and for the destitute.')
>
> (*al-Dhāriyāt*, 51: 19)

The needy who may ask for help does not include beggars who may have taken up begging as a profession. Instead it means a person whose need impels him to approach you with a request for help. Having satisfied yourself about his need, and if you are in a position to extend the desired help, you have no option but to discharge your responsibility towards those who are actually asking you for their 'right'. As for those who for some reason are prevented from approaching you with their request, they also have the right to their share of your affluence, once you have confirmed their need.

In addition to the 'Rights of Men' (*Ḥuqūq al-ʿIbād*), Islam has also enjoined Muslims to spend 'in the Way of Allah', thereby establishing the rights of the society and the state on their wealth. The import of this injunction is that a Muslim is required to be generous, magnanimous, compassionate and considerate, and should spend his money open-heartedly in every good cause and in the service of his religion and society, not inspired by any selfish motive, but purely for the sake of Allah's Pleasure. Islam injects a powerful moral passion in every individual through its education and training, and through the environment that it creates in a Muslim society which motivates a person to volunteer his services for every good cause, not due to any compulsion but out of his own will.

5.3.4. *Zakāh*

Zakāh is the most outstanding feature of the economic system of Islam. In addition to '*Infāq fī Sabīlillāh*' (voluntary spending in the Way of Allah), *Zakāh* is levied on the prescribed amount of capital saved, on trade goods, business and commerce, agricultural produce and livestock, in order to lend support to those members of society who have lagged behind economically. The mandatory charity of *Zakāh* and the voluntary spending in the Way of Allah (*Ṣadaqāt*) are like regular and supererogatory Prayers. There is no limit to the supererogatory Prayer and one can offer as much as he likes for his spiritual advancement and nearness to the Lord. However, the regular Prayer is mandatory, and the supererogatory Prayers, even if they are countless, cannot take its place. Similarly, *Ṣadaqāt* cannot absolve one of the obligation to pay *Zakāh*.

Zakāh should not be mistaken for a 'holy' tax. It is not a tax, but *'ibādah* or an act of worship, and like regular Prayer is one of the five Pillars of Faith. A tax is an amount that is levied by force on a person, which he may or may not like. A person who is taxed hardly feels honoured or gratified, nor does he regard it as an act of mercy and benevolence. In fact, even in developed economies, one can find plenty of people who try to seek a way to evade its application and avoid payment. Tax differs in principle from *Zakāh*. Tax is levied to generate revenue to meet expenditure on services, the benefits of which eventually return to the taxpayer. The basic concept governing a taxation system is that you are required to contribute a certain amount from your income for the facilities you expect the government to provide you with. Your tax is, therefore, the contribution that you make for the services of which you are a beneficiary as a taxpayer.

On the contrary, *Zakāh* is an act of worship, just like *Ṣalāh*. It is imposed not by an act of Parliament or a legislature, but has been made mandatory by Allah *subḥānahū wa ta'ālā* and, as a believer, every Muslim is duty-bound to pay it willingly and never try to avoid its payment. Even in the absence of any official machinery to collect *Zakāh*, the faithful makes his own calculations to ascertain the amount payable by him on the due date. *Zakāh* is not meant to satisfy the social needs of the people. It is exclusively for the benefit of those who have somehow lagged behind or remained deprived of their due share of the national wealth and are in need of assistance, whether temporarily or permanently. Therefore, *Zakāh* is absolutely different from tax in its essence, objectives, form and content. It is collected or paid not for the construction of roads, rails, canals or to run the country's administration, but has been levied by the Lord to help the deserving get his due; the only dividend one should look for on its payment is Allah's Pleasure and the reward of the Day of Reckoning.

There has been a misperception that there is no tax in Islam other than *Zakāh* and *Kharāj* (land tax). The fact is that the Holy Prophet (*pbuh*) has himself declared: اِنَّ فِی الْمَالِ حَقًّا سِوَی الزَّکوٰۃ ['There is a right (of the state) in (Muslims') property other than *Zakāh*]. There are taxes which Islam does not approve of. These include taxes such as those levied by the Caesars, Khosraus and despotic princes, which were deposited in royal coffers as their personal property and for which they were accountable to none but themselves. The *Sharī'ah*, however, puts no restriction on the taxation levied by an Islamic government that is run on the principles of popular participation or *Shūrā*. The revenue thus gathered forms part of the public treasury and is spent with the people's consent in the national interest, and the government is held responsible for its proper utilization. In the case of an economic imbalance created in the society prior to the establishment of an Islamic government, or wealth being amassed through illicit means by certain classes, the malaise cannot be remedied by the confiscation of property, but by levying direct taxes. The concentration of wealth in a few hands can also be effectively checked with the help of relevant Islamic laws. Allowing the rulers to confiscate property would naturally lead them to strengthening their hands with repressive laws, thereby giving them a license to grow even more oppressive and commit more injustice and transgressions.

5.3.5. *Law of inheritance*

Islam's law of inheritance has been framed with the sole objective of allowing the wealth, big or small, that is left behind by the deceased to pass on to a larger group of his heirs and next of kin in a well-defined manner. His mother, father, wife and children are among the prime beneficiaries, followed by his brothers and sisters and close relatives. If a person has no legal heir, the community as a whole becomes the heir and the legacy goes to the public treasury.

These are the basic principles and parameters that are set by Islam for the economic well-being of a society. We are free to devise an economic system of our own within these parameters; it is for us to finalize the details, as demanded by the situation in our time. What we are strictly required to do is to follow neither the capitalist path of an unbridled economy, nor the communist method of taking all the economic resources under state control. We have to adopt a system of free economy that is restricted by certain limits, a system that leaves all avenues open to the individual for the moral growth and development of his personality; a system that will rarely need any legislation to mobilize everyone to doing their bit for the welfare of society; a system that leaves no room for the emergence of classes through unfair means and should promote cooperation among the legitimately existing natural classes, rather than conflict. Every means of livelihood that is declared *Ḥarām* by Islam will remain unlawful under this system, and only those means proclaimed *Ḥalāl* will be legal. The rights that are guaranteed by Islam for acquiring and disposing of wealth earned through lawful means will remain secure. The state will have a proper mechanism for the compulsory collection of *Zakāh* and its disbursement. Property that is left by the deceased will get distributed according to the law of inheritance, and every individual will be free to conduct his economic activities within the approved parameters, with no legislation to curtail this freedom. The law will not interfere in the unrestrained economic activities of individuals, so long as they continue to abide by the norms of justice and fairplay. However, if they transgress the prescribed limits or try to establish monopolies and cartels, the law would then definitely take action, not to deny them their basic freedom, but to keep them firmly on the path of justice and to prevent any transgression and derailment.

I have discussed the first part of the question so far. Now let us move on to the second part concerning the position of land, labour, capital and organization in the blueprint of an Islamic economic system.

5.4. Position of labour, capital, and organization

To understand the exact position that labour, capital and organization occupy in the economic system of Islam, I would recommend studying the laws concerning '*Muzāraʿah*' and '*Muḍārabah*' that are explained and elaborated in the books of Islamic jurisprudence. The way that modern day books on economics define land, labour, capital and organization as economic factors is quite different from the way these are treated in works of scholarship by pioneer Muslim jurists and scholars. They did not write books dealing exclusively with economics, but contributed detailed chapters on principal issues concerning the subject. The wording used was very different from the jargon-laden language of today's books on economics as a discipline. Except for those who are held captive by these high-sounding terms and phraseologies, anybody who is interested in economics and issues of economic relevance can easily understand the significance and import of the various themes discussed in juristic language and the concepts underlying them. The Islamic law of *Muzāraʿah* and *Muḍārabah* that the books of jurisprudence discuss in detail provides the necessary guidance about the Islamic approach to land, labour, capital and organization.

Muzāraʿah is a method of farming where the land belongs to one person but is cultivated by another and both share the profits on its produce. *Muḍārabah* is a form of investment wherein the capital belongs to one person and is used by another for business and trade and both share the profits. The way that the rights of both the landowner and the investor, as well as those who 'labour' in these transactions have been reaffirmed and safeguarded by Islam clearly shows that, according to Islam, land, human labour, enterprise and capital are all economic factors which are jointly eligible to a share in the profit. Initially, Islam leaves the onus for determining the share-ratio of the different production factors to common sense, in order to let people settle their matters amicably among themselves without the law having to intervene. But this is true only as long as people handle their affairs judiciously according to the dictates of conscience and good sense. In the case of any injustice, however, the law definitely takes action. For example, if I as the owner give my farmland to someone else for cultivation, employ somebody on wages to till it or give it on a contract basis to someone for farming and settle the terms with the other party in a proper manner, the court will have no reason to intervene. But if I commit an injustice and violate the terms of the contract, the court will then intervene to ensure justice for the aggrieved party. The law can determine the rules and regulations by which such disputes should be settled so that neither the owner of the land nor the labour engaged in farming suffer on any count. Similarly, when an investor, the labourers and the organization manage their affairs amicably by mutual consent, the law has no cause to intervene. But when any one of these is high-handed and violates the other side's rights, the law will be required to settle the matter justly and provide rules and regulations guaranteeing the equitable distribution of dividends among all stakeholders.

5.5. *Zakāh* and social welfare

Now, let us turn to the second question about the admissibility of *Zakāh* and *Ṣadaqāt* funds for use in welfare-related schemes. To put it briefly, *Zakāh* and *Ṣadaqāt* are meant to satisfy the people's welfare needs. However, it must be borne in mind that, in the context of mandatory and normal acts of charity, the term 'Social Welfare' cannot be taken to include the entire state and all the segments of its population. These funds are not allowed to be used for the economic uplift of the country as a whole. As explained earlier, *Zakāh* is meant to satisfy the essential needs of the deserving and the needy. It ensures that no member of the society remains deprived of his basic needs – food, clothing, shelter, health care, childcare and the basic education of children. It also guarantees any necessary help and the satisfaction of the subsistence needs of those who are either unable to earn their living, like destitute women and children, the old and the handicapped; or those who are temporarily unemployed and without the means to earn their living, but are capable of standing on their own feet once they have been provided with the necessary financial and material support; or those who have incurred a loss. *Zakāh* has been enjoined on the Muslim community to take care of all such deserving cases. As for the general economic uplift of the country and its citizens, the state has the means to exploit other resources.

5.6. Interest-free economy

Coming to the third question regarding the possibility of successfully introducing and running an interest-free economy, my answer to this is decidedly in the affirmative. An interest-free system has been practiced for centuries in the past and can be re-established even today without too much difficulty, provided we stop blindly following others. Before the advent of Islam, the world's fiscal system had been running on usury and interest, as it is today. Islam discarded this system and banned usury in all its forms. It was first banned in Arabia, and the ban then continued extending to all the territories which subsequently came under its benign rule; the economies of the Muslim lands remained interest-free not for one or two, but for many centuries. There is no reason why this system should be dysfunctional today. If we have the capability to reinterpret our juridical issues (*Ijtihād*), if we are firm in our faith (*Īmān)* and have the resolve to do away with a moth-eaten system declared *Ḥarām* by Allah *subḥānahū wa taʿālā*, then we are bound to succeed in replacing the interest-based system with an interest-free system of economy and in managing all our financial and economic matters efficiently. I have already explained in my book '*Sūd*' (Interest) in greater detail that there are no insurmountable hurdles in the way and the matter is quite simple and plain. Capital in the form of loans has no right to take the centre stage and draw maximum benefit through a fixed profit, regardless of whether the workers and organization receive a profit commensurate to the services rendered or not. The real drawback in an interest-based system is that an individual or organization lends capital as a loan and receives a certain amount of profit fixed in advance. They care little whether the debtor has lost or gained in his enterprise, or what his rate of the profit has been if he has gained. The investor goes on receiving the predetermined profits on his loan on a yearly or monthly basis, while also remaining entitled to the return of the principal amount he advanced on the loan. This is a tyranny that Islam seeks to abolish. It is an unjust system that can hardly be defended. On the contrary, the principle enunciated by Islam states that if you have offered somebody a loan, it should only be a loan and not a tool of exploitation. You are only entitled to get back the principal amount of your loan. However, in case you wish to earn a profit as well, then you should be a partner or shareholder. The capital that you wish to extend on loan in agriculture, trade or industry should be offered on the condition that whatever profit is earned on your investment will be distributed equitably among you and your other partners or shareholders. That is what justice demands and is also how the economy can prosper. What is the problem after all in giving up an interest-based system in favour of a system involving no interest? The amount that is being invested today as loans can very well be used on a partnership basis in the future. The way that profits are calculated on interest-based transactions can also be calculated using an interest-free system. There is very little problem involved in this, except that we have become used to blindly following. We need instead to carve out our own more respectful and more profitable way through a scholarly reinterpretation of emerging issues in the light of the Holy Qur'ān and the *Sunnah.* The *Mawlawī* is unnecessarily blamed for 'blind followership' *(Ṭaqlīd)* and avoiding *Ijtihād*, while the so-called 'enlightened' ones among us have remained intellectual slaves and blind followers of others and are least ready for serious homework. If it were not for this intellectual servitude, the problem could have been resolved much earlier.

5.7. Interrelationship between economic, political and social systems

Let us finally examine the last question regarding the interrelationship of the economic, political, social and religious systems in Islam. The brief answer to this is that it is a relationship like that of the stems with the roots, of the branches with the stems and of the leaves with the branches of a single tree. The Islamic system is a unified whole. It is a system that evolves out of Faith in the Oneness of God and the Finality of Prophethood. It is out of this root that emerges the system of moral conduct, the system of Divine Worship, the economic system and the political system. All of these are inter-related with each other. If you believe in God and His Apostle and accept the Qur'ān as the Book of God, you will inevitably have to practise the moral principles preached by Islam, follow the political precepts taught by Islam, reconstruct your social order on Islamic values and run the entire affairs of your economy on the basis of Islamic norms and principles. The Faith is the basis on which you offer Prayer; you will have to conduct your business and all economic activities on that same basis. The Religion that governs your fasting and pilgrimage, that very Guidance has to be followed in the conduct of your affairs in your law courts and the market system. There is no multiplicity of independent orders, religious, political, economic and social, in Islam. It is a unified system with its different wings and parts interlinked with each other, drawing sustenance and strength from one another. Without a firm Faith in the creed of Monotheism, the Finality of Prophethood and the Day of Reckoning, and without the social conduct produced by this Faith, it will never be possible to establish the Islamic economic system and run it successfully. Similarly, the political system of Islam cannot be established, nor can it be successfully maintained, unless we are firm in our faith in Allah *subḥānahū wa taʿālā*, His Prophet, the Day of Reckoning and the Qur'ān. As we are all aware, the political system that Islam offers is based on the belief that supremacy belongs to Allah; His Holy Prophet (*pbuh*) is His Messenger; the Qur'ān and the *Sunnah* must be obeyed as the embodiment of the Divine Guidance; and we are ultimately held to account for all that we do before Him on the Day of Judgment. It is therefore wrong to think that there can be any political or economic system in Islam independent of its religious and moral systems. He who has a knowledge of Islam and believes in it cannot even think of any part of his life, whether political or economic, as separate from his religious being, or think that he can lead an Islamic life simply by performing certain mandatory rituals without carefully observing the principles and guidance provided to him by Islam in the political, economic, judicial and legal fields.

6 Some Basic Principles of Economic Life

6.1. Basic values of Islamic society

إِنَّ ٱللَّهَ يَأْمُرُ بِٱلْعَدْلِ وَٱلْإِحْسَٰنِ وَإِيتَآيِٕ ذِى ٱلْقُرْبَىٰ وَيَنْهَىٰ عَنِ ٱلْفَحْشَآءِ وَٱلْمُنكَرِ وَٱلْبَغْىِ ۚ يَعِظُكُمْ
لَعَلَّكُمْ تَذَكَّرُونَ ﴿٩٠﴾

('Surely Allah enjoins justice, kindness and the doing of good to kith and kin, and forbids all that is shameful, evil and oppressive. He exhorts you so that you may be mindful.')

(*al-Naḥl*, 16: 90)

In this brief Qur'ānic statement, we are enjoined to observe three traits on which the health of the entire human society depends.

The first of these is *ʿAdl* (justice), which involves a combination of two permanent values of human society: (i) balance and harmony among the people in their rights; and (ii) each person getting his rights honorably and with no strings attached. *ʿAdl* is generally translated in Urdu by the word *Inṣāf*, which gives an incorrect impression that the division of rights between two persons should be on a 'fifty-fifty' basis. It is this wrong connotation that has given rise to the misperception that the Qur'ānic term implies equality in the division of rights, which is absolutely contrary to the dictates of nature. According to the Qur'ānic concept of *ʿAdl*, an equilibrium and balance is established, not equality. In certain matters, however, *ʿAdl* does seek to secure equality among all members of the society, as for example in the case of citizenship. But in social and moral matters, for example, equality between parents and children, or parity in rewards for those rendering services of greater and lesser value, would be quite contrary to the concept of *ʿAdl*. What the All-Merciful has commanded is, therefore, not parity in rights, but balance and equilibrium. His Command demands that everybody get his moral, social, economic, legal, political and civil rights honestly and faithfully.

The second trait that we have been enjoined to observe in this Divine Command is the quality of *Iḥsān*, which means kindness, fair dealing, magnanimity, tolerance, courtesy, caring for each other, mutual respect, giving another person more than their due and accepting for oneself less than one's right. *Iḥsān* is an attribute that combines all of these most noble traits of human character, and is thus over and above the quality of 'justice'. Its significance in social life is, therefore, higher than *'Adl*. If *'Adl* is taken to be the foundation stone of a human social structure, *Iḥsān* may be viewed as its beauty and grandeur. If *'Adl* safeguards the society from imbalance and bitterness, *Iḥsān* fills it with pleasure and sweetness. No society can be sustained solely on the basis of a dispassionate attitude where every individual is strictly concerned with what is due to him as his right and what must he pay to others as an obligation. There may arise no occasion of crisis or conflict in such a frigid social set-up, but it will inevitably remain deprived of the higher values of love, gratitude, magnanimity, tolerance, sincerity and compassion, which are actually those values that make life livable and sweet and promote an atmosphere of goodness and harmony in society.

The third trait that the Almighty has ordered us to inculcate within ourselves is the quality of love and care for the bonds of kindred. This does not simply mean that one should treat his kith and kin well, be at their side in times of happiness and distress and lend them whatever support he can within permissible limits. It also means that a financially capable person should not remain content simply with discharging his obligations properly towards himself and his family, but is also obliged to give his kith and kin their rights from the resources at his disposal. The Islamic *Sharī'ah* makes it incumbent on all affluent members of a family to look after the less fortunate among their close relations and those at the mercy of the vagaries of time. A society where a person is allowed to live in luxury while his relatives are unable even to make both ends meet is viewed by Islam as one that is guilty of the worst kind of apathy. According to the *Sharī'ah*, the family is the vital constituent unit of human society. Every poor member of the family therefore has, as a matter of principle, a right first on every affluent person in the family and then on others in the society, for the fulfilment of his basic needs. This is further explained in various Traditions of the Holy Prophet (*pbuh*). We have been told that parents, wife and children, brothers and sisters are the prime responsibility of a man, followed by his next of kin and then others near to them. Based on this principle, the Second Caliph Ḥaḍrat 'Umar, may Allah be pleased with him, instructed the paternal cousins of an orphan child to shoulder the responsibility of their upkeep and maintenance. In another case, he said that, had there been even a distant relative of that orphan alive, he would have made it obligatory for him to take care of the child. It can readily be imagined how easily a society could reach greater heights of economic prosperity, achieve an extraordinary level of social harmony and goodwill and enjoy a spirit of moral excellence when every unit makes itself available to take care of each and every individual under its jurisdiction!

In contrast to these three virtues that are enjoined, Allah *subḥānahū wa taʿālā* has forbidden three vices which corrupt a person when done individually and the society as a whole when committed collectively.

The first of these is *Faḥshā'*, which includes all shameful deeds and acts of immorality and immodesty. In the Arabic language, every vice that is extremely detestable in itself is called *Fuḥsh.* For example, miserliness, fornication, illicit sex, nudity, sodomy, incest, theft, intoxicants, abusive language, etc. are all *Fuḥsh* acts. Indulging in such vices in public or attempting to spread immorality and promiscuous behaviour in society is also called *Fuḥsh.* This additionally includes false propaganda, defamation, publicity of crimes committed in secret, sexually inciting stories, plays and movies, seductively clad and made up women masquerading in public, men and women mixing publicly, stage-performance by female dancers and coquettes, people adopting begging as profession, etc.

The second vice is *Munkar*, which means evil and includes everything objectionable that people generally disapprove of as bad and have always seen as such. These are the vices that are forbidden in all Divine creeds.

The third forbidden trait is *Baghy*, which means revolt, transgression of limits and oppressive acts. It includes all attempts to violate another's rights, whether of the Creator or His creatures.

These are the basic values on which the edifice of a truly Muslim society stands, and to safeguard these is the responsibility of the individual, the society and the government. All the forces of law and morality are to be pressed into service in order to preserve these in an Islamic state.

6.2. The Islamic path of moral and economic rejuvenation

فَـَٔاتِ ذَا ٱلْقُرْبَىٰ حَقَّهُۥ وَٱلْمِسْكِينَ وَٱبْنَ ٱلسَّبِيلِ ۚ ذَٰلِكَ خَيْرٌ لِّلَّذِينَ يُرِيدُونَ وَجْهَ ٱللَّهِ ۖ وَأُو۟لَـٰٓئِكَ هُمُ ٱلْمُفْلِحُونَ ﴿٣٨﴾

('So give what is due to the near of kin, and to the needy, and to the wayfarer. That is better for those who desire to please Allah. It is they who will prosper.')

(*al-Rūm*, 30: 38)

The above *Āyah* does not tell us to give charity to our kith and kin, the needy and the wayfarer. It declares that they should receive their rights, which we are exhorted to give to them. The spirit that the *Āyah* seeks to generate within us is one of benign beneficence and thankfulness to the Lord for enabling us to satisfy the needs of the deserving. Islam believes in a charity where the left hand does not know what the right hand is doing. The almsgiver, instead of exulting with a sense of pride for his good work, is required to feel beholden to the recipient for gaining fulfilment through him. We are reminded time and again that what we own is not actually ours; we are merely custodians. The ownership of everything we have belongs to the Lord, and therefore when we spend out of the wealth at our disposal to satisfy others' needs, we are actually transferring to them what they had a right to receive. We must also, therefore, thank the Lord that we rose up to this level of His Command and succeeded in passing the test that we were given concerning the wealth under our control.

When one looks into this Divine Command and the guiding spirit behind it, it immediately becomes clear that the path of moral and spiritual rejuvenation proposed for mankind by the Book of God necessitates an unfettered society and a liberal economy. The rejuvenation foreseen is not possible in a social set-up where people are denied their basic rights, including the right to own; where the state takes under its control all the resources of the land, and the distribution of the means of living is done entirely through the government machinery; where an individual is reduced to a level where he is unable to recognize his duties to others; or where nobody can get anything from anyone and have a sense of gratitude in his heart. The economic system of communism, which attempts are now being made to introduce in our country under the deceptive slogan of 'Islamic Socialism,'[1] is absolutely in conflict with the Qur'ān and the *Sunnah*. As it has done in its birthplace, the system seeks to completely deny the individual the prospects for unhindered growth and development of his personality and the flowering of his personal conduct. The Qur'ānic scheme can only function in an environment where the people enjoy the right to own the means of production, have the right to handle them freely and can use their free will sincerely to pay to God what is due to Him, and to His subjects what is due to them. Only in this kind of society can an individual acquire and develop the traits of compassion, sincerity, kindness, altruism, sacrifice and the correct observance of rights and obligations; while those who get a better treatment from others can develop within their hearts the noble sentiments of regard, gratitude, love, sincerity and fellow-feeling: هَلْ جَزَآءُ ٱلْإِحْسَـٰنِ إِلَّا ٱلْإِحْسَـٰنُ ('Can the reward of goodness be any other than goodness?') (*al-Raḥmān*, 55: 60).

This atmosphere may eventually lead to the ideal situation, where stopping vice from spreading and helping virtue to grow from strength to strength will

[1] 'Islamic Socialism' was the popular slogan of Prime Minister Zulfikar Ali Bhutto's government in Pakistan during early 1970s, which saw its demise with his passing away. – Translator.

not depend on the intervention of any external force, but the people themselves will emerge as the upholders of goodness and virtue.

6.3. The concept of earning and spending

وَلَا تَمُدَّنَّ عَيْنَيْكَ إِلَىٰ مَا مَتَّعْنَا بِهِۦٓ أَزْوَٰجًا مِّنْهُمْ زَهْرَةَ ٱلْحَيَوٰةِ ٱلدُّنْيَا لِنَفْتِنَهُمْ فِيهِ ۚ وَرِزْقُ رَبِّكَ خَيْرٌ وَأَبْقَىٰ ﴿١٣١﴾

('Do not turn your eyes covetously towards the embellishments of worldly life that We have bestowed upon various kinds of people to test them. But the clean provision bestowed upon you by your Lord is better and more enduring.')

(*Ṭā Hā*, 20: 131)

The meaning of the word '*rizq*' that appears in this *Āyah* is provision or the means of subsistence, and includes only the *Ḥalāl* (lawful) and not the *Ḥarām* (forbidden) means. Allah *subḥānahū wa ta'ālā* warns Muslims, through His Holy Prophet (*pbuh*), against following the life-pattern of those who are disobedient to the Lord and are morally depraved and profligate, those to whom worldly splendour is everything and who remain busy throughout their lives amassing wealth by fair means or foul. It is impressed upon us that the glitter of worldly pomp and show must not be an object of envy or heart-burning for us because the provision that we get through lawful means, however meagre that might be, is 'better and more enduring' both for this world and the Hereafter:

...وَٱللَّهُ يَرْزُقُ مَن يَشَآءُ بِغَيْرِ حِسَابٍ ﴿٣٨﴾

('... for Allah grants whomsoever He wills beyond all measure.')

(*al-Nūr*, 24: 38)

...وَيْكَأَنَّ ٱللَّهَ يَبْسُطُ ٱلرِّزْقَ لِمَن يَشَآءُ مِنْ عِبَادِهِۦ وَيَقْدِرُ... ﴿٨٢﴾

('...Alas, we had forgotten that it is Allah Who increases the provision of those of His servants whom He will and grants in sparing measure to those whom He will.')

(*al-Qaṣaṣ*, 28: 82)

This means that affluence and poverty are both from the Lord, Who knows what is in our best interests. If someone revels in his riches, it does not necessarily mean that the Lord is highly pleased with him and that what he is enjoying in this world in terms of health, happiness and material gain is essentially a reward from Him. It is common to witness a person, otherwise worthy of His Wrath, continuing to thrive materially until the time comes when the very symbols of his status in life turn into curse for him and a sign of Allah's Displeasure. On the contrary, if a person lives from hand to mouth and is apparently less fortunate materially, this in no way means that the Almighty is displeased with him or that he is being punished by Him. It often happens that Allah's most loved ones pass through tough times, and ultimately this apparent misery and misfortune turns out to be His great Blessing. It is because of this common misperception that every affluent person in our society is generally viewed with envy, although in reality he may be worthy of Allah's Wrath.

...فَإِلَٰهُكُمْ إِلَٰهٌ وَاحِدٌ فَلَهُۥٓ أَسْلِمُوا۟ ۗ وَبَشِّرِ ٱلْمُخْبِتِينَ ﴿٣٤﴾ ٱلَّذِينَ إِذَا ذُكِرَ ٱللَّهُ وَجِلَتْ قُلُوبُهُمْ وَٱلصَّٰبِرِينَ عَلَىٰ
مَآ أَصَابَهُمْ وَٱلْمُقِيمِى ٱلصَّلَوٰةِ وَمِمَّا رَزَقْنَٰهُمْ يُنفِقُونَ ﴿٣٥﴾

('So submit yourself to Him alone. And give, (O Prophet), glad tidings to those that humble themselves (before Allah). Whose hearts shiver whenever Allah is mentioned, who patiently bear whatever affliction comes to them, who establish Prayer, and who spend (for good purposes) out of what We have provided them.')

(*al-Ḥajj*, 22: 34-35)

As stated earlier, 'glad tidings' from Allah *subḥānahū wa ta'ālā* are conveyed to those devotees who, apart from their other qualities, spend generously in His Way out of what He has bestowed upon them, involving the *Ḥalāl* means of subsistence. No charity is acceptable if the wealth is gathered through foul means. The quality of magnanimity in spending does not include all kinds of expenditure. It covers only the amount of money spent to satisfy the legitimate needs of oneself, one's family, relatives, neighbours and the needy, and that spent on schemes of public welfare and for Islamic causes. The Qur'ānic term '*Infāq*' (spending) does not, therefore, apply to lavish spending on luxuries, pomp and show. The terms that are used by the Book of God for such prodigality are '*Isrāf*' (intemperance) and '*Tabdhīr*' (extravagance with and squandering of wealth). Stinginess is the opposite of the desired quality of *Infāq*. The *Sharī'ah* does not also approve of reluctance to spend on the legitimate needs of oneself and one's family or to help others if one is financially capable. This kind of attitude has been condemned as '*Bukhl*' (miserliness) and '*Shuḥḥa al-Nafs*' (covetousness, envy and greed).

6.4. Principles of spending

... كُلُوا۟ مِمَّا رَزَقَكُمُ ٱللَّهُ وَلَا تَتَّبِعُوا۟ خُطُوَٰتِ ٱلشَّيْطَٰنِ ۚ إِنَّهُۥ لَكُمْ عَدُوٌّ مُّبِينٌ ﴿١٤٢﴾

('Eat of the sustenance that Allah has provided you and do not follow in the footsteps of Satan, for surely he is your open enemy.')

(*al-An'ām*, 6: 142)

According to this *Āyah*, Allah *subḥānahū wa ta'ālā* likes us to bear in mind that the garden, the farm, the cattle herds and everything else at our disposal have all been gifted by Him alone and noone else. This is why we owe our thankfulness to Him alone and there actually is none other than Him to merit our gratitude. We also have to keep in mind that, since everything we have is a gift from God, we are duty-bound to observe the rules set by Him for its use, and nobody has the authority to impose a new set of restrictions for the bounties of God. In fact, to observe such restrictions and bow to others in thankfulness are grievous acts of transgression. The third aspect that is brought home to us in this *Āyah* is that the Lord has created His bounties for us to eat, drink and make use of, and not to abstain from them and impose unwarranted restrictions on their use because of superstitions and taboos for which there is no sanction from the Lord:

يَٰٓأَيُّهَا ٱلَّذِينَ ءَامَنُوا۟ لَا تُحَرِّمُوا۟ طَيِّبَٰتِ مَآ أَحَلَّ ٱللَّهُ لَكُمْ وَلَا تَعْتَدُوٓا۟ ۚ إِنَّ ٱللَّهَ لَا يُحِبُّ ٱلْمُعْتَدِينَ ﴿٨٧﴾ وَكُلُوا۟
مِمَّا رَزَقَكُمُ ٱللَّهُ حَلَٰلًا طَيِّبًا ۚ وَٱتَّقُوا۟ ٱللَّهَ ٱلَّذِىٓ أَنتُم بِهِۦ مُؤْمِنُونَ ﴿٨٨﴾

('Believers! Do not hold as unlawful the good things which Allah has made lawful to you, and do not exceed the bounds of right. Allah does not love those who transgress the bounds of right. And partake of the lawful, good things which Allah has provided you as sustenance, and refrain from disobeying Allah in Whom you believe.')

(*al-Mā'idah*, 5: 87-88)

The above *Āyāt* contain two injunctions. The first cautions us against assuming the position of a self-appointed law-giver, because the authority to declare anything *Ḥalāl* or *Ḥarām* rests with none but the Lord and His Apostle (*pbuh*). If anybody tries to make lawful something declared unlawful by the Lord, or to treat as unlawful that which is lawful according to the *Sharī'ah*, he is then not following the Divine Law but his own whim. The second instruction we get here is that Muslims are not supposed to renounce legitimate worldly pleasures that are gifted to us by the Lord and follow the life-pattern of the Christian monks, Hindu yogis, Buddhist monks, mystics or 'saints'. Generally, religiously-oriented pious men have been prone to view the gratification of the demands of the body and the self as detrimental to their spiritual progress. They tend to believe that self-torture, the renunciation of worldly pleasures and distancing themselves from the means of human subsistence are in themselves acts of virtue, without which it is impossible to achieve Divine Favour. A few of the Companions of the Holy Prophet initially appeared to hold the same notion. At one time, the Holy Prophet came to know that some of his Companions had pledged to observe their day fasting and their nights praying perpetually, and to abstain completely from meat and every kind of rich diet and avoid all contact with their wives. At this, the Prophet of God (*pbuh*) went up into the pulpit and delivered a sermon in which he unequivocally declared:

> 'I have not been enjoined such things. Your own self has a right upon you. Observe fast and also enjoy food and drink. Do pray at night, but also go to bed. Look at me. I sleep as well as stand awake in Prayer. I keep fast and also don't keep. I take meat and butter oil too. Whosoever is averse to my life-style, is, therefore, not my follower.'

Sayyidunā Rasūl Allah then added:

> 'What has gone wrong to some people? Why have they banned upon themselves women, perfume, good food, sleep at night and other blessings of this world. I have never instructed you to become a hermit or a monk. In my Religion there is neither any abstinence from women or meat, nor any seclusion and living the life of a recluse. We have to fast for self-restraint. All the benefits of a stoic life are available to us from *Jihād*. Worship the One and Only God and assign no partner unto Him. Perform *Ḥajj* and *'Umrah*; establish the order of *Ṣalāh* and *Zakāh*; and observe the *Ṣawm* of Ramaḍān. Those destroyed before you were put to their sad end due to that kind of intemperance. When they became hard on themselves, Allah also subjected them to hardship. Those found in monasteries and hermitages are the remnants of those very people.'

It is narrated in the same context that, when the Holy Prophet (*pbuh*) came to know that one of his Companions was keeping away from his wife and remained busy praying day and night, he called for him and ordered him to go at once to his wife. On his submission that he was fasting, the Holy Prophet instructed him to break his fast and do as directed.

During the reign of the Second Caliph Ḥaḍrat 'Umar, may Allah be pleased with him, a woman complained that her husband spent his day fasting and his night praying. The Caliph referred her case to the Court of the eminent Jurist

Ka'b bin Sawr al-Azdī, who decreed that the husband of that lady could use only three nights for prayers, but the fourth night as a matter of right belonged to his wife, which he must keep spare for her.

The transgression of the 'bounds of right', to which the above *Āyāt* refer, has a broader connotation. To ban oneself of the things declared lawful by the Lord as though they were *Ḥarām* is one kind of transgression, while another kind is extravagance and intemperance in the use of *Ḥalāl* things. The third category of transgression is to cross the boundaries of the *Ḥalāl* to make use of the *Ḥarām*. Allah *subḥānahū wa ta'ālā* has disapproved all of these three categories of transgression.

6.5. Principles of moderation and balance

وَالَّذِينَ إِذَا أَنفَقُوا لَمْ يُسْرِفُوا وَلَمْ يَقْتُرُوا وَكَانَ بَيْنَ ذَٰلِكَ قَوَامًا ﴿٦٧﴾ وَالَّذِينَ لَا يَدْعُونَ مَعَ اللَّهِ إِلَٰهًا آخَرَ وَلَا يَقْتُلُونَ
النَّفْسَ الَّتِي حَرَّمَ اللَّهُ إِلَّا بِالْحَقِّ وَلَا يَزْنُونَ وَمَن يَفْعَلْ ذَٰلِكَ يَلْقَ أَثَامًا ﴿٦٨﴾ يُضَاعَفْ لَهُ الْعَذَابُ يَوْمَ الْقِيَامَةِ
وَيَخْلُدْ فِيهِ مُهَانًا ﴿٦٩﴾

('The true servants of the Merciful One are) those who are neither extravagant nor niggardly in their spending but keep the golden mean between the two; who invoke no other deity along with Allah, nor take any life – which Allah has forbidden – save justly; who do not commit unlawful sexual intercourse – and whoso does that shall meet its penalty; his torment shall be doubled for him on the Day of Resurrection, and he will abide in it in ignominy.')

(*al-Furqān*, 25: 67–69)

Instructing us in the traits of balance and moderation, these *Āyāt* tell us that the servants of the Most Merciful Lord are those who follow the path of righteousness and the love of God and His subjects, and who avoid extremes. When they spend they are neither extravagant nor niggardly, but keep a proper balance. In our context particularly, this means that true Believers are not supposed to squander away their hard-earned income on pomp and show, luxuries, costly wedding ceremonies, alcoholic drinks, gambling and other forbidden pastimes, or on living beyond our means. Nor are we expected to live like a worshipper of wealth, avoiding even rightful expenditure on ourselves, our family, our kith and kin and those who deserve our help. The Arabia of the Holy Prophet's time had both of these categories of people: those who indulged in personal aggrandizement, pomp and show and liked to be known as the most generous of their tribe; and those who were notorious for their miserliness. It was hard to find people of a balanced mindset. Between the two extremes, the small group of believers led by *Sayyidinā* Rasūl Allāh (*pbuh*) stood out as the only example of moderation and virtue.

It is pertinent here to underscore what Islam means by the terms *Isrāf* (intemperance) and *Bukhl* (miserliness). *Isrāf* stands for the following three traits:

- spending money on unlawful deeds, even if the amount spent is only a penny;
- crossing the boundaries of good sense and balance when spending on one's legitimate needs, either by going beyond one's means or by consuming his riches on personal aggrandizement and luxuries; and
- spending generously in acts of charity purely for personal fame and to show off, and not sincerely for Allah's Pleasure.

Bukhl, on the other hand, implies the following two facets: (i) a person's reluctance to spend in proportion to his ability and status on the legitimate needs of himself, his family and his children; and (ii) stinginess in spending out of his pocket on the causes of public good.

Islam's path runs midway between these two extremes. It is the path of moderation and balance. What the Holy Prophet (*pbuh*) has said in this respect must always be our motto as the golden principle to guide our economic life:

مِن فِقهِ الرَّجُلِ قَصدُه فِى مَعِيشَتِه

('Among the signs of one's prudence is his moderation in his style of living.')

(Narrated by Imām Aḥmad and Ṭabarānī from Abū al-Dardā')

6.6. Economic honesty and justice

...قَالَ يَـٰقَوْمِ ٱعْبُدُوا۟ ٱللَّهَ مَا لَكُم مِّنْ إِلَـٰهٍ غَيْرُهُۥ ۖ قَدْ جَآءَتْكُم بَيِّنَةٌ مِّن رَّبِّكُمْ ۖ فَأَوْفُوا۟ ٱلْكَيْلَ وَٱلْمِيزَانَ
وَلَا تَبْخَسُوا۟ ٱلنَّاسَ أَشْيَآءَهُمْ وَلَا تُفْسِدُوا۟ فِى ٱلْأَرْضِ بَعْدَ إِصْلَـٰحِهَا ۚ ذَٰلِكُمْ خَيْرٌ لَّكُمْ إِن كُنتُم مُّؤْمِنِينَ ﴿٨٥﴾

('He [Shu'ayb] exhorted them: "O my people! Serve Allah, you have no god other than He. Indeed a clear proof has come to you from your Lord. So give just weight and measure and diminish not to people their things, and make no mischief on the earth after it has been set in good order. That is to your own good, if you do truly believe".')

(*al-A'rāf*, 7: 85)

وَقَالَ ٱلْمَلَأُ ٱلَّذِينَ كَفَرُوا۟ مِن قَوْمِهِۦ لَئِنِ ٱتَّبَعْتُمْ شُعَيْبًا إِنَّكُمْ إِذًا لَّخَـٰسِرُونَ ۝

('The disbelieving elders of his nation said: 'Should you follow Shu'ayb you will be utter losers'.')

(*al-A'rāf*, 7: 90)

According to the first of these *Āyāt*, the Prophet Shu'ayb's people suffered from two major vices: polytheism and dishonesty and fraud in business and trade. Prophet Shu'ayb was sent to his people to reform them of these vices. The response of the elite class to the Prophet's exhortations merits a careful study. What the leaders and notables of Midyan sought to convey and impress upon the people was that the qualities of honesty and righteousness and the eternal virtue of good conduct, which Prophet Shu'ayb would like them to observe in their social and economic lives, actually sounded the death-knell for them and their society. They audaciously countered the Prophet with questions: 'How can we conduct our trade if we sincerely and honestly observe the rules being preached by you?' 'As a nation sitting astride the confluence of the world's two major trade-routes and serving as a link between the two dominant civilizations of the day, the Egyptian and the Mesopotamian, how can we prevent ourselves from benefiting from this envious position and let the trade caravans pass in peace?' 'If we forego this privilege, how can we draw on the advantages of our geographic location and what would then happen to the economic and political gains now accruing to us?' 'Wouldn't our righteous conduct deprive us not only of our economic ascendancy, but also weaken our clout politically among the neighbouring peoples?' Such arguments, which apparently sound quite logical and convincing, were not specific to the people of Prophet Shu'ayb alone. In fact they reflect a familiar approach for deluded people throughout human history. Wrongdoers have always discovered similar setbacks and losses in righteous conduct. They have always been of the view that political and economic activities cannot run effectively without recourse to lies, dishonesty and other misconduct. Among the arguments advanced everywhere at all times to counter the eternal mission of truth and righteousness (Islam), the most familiar has always been: 'Deviation from the worldly ways that rule the roost in favour of an honest and righteous approach will be contrary to the supreme interest of the nation and the state!'

6.7. Distributive justice

The golden rule of distributive justice Islam has given to humanity is explained succinctly in the following verse of the Holy Qur'ān:

مَّآ أَفَآءَ ٱللَّهُ عَلَىٰ رَسُولِهِۦ مِنْ أَهْلِ ٱلْقُرَىٰ فَلِلَّهِ وَلِلرَّسُولِ وَلِذِى ٱلْقُرْبَىٰ وَٱلْيَتَـٰمَىٰ وَٱلْمَسَـٰكِينِ وَٱبْنِ ٱلسَّبِيلِ كَىْ
لَا يَكُونَ دُولَةًۢ بَيْنَ ٱلْأَغْنِيَآءِ مِنكُمْ ۚ وَمَآ ءَاتَىٰكُمُ ٱلرَّسُولُ فَخُذُوهُ وَمَا نَهَىٰكُمْ عَنْهُ فَٱنتَهُوا۟ ۚ وَٱتَّقُوا۟ ٱللَّهَ ۖ إِنَّ ٱللَّهَ
شَدِيدُ ٱلْعِقَابِ ﴿٧﴾

('Whatever (from the possessions of the towns' people) Allah has bestowed on His Messenger belongs to Allah, and to the Messenger, and to his kinsfolk, and to the orphans, and to the needy, and to the wayfarer so that it may not merely circulate between the rich among you. So accept whatever the Messenger gives you, and refrain from whatever he forbids you. And fear Allah: verily Allah is Most Stern in retribution.')

(*al-Ḥashr*, 59: 7)

This is one of the most important verses, containing guiding principles for an Islamic social order and the economic policy of an Islamic government. According to the financial rule of Islam, wealth should be free to circulate within the entire social fabric of the Muslim society. Islam does not approve clogging of this lifeblood in the arteries of the society due to accumulation of wealth within few hands. The basic consideration behind this injunction is to prevent the rich from growing richer and the poor poorer. This golden principle has been enunciated not just as a policy matter, but ground rules have also been laid down for its implementation.

In this context, Islam has forbidden all forms of interest and interest-based transactions; *Zakāh* has been made mandatory on wealth exceeding a prescribed limit; *Khums* has been levied on war gains; and ʿ*Ushr* on agricultural produce. In addition to these mandatory levies, Islam has repeatedly encouraged the well-off of the Muslim society to generously contribute in voluntary charities. Different forms of expiatory gifts have been prescribed as penance for lapses committed in performance of religious duties.

The guiding principle behind these injunctions is to divert the flow of wealth to the poorer sections of the society. The Islamic Law of Inheritance is also based on the same principle, i.e. to avoid concentration of wealth within few hands and let it flow to a wider circle.

Islam has similarly disapproved stinginess as an unethical trend and declared generosity as one of the best personal traits of a believer. It has impressed upon the affluent segment of the society to keep in mind the essential Islamic principle that the less affluent and deprived lot has a right in their riches, which they have to return to them not as a matter of charity, but as if they owed that amount to the deserving.

According to the law concerning public funds that form the largest part of the Islamic government's revenue, the government is under obligation to spend its major portion on the welfare and support of the less affluent people. It must also be kept in mind that the main source of income of an Islamic government are (i) *Zakāh;* and (ii) *Fay',* which is based on the revenue generated from different sources including *Jizyah* (capital tax, levied on non-Muslim subjects in return for the Islamic state's guarantee of protection for their life, property and honour – nominal in terms of money and much less than *Zakāh* mandatory for the Muslim subjects) and *Kharāj* (land tax), much less than the amount deducted as *Khums* and *'Ushr* from the Muslim subjects. The poor has the largest share of this revenue generated as public funds. This fundamental Islamic principle remains the mainstay of the economic policy of Islam: that the state is bound to frame its policies in such a manner that the wealth has a wider circulation and does not concentrate within the hands of a few privileged ones; the state resources must not be allowed to be monopolized by the rich; and the flow of wealth must invariably be from the rich to the poor and not vice versa.

According to the [illegible] accounts, the [illegible] funds [illegible] separation [illegible] the Islamic government [illegible] its major [illegible] support to the [illegible] quality [illegible] the [illegible] that [illegible] government [illegible] (1) Zakat [illegible] organised [illegible] different sources [illegible] and [illegible] for the Islamic state [illegible] and [illegible] common [illegible] and much [illegible] than Zakat [illegible] therefore [illegible] the Muslim [illegible] and [illegible] as [illegible] from the Muslims [illegible] the [illegible] taxes [illegible] share of [illegible] public funds [illegible] fundamental Islamic principle [illegible] that the state [illegible] the [illegible] shall [illegible] not be [illegible] by the [illegible] wealthiest [illegible] from the [illegible] and vice versa.

PART TWO

THE ECONOMIC SYSTEM OF ISLAM: SOME BASIC FEATURES

7 The Question of Land Ownership

[The question of land ownership is one of the most serious issues of our times. It has been the subject of so much discussions and debate that the actual issue has become buried under the debris of conflicting opinions, making it difficult to review the matter dispassionately from a correct perspective. There are those who vehemently support the capitalist form of private ownership, and those on the opposite extreme championing a communist-style state ownership. The latter straightaway label anybody that speaks in favour of an individual's right to own land as an agent of feudalists and capitalists. Those opposed to the existing feudal system and the curse of landlordism are unfortunately not even ready even to think of any alternative other than the communist recipe of public ownership. Due to this confused state of affairs, it has become extremely difficult today to understand the concept of private ownership in Islam properly. The author has contributed a great deal on the subject and we have attempted in the ensuing pages to present some significant excerpts from his writings. These have been rearranged so as to explain a correct perspective about the Islamic economic system succinctly. The Islamic concept of ownership needs to be examined against the backdrop of the Islamic social order and economy alone, and not in context of any other system.

Another basic fact which needs to be borne in mind here is that the institution of private ownership is much older than the capitalist system. Certainly it has been exploited by the capitalists, who have given it a particular shape. The perversion of this institution has mainly been possible due to the very character, aims and objectives, as well as the institutional malaise, of private ownership. While examining the issue, we must therefore avoid falling into the trap of either the communists or the capitalists, who have both distorted the actual issue and damaged it beyond recognition. – Editor.]

7.1. The Holy Qur'ān and the question of private ownership*

Let me first recall to your mind the universal rule that the law's reticence about a common occurrence always implies its consent and approval. For example, if

* Adapted from the author's book 'The Question of Land-Holdings' (*Mas'alah-i-Milkī-yat-i-Zamīn*). – Editor.

a place is being used by the people as a thoroughfare and the authorities have not notified the public of any issue concerning this, it would mean that there is no restriction on the use of that place as a thoroughfare. No formal permission is needed to reaffirm this position because the absence of a restriction is in itself an implied permission. The question of land ownership is of the same nature. People have owned land since time immemorial. The Qur'ān did not forbid this ownership, issue a decree to check this practice, promulgate a law to replace the existing situation or even make a critical reference to this common practice. This would obviously indicate that Allah *subḥānahū wa taʿālā* has accorded His consent to the practice of people owning land. The Muslims have therefore followed the age-old tradition of acquiring property in the same way it was done in ancient times. If somebody holds a different view and considers private ownership impermissible, the burden of proof will naturally fall on him and he will be required to justify and prove his standpoint.

However, the matter does not rest here. The Qur'ān has not only allowed private ownership to continue, it has also approved it by inference and thus we see relevant rules and regulations governing our social life and economy in this context.

Man essentially needs land for two purposes: agricultural and residential. The Book of God acknowledges the right to own land for both of these. The Lord says in *Sūrah al-Anʿām*:

... كُلُواْ مِن ثَمَرِهِۦٓ إِذَآ أَثۡمَرَ وَءَاتُواْ حَقَّهُۥ يَوۡمَ حَصَادِهِۦ ... ﴿١٤١﴾

('Eat of their fruit when they come to fruition and pay His due on the day of harvesting.')

(*al-Anʿām*, 6: 141)

The injunction to 'pay His due' refers to the 'due' of the Lord, Who enabled us to own land and put it to proper use. This 'due' is to be paid in the form of *Zakāh* and *Ṣadaqāt*. To pay and receive *Zakāh* obviously cannot be possible unless someone owns the land and others do not. The above directive could not have been issued in the case of land being state-owned. The owner of land is therefore ordered here to make the best use of the land in his possession and at the same time not forget paying to the poor from that part of its produce which belongs to the Lord. This Qur'ānic injunction has thus ratified the age-old practice of the private ownership of land. This is further supported by yet another *Āyah*:

يَٰٓأَيُّهَا ٱلَّذِينَ ءَامَنُوٓاْ أَنفِقُواْ مِن طَيِّبَٰتِ مَا كَسَبْتُمْ وَمِمَّآ أَخْرَجْنَا لَكُم مِّنَ ٱلْأَرْضِ ... ﴿٢٦٧﴾

('Believers! Spend (in the Way of Allah) out of the good things you have earned and out of what We have produced for you from the earth.')

(*al-Baqarah*, 2: 267)

According to the unanimous view of the jurists, the injunction about spending in the Way of Allah out of the good things earned from the land concerns *Zakāh* and *Ṣadaqāt*. Unless one owns land, he cannot carry out the command and nobody can give or receive charity unless he owns property and other means of living. The Qur'ān, therefore, guides us also with respect to those who are eligible to receive *Zakāh* and *Ṣadaqāt*:

لِلْفُقَرَآءِ ٱلَّذِينَ أُحْصِرُواْ فِى سَبِيلِ ٱللَّهِ لَا يَسْتَطِيعُونَ ضَرْبًا فِى ٱلْأَرْضِ ... ﴿٢٧٣﴾

('Those needy ones who are wholly wrapped up in the cause of Allah, and who are hindered from moving about the earth in search of their livelihood, especially deserve help.')

(*al-Baqarah*, 2: 273)

إِنَّمَا ٱلصَّدَقَٰتُ لِلْفُقَرَآءِ وَٱلْمَسَٰكِينِ وَٱلْعَٰمِلِينَ عَلَيْهَا وَٱلْمُؤَلَّفَةِ قُلُوبُهُمْ وَفِى ٱلرِّقَابِ وَٱلْغَٰرِمِينَ وَفِى سَبِيلِ
ٱللَّهِ وَٱبْنِ ٱلسَّبِيلِ فَرِيضَةً مِّنَ ٱللَّهِ وَٱللَّهُ عَلِيمٌ حَكِيمٌ ﴿٦٠﴾

('The alms are meant only for the poor and the needy and those who are in charge thereof, those whose hearts are to be reconciled, and to free those in bondage, and to help those burdened with debt, and for expenditure in the Way of Allah and for the wayfarer. This is an obligation from Allah. Allah is All-Knowing, All-Wise.')

(*al-Tawbah*, 9: 60)

As for the second purpose for which one needs land, the Lord says:

يَٰٓأَيُّهَا ٱلَّذِينَ ءَامَنُواْ لَا تَدْخُلُواْ بُيُوتًا غَيْرَ بُيُوتِكُمْ حَتَّىٰ تَسْتَأْنِسُواْ وَتُسَلِّمُواْ عَلَىٰٓ أَهْلِهَا ذَٰلِكُمْ خَيْرٌ لَّكُمْ
لَعَلَّكُمْ تَذَكَّرُونَ ﴿٢٧﴾ فَإِن لَّمْ تَجِدُواْ فِيهَآ أَحَدًا فَلَا تَدْخُلُوهَا حَتَّىٰ يُؤْذَنَ لَكُمْ ... ﴿٢٨﴾

('Believers! Enter not houses other than your own houses until you have obtained the permission of the inmates of those houses and have greeted them with peace. This is better for you. It is expected that you will observe this. Then if you find no one in them, do not enter until you have been given permission (to enter) ...')

(*al-Nūr*, 24: 27 and 28)

These *Āyāt* affirm the right of ownership and possession of land by individuals for residential purposes as well. They also affirm the owner's right of privacy, and trespassing of his premises by an outsider is therefore disapproved of.

Let us now turn to the Prophetic Tradition and the precedents of his Rightly-Guided Caliphs (*al-Khulafā' al-Rāshidūn*). When we carefully study the sayings of the Holy Prophet (*pbuh*) and the practices followed during his golden era and that of his illustrious successors, we come to the same conclusion – that the *Sharīʿah* not only approves an individual's right to own land, but it also never imposes a limit on that ownership.[1] In addition, the owner of the land is authorized to let his land on lease or rent for farming in the event that he is unable to till the land himself.

7.2. Precedents of the Holy Prophet and his Caliphs

In order to understand how the Holy Prophet (*pbuh*) and his illustrious successors, the four Caliphs, managed the land, we must keep in mind that, according to the Islamic *Sharīʿah*, any land that falls under the state's jurisdiction is divided into the following four broad categories:

- land belonging to those who embraced Islam;
- land owned by unbelievers, living as citizens of the Islamic State;
- land owned by those subdued into submission by force; and
- land belonging to nobody.

Let us now discuss precedents from the Holy Prophet and four Caliphs in respect of each one of these four categories.

7.2.1. *First category of land*

The Prophet of God (*pbuh*) observed the following principle in respect of the first category of land:

---

[1] It may be noted that this is the general rule. But in exceptional circumstances, the Islamic government can impose some restrictions in the interests of justice and the rights of God and His subjects. Details of this are available in books of Islamic jurisprudence. Similarly, if the need arises, a particular industry or land can also be nationalized through proper legal proceedings. The state's overall system will have to be developed and organized, however, on the basis of private enterprise. As far as I have studied the issue in the light of the Islamic Law and jurisprudence, I can clearly state that Islam does not adopt a program of nationalization of the means of production as a matter of principle. This is contrary to the very social order that Islam seeks to establish. From an Islamic perspective, it is not a right solution to a country's economic problems to nationalize the entire means of production. However, if experience shows that a certain industrial unit or commercial enterprise cannot be developed and sustained in private custody, it can then be taken over by the state in the public interest. – Author.

إِنَّ القَومَ إِذَا أَسلَمُوا أَحرَزُوا دِمآءَهُم وَ أَموَالَـهُم

('When the people embrace Islam, they make their blood and property secure.')

(*Kitāb al-Kharāj*)

إِنَّهُ مَن أَسلَمَ عَلى شَيءٍ فَهُوَلَهُ

('What a person owns when embracing Islam will remain his property.')

(*Kitāb al-Amwāl*)

This rule was applied to both movable and immovable property, and to agricultural as well as non-agricultural lands. The entire treasure-house of the Prophetic Traditions and the precedents of his illustrious successors bear witness to the fact that the Islamic State of Arabia left the property that belonged to those who entered the portals of Islam untouched. Whatever one owned as an unbeliever continued to be owned as a Muslim. Imām Abū Yūsuf explained this *Sharī'ah* precedent as follows:

> 'Those who embrace Islam, their blood becomes sacrosanct. Whatever they own by way of wealth while embracing Islam will remain theirs. Similarly, their land will continue to be their property, with *'Ushr* (one tenth of the value of its produce payable on them as in case of agricultural land of other Muslims). The precedent in this is the example of Madinah, where inhabitants embraced Islam at the hands of the Holy Prophet (*pbuh*) and remained owners of their lands and *'Ushr* was levied on them. The same precedent was followed with the people of Ṭā'if and Bahrain. The Badawīs (Bedouins, or desert dwellers) were also treated similarly and were recognized as owners of their lands, oases and natural springs as they embraced Islam ... *'Ushr* was levied on their lands from which they were not evicted. They enjoyed the rights of sale, purchase and inheritance on these. In line with the same precedent, wherever the people embrace Islam, they will continue enjoying proprietary rights of what they own.'
>
> (*Kitāb al-Kharāj*, p.35)

Another eminent scholar of Islam's economic system, Imām Abū 'Ubayd al-Qāsim bin Sallām, observed:

> 'The tradition coming down to us from the Holy Prophet and his Caliphs offers us three categories of injunctions. The first relates to those lands

whose owners embraced Islam. They remained owners of the lands in their possession and no tax other than *'Ushr* was levied on them.'

(Abū 'Ubayd, *Kitāb al-Amwāl*, p.55)

Abū 'Ubayd further said: 'Those who embraced Islam remained owners of their lands, as in Madinah, Ṭā'if, Yemen and Bahrain. In case of Makkah as well, which was conquered militarily, the Holy Prophet (*pbuh*) obliged the Makkans and graciously spared them their lives and property ... When they embraced Islam, they were allowed to keep their lands in their possession and pay *'Ushr* on them.'

(*Kitāb al-Amwāl*, p.512)

'Allāmah Ibn al-Qayyim wrote in his compendium, *Zād al-Ma'ād*:

'It was the practice of the Holy Prophet (*pbuh*) to leave in custody whatever one possessed when he embraced Islam. He was not checked about its ownership prior to Islam and was allowed to retain it in his possession as before.'

(*Zād al-Ma'ād*, vol.II, p.96)

This is thus a general rule, and no exception can be found in the established practice and precedents of the golden era of the Holy Prophet and his *al-Khulafā' al-Rāshidūn*. The reforms that were introduced by Islam into the economic life of its followers were for the future, but it left what they already possessed untouched.

7.2.2. *Second category of land*

The second category of land involved that which belonged to those who remained unbelievers, but willingly chose to live as citizens of the Islamic State. The rule enunciated by the Holy Prophet (*pbuh*) for these people was that the State should follow in letter and spirit the terms and conditions of any agreements made with them. *Sayyidinā* Rasūl Allāh said:

'The people engaged with you in war may approach you later seeking amnesty for themselves and their families, in return for their property (which they may offer as ransom) and then you arrive at peace agreement with them. In such a situation you are to demand from them nothing else over and above the agreed terms, because anything in addition to that is not lawful.'

(Abū Dāwūd and Ibn Mājah)

> 'Beware! Anybody, who did wrong to a *Dhimmī*,[2] curtailed his rights guaranteed to him by the state, forced him to bear a burden beyond his capacity or took away from him anything without his consent, I would be his Plaintiff on the Day of Judgement.'
>
> (Abū Dāwūd)

It was on the basis of this rule that the Holy Prophet (*pbuh*) allowed the non-Muslims in Najrān, Aylah, Azru'āt, Hijr and other places, as well as those tribes with whom he entered into peace treaties, to retain their land holdings, properties, industries, businesses and trade. They were required as per their agreement to pay only *Jizyah* (capital tax) and *Kharāj* (land tax). The same practice was followed by *al-Khulafā' al-Rāshidūn*. In Iraq, Shām (Levant), al-Jazīrah, Egypt and Armenia, the towns and settlements that followed the path of peace and surrendered themselves to the Islamic Caliphate were allowed to retain control of whatever they possessed, except for the tax which they had to pay according to the peace deal. During the glorious reign of the second Caliph Ḥaḍrat 'Umar, when the people of Najrān had to be moved to Shām and Iraq in the interests of the state, they were offered the same amount of residential and farmland in their new settlements as they had possessed at Najrān. The Governors of Shām and Iraq were issued with decrees making it binding on them to 'generously provide them (over and above their rightful claims) from the available state lands' (*Kitāb al-Amwāl*, Abū 'Ubayd, p.189).

There was no exception to this rule, either during the era of the Holy Prophet or during the reigns of his illustrious successors. As such, it remains a legal precedent unanimously agreed upon by eminent Muslim jurists. Imām Abū Yūsuf discusses this as an act of law in his book *Kitāb al-Kharāj*. He says:

> 'Those among the non-Muslims with whom a peace treaty has been signed by the Islamic government making it incumbent upon them to be lawful subjects of the state and pay land tax, they are under the state covenant (*Ahl al-Dhimmah*). Their land belongs to the category on which the state collects *Kharāj* (land tax). They would pay only that much which they have pledged to do under the peace deal and the state would honour its commitment to them, without imposing on them anything extra.'
>
> (*Kitāb al-Kharāj*, p.35).

[2] *Dhimmī* was a non-Muslim subject of the Islamic state who was under the state covenant (*Ahl al-Dhimmah*) and enjoyed full protection and safety in return for paying a token capital tax called *Jizyah*, which was much less than the mandatory charity of *Zakāh* that was levied on Muslim subjects. – Translator.

7.2.3. *Third category of land*
For those who continued fighting the Islamic forces until they were vanquished and subdued into submission, there are three different precedents concerning their property during the era of the Holy Prophet and *al-Khulafā' al-Rāshidūn.*

The first example that has come down to us is the unprecedentedly magnanimous declaration of the Holy Prophet following his bloodless conquest of the pagan state of Makkah: لَا تَثْرِيبَ عَلَيْكُمُ الْيَوْمَ ('No blame lies with you today'). This was a glad tiding for the blood-thirsty Makkans, that they could receive a general amnesty. As a result, they remained the owners of their lands and property and, as they eventually embraced Islam, '*Ushr* was levied on their agricultural land.

The second precedent concerns the Prophet of Islam's actions at Khayber. There he declared that the conquered land was a part of the war-gains. The erstwhile owners therefore had to forego their ownership rights to it. A part of this was taken into the public treasury as belonging to Allah and His Apostle, and the remaining portion was distributed among the soldiers who took part in the expedition. They were notified that they were the owners of the land that came into their possession and '*Ushr* was levied on that. (*Kitāb al-Amwāl*, Abū 'Ubayd, p.513).

The third case in point concerns the stand that was initially taken by Ḥaḍrat 'Umar in Shām and Iraq, and subsequently in other conquered territories. Instead of distributing the land of the conquered territories among members of the fighting force, he declared it to be a common property of the Muslims, with their Caliph as the custodian to administer it on their behalf. He left these lands in possession of their original owners who were proclaimed as *Dhimmīs*, or free subjects, who enjoyed the Islamic State's protection in return for the nominal tax they had to pay to claim this right. *Jizyah* (capital tax) and *Kharāj* (land tax) were levied on these lands. The tax revenue thus collected was spent on the welfare of the Muslim public, as they were the actual owners of the conquered land according to the concepts of war and peace in Islam.

There is some semblance of the socialist approach to public ownership in this last precedent. When seen in its correct perspective, however, it becomes evident that there is no relation to the socialist concept. The actual position is that, when the vast territories of Egypt, Shām and Iraq came under Islamic control, a few of the Companions of the Holy Prophet demanded that Ḥaḍrat 'Umar distribute the lands and properties of the conquered territories among the fighting forces, as had been done in Khaybar. Ḥaḍrat 'Umar declined to do this, and his stand was supported by eminent and senior Companions of the Holy Prophet such as Ḥaḍrat 'Alī, Ḥaḍrat 'Uthmān, Ḥaḍrat Ṭalḥa and Ḥaḍrat Mu'ādh bin Jabal, may

Allah be pleased with them all. The speeches made on this occasion throw some light on the *raison d'être* for this revolutionary approach.

> Ḥaḍrat Mu ʿādh said: 'If you distribute the land as war gains, its consequences by God would be such as you may never like. Big chunks of fertile land would get divided among the fighting forces. When they expire, some of these might be inherited by a woman or a child. Then, the govt will have nothing to offer to those who succeed them to defend the frontiers of Islam. Therefore, do something which may leave room for the present lot as well as for those who would follow them in future.'
>
> Ḥaḍrat ʿAlī observed: 'Please leave the farmers' community of the land as they are so that they may become the means of economic strength for the Muslims.'
>
> Ḥaḍrat ʿUmar declared: 'How is it possible that I distribute the land amongst you and leave nothing for your successors to get as their due … After all, what would then be left for the future generations? … Would you like those succeeding you in future to get nothing? … I am also afraid that if the land is distributed, you may start quarrelling amongst yourselves over water.'

On the basis of this informed debate and mutual consultations, it was unanimously decided to leave the land in possession of its original owners; as *Dhimmīs* they should pay the tax, while the revenue thus generated should be spent on schemes of public welfare. The historic decree conveying this decision by *Amīr al-Mu'minīn* ʿUmar to his Governor in Iraq, Sa ʿd bin Abī Waqqāṣ, read:

> فَانظُر مَاأَجلَبُوا بِهِ عَلَيكَ فِى العَسكَر من كرُاعٍ أَو مالٍ فَأَقْسِمهُ بَينَ مَن حَضَرَ مِنَ المُسلِمِينَ. وَاترُكِ الأَرضِينَ وَالأَنهَارَ لِعُمَّالِهَا لِيَكُونَ ذٰلِكَ فِى أُعطِيَاتِ المُسلِمِين. فَإِنَّا إِن قَسَمنَاهَا بَينَ مَن حَضَرَ لَم يَكُن لِمَن بَعدَهُم شَئٌ
>
> ('Whatever movable property the soldiers of Islam have acquired as war gains and deposited it in the camp, should be distributed among them. But let the immovable property, the lands and rivers, remain with those who are engaged with these, so that the revenue generated from them may serve to cover the welfare needs of the Muslims. That is because if we distribute these amongst those present, nothing would be left for those to follow in future.') [3]

---

[3] For greater details of this debate, please see Abū Dāwūd, *Kitāb al-Kharāj* (pp.20-21) and Abū ʿUbayd, *Kitāb al-Amwāl* (pp.57-63). – Author.

The basic idea governing the new dispensation was as discussed; i.e. the conquered lands belonged to the Muslims and their erstwhile owners became farmers, while the government has to take control as an agent and the legal authority representing the people.[4] Practically, however, the rights that were granted to the *Dhimmīs* were in no way different from ownership rights. They continued to occupy the lands they had in their possession with only a small amount of land tax (*Kharāj*) required of them to pay. They enjoyed every right of sale, mortgage and inheritance on the property in their possession, as before. Imām Abū Yūsuf explains this as an act of law as follows:

> 'The Muslim ruler is authorized to distribute among the soldiers the land coming under his jurisdiction as a result of the victory in a decisive battle. This land would then be treated as *'Ushri* (with its new owners paying *'Ushr*). If the ruler, however, does not deem it fit to distribute the land among soldiers and decides in favour of allowing its erstwhile occupants to retain it in their possession, as was done by Ḥaḍrat 'Umar in Iraq, the land would then become *Kharājī*. The ruler cannot then take it back from them once they start paying *Kharāj*. They would be treated as its de facto owners, eligible to transfer it to their descendants in inheritance and also for its sale and purchase.'
>
> (*Kitāb al-Kharāj*, pp.35-36)

7.2.4. *Fourth category of land*

The three categories of lands discussed above involved those which were already in possession of different people, and the previous ownership was either ratified by the Islamic state or there was a slight reshuffling due to the change of hands, without changing the system of ownership itself. Let us now examine the case of lands owned by nobody and the precedent of the Holy Prophet (*pbuh*) and his illustrious Caliphs in that respect.

This category of land, in possession of the state, consisted of two major classifications:

- The *Mawāt* or wasteland, with no owners or whose owner had died a long time ago, and also land inundated by floods or rendered useless by wild growth or swamps.

[4] This concept is further explained by the following incident. 'Utbah bin Farqad once came to see Ḥaḍrat 'Umar and informed him that he had purchased a piece of land on the banks of the Euphrates. Amīr al-Mu'minīn 'Umar asked him, whom he had bought it from? He replied, from its owners. The Second Caliph retorted, pointing his fingers to the *Muhājirīn* and *Anṣār*: 'Its owners are sitting right here.' (*Kitāb al-Amwāl*, p.74).

- The *Khāliṣah* or land declared as state property. This includes the following types of lands: (i) those abandoned by their owners authorizing the government to put them to use as deemed fit;[5] (ii) lands annexed by the Islamic State as a punishment for their owners' anti-state activities and intrigues against its security, as was done with the lands of the treacherous Jewish tribe of *Banī Naḍīr* on the outskirts of Madinah; and (iii) lands declared *Khāliṣah* (state property) in a conquered territory, such as the lands belonging to Kisrā (Khosrau) and his family members in Iraq, and enemy lands whose owners were killed in battle or who fled to some other country.

Let us now discuss the rules applied to these two types of lands in greater detail: *Mawāt* and *Khāliṣah.*

7.3. Ownership right on the basis of settlement

The Holy Prophet (*pbuh*) revived and regulated the oldest human practice of *Mawāt* (wasteland occupied by nobody). As mankind started settling on the earth, the rule followed was to occupy the piece of land he needed for himself and family. This was harnessed for cultivation and other uses and was treated as belonging to him as a matter of right. This practice provided the basis for humankind's ownership right on the bounties of nature. As a matter of principle, it was thus established that whoever rehabilitated a piece of land that belonged to nobody was its rightful owner. This same rule was ratified by the sayings of the Holy Prophet. Some Prophetic Traditions in this context are quoted below:

عَن عَائِشَةٍ عَنِ النَّبِیّ صَلَّی اللهُ عَلَیهِ وَسَلَّم قَالَ: مَن عَمَّرَ اَرضاً لَیسَت لِاَحَدٍ فَهُوَ
احَقُّ بِهَا قَالَ :عُروةُ قَضَیٰ بِه عُمَرُ فِی خِلاَفَتِه

('Sayyidah 'Ā'ishah, may Allah be pleased with her, that the Holy Prophet, (*pbuh*), said: "He who rehabilitates the land belonging to nobody, deserves it the most." 'Urwah bin Zubayr, nephew of *Sayyidah* 'Ā'ishah, was quoted as having added that Ḥaḍrat 'Umar acted according to the same principle during his reign as Caliph')

(Bukhārī, Aḥmad and Nasā'ī)

---

[5] As narrated by 'Abd Allāh bin 'Abbās, the Anṣār (followers of the Holy Prophet in Madīnah, who helped him and the emigrants from Makkah at the time of Hijrah) gave all their lands which remained unirrigated due to lack of water to the disposal of the Holy Prophet for use as he considered fit. (*Kitāb al-Amwāl,* p.282) – Author.

عَن جَابِرٍ اَنَّ النَّبِّیَ صَلَّی اللهُ عَلَیهِ وَسَلَّم، قَالَ : مَن اَحیىٰ اَرضاً مَیتَةً فَهِیَ لَه

(Jābir bin ʿAbdullāh that the Holy Prophet (*pbuh*) said: 'He who revives a dead piece of land, it is then his.')

(Aḥmad, Tirmidhī, Nasā'ī and Ibn Ḥibbān)

عَنْ سَمُرَه بِن جُندُب عَنِ النَّبِّیَ صَلَّی اللهُ عَلَیهِ وَ سَلَّم، قَالَ: مَنْ أَحَاطَ حَائِطاً عَلىٰ أَرْضٍ فَهِيَ لَه

(Samurah bin Jundub that the Holy Prophet (*pbuh*) said: 'He who erects a boundary wall round a piece of (unclaimed waste) land it would then be his.')

(Abū Dāwūd)

عَن اَسمَر بِن مُضَرَّسٍ عَنِ النَّبِّیَ صَلَّی اللهُ عَلَیهِ وَسَلَّم، قَالَ: مَن سَبَقَ اِلی مَاءٍ لَم یَسبِق اِلَیه مُسلِمٌ فَهُوَ لَه

(Asmar bin Muḍarras that the Holy Prophet (*pbuh*) said: 'He who discovers a well before anybody else from among his fellow Muslims it then belongs to him.')

(Abū Dāwūd)

عَن عُروَه قَالَ، اَشهَدُ اَنّ رَسُولَ الله صَلَّی اللهُ عَلَیهِ وَسَلَّم قَضىٰ اَنَّ الاَرضَ اَرضُ الله والعبادُ عبادُ الله، مَن اَحیىٰ مَواتاً فَهُوَ اَحَقُّ بِهَا. جَاءَ نا بهذا عَنِ النَّبى صَلىَّ اللهُ عَلَيهِ وَسَلَّم الّذِينَ جَاؤُا بِالصَّلوٰةِ عَنهُ

(ʿUrwah that he said: 'I bear witness to what the Holy Prophet (*pbuh*) decreed that the 'land belongs to God and His subjects belong to Him as well and he who revives a dead piece of land deserves it the most.' The decree has been quoted to me from the Holy Prophet (*pbuh*) by those very Companions of his through whom we have come to learn about *Ṣalāh*.')

(Abū Dāwūd)

While reviving and ratifying this natural legal right, the Holy Prophet (*pbuh*) also laid down the following two rules: (i) a person rehabilitating another's property would not be entitled by this act to claim ownership of it; and (ii) anybody who takes hold of a piece of unclaimed land and, in order to claim his right, erects a boundary-wall or draws a line round it without actually rehabilitating it and making the land productive, would lose his right of occupancy after three years. The first rule has been explained thus:

عَن سَعِيد بِن زَيدٍ قَالَ، قال رَسُولَ الله صَلَّى اللهُ عَلَيهِ و سَلَّم، مَن اَحيىٰ اَرضاً مَيتَةً فَهِىَ لَهُ وَ لَيسَ لِعِرقٍ ظَالِـمٍ حَقٌّ

(Sa'īd bin Zayd that the Prophet of God (*pbuh*) said: 'He who revives a dead land, it will belong to him. But rehabilitation of other's land unauthorized by a miscreant entitles him to no such title.')

(Aḥmad, Abū Dāwūd and Tirmidhī)

The following Traditions are the source of the second rule:

عَن طَاؤُس قَالَ، قال رَسُولَ الله صَلَّى اللهُ عَلَيهِ وَسَلَّم، عَادِىُّ الاَرضِ لله وَلِلرَّسُولِ ثُمَّ لَكُم مِن بَعد. فَمَن اَحيَا اَرضاً مَيتَةً فَهِىَ لَهُ وَلَيس لِـمُحتَجِرٍ حَقٌّ بَعد ثَلٰثِ سِنِين

(Ṭāwūs that the Prophet of God said: 'The unclaimed land belonging to nobody is for Allah and His Apostle and thereafter, for you. As for the desolate piece of land, it belongs to him who rehabilitates it. Nobody can, however, claim any right to the land kept idle by him for three years.')

(Abū Yūsuf narrates in his *Kitāb al-Kharāj*)

عَن سَالِمِ بِن عَبدِا لله بِن عُمَر اَنَّ عُمَر بِن الخَطَّاب قَالَ عَلَى الـمِنبَرِ، مَن اَحيَا اَرضاً مَيتَةً فَهِى لَهُ وَلَيسَ لَـمُحتَجِرٍ حَقٌّ بَعد ثَلٰث سِنِين وَذٰلِكَ اَنَّ رِجَالاً كَانُوا يَحتَجِرُونَ مِنَ ا لاَرضِ مَالاَ يَعمَلُون

(Sālim bin 'Abd Allāh bin 'Umar as saying that Ḥaḍrat 'Umar declared at the pulpit that 'whosoever revives a dead land it would become his. But nobody has the right over the unclaimed land after keeping it idle for three years.' The ruling was given as some people kept idle their acquired lands.)

(Imām Abū Yūsuf quotes in his *Kitāb al-Kharāj*)

Senior Muslim jurists unanimously support this view. They have, however, differed on the question of whether the mere act of rehabilitating unclaimed land entitles one to ownership, or whether this ownership has to be duly approved and authenticated by the state. Imām Abū Ḥanīfah considers the state's approval essential. Imām Abū Yūsuf, Imām Muḥammad, Imām Shāfi'ī and Imām Aḥmad bin Ḥanbal, however, are of the view that no government approval is necessary and that the person rehabilitating the land automatically becomes its owner on the basis of the right granted to him by Allah and His Apostle. The state's role begins when the case is moved to it for authentication, or in the event of a dispute for consolidation. Imām Mālik differentiates between land in the vicinity of a settled habitation and desolate lands in far-flung areas. He believes that the first category of land is exempt from the purview of the rule and should remain state property. As for the second category, this would automatically become the property of the person who rehabilitates it without any formal sanction by the government.

According to the established practice of Ḥaḍrat ʿUmar and the Caliph ʿUmar bin ʿAbd al-ʿAzīz, as recorded by Imām Abū Yūsuf *(Kitāb al-Kharāj)*, Abū ʿUbayd *(Kitāb al-Amwāl)* and Shaykh ʿAlī Muttaqī (*Kanz al-ʿUmmāl*), a person who can irrefutably confirm his ownership in respect of land which someone else rehabilitated, thinking it was desolate and unclaimed for, will be given the option either to reoccupy it after paying compensation to the one who rehabilitated it, or to transfer the land's proprietary right to that person by obtaining its cost from him.

7.4. Award of state land

The Holy Prophet (*pbuh*) had awarded the title of both the categories of lands to people – *Mawāt* (unclaimed desolate land) and *Khāliṣah* (state land). This same practice was then followed by *al-Khulafāʾ al-Rāshidūn*. Some of the precedents recorded in books of *Aḥādīth* (Prophetic Traditions) and history in this context are quoted below:

- Imām Aḥmad narrated in his *Musnad* from ʿUrwah bin Zubayr quoting ʿAbd al-Raḥmān bin ʿAwf that, 'the Holy Prophet (*pbuh*) awarded him and Ḥaḍrat ʿUmar titles of some lands. During the reign of Third Caliph Ḥaḍrat ʿUthmān, ʿUrwah's father, Zubayr purchased from the family of Ḥaḍrat ʿUmar the part of land belonging to them. Ḥaḍrat Zubayr then went to the Caliph for approval of the deal. As witness, he quoted the testimony of ʿAbd al-Raḥmān bin ʿAuf reaffirming the land's ownership by Ḥaḍrat ʿUmar's family on the basis of its award to the late Second Caliph by the Holy Prophet (*pbuh*). Ḥaḍrat ʿUthmān accepted the testimony saying that ʿAbd al-Raḥmān was a man of truth and he could never give a wrong witness even if it went against him.'
- 'Alqamah bin Wāʾil narrates from his father Wāʾil bin Hujr that he was given by the Holy Prophet (*pbuh*) a piece of land in Ḥaḍramawt.' (Abū Dāwūd and Tirmidhī).
- 'Sayyidah Asmāʾ bint Abī Bakr said that the Holy Prophet (*pbuh*) had given her husband Zubayr a plot of land in Khaybar, which had also date-garden and other trees. Her son ʿUrwah bin Zubayr added that his father was also granted an oasis from the lands of Banī Naḍīr. According to ʿAbdullāh

bin ʿUmar, Ḥaḍrat Zubayr was also given a vast tract of land by the Holy Prophet for which he was asked to let his stallion gallop and the areas thus covered upto the point where the horse stopped would all belong to Zubayr.' (Imām Bukhārī, Imām Aḥmad, Abū Dāwūd, *Kitāb al-Amwāl* by Abū ʿUbayd).

- ʿʿAmr bin Dinār said that when the Holy Prophet (*pbuh*) arrived in Madinah, he gave lands to both Ḥaḍrat Abū Bakr and Ḥaḍrat ʿUmar.' (*Kitāb al-Kharāj* by Imām Abū Yūsuf).
- 'Abū Rāfiʿ said that his family members were given land by the Holy Prophet (*pbuh*), which they, however, couldn't rehabilitate and sold in eight thousand Dinars during the reign of Ḥaḍrat ʿUmar.' (*Kitāb al-Kharāj* by Imām Abū Yūsuf).
- 'Ibn Sīrīn narrates that the Holy Prophet (*pbuh*) had given a piece of land to a person from Anṣār, named Sulayṭ. He had to leave Madinah quite often to look after that land. On return, whenever he learnt about the number of *Āyāt* revealed to the Holy Prophet during his absence, he felt greatly perturbed. Once he requested the Prophet that he wished to return the land back to the State, as it had been a barrier between him and the Holy Prophet and he was graciously allowed to do so.' (*Kitāb al-Amwāl* by Abū ʿUbayd).
- 'Bilāl bin Ḥārith Muzanī narrates that the Holy Prophet (*pbuh*) awarded him the entire area of ʿAqīq.' (*Kitāb al-Amwāl*).
- ʿʿAdī bin Ḥātim narrates that the Holy Prophet gave Furāt bin Ḥayyān 'Ijlī a plot of land in Yamamah.' (*Kitāb al-Amwāl*).
- 'Nāfiʿ, son of the Arabia's famous physician Ḥārith bin Kaldah, requested Ḥaḍrat ʿUmar to give him a piece of land available in Basrah which was neither part of state land on which *Kharāj* was levied, nor was of interest to any local Muslim. He sought the land to grow fodder for his horses. Ḥaḍrat ʿUmar wrote to his Governor Abū Mūsa al-Ashʿarī permitting the award of land to Nāfiʿ if its status was the same as described by him.' (*Kitāb al-Amwāl*).
- 'Mūsā bin Ṭalḥah narrates that the third Caliph Ḥaḍrat ʿUthmān awarded lands to Zubayr bin al-ʿAwwām, Saʿd bin Abī Waqqāṣ ʿAbd Allāh bin Masʿūd, 'Usāmah bin Zayd, Khabbāb bin al-Aratt, ʿAmmār bin Yāsir and Saʿd bin Mālik, may Allah's peace be upon them all.' (*Kitāb al-Amwāl*).
- ʿʿAbd Allāh bin Ḥasan narrates that on the request of Ḥaḍrat ʿAlī, Ḥaḍrat 'Umar gave him the land of Yambuʿ.' (*Kanz al-ʿUmmāl*).
- 'Imām Abū Yūsuf narrates from different authentic sources that Ḥaḍrat 'Umar declared as *Khāliṣah* all lands, which were left by Khusrau and his

household, those abandoned by their owners, or whose owners were killed in battle and also the lands affected by floods, swamps, or wild growth. Whatever he awarded to the people was from these state lands.' (*Kitāb al-Kharāj*).

7.5. The *Sharī'ah* perspective on the award of state lands

The procedure followed by the Caliphs for awarding the titles of state lands was very unlike the feudal custom of royal decrees and baksheesh that favoured a coterie of sycophants and courtiers. It followed a strict, well-defined pattern governed by certain rules and regulations. As recorded by the Prophetic Traditions and books of history, these rules may be summed up as follows:

- During the days of the Holy Prophet (*pbuh*) and his illustrious Caliphs, the first eligibility rule for a person seeking the award of the title to state land was that he must have rendered meritorious services for the cause of his Religion and State. Only those who had actually rendered extraordinary services in the national interest or were then engaged in such service merited the award. The land could also be awarded to someone if such a gesture was considered appropriate for the community's collective good.
- The one so awarded a title of state land was then bound under the law to put the land to productive use. If he failed to do so for three consecutive years, the award was deemed to be cancelled. Imām Abū Yūsuf quoted in this respect the precedent of *Sayyidinā* Rasūl Allāh (*pbuh*), who allowed others to make use of lands following the failure of the Muzaynah and Juhaynah tribes to put the lands to use that had earlier been awarded to them. When people from these tribes approached Ḥaḍrat 'Umar during his rule to cancel the titles of those who had subsequently rehabilitated the land, he replied that, had the award been made by him or Ḥaḍrat Abū Bakr, he might have considered their request; however, as it was done by no less a person than the Prophet himself, he could not do this. He added that the rule remained the same:

مَـنْ كَانَتْ لَهُ اَرضٌ ثُمَّ تَرَكَهُ ثَلٰثَ سِنِينَ فَلَمْ يُعَمِّـرهَا فَعَمَّـرَهَا قَـومٌ آخَرُونَ فَهُمْ اَحَقُّ بِهَا

('He who had a piece of land in his possession, but left it unutilized for three years without putting it to any productive use and then some others rehabilitated it, the latter would have a better claim over it than the former.')

(Abū Yūsuf, *Kitāb al-Kharāj*)

- The third rule was to review the award if the land was not being correctly used. To support this, Abū ʿUbayd in his *Kitāb al-Amwāl* and Yaḥyā bin Ādam in his book *al-Kharāj* quoted the precedent of Ḥaḍrat ʿUmar, who did not allow Bilāl bin Ḥārith Muzanī to retain the entire ʿAqīq valley, which had been gifted to him by the Holy Prophet (*pbuh*), because of his failure to put the whole of it to use. Ḥaḍrat ʿUmar told him that the gift was made in the interests of the nation, and the Holy Prophet (*pbuh*) had wanted him to make the best possible use of the land rather than leave it idle. He was therefore advised to retain only the amount that he could utilize and return the rest for others to care for. On his reluctance to do this, Ḥaḍrat ʿUmar left with him part of the land he could use and confiscated the rest to distribute it among those better qualified to rehabilitate it.
- The fourth rule was that the government was authorized only to distribute from the state lands of *Mawāt* and *Khāliṣah* catagories and could not take away the personal property of an individual to gift it to another. The government was also not entitled to impose on the actual allottees/owners of the land another person as their landlord, nor could a feudal supremo obtain ownership rights and reduce the actual owners to the status of farm-labour and peasants.

7.6. Feudal estates and Islamic *Sharīʿah*

According to the Islamic *Sharīʿah*, it is not lawful for rulers to gift state lands to their favourites. No tyrants or autocrats are allowed to hand out state lands as favours to their cronies, sycophants and those engaged in their service, or to promote their own personal interests and perpetuate their image.

The above rule has been explained by Imām Abū Yūsuf thus in his monumental *Kitāb al-Kharāj*:

> 'An honest and upright leader (of the Muslim nation) is entitled to offer as gifts and awards from the state property which belongs to no third person to those who may have rendered meritorious services for the Muslims and Islam … A person so awarded any piece of land by a righteous ruler cannot be deprived of his award. But the land snatched away by a ruler from one person to gift to another would be treated like usurping one's right in favour of the other.'

He further says:

> 'Of the lands we mentioned as lawful for the Imām (national leader of the Muslims) to award, those gifted by the righteous rulers in Iraq, Arabia

and al-Jibāl area cannot be taken back by future Caliphs. They cannot also dispossess the present owners of these lands, which they possess now either by inheritance, or by purchasing them from their erstwhile owners or heirs.'

Imām Abū Yūsuf concludes:

> 'These precedents thus establish that the Holy Prophet (*pbuh*) himself awarded state lands and this was done also by his illustrious Caliphs. The Holy Prophet kept it in view that whosoever gets the land, he gets it purely on the basis of merit and in best interest (of the nation and the state). To win the hearts of the new converts and rehabilitation of a barren piece of land were other considerations. Al-*Khulafā' al-Rāshidūn* also gifted lands on the basis of one's meritorious service for an Islamic cause or his role against the enemies of Islam or in national interest.'
>
> (*Kitāb al-Kharāj*, pp.32-33)

These statements by Imām Abū Yūsuf were actually a response to the Abbasid Caliph Hārūn al-Rashīd's query about the *Sharī'ah* standpoint on feudal estates and how far a ruler is authorized to exercise his authority and discretion in this respect. The Imām's reply shows that the awarding of state lands was in itself a lawful act, but this has to be governed by certain rules. All those who award land are not the same, nor are the recipients. The state award is to be conferred by a fair, righteous and God-fearing ruler. He must use his authority and discretion justly and offer state-awards to the true servants of religion and state, to those who merit such awards and also for a noble cause whose advantages may eventually return to the state and the nation. The award should also be offered from funds or lands which rightly fall under the Muslim ruler's dispensation. Another type of award is that which tyrants and autocrats make to those who are as bad as they are. These are given generally for no plausible purpose and are often lavished recklessly out of the funds and lands which the self-serving rulers are not legally authorized to use. There are thus two distinct categories of awards and the two must be treated differently. The first category of state awards are lawful, and justice demands that these be upheld. The second category is definitely illegal and, according to the dictates of justice, these must be annulled. It is certainly wrong to treat the two in the same way.

7.7. Respect for ownership rights

The testimony and precedents of the golden era of the Holy Prophet (*pbuh*) and his illustrious Caliphs provide us with a blueprint for the way the Qur'ānic injunctions should be translated into practice. This blueprint leaves with no doubt about Islam's standpoint on private ownership. Instead of favouring public ownership at the cost of an individual's right to own, it reaffirms that Islam considers private ownership as the natural and correct way of putting the land to better use. This is the reason why the Prophet of God (*pbuh*), in most of the cases cited above, not only allowed previous ownerships to continue, but also, soon replaced those that were cancelled with new ownerships and paved the way for future ownerships as well. He also granted ownership rights by distributing state lands among the most deserving and meritorious persons of his time. This clearly proves that the old system of private ownership was retained by the Holy Prophet not as a *necessary evil* but as a *rightful precedent*, and the same was considered fit for the future.

To illustrate this point further, we may cite the orders that the Holy Prophet (*pbuh*) gave to respect the right of the individual to own. Imām Muslim narrated from different authentic sources that a woman lodged a lawsuit against Sa'īd bin Zayd, the brother-in-law of Ḥaḍrat 'Umar, during the reign of Marwān bin al-Ḥakam, accusing him of having occupied part of her land. In reply to that petition, Ḥaḍrat Sa'īd stated: 'How could have I deprived her of her portion of land when I have myself heard the Holy Prophet (*pbuh*) pronouncing the following judgement?':

مَن اَخَذَ شِبراً مِنَ الاَرضِ ظُلَماً طُوِّقَهُ اِلَى سَبعِ اَرضِين

('Whoever grabs even a foot of the ground unfairly, he would get enwrapped round his neck seven layers of that piece of land.') (Narrated by Sa'īd bin Zayd, Abū Hurayrah and Sayyidah 'Ā'ishah, may Allah be pleased with them all).

(Muslim)

Abū Dāwūd, Nasā'ī and Tirmidhī recorded from different sources that the Holy Prophet (*pbuh*) said: لَيسَ لِعَرقٍ ظَالِمٍ حَقٌّ ('... rehabilitation of other's land unauthorized by a miscreant entitles him to no right').

Rāfi' bin Khudayj narrates that the Holy Prophet (*pbuh*) said:

مَن زَرَعَ فِى اَرضِ قَومٍ بِغَيرِ اِذنِهِم فَلَيسَ لَهُ مِنَ الزَرّعِ شَىءٌ وَلَهُ نَفَقَتُه

('Anybody who did farming in somebody else's land without his consent, has legally no right on its produce. The expenses he incurred would, however, be payable to him.')

(Abū Dāwūd, Ibn Mājah, Tirmidhī)

> ʿUrwah bin Zubayr narrates that a petition was submitted to the Holy Prophet (*pbuh*) about a person who had planted date-palm trees in the lands of an Anṣārī. The Holy Prophet (*pbuh*) ordered in his ruling that the plants should be removed and the land returned to its rightful owner.
>
> (Abū Dāwūd)

The injunctions contained in the foregoing paragraphs further support the idea that Islam has never been in favour of eliminating private ownership and promoting a public monopoly or state control on land and its resources.

7.8. Islamic social order and private ownership

The injunctions of the Holy Qur'ān and *Sunnah* are never in conflict with each other. They make a mutually harmonious whole. It is this outstanding feature of the Islamic law and *Sharīʿah* injunctions that has been cited by Allah *subḥānahū wa taʿālā* Himself as an irrefutable testimony of their Divine origin. Let us presume for a while that *Muzāraʿah*[6] is not allowed by the *Sharīʿah* and that Islam prefers ownership rights to be restricted exclusively to the land tilled by the owner himself, and that farmland he does not cultivate personally should remain idle or be distributed to others without paying him a farthing in return. With a little closer inspection, it is clear that such a rule is totally incompatible with the benign spirit of the *Sharīʿah* and the legal system of Islam. The inherent contradictions of such a provision can be summarised as follows:

- In Islam, the right to own is not restricted to the able-bodied male members of the society. It is also applicable to women, children, the ailing and the old. If *Muzāraʿah* (Sharecropping contract) were illegal, this would debar all the weaker segments of the society from owning agricultural lands.
- According to the Islamic law of inheritance, just as the legacy of the deceased gets divided among his heirs, so in the same way the shares of inheritance from many dead relatives can be transferred to a single person. Therefore, it would be strange to believe that, while Islam's law of inheritance allows a single person to own hundreds of acres of land, its agrarian law makes it unlawful for him to benefit from all the land in his possession, except for that part which he himself cultivates.
- The Islamic law of sale and purchase has imposed no restriction on a person's right to buy or sell items sanctioned by the law. Just as there is no curb on one's right to sell or purchase anything lawful, there is similarly no

[6] *Muzāraʿah* is that form of cultivation where the land belongs to one person and the farming is done by another, and the two share the produce. In Urdu, it is commonly known as *Batā'ī*. – Author.

restriction on a farmer in respect of his land. Seen from this perspective, it would appear strange that a person should be eligible according to civil law to purchase any amount of land, but according to agrarian law could not take advantage of his farmland beyond the certain limit which he tills himself.

- Islam has imposed no restriction on any kind of ownership with respect to its quantity or size. Anything lawful that is acquired and owned through fair means can be kept in possession and put to unlimited profitable use, subject only to the clearance of dues and other obligations under the law. No restriction has been imposed by the *Sharīʿah* on the amount of ownership of items like money, cattle-herds, consumer goods, residential accommodation, means of transport, etc. If this is the case, why should curbs be imposed on the purchase, proprietorship and use of agricultural land and property?
- Islam has taught us to be generous and magnanimous in every area of our lives. But according to the established norms of *Sharīʿah*, once the observance of obligatory duties is ensured, not even magnanimity can be imposed as mandatory on an individual. For example, Islam greatly values *Ṣadaqāt* and inspires us to be charitable and spend generously in good causes, and this over and above the mandatory contribution of *Zakāh*. However, it does not make this additional act of charity binding on anyone. Nor does it make it unlawful for someone to extend a loan to the needy or to participate in a business as a partner on the principle of *Muḍārabah*.[7] Similarly, if a person has many houses as residential accommodation, the biggest one may suffice his needs and it may be best for him to donate his additional accommodation to the homeless. But Islam does not impose these actions on its followers. The letting of this additional accommodation for rent or selling it to earn money is also lawful. If this is the case, why would the *Sharīʿah* modify its general rule only for agricultural land and compel the landowner to distribute free of cost his excess land among the landless, after he has paid *Zakāh* on its produce, and do no business with anyone on the principle of partnership (*Muzāraʿah*)?
- According to the Islamic *Sharīʿah*, everyone is fully entitled to enter into commercial, industrial and business deals on the principles of *Mushārakah* (equity participation on a profit and loss sharing basis) or *Muḍārabah* (partnership or trustee-financing). One person can lend capital to another

---

[7] *Muḍārabah* is that form of business wherein the capital belongs to an entrepreneur and the labour to another, and the two share the profit as partners in the business. – Author.

in *Muḍārabah* and can jointly do business with others by sharing capital and labour in *Mushārakah.* The capital can be given in the form of a building, machine, car, boat or plane, and he can tell him to do business with these and pay back a certain amount of their profit on the income. Why should the same principle not be applied to agricultural land, and why can the landowner not give another person his land to farm and get in return one-third or one-quarter of its produce on the principle of *Muzāraʿah*?

7.9. The question of delimitation of agricultural land

The following two questions were addressed to Sayyid Mawdūdī by a religious scholar seeking his considered opinion[8]:

Q.i: Will you please elucidate the *Sharīʿah* point of view in respect of confiscating feudal lands beyond the approved limit under the agricultural reforms, as the Tradition says that the Holy Prophet (*pbuh*) had granted vast tracts of land to Ḥaḍrat Zubayr?

Q.ii: As for the ejection of peasants, it is evidently not permissible until the harvest has been done. There is, however, no other reason to make it impermissible. Please let us have your views about this as well.

A: As to the first query, you may bear in mind, as a matter of principle, that the proprietary rights of feudal lords are not established on the feudal estates, doled out to them by any government, past or present, the way those are confirmed on lands purchased by someone or acquired by him through inheritance. The government can always review the case of a feudal estate and, if it is found to be unfair, can amend or even cancel the decree.

The books of Islamic history and *Aḥādīth* provide us with many precedents in this regard. The Holy Prophet (*pbuh*) granted Abyaḍ bin Ḥammāl M'azinī a tract of land in the salt range of Ma'ārib in Yemen. Subsequently, however, when the Holy Prophet realised that it was a major salt mine, he cancelled the decree in the public interest. We may deduce from this that a decree about the official gift of state lands can always be reviewed, and also that it is contrary to the public interest to favour someone with state awards of an unspecified value. This is further confirmed by another precedent. The first Caliph Abū Bakr awarded a

[8] *Tarjumān al-Qur'ān,* June, 1951 – Translator.

gift of land to Ṭalḥah and asked him to have the deal ratified by a certain number of signatures as witnesses. These witnesses included 'Umar. When Ṭalḥah came to him, he refused to put his seal on the deal and said: أَهٰذَا كُلُّهُ لَكَ مِن دُونِ النَّاسِ ('How can all this be for you alone over and above others?') (*Kitāb al-Amwāl*, Abū 'Ubayd, pp.275-76).

As for the gift of land to Ḥaḍrat Zubayr, the challenge facing the state then was the rehabilitation of vast tracts of idle land. The Holy Prophet (pbuh) therefore awarded large chunks of these lands to many competent followers to put these to productive use.

Regarding the second question, the government is authorized to pass legislation banning the eviction of landless farm labour/tenant by the landlord without offering a plausible reason. This is one of those prerogatives that the Islamic *Sharī'ah* grants to the chief executive in order to ensure the rule of law and public safety and to provide a check on social unrest and injustice. As the vast majority of our population now depends entirely on land for its sustenance, it cannot therefore be in the public interest to give landlords unbridled powers to eject a tenant from the land without offering any cogent reason. Such an unhealthy trend would involve giving the tenant no breathing space and letting the all-powerful landlords' 'sword of Damocles' consistently hang over the heads of millions of poor farmers engaged generations after generations in this profession .

7.10. Sharecropping between landlord and farmer[9]

There is nothing wrong in principle with the practice of *Muzāra'ah*. According to this mode of farming, the landlord and farmer distribute the shares of their produce equitably among themselves, which traditionally grants 2/5 to the landlord and 3/5 to the farmer. However, in order to fulfil the dictates of justice, the landlord will have to provide the farmer with at least enough land that his share of its produce will give him sufficient to fulfil his needs. The landlord is also required to determine physically, according to the demands of justice and irrespective of customary practice, the actual proportion of the produce to be shared by himself and the farmer. There can be no hard and fast rule in this respect because of the differences in farming conditions and the quality of agricultural lands from place to place. It would seem contrary to the norms of justice and fairplay that, merely by virtue of owning the land, the landlord should seek seed and farming equipment from the farmer in addition to his labour, but should not be willing to change the age-old proportions of 2/5 and 3/5.

[9] In response to a query in *Tarjumān al-Qur'ān*, October, 1950.

It is therefore essential for the landlord not simply to rest content with improving his approach to conform to the dictates of *Sharīʿah*, but also to be ready to do justice and be magnanimous.

The landlord is entitled to monitor any unfair means that the farmer may be tempted to use before the division of the produce to ensure that the rules of the game are correctly observed. However, this supervision must not be extended to a level where the farmer becomes his serf or subservient to his supervisory staff. The status of a farmer is not that of a servant or labourer, but that of a partner and stakeholder in the business. The landlord must deal with him accordingly. I would thus like landlords to bring about a drastic change in their feudal mindset and reform their approach.

7.11. Principles of property management

وَلَا تُؤْتُوا۟ ٱلسُّفَهَآءَ أَمْوَٰلَكُمُ ٱلَّتِى جَعَلَ ٱللَّهُ لَكُمْ قِيَـٰمًا وَٱرْزُقُوهُمْ فِيهَا وَٱكْسُوهُمْ وَقُولُوا۟ لَهُمْ قَوْلًا
مَّعْرُوفًا ﴿٥﴾ وَٱبْتَلُوا۟ ٱلْيَتَـٰمَىٰ حَتَّىٰٓ إِذَا بَلَغُوا۟ ٱلنِّكَاحَ فَإِنْ ءَانَسْتُم مِّنْهُمْ رُشْدًا فَٱدْفَعُوٓا۟ إِلَيْهِمْ أَمْوَٰلَهُمْ ۖ وَلَا تَأْكُلُوهَآ
إِسْرَافًا وَبِدَارًا أَن يَكْبَرُوا۟ ۚ وَمَن كَانَ غَنِيًّا فَلْيَسْتَعْفِفْ ۖ وَمَن كَانَ فَقِيرًا فَلْيَأْكُلْ بِٱلْمَعْرُوفِ ۚ فَإِذَا دَفَعْتُمْ إِلَيْهِمْ
أَمْوَٰلَهُمْ فَأَشْهِدُوا۟ عَلَيْهِمْ ۚ وَكَفَىٰ بِٱللَّهِ حَسِيبًا ﴿٦﴾

('Do not entrust your properties – which Allah has made a means of support for you – to the weak of understanding, but maintain and clothe them out of it, and say to them a kind word of advice. Test the orphans until they reach the age of marriage, and then if you find them mature of mind hand over to them their property and do not eat it up by either spending extravagantly or in haste, fearing that they would grow up (and claim it). If the guardian of the orphan is rich let him abstain entirely (from his ward's property); and if he is poor, let him partake of it in a fair measure. When you hand over their property to them let there be witnesses on their behalf. Allah is sufficient to take account (of your deeds).')

(*al-Nisāʾ*, 4: 5-6)

The above *Āyāt* are comprehensive in their meaning. They tell the Muslim *Ummah* how to safeguard the rights and responsibilities concerning property. We have been instructed not to let property that Allah *subḥānahū wa taʿālā* has made a means of support for us pass on to immature persons, lest by their inadvertent use they disrupt the socio-economic fabric and ultimately the ethical foundations of society. The rights of private ownership that are available to an individual under the Islamic *Sharīʿah* are not without checks and balances. Nobody has unlimited powers over the property they own. No one is free to use or abuse it recklessly and thus disturb the socio-economic balance and the moral fabric of society. Therefore, as far as the basic necessities of one's life are concerned, these must be fulfilled; but as for the freedom to use one's ownership rights, this must be kept in check so as to prevent any harm coming to the society's economic structure and moral complexion. According to the injunctions contained in these *Āyāt*, the owners at the micro-level have to be careful when passing over their property to someone to ensure that the person is capable of its proper custody and use. At the macro-level, an Islamic government is responsible to take under its custody the property of those who may not be capable of managing it themselves, or who are found using it wrongly. The government will also have to look after the basic necessities of these persons and deal with them tenderly and with affection.

Another instruction contained in these *Āyāt* enjoins the guardians and custodians of the under-aged to help them grow in an atmosphere of love and care conducive for their healthy physical and mental growth. The preconditions that are laid down for transferring the management of their property to them are: (i) that they attain the age of physical maturity (puberty); and (ii) that they are of sound judgment or have the ability to manage it correctly. As for the first precondition, the leading jurists of Islam are unanimous in its interpretation. There is, however, a difference of opinion regarding the second. Imām Abū Yūsuf, Imām Muḥammad al-Shaybānī and Imām Shāfi'ī are of the view that the quality of *rushd*, or *maturity of mind*, is essential before the transfer of property to 'the weak of understanding'. It is appropriate in light of this viewpoint that the matter in such cases be referred to the Islamic law court and, if the scrutiny of the *Qāḍī* (Judge/Magistrate) confirms a lack of the quality of *rushd* in a person, the custody of their property should be entrusted by the judge to a supervisory board to manage it on their behalf.

8 The Question of Interest[1]

8.1. Islamic injunctions concerning interest

Let us try first to understand what *Ribā* or interest is, according to the Qur'ān and the *Sunnah*. What are its parameters? What are the specific cases on which the injunctions regarding its prohibition apply? What are the alternatives that Islam offers for the economic well-being of man, and how would it like to resolve the economic problems?

8.1.1. *Meaning of Ribā*

The Holy Qur'ān uses the word *Ribā* for interest/usury. The root of this word consists of the letters (ر+ب+و), which mean addition, growth and increase. Hence, it is said: ربا فُلان الرَّابِيَة, i.e. 'Someone climbed up the mound'; ربا فِي حِجرِفُلان, 'He grew up under someone's patronage'; and أربى الشيء, 'He made the thing grow'. In Arabic, *Rabwah* (رَبْوَة) means raised ground or a hillock. The word and its derivatives have been used in the Holy Qur'ān to mean *increase*, *growth* and *swelling*, as well as interest. Here are a few examples:

...فَإِذَآ أَنزَلْنَا عَلَيْهَا ٱلْمَآءَ ٱهْتَزَّتْ وَرَبَتْ ... ﴿٥﴾

('... and no sooner than We send down water upon it, it begins to quiver and swell.')

(*al-Ḥajj*, 22: 5)

[1] The author has contributed a remarkable book on the subject entitled *Sūd*. In this, he discussed in depth the question of interest from its historical, logical and *Sharī'ah* perspectives. Tracing the history of the growth and development of the modern banking system, he established that this interest-based institution was the worst instrument of economic abuse and exploitation. Exposing the absurdity of the notion about the difference between commercial and non-commercial interest, he offered in the book an outline of an interest-free economy. For the student of Economics, a study of this book and the issues raised in it is of immense value. We have tried to include in this Chapter only those topics concerning interest that are more relevant for our context. For this we have drawn, in addition to the information available in the book *Sūd*, upon his magnum opus *Tafhīm al-Qur'ān* and *Rasā' il-wa-Masā'il*. – Editor.

يَمْحَقُ ٱللَّهُ ٱلرِّبَوٰاْ وَيُرْبِى ٱلصَّدَقَـٰتِ ... ﴿٢٧٦﴾

('Allah deprives interest of all blessing, whereas He blesses charity with growth.')

(*al-Baqarah*, 2: 276)

...أَن تَكُونَ أُمَّةٌ هِىَ أَرْبَىٰ مِنْ أُمَّةٍ ... ﴿٩٢﴾

('... so that one people might take greater advantage than another.')

(*al-Naḥl*, 16: 92)

...وَءَاوَيْنَـٰهُمَآ إِلَىٰ رَبْوَةٍ ... ﴿٥٠﴾

('... and We gave them refuge on a lofty ground.')

(*al-Mu'minūn*, 23: 50)

...وَذَرُواْ مَا بَقِىَ مِنَ ٱلرِّبَوٰاْ ... وَإِن تُبْتُمْ فَلَكُمْ رُءُوسُ أَمْوَٰلِكُمْ... ﴿٢٧٩﴾

('... and give up all outstanding interest ... If you repent even now, you have the right of the return of your capital.')

(*al-Baqarah*, 2: 278-279)

وَمَآ ءَاتَيْتُم مِّن رِّبًا لِّيَرْبُوَاْ فِىٓ أَمْوَٰلِ ٱلنَّاسِ فَلَا يَرْبُواْ عِندَ ٱللَّهِ ... ﴿٣٩﴾

('Whatever you pay as interest so that it may increase the wealth of people does not increase in the sight of Allah.')

(*al-Rūm*, 30: 39)

It is evident from the above *Āyāt* that any addition to the principal amount comes under the category of *Ribā*. However, the Book of God does not prohibit every addition and increase on the principal amount. It has banned only a particular kind of addition, and this is why it is called *al-Ribā* (ٱلرِّبَوٰاْ) (with the definite article 'al-'), which is the Qur'ānic term for all forms of interest and usury. Usury was a normal form of transaction in pre-Islamic days. The *Jāhilī* Arabs (of the Days of Ignorance) equated it with business and trade. Islam told them that an increase on the principal amount caused by *al-Ribā* is different from an increase gained through business and trade (*al-Bay'*):

...ذَٰلِكَ بِأَنَّهُمْ قَالُوٓاْ إِنَّمَا ٱلْبَيْعُ مِثْلُ ٱلرِّبَوٰاْ وَأَحَلَّ ٱللَّهُ ٱلْبَيْعَ وَحَرَّمَ ٱلرِّبَوٰاْ ... ﴿٢٧٥﴾

> ('Seized in this state they say: "Buying and selling is but a kind of interest", even though Allah has made buying and selling lawful, and interest unlawful'.)
>
> (*al-Baqarah*, 2: 275)

As the exact nature of *al-Ribā* and its negative impact on the *Jāhilī* society was well known, the Qur'ān made no further elaboration on this and simply commanded the believers to give up this abominable form of economic dealing.

8.1.2. Ribā *of the Days of Ignorance*

In Pre-Islamic Arabia, various forms of *al-Ribā* were practiced. According to *Qatādah*, a merchant often sold a commodity to a person in return for an amount that would be paid after a certain period. When the deadline expired, the payment time was extended to a new date and the amount raised for the commodity sold. Another form of usury in practice during *Jāhilīyah*, as narrated by Mujāhid, was that the debtor seeking a loan used to assure the lender that he would pay them so much extra in addition to the principal amount of loan (Ibn Jarīr, vol. 3, p.62). Abū Bakr al-Jaṣṣāṣ has also cited similar kinds of *Ribā* in his *Aḥkām al-Qur'ān* (vol.1). According to Imām Rāzī, the most common *jāhilī* practice was to lend somebody a loan on the condition that he would pay a predetermined amount of interest for a certain period on a monthly basis, and on the expiry of that period would return the principal amount. If the debtor failed to repay the loan on the agreed date, he was offered a fresh deadline on an enhanced rate of monthly interest (*Tafsīr al-Kabīr*, vol-2, p.351).

These were the popular forms of interest-based transactions, which the Pre-Islamic Arabs called *al-Ribā*; it was this practice, in all its various forms, that the Holy Qur'ān declared as unlawful and strictly forbidden.

8.1.3. *Basic difference between* Ribā *and* Bayʿ

Now let us examine the following: (i) What is the difference in principle between the normal way of trade and business (*Bayʿ*) and *al-Ribā* (interest-based transactions)? (ii) What are the basic features of *al-Ribā* that make it different from *Bayʿ*? (iii) Why has Islam prohibited *al-Ribā* while allowing *Bayʿ*?

In normal trade and business deals (*Bayʿ*), the seller offers a certain commodity for sale at a price fixed by him and the buyer negotiates, and thus a deal is agreed by mutual consent. This transaction is inevitably marked by either of the following two conditions: the seller producing the commodity himself through his own personal labour and capital; or the seller acquiring it by purchasing it from a third source. In both cases, he adds to his capital, which he invested in producing or acquiring the commodity, an amount of his labour which entitles him to his profit. *Ribā,* on the other hand, is a form of transaction where a person lends his capital to somebody on the condition that he will charge an added payment during a certain period over and above the principal amount of the loan. This is a deal of capital versus capital, with an additional sum that is determined beforehand for the grace period. It is this additional sum which is Ribā, or interest, and which is not charged in return for any goods or services, but just in lieu of the grace period. In the case of *Bayʿ* or a trade deal, if the seller imposes an additional amount on the buyer over and above the actual price of the commodity, should the latter fail to settle payment after the mutually agreed date, any addition to the actual price would fall under the category of *Ribā.*

Ribā or interest can, therefore, be defined as the amount added to the principal sum in return for the grace period and determined beforehand as a precondition. There are thus three constituent parts of *Ribā*: (i) an addition to the principal sum; (ii) determination of this addition according to a fixed term; and (iii) the deal being conditional on the payment of an additional amount. A loan deal that consists of these three ingredients would be an interest-based transaction, irrespective of the nature of loan – whether it is taken to satisfy one's personal needs or as an investment in a production venture, and whether the borrower is a rich or poor person.

The difference in principle between *Bayʿ* and *Ribā* may be further elucidated as follows:

- In *Bayʿ*, the profit is exchanged between buyer and seller on an equal footing because the buyer gets a benefit from the goods purchased from seller and the seller gets the benefit of the labour, enterprise and time he contributed in making the goods available to the buyer. Conversely, there is no such exchange of profits in an interest-based transaction. The person receiving interest does secure a fixed amount of money, which is definitely beneficial to him; but the one who pays interest only gets in return a grace period which he is never sure if it will benefit him or not. If the borrow has obtained a loan for his personal needs, the grace period offered to him is definitely harmful and not beneficial. But if the loan has been taken to improve his business, trade, agriculture, industry or any other commercial venture, there is an equal chance of profit or loss for the borrower. The lender, on the other hand, has nothing to worry him and is always assured of getting a fixed amount of interest on his principal sum. He is completely unconcerned whether the borrower is suffering losses or enjoying gains.

Hence, interest-based deals are either made for the gain of one party and the loss of the other; or for the definite and pre-determined gains of one and the uncertain and undefined gains of the other.

- In business and trade deals, the seller receives the amount of profit he determines for his commodity only once from his client. In the case of *Ribā*, however, the capitalist extending a loan continues drawing interest on his principal sum and the amount of interest continues multiplying with the passage of time. Whatever the quantum of benefit that is earned by the borrower, it cannot exceed a certain limit. However, the advantages drawn in return by the lender are unlimited. It may happen that the benefit accrued to the lender through interest may exceed his entire resources of wealth, and even then continue multiplying endlessly.
- In trade, the matter ends once the buyer and seller have concluded a deal. After making payment, the buyer owes nothing more to the seller. In an interest-based transaction, however, the borrower has not only to return the principal sum after making use of the loan, but also the amount of interest accrued thereon.
- In an agricultural, industrial and commercial venture, the entrepreneur invests his labour, capital and time and reaps the harvest of dividends. In an interest-based venture, however, the lender invests his capital, which comes from the excess of his needs, and becomes the controlling partner in the earnings of other stakeholders without putting in his own personal labour or money. His position is not that of the customary shareholder, who shares both loss and gain in proportion to his investment. The lender is a partner who enjoys the dubious benefit of a claim to a fixed and pre-determined amount of interest, regardless of whether the venture runs into loss or profit and irrespective of the actual proportion of the profit earned.

8.1.4. *Rationale for prohibition*

These are the factors behind why the All-Merciful has declared *Bayʿ Ḥalāl* and *Ribā Ḥarām.* In addition to the reasons mentioned above, there are other factors for the illegality of interest. On ethical grounds, one cannot justify interest in any form. It is a system that gives rise to the traits of stinginess, selfishness, apathy and capital-worship, as well as the materialistic trend in society. It sows the seeds of discord among nations and communities and weakens the bonds of compassion and cooperation among fellow humans. It sets the trend of amassing wealth and promoting only self-interest. It prevents the free flow of capital in society and actually reverses the direction of its flow from the have-nots towards the haves. Because of this, the resources get concentrated into the hands of the moneyed class, which eventually leads to a total collapse of the social structure. Those with an insight into the realms of economics and the social sciences are aware of this fact all too well.

One also cannot deny the fact that an interest-based system of economy is in total disharmony with the blessed blueprint, according to which Islam wants to rebuild human civilization and culture, reorganize society economically and rejuvenate individuals morally. Even some apparently inconsequential types of interest-based transaction are too damaging for this blueprint. This is the reason why the Lord has sternly commanded the believers to give up all transactions involving usury or modern-day interest:

يَـٰٓأَيُّهَا ٱلَّذِينَ ءَامَنُواْ ٱتَّقُواْ ٱللَّهَ وَذَرُواْ مَا بَقِىَ مِنَ ٱلرِّبَوٰٓاْ إِن كُنتُم مُّؤْمِنِينَ ۝٢٧٨ فَإِن لَّمْ تَفْعَلُواْ فَأْذَنُواْ بِحَرْبٍ مِّنَ ٱللَّهِ وَرَسُولِهِۦ... ۝٢٧٩

('Believers! Have fear of Allah and give up all outstanding interest if you do truly believe. But if you fail to do so, then be warned of war from Allah and His Messenger.')

(*al-Baqarah*, 2: 278-279)

8.1.5. *Strict nature of ban*

There are many other sinful acts for which the believers have been warned by the Holy Qur'ān of punishment in the Hereafter. No crime has, however, been dealt with in such harsh terms as usury and interest. The Holy Prophet (*pbuh*) therefore tried his best to eliminate all forms of interest within the Islamic Caliphate. The treaty he signed with the Christians of Najran contained a particular clause making it binding on them not to indulge in any interest-based activities, or the treaty would be deemed to be cancelled and they would be liable for attack by the defenders of the Islamic social order. The usury dealers of *Banī Mughīrah* were notorious for their practice throughout Arabia. After the conquest of Makkah, the Holy Prophet (*pbuh*) cancelled all of their interest deals. He wrote to the Makkah Governor declaring he would wage war against them if they dared challenge the law and re-start their age-old practice. Ḥaḍrat ʿAbbās, the well-revered uncle of the Prophet of Islam, was himself an established moneylender in Makkah. During his Farewell Pilgrimage (*Ḥajjat al-Wadāʿ*), *Sayyidinā* Rasūl Allāh declared that he annulled all deals according to which the borrower had to pay interest on his loan, and all of the interest accumulated on loans extended earlier by his uncle ʿAbbās was also no longer valid. The Holy Prophet (*pbuh*) added: 'He who takes interest, or offers interest, or writes deeds of interest-based deals, or stands witness to such deals, are all accursed by the Lord'.

The purpose of these injunctions was not just to prohibit a particular form of interest or usury that was in practice in those days and keep the doors open for all other forms of financial exploitation. Instead, the objective was to ban forever every form of interest and thereby do away with the capitalist mindset and the exploitative economic systems and social behaviour. These injunctions also aim at establishing a new socio-economic order that is marked by compassion and cooperation instead of selfishness, magnanimity instead of miserliness, *Zakāh* instead of interest and *Bayt al-Māl* instead of banking. The Qur'ānic injunctions seek to check the consequences of the capitalist system which compel a community to set up cooperatives, insurance companies, the system of provident funds and also the unnatural system of communism.

8.2. Need for interest: a rational reassessment

So far, we have discussed the question of usury and interest in light of the teachings of the Holy Qur'ān and the *Sunnah* (Tradition of the Holy Prophet). Let us now look at this from the standpoint of reason and common sense.

To begin with, let us ask whether interest is really plausible? Is it reasonable for a person to ask for an extra amount in addition to the sum extended on loan? Does it conform to the dictates of justice to ask for an additional amount over and above one's principal sum? These are a few of the most pertinent questions on the basis of which a major part of the debate on the subject gets settled automatically and a majority of the issue is resolved. If interest is something that is plausible, the question of its prohibition obviously loses significance. But if it cannot be justified from the standpoints of reason and justice, then the question naturally arises why people insist on retaining such an anti-social and irrational practice?

Let us examine the plausibility of the arguments that are generally advanced by advocates of an *interest*-based system of economy.

8.2.1. *Compensation for elements of risk and sacrifice*

The most favourite plea in support of interest is that a person giving a loan to somebody out of his hard-earned and carefully saved money is actually taking a risk of the borrower defaulting. He lends money which he could have used himself, and there is thus also an element of sacrifice in his gesture. If the borrower takes a loan to satisfy some of his personal needs, he ought to pay rent on the money obtained through the loan in the way he does for the house he hires or the furniture and means of conveyance that he borrows. The interest that the borrower thus pays covers this element of risk that the lender has taken by offering him a loan, while at the same time being a compensation for the sacrifice of extending on loan an amount he could have utilized for his personal needs. If the borrower uses the loan in a profitable venture, the lender is then even more justified in demanding interest on his principal sum. If the borrower is getting a benefit from the lender's money, why should the lender forego his dividend?

As for the first part of this plea, it is absolutely correct that the lender risks the default of the money, and that there is also an element of sacrifice in offering a loan to someone rather than making use of the amount himself. The question, however, arises: How does this justify the lender's right to demand that the borrower should pay him on a monthly, half-yearly or annual basis five or ten percent extra as a compensation for the risk he may have taken or sacrifice he made? The best he could do to counter the element of risk is: (i) retain as a mortgage (*Rahn*) something of equal value from the borrower; (ii) extend a loan on the basis of some surety (*Kafālah*); (iii) ask the borrower to furnish a guarantor (*Ḍāmin*); or (iv) refuse a loan if he is not satisfied, rather than take the risk. The element of risk is not a commercial commodity that has its cost, nor is it a house or a means of conveyance to justify rent.

As for the aspect of sacrifice, it remains a *sacrifice* as long as it does not degenerate into a commercial deal. If somebody is willing to sacrifice for someone in need, he should do it in a true spirit of sacrifice and then rest content with the moral dividends of a moral act. But if he seeks a financial return for his sacrifice, he would then simply be a merchant and would have to justify why he should be paid an extra amount on a monthly, half-yearly or yearly basis over and above the actual sum extended to somebody in need of a loan. We may further ask: Wasn't the amount of money the lender offered as a loan in excess of his own needs? If not, how could he have afforded to advance it as a loan? It is therefore evident that the lender, by extending a loan on interest, is not performing an act of charity or benevolence, nor is it an act of sacrifice by him.

Let us now examine the claim of equating interest with rent. Is it justifiable to take the additional amount that a lender imposes on the principal sum of a loan as rent? Rent is an amount of money which is charged on the use of items which their owner spends his time, labour and capital maintaining and which are devalued and subject to wear and tear during their use by those who hire them. The above definition of rent is applicable to things that are commonly used, such as residential accommodation, means of transport, furniture items, etc. It cannot, however, be applied either to consumer goods, like wheat, rice, fruit, vegetables, etc., nor on currency, which is just a medium of exchange for goods and services.

What a lender can claim from the borrower is that, because he is offering the opportunity to benefit from his personal money, he therefore deserves to share in the benefits. This seems to sound logical. But the question arises: "Do you think that the poor man who has to borrow a paltry sum of money from you to feed himself and his family is reaping such a large benefit to entitle you to seek an extra amount from him each month as a dividend for the sum advanced to him on loan? He has certainly benefited, and it is you who have provided him with the opportunity for this benefit by lending him money. But on what grounds, be they reason, justice, social service or commercial ethics, does this authorize you to determine a certain value of the *benefit* accrued to the poor borrower and to add to his worries by demanding that he pay you an additional sum of money? How can you justify your action, which results in the rate of your dividends continuing to rise with the increase in the borrower's sufferings? If you don't have the heart to feel for the hard-pressed and give money to the needy that is in excess of your personal needs, the least you can do is lend them the required amount after satisfying yourself of its return. If you don't feel like offering them the loan, nobody will force you to do this and you can rest content with your riches. But how on earth can you justify your cruel act of taking advantage of someone else's worries? Is this a plausible kind of business, turning the hardship and suffering of a person into an opportunity for making money and reducing the hungry and the dying into investment avenues? How is it that, the more humanity suffers, the better the prospects are for lenders to reap a bumper harvest of the money they have advanced on interest[2]?

The financial worth of an *opportunity* given to someone to *benefit* from a loan that is extended to him can only really be of value if it has been advanced for a business or commercial enterprise. In this case, the lender has a reason to demand a share of the benefit the borrower has got from the loan. It is obvious, however, that capital in itself has no capacity to generate dividends. It is only through human labour and enterprise that it can become an instrument of benefit. In addition, this benefit does not start flowing at once, but it takes time

---

[2] The adverse impact of interest is not confined to individual borrowers alone. Under this system the poor nations of the world have become poorer and their economic worries aggravated manifold. Those nations that have been lured into borrowing from the World Bank, IMF, multinational consortiums, regional development banks or international financial institutions, and their balance of payments' position, trade deficits and budgetary imbalances continue to grow from bad to worse. While reducing the common man to the level of an *economic animal*, these money barons have raised their own favourites within poor nations who enjoy fleecing everyone else to fill their own coffers and safeguard their patrons' interests. – Translator.

for the labour and enterprise to produce results. Moreover, one never knows how much time the labour, capital and enterprise will take to bear fruit. He similarly does not know if the return he is expecting will be as planned, or whether he will suffer losses and may even go bankrupt. If this is the position of every enterprise and entrepreneur in reality, how rational is it on the part of the lender to demand dividends on his loan from a time before the principal sum has even been put to use? How can he expect the entrepreneur to determine beforehand the rate and quantity of his profits? How can the borrower be sure of the amount he may gain in return or the loss he may suffer in spite of his best efforts?

The only plausible option for the capitalist extending a loan is to become a partner with the borrower and share the profit or the loss of the joint venture. The lender may become a shareholder with the entrepreneur, participating with him in the profit and loss of the enterprise at a predetermined rate. However, he has no right to demand that the borrower pay him a fixed amount of interest on a month-to-month or year-to-year basis on the loan he extends, without taking into consideration the gestation period of the loan before it bears fruit, as well as the chances of profit and loss. Is it rationally acceptable to allow the lender to press the borrower to pay a predetermined amount of interest, even if the borrower may have suffered a loss, earned less or only made enough profit to pay the interest? Is it justifiable that a person who invests his entire physical and intellectual capabilities, his time and his resources to see a venture grow should be forced to let a major portion of his gains pass on to a lender whose only contribution is a certain amount of money in a loan? Even the bull toiling in an oil-expeller is entitled to fodder at the end of his hard day's labour. Unfortunately, however, the capitalist would not like an entrepreneur to get the dividends of his labour which rightly belong to him.

Let us presume that the profit earned by an entrepreneur is more than the amount of interest fixed by the capitalist on his loan. Even in this case, how can one justify the capitalist's right to predetermine and impose interest over the loan extended from his excess finances; while traders, craftsmen, industrialists, farmers and all those who are the actual producers and who contribute their time, physical energy, intellectual faculties and the entire resources of their bodies and minds to produce and provide society with its essential requirements have no security at all of a profit or guarantee against any possible loss? Is it right to let the entrepreneur face the risk of fluctuating rates of profit and the vagaries of an unpredictable market, while the money-lender may sit back comfortable and smug, assured of receiving a guaranteed amount on a monthly or yearly basis over and above the principal sum he invested as a loan?[3]

8.2.2. *Compensation for opportunity and grace period*

The preceding discussion makes it abundantly clear that the plea for the permissibility of interest, which initially sounded reasonable, becomes untenable once it is viewed logically. There is definitely no justification for any amount of interest on a loan that is taken to meet one's pressing personal needs. Even the advocates of interest-based deals are now reluctant to justify this kind of interest. As for a loan obtained for commercial purposes, the questions that defy an answer remain: 'What is the nature of the commodity, the cost of which one is made to pay a certain amount of interest to cover'? 'What is the substantial object that the lender is giving to the borrower in addition to the principal sum of the loan, and what is its value, in lieu of which he is entitled to demand a fixed amount of interest not only once, but on a month-to-month or year-to-year basis?' These are questions, which have bogged the minds of even the champions of an interest-based system. According to some, it is the *opportunity* to benefit which entitles the lender to claim a certain amount of *interest* from the borrower. But, as noted earlier, this *opportunity* cannot entitle him to demand as a *cost* a predetermined, definite amount on a multiplying basis.

There are also those who try to justify the system of interest on the basis that it is in lieu of the grace period allowed to a borrower for use of the principal sum. This period of time, they claim, has its own value and that value goes on increasing with each passing day. From the moment that the entrepreneur invests the amount of the loan in his enterprise until the time he brings his product to the market, each and every moment is precious. If he is allowed no grace period and the capital is immediately taken back from him, he cannot run his enterprise and the commercial venture will go to waste. The lender, therefore, has every right to demand his share of the benefit that is earned by the borrower utilizing this period of grace that has enabled him to bring his finished product to the market. The lender is thus justified in determining the cost of this period on the basis of its length and duration.

The following most pertinent questions still remain unanswered, however: (i) How can the person lending money foresee that the borrower will definitely

---

[3] On the analogy of interest, one may very well object to a fixed amount of land revenue because the farmer can also never be sure of his produce until it is harvested. I endorse this point and have a different view about the permissibility of a predetermined amount of land revenue per acre, as this would be identical to a fixed rate of interest. My viewpoint in this respect is that the right kind of farmland management, according to the *Sharīʿah*, is *Muzāraʿah*, i.e., the landlord and the farmer distributing the produce equitably among themselves. This is a deal similar to sharing the profit in a commercial venture (*Mushārakah*). For details, one may refer to my book *Mas'ala-i-Milkīyat-i-Zamīn* (The Question of Land-Holdings). – Author.

earn a profit from that money and that there are no chances of him incurring a loss? (ii) How can he determine in advance the rate of that profit, on the basis of which he is justified to demand a definite amount as his share? (iii) On what basis can he precisely calculate the monthly or yearly rate of profit that the borrower will earn during the grace period in advance so that he can justify a claim to a predetermined sum of interest on a monthly or annual basis? The advocates of the system have no convincing answers to satisfy these questions. This naturally leads us to one conclusion: that the only plausible option for the capitalist is to participate with the borrower in his commercial venture as a shareholder on a profit and loss sharing basis.

8.2.3. *Sharing of profit*

A group supporting interest believe that profitability is intrinsic to capital, and the mere fact of someone using another's money to his advantage is therefore in itself a cogent reason entitling the lender to demand interest from the borrower. According to them, it is thus incumbent upon the latter to pay the former the desired amount. Capital has the power to support production and supply goods for public use. It helps in boosting production, which is not possible without the support of capital. A greater amount of capital leads to better quality and more value-addition, and consequently better access to the market. Conversely, less capital means poorer quality, less value-addition and even less production, limiting access to markets and lowering the price for a poorer quality product. They would say that this proves the real worth of capital and its intrinsic quality of profitability, and hence the fact that mere use of capital by the borrower for his commercial venture makes it incumbent on him to pay his lender an additional amount of interest on the principal sum.

To begin answering this, the very premise of profitability as intrinsic to capital is self-evidently wrong, and the claim that is based on this is, to say the least, fallacious. The quality of profitability is generated in capital only when it is invested by an entrepreneur in a productive venture. It is only at this point that one can argue that the lender should also have a share in the profit of the enterprise. In the case of a loan being used by the borrower for the payment of medical bills, to meet the expenses of funeral charges, to support pressing domestic needs or other similar contingencies, how can one justify that it is profitable and force the borrower to pay interest over and above the principal sum of the loan that he was compelled to obtain to meet a dire need?

Secondly, capital invested in profitable ventures does not necessarily add more value to justify the premise that it is profitable in itself. Sometimes the investment of more capital in an enterprise proves counter-productive and, instead of bringing greater dividends, actually causes a loss. The root cause of the crisis through which the world of trade and commerce is passing today is the fact that capitalists have too much money and go on investing fervently in profitable ventures. The rapid increase in the volume of production, however, automatically leads to a decline in the prices of the goods produced, and the increased supply to markets eventually causes an erosion of their value and a loss of profitability. The result is that the entrepreneur is ultimately compelled to beg for anti-dumping measures. This shows that capital's innate profitability faces a big question mark, and the entrepreneur loses all hope of reaping a good return for his investment.

Moreover, whatever potential quality the capital may have depends entirely for its fruition on so many other factors. These include hard work, the physical and intellectual potential and experience of its users, congeniality of the economic and socio-political atmosphere at the time of use and safety from natural calamities and disasters. These are among the essential preconditions for capital to bear fruit. In the absence of any one of these, not only is the profitability of capital lost, but the principal amount also often suffers loss. A capitalist who invests in interest-based ventures, however, neither shares the responsibility for the fulfilment of these preconditions, nor is he ready to forego his interest in the event of any mishap. His plea remains that the use of his capital alone entitles him to the extra amount of the interest, regardless of whether the borrower makes any gains or even suffers a loss.

Hypothetically speaking, even if we accept the claim about capital's profitability, how can this rate of profitability be calculated in advance in order to determine the rate of interest? We fail to understand how a capitalist who advances a loan in 1949 to a commercial concern for a ten-year term and to another for twenty years can be sure of the rate of his capital's future profitability, especially when the market interest rate in 1959 is likely to be different from that in 1949, with further change by 1969? How can he justify his premature calculation of the rate of interest, regardless of the future realities and the interplay of market forces ten and twenty years ahead?

8.2.4. *Compensation for time*

The last plea in this context has been more intelligently devised. This seeks to press the following points: One is naturally keen to get an immediate return on an investment, preferring today's cash over tomorrow's credit. A longer term investment decreases the value of any benefits promised. The gains that accrue today are much more attractive and precious than those expected later on. The satisfaction of an immediate need is better than future promises of even greater gains.

On the basis of this hypothesis, the certain gains of today naturally have precedence over the dubious benefits of tomorrow. The value of a loan that a person takes today is therefore much greater than the amount he would pay back to the lender tomorrow. The interest is thus the additional value that compensates for the loss a lender incurs in the intervening period on his principal sum. The argument can be illustrated further by the following example. Someone comes to a moneylender with a request for a loan of one hundred rupees. The terms that moneylender offers to agree the deal is that the borrower will pay him one hundred and three rupees in return a year later. The deal in fact envisages an exchange of Rs.103/- for Rs.100/-, and the additional sum of Rs.3/- is intended to balance the psychological rather than the economic difference between its value today and a year later. If this additional amount is not included, the principal amount will not be equal to the future value that the lender has determined for it at the time of lending.

The argument seems to sound logical. However, the way that the psychological difference between the present and future value of the principal sum has been determined is, in fact, fallacious.

Is it factually correct that human nature tends to value the present much more than the future, and that the future is of lesser worth than the present? If this is the case, why is it that the majority of people prefer to save as much as they can afford for the future, rather than spending all their earnings today? Perhaps you may not have come across even one percent of those carefree persons who have no interest in their future and the future of their families, and who are willing to sacrifice their tomorrows for the luxuries and comforts of today. At least 99% of men and women are by their very nature always aware of the need to strive for a better future, for which they are ready even to forego their present day comforts. They are impelled by this instinct to save from their income for the future. Islam has therefore established the institutions of *Zakāh* and *Ṣadaqāt* to check the *haves*, on the one hand, from becoming too money-minded; and on the other, to ensure a better living and secure future for the *have-nots*.

Even if we accept for a while the hypothesis that one can forego tomorrow's loss for today's gain, the overall argument remains untenable as far as the question of interest is concerned. At the time of the loan deal, the value of the lender's Rs.100/- was assessed to be Rs.103/- a year later. However, did the actual value remain as was predetermined when the borrower went to pay his loan after one year? If he failed to pay this amount on the due date, will the borrower have to pay the lender Rs.106/- another year later? Can anybody predict the money's future value with certainty? Who can guarantee its upward trend? *Is* the exchange rate of the rupee higher today than it was in the past? Can you claim that the actual worth of the principal sum of a loan will go on multiplying with each passing day? Can you rule out the possibility of a recessionary trend in the market and an inflationary trend in the cost of goods and services that would continue eroding the worth of your money? Can you justify, in light of the answers to these queries, your demand for an extra amount over and above what you have extended to the borrower as a loan?

8.2.5. *Reasonableness of an interest rate*

This is the total sum of arguments advanced by protagonists of an interest-based system of economy. The above analysis has exposed the hollowness of their ideas. There is little weight in their arguments to justify why interest should be offered or claimed. It is really quite intriguing how intellectuals and scholars in the West have willingly accepted a phenomenon that is so irrational and untenable as an economic system and become an established fact! It is equally surprising how they could feel so inspired by this that they focus so greatly on the rate of interest as though the whole concept was something completely 'reasonable'! It is difficult to find any discussion on interest itself in modern Western literature and whether interest-based deals are justified at all. Instead, their arguments have remained focused on the rate of interest and whether a certain rate is a bit on the high side, and hence objectionable, or whether it is 'reasonable' and, therefore, acceptable.

Leaving aside the question about the reasonableness of a certain rate of interest, which in itself is hardly justifiable or rationally acceptable, let us examine the grounds for describing a particular rate of interest as reasonable, and the basis on which one can approve or disapprove of it? Let us look into the criteria on the basis of which the world has been determining rates of interest for interest-based transactions, and whether any rationale has been followed in this?

As we examine the question critically, the fact that immediately grabs our attention is that the world has so far known no rate of interest that can be claimed as *reasonable*. Different rates that were declared as *reasonable* on different occasions were eventually rejected as unrealistic and unreasonable. The same rate of interest has often been found acceptable in one place and unrealistic in another. The Aryan intellectual Kautilya regarded a rate of interest between 15 and 60 percent as quite reasonable, which could then go even higher if the risk level rose. During the period from the mid-eighteenth to the early nineteenth century, the financial deals of India's Princely States with the local moneylenders and the East India Company were generally franchised at an annual interest rate of 48 percent. During the First World War, the British Indian Government obtained war loans at a 6½ percent annual interest rate. From 1920-30, the rate of interest for cooperative societies remained between 12 and 15 percent; while local courts designated a nine percent annual interest rate as reasonable from 1930-40. During the time leading up to the Second World War, the 'discount rate' of the Reserve Bank of India was fixed at three percent per annum, and this continued even during the War.

This was the situation in our own subcontinent. You will notice a very similar situation in Europe as well. During the sixteenth century, a 10 percent rate of interest was viewed as reasonable in England. In the 1920s, the Central Banks of some European countries charged eight to nine percent interest. The League of Nations endorsed the same rate. Today, both the US and the West as a whole reject the old rates as too hard and exploitative. They have now settled on new rates ranging from 2½ to a maximum of 4 percent. This rate goes down even further to ½ or ¼ percent in certain situations. In sharp contrast to this, the rate of interest allowed by Britain under its 'Money Lenders Act' of 1927 for loans extended to poor people is to 48% per annum; while the US courts have permitted the American money-mafia to charge interest at a rate ranging from 30 to 60 percent per annum. Now, which of these varying rates of interest can be declared as 'reasonable' and 'rational', and which others are 'atrocious' and 'criminal'?

Let us now move on to the question of whether a particular rate of interest can be logically natural and reasonable. The moment that you begin to ponder this question, your common sense comes to the conclusion that, if anyone is in a position to determine in advance the exact value of benefit the borrower is likely to get from a loan he is offered, it may then be considered as 'natural' if a particular rate of interest is imposed on him. So, for example, if anybody could foresee with certainty that the use of one hundred rupees for one year will definitely fetch dividends worth Rs.25.00, it would then be possible to determine the lender's share in the value of dividends at a rate of 5, 2½ or 1¼ percent. However, it is obviously not possible to pre-determine the amount of profit the capital will fetch. On the other hand, the money mafia that determines the market rate of interest never takes into consideration the aspect of profitability or otherwise of the money loaned by the borrower. Actually, the normal practice of moneylenders is to fix the rate of interest in terms of the borrower's constraints and needs; while rates of commercial interest are fixed by market manipulators on considerations that have hardly any relevance to reason or the dictates of justice and fair play.

8.2.6. *Rationale for varying rates of interest?*
In the money business, the basic factor encouraging moneylenders to determine an interest rate is the gravity of the borrower's need. The more helpless he is, the better are the prospects for the money barons to squeeze more out of him. If the borrower is not very hard-pressed or is seeking a larger amount to loan, the rate of interest will naturally go down. However, the rate will continue to swell with a rise in the gravity of the borrower's need. The heartlessness of the interest-based system is such that, in the case of loan being sought by a poverty-stricken father for the treatment of his desperately ill son, the interest rate of a moneylender could rise as high as four to five hundred percent. The criterion for a 'rational' rate of interest in this situation would be the same as that practised by, for example, the Sikh vendor at Amritsar Railway Station in 1947 who demanded Rs.300/- for a glass of water from a Muslim refugee migrating to Pakistan, who desperately needed the 'aqua vitae' for his child that was dying of thirst.

As for the second category of interest, the commercial interest that the market manipulators determine, the economists generally hold one of the following two opinions.

- One group of economists is of the view that the law of supply and demand is the basis for the rise and fall in the rate of commercial interest. When investors are few in number and investment-worthy capital is growing, the rate of interest continues to decline until a time comes when it reaches a lowest ebb and borrowers rush to use the opportunity to obtain more loans to invest in their businesses and trade. When demand for money surges and loan-worthy capital records a downward trend, the rate of interest then registers a sharp rise until it reaches a point where demand for loans comes to a halt.

  Let us peep through the smokescreen created by this phenomenon. We see that the capitalist is not willing to participate in a proper and judicious manner with the entrepreneur, sharing both the profit as well as any loss in a venture. Instead, he speculates about the likely benefit accruing to the entrepreneur on the sum of the loan being advanced, and accordingly determines in advance the rate of interest. On the other hand, the entrepreneur also speculates about the dividends he is likely to earn, and on this basis tries not to let the interest on a loan exceed his profit. Both parties thus resort to speculation. The capitalist naturally ensures a rosy picture for himself, and his expected profit is always on the higher side; while the entrepreneur is more cautious and keeps in view the prospects of both gain and loss. A 'tug of war' is therefore inevitable between the two because of the conflicting nature of their interests, rather than a congenial relationship of cooperation and consideration. When an entrepreneur seeks to invest in a venture with the hope of better dividends, the money baron starts raising the value of his capital until it finally becomes barely possible for the entrepreneur to avail himself of a loan due to the unreasonably high rate of interest. This prevents further investment, and the whole process of an economic upswing comes to a grinding halt. When a recession takes over, the economic realm and the capitalist realize that their own doom is around the corner. The rate of interest is then lowered to a level that inspires those in commerce and business to take loans at cheaper rates, with the expectation of earning a higher rate of profit and capital starts pouring in to aid the market's buoyancy. It is thus quite obvious that, due to the absence of a reasonable and healthy relationship of participatory cooperation between the capitalist and the entrepreneur, the global economy suffers tremendously and faces alternative highs and lows that adversely affect the world's economic health. The capitalist's stranglehold has helped to boost the spirit of speculation and minting of money through interest. This has naturally poisoned the bilateral relationship between capital and enterprise, and the raising and lowering of interest rates are now done in such a way as to keep the entire world's economic health always in risk.

- According to the second viewpoint, fluctuations in the rate of interest are justified on the grounds that a capitalist raises the interest rate only when he thinks that he needs capital for his own use; but when he has no such urge, he lowers its rate. As for why the capitalist prefers to retain his money in cash, it is said that he does this mainly because he is keen to save money for his personal or commercial needs, and also to meet other contingencies. Furthermore, the capitalist prefers to have enough cash in reserve to help him maximize his profit in the event of a decline in the currency's value or a rise in the interest rate. As the capitalist's desire to retain his wealth for better gains in the future may vary due to various personal, social, political or economic factors, he is therefore justified in raising the interest rate as this desire grows, and to lower it when he feels he has less need to retain his capital.

When viewed dispassionately, this apparently plausible justification for the capitalist's desire to make use of his money as he likes is shown to be as fallacious as the first one. So far as his personal needs are concerned, the capitalist's desire to keep his capital intact to meet various contingencies should affect no more than five percent of his wealth, and hence this is not a cogent reason to justify his manipulation of the capital market. The actual reason for withholding 95 percent of his money at some times, and letting it flow through the market's loan channels at others is entirely different. It is in fact the capitalist's extremely selfish mindset and the narrow outlook through which he perceives the world situation and the scenario at home, which is responsible for the rise and fall in interest rates. He views everything in a lopsided manner, and is always eager to keep the weapon in his control that he may use when society faces hardships, calamities and problems in order to exploit these for his own interest and thereby add to his riches. He therefore withholds his capital for the sake of speculation, raises the rate of interest, abruptly stops the flow of capital to local trade and industry and opens up the floodgates of economic recession. When he subsequently realizes that he has reaped the best harvest of his gains through these unhealthy means and can earn no more, or rather faces the risk of a loss, his actions take a new turn and he tries to entice and attract entrepreneurs with the lure of loans offered at lower rates of interest. He announces that he has plenty of money which they can use at reduced rates of interest in trade and industry.

These are the two factors that, according to today's economic experts, play a major role in determining rates of interest. However, there remain questions that have continued to defy answers: How can anyone justify as rational and logical the capitalist's desire to earn an extra amount over and above his principal sum as interest? How can he be indemnified and allowed to manipulate the money market for his narrow personal gains at the cost of the vast majority who suffer? We thus arrive at the inevitable conclusion that the interest-based system of economy is actually the most exploitative and injurious for humanity's economic health.

8.3. 'Economic benefits' of interest?

The protagonists of an interest-based system speak of the benefits that accrue to individuals and institutions. They are of the view that interest is an economic necessity, and without it the economy cannot achieve progress. The reasons they advance about the advantages that supposedly flow from interest may be summed up as follows:

- The human economy is entirely dependent on the pooling of financial resources. This is not possible unless people exercise restraint on their desires and needs and, instead of spending all their income on themselves, save a certain amount as well. In order to inspire someone to sacrify his ambitions and curtail his needs, one must have incentives for better dividends on his savings. Interest is thus the incentive which encourages him to save money and invest it in lucrative schemes. This incentive cannot be offered if interest is discarded and capital is not allowed to accumulate and serve the needs of economic development?

- The easiest access to capital for business and commerce is only possible by letting people open the doors of their savings for investment in interest-based deals. It is this lure of easy money earned through interest that makes people take their wealth from safe custody and pass it on to commercial banks, business magnates and stock dealers, rather than keeping it idle and unproductive. To shut this door of profitability would mean not only removing the most important stimulant for investment, but also denying even the little amount of capital in deposit any access to business and trade.
- Interest helps not only in investment and attracting capital to business and trade, but also in preventing unproductive uses. The rate of interest helps to determine the channel for the free flow of capital automatically towards the most lucrative option available to the investor for earning extra money. There is no other means to distinguish the more profitable from the less profitable ventures to facilitate this flow of capital. If you abolish interest, people will start recklessly using their capital and investing in all sorts of schemes, regardless of their loss or gain.
- A loan is among the inevitable needs of human life. It is a need felt by both a common man and an entrepreneur, by governments as well as institutions, in their day-to-day domestic and economic activities. Is it possible to make the required sum available to them on such a large scale purely on a charity basis? If you do not offer the capitalist the incentive of interest and the guarantee of continued dividends on his principal sum, how can you compel him to hand over his wealth on loan? Would not such a blockade of loans be disastrous for the economic life of the country and the nation? A poor man can at least get a loan from the moneylender because of the lure of interest. Except for this lure, nobody would have come to his help, even to arrange a shroud for his dead body. The businessman gets a loan when he is hard pressed for cash, and this is how he manages to keep his venture afloat. Had there been no avenue open to him to get a loan due because there was no provision of interest, he would have failed to support his venture with the much-needed cash, which is the life-blood for business and industry. Similarly, governments

would have been left high and dry without success in pooling millions through public loans for financing their development schemes.

8.4. Need and utility of interest?

Now let us examine in turn the so-called 'need' and 'utility' of interest to see if there really is any such need and benefit, or whether this is all merely a hoax?

The first misperception concerns the actual worth and advantage of frugality and money-mindedness. To save money by hook or by crook is regarded as being in the interests of economic health of both individuals and nations. Actually, it is just the opposite. Factually speaking, economic growth and prosperity depend on a community's ability to produce more and the market's buoyancy in order to sell all that it receives to satisfy the demands of consumers, thereby maintaining the balance and pace of the cycle of production and consumption. This is only possible when people get used to utilizing the amount of money they earn through their economic struggle properly, and are magnanimous enough to spend what is more than they actually need in helping the needy and the indigent of their community, enabling them to purchase their required items. National wealth thus shifts automatically to the areas where it is most needed. Conversely, the champions of an interest-based system teach people who have gathered more than they actually need to stockpile and preserve their wealth by pursuing a course of miserliness, which they interpret as self-restraint and sacrifice. They ask those who earn to be frugal in spending their money even for their personal needs. They believe that the capital thus saved serve to promote trade and industry. Actually, however, the market becomes the greatest loser, because a major portion of the goods produced remains unused. Consumers with less purchasing power are unable to get even the goods they desperately need; while those with a better purchasing capacity and the moneyed class prefer to avoid costlier items and are unwilling to transfer wealth to others, but keep it hoarded in their bank accounts and coffers. When consumers who are blessed with purchasing power and affluent people withhold a good part of their wealth from purchasing goods themselves and do not let that capability pass on to those who have a greater need for it, instead simply amassing wealth, then a natural corollary is that a major part of the community's economic product remains unsold in each economic cycle. The decline in consumption thus leads to a decline in job avenues; this decrease in jobs causes a decrease in income; and the decrease in income in turn results in a further decline of the consumption level of finished goods. The accumulation of wealth within a few hands thus leads to the economic ruin of many, eventually turning the tables against capital-worshippers themselves because the wealth they have amassed, when it is used to produce more goods, has no market to consume them and give the money barons the desired return.

As we examine this eventuality more carefully, we come to the conclusion that the actual economic requirement is to remove the causes and factors due to which, instead of spending, people are led to withhold and stockpile their income. The community's welfare demands that there should be, on the one hand, a sound arrangement in place which allows every member to get the required assistance in times of need so that everyone may enjoy a sense of security about his future, rather than being tempted to suppress his needs and save for a 'rainy day'. On the other hand, *Zakāh* should be levied on the surplus saved in order to discourage the affluent from amassing wealth and providing a channel for at least a part of this accumulated capital to reach those who may have lagged behind and can only get a small share from the money in circulation. In sharp contrast to this, the champions of an interest-based system encourage those given to greed and lust for money to be more miserly on the pretext of better dividends in the form of interest; while those not susceptible to such traits are being advised to save and make more money instead of spending it on personal needs and noble causes.

The capital thus gathered, contrary to the imperatives of public welfare, is then diverted towards the process of producing wealth, and this through the charging of interest. This is yet another crime of the capitalists against the public interest. Had the accumulated wealth been invested in business and trade, with the capitalist getting a proportionate share of the dividends, even this would have been fair. Unfortunately, however, everything is directed towards hoisting him higher on the money market and ensuring a guaranteed return in the shape of dividends, regardless of the business suffering loss or gain and the rate of profit being high or low. The protagonists of an interest-based system have thus let the national economy suffer a double loss: the first caused by preventing the capital from flowing into the market; and the second through the return of that accumulated wealth to the national economy not through participation in business on the principle of partnership, but as loans lying heavy on the shoulders of the society's entire trade and industry. The capitalist is thus the sole beneficiary enjoying a legally guaranteed rate of profit. The system thus impels the majority of people to hold back their purchasing power from buying national products, and instead to invest the money saved in more and more interest-based loans. The community is then faced with the dilemma of how to get rid of the rising burden of interest and loans, while the market is unable to find a sufficient number of consumers for the goods produced from that capital. While millions are unable to purchase goods, as they have no money to buy, there are thousands who do not purchase because they prefer to hold back their purchasing power to convert it into more interest-based loans.

According to the advocates of an interest-based system, interest is helpful in inspiring businessmen to avoid wasteful use of capital and to utilize it gainfully. They take it as one of the wonders of the interest-based system that it discreetly guides those in business and trade to seek the most lucrative channel for investment. However, if they care to look behind the smokescreen of such superficial claims, they will notice the damage done by this system. The first setback of the system is that it has altogether changed the concept of 'profit and gain', by which everyone today means simply 'material gain' and 'financial profit'. The capital has thus been prevented from flowing into those channels where profits and gains do not stand essentially for material and fiscal dividends. It has instead been directed directly to a more mundane use, where it is sure to reap profit for investors at a predetermined rate. Another setback of the system is that the sole criterion of the capital's fruitful use is now the gains reaped by the capitalist, and not the community. The predetermined rate of interest guarantees him at least six percent profit per annum for his capital's investment in ventures. Investment in anything less advantageous to him, though much more beneficial to the community, is hardly attractive. For example, there is a low-income housing project for the poor on the one side and on the other a scheme for a grand cinema complex. The former carries a rate of profit below six percent, while the latter offers a much higher rate of interest. Under normal circumstances, the capital should have flowed generously to the financially less-attractive scheme. But the lure of additional income through an enhanced rate of interest makes the capitalist shy of investing in a less profitable project. Furthermore, a businessman is often tempted to use even unethical means to keep his profit higher than the interest level fixed by the money baron. For example, if someone establishes a film company in which the capital invested carries an annual interest rate of six percent, he will have to produce movies which bring in more money to enable him pay back the amount of interest to his investors and also earn a profit. He will even avoid producing educational and healthy films in favour of vulgar movies, and through sexplosive advertisements he will try to entice the unwary public to gate-crash cinema halls and bring him a windfall of profit.

This is the actual position about dividends earned through an interest-based system. Now, let us examine the need for a loan which, according to the money barons, cannot be satisfied without interest. Without doubt, the loan is one of the dire needs of human society: people need it for their personal necessities; it is required in the fields of trade, business, industry and agriculture; and governments and social institutions also need loans. But to say that a loan cannot be available interest-free is absolutely wrong. In fact, the present situation, where neither individuals nor institutions, either public or private, can get a loan free of interest, is due entirely to the legalized system of interest. On the other hand, there is no legal cover in an interest-free system of economy. Once interest is declared unlawful and the state adopts the economic and social systems of Islam, then it will be evidently clear how easy it is to get a loan for everything, starting from one's personal needs up to the social and economic requirements of the public and private sectors. Even donations will start pouring in. This is a historical fact that centuries of experience of an Islamic social order has practically vindicated. The Muslim society continued to manage its affairs for centuries, including everything concerning its economy, in a much better way without recoursing to interest. Before the introduction of the interest-based system, the Muslim community had never witnessed an accursed phenomenon like a person's dead body lying unsolicited because of his heir's inability to put together a paltry sum in a loan to arrange for a shroud and a decent burial; or a commercial, industrial or agricultural venture collapsing due to the want of *al-qarḍ al-ḥasan* (an interest-free loan, with no stipulated due date); or Islamic governments of the day failing to implement their public welfare schemes or Jihad expeditions as a result of the reluctance of their Muslim subjects to invest in such schemes. The claim that the scheme is not practicable and the practice of debit and credit can only flourish on the foundation of interest is, therefore, logically untenable. The flimsiness of such statements lies exposed by the glorious record of our centuries-old practice.

8.5. Demerits of interest

...فَمَن جَآءَهُۥ مَوۡعِظَةٞ مِّن رَّبِّهِۦ فَٱنتَهَىٰ فَلَهُۥ مَا سَلَفَ وَأَمۡرُهُۥٓ إِلَى ٱللَّهِۖ وَمَنۡ عَادَ فَأُوْلَٰٓئِكَ أَصۡحَٰبُ ٱلنَّارِۖ
هُمۡ فِيهَا خَٰلِدُونَ ٢٧٥ يَمۡحَقُ ٱللَّهُ ٱلرِّبَوٰاْ وَيُرۡبِي ٱلصَّدَقَٰتِۗ وَٱللَّهُ لَا يُحِبُّ كُلَّ كَفَّارٍ أَثِيمٍ ٢٧٦

('Hence, he who receives this direction from his Lord, and then gives up (dealing in interest), may keep his previous gains, and it will be for Allah to judge him. As for those who revert to it, they are the people of the Fire, and in it shall they abide. Allah deprives interest of all blessing, whereas He blesses charity with growth. Allah loves none who is ungrateful and persists in sin.')

(*al-Baqarah*, 2: 275-276)

In the above *Āyah*, Allah *subḥānahū wa taʿālā* did not grant absolute pardon to the moneylender for the interest-money he took and consumed prior to the promulgation of the decree banning interest. The Lord just said: '... it will be for Allah to judge him'. The pardon in this case is, therefore, a legal clemency, absolving him from returning the additional sum he consumed earlier, because otherwise it would have been difficult to put an end to the litigations from those seeking the return of extra amounts of interest that the moneylenders had taken and consumed. Ethically speaking, however, the amount earned in interest earlier remains undesirable. The moneylender who underwent a social and moral transformation after embracing Islam was inspired on his own not to put the money earned as interest to personal use, but to return it wherever possible and, in cases where borrowers were difficult to trace, to spend it on schemes of public welfare rather than enjoying its benefits himself.

Āyah 276 speaks of a truth that is absolutely correct morally and spiritually, as well as from social and civilizational points of view. Apparently, wealth seems to grow by interest and looks to recede through donations to charities and almsgiving. However, the reality is just the opposite. According to the Divine law of nature, interest is a barrier in the way of humanity's moral, spiritual, economic and civilizational growth. It is in fact a major cause of degradation. *Ṣadaqāt* (Charity), on the other hand, which also include *al-qarḍ al-ḥasan*, are helpful in preserving and promoting everything from morality and spiritualism to the economy and civilization.

Viewed from the moral and spiritual perspectives, it is quite clear that the phenomenon of usury and interest is an offshoot of traits such as selfishness, miserliness, petty-mindedness and heartlessness. These are the qualities that *Ribā* promotes in human beings. Conversely, *Ṣadaqāt* are the result of such noble attributes as magnanimity, compassion, large-heartedness and broad-mindedness. By adopting *Ṣadaqāt* as a life pattern, these qualities go on flourishing among humans. Who can deny that the former set of traits is the worst and the latter the best for both individuals and the community?

From a civilizational point of view, it is also quite easy to understand how weak the social fabric of a society will become if individuals treat each other selfishly; if nobody is of any use to another unless his personal benefit is involved; if the need of one is fodder for the greed of another and the 'haves' are always ready to exploit the misery of the 'have-nots'; and if the interests of the moneyed class stand counter to the interests of the common man. Members of this kind of society can never expect to enjoy an atmosphere of mutual love, trust and respect. They are instead exposed to an air of mutual distrust, rancour, apathy and a lack of compassion. An atmosphere of chaos, confusion and even conflict is bound to be the hallmark of such a society. Conversely, a society whose structure is based on compassion and mutual trust, where members treat each other with magnanimity, where to live is to love and be helpful to one another and where those with resources treat those in need with kindness and a spirit of cooperation, this social set-up can only prosper, with justice, fairplay, love and an atmosphere of fellow-feeling prevailing. Members of a blessed society like this are certainly bound together in a strong bond of cohesiveness and mutual care; no internal conflict or major discord will ever rupture its harmony. With the qualities of cooperation and care underlying a society, it is destined to progress at a much faster pace than its counterpart.

Now let us examine this issue from the economic angle. From an economic perspective, interest-based loans can be of two types: those taken by the needy to satisfy their personal needs; and those obtained by entrepreneurs to support their commercial, industrial, agricultural and other ventures. Concerning the first category of loans, it is an established fact that these play a devastating role in the lives of poverty-stricken people. There is hardly any country in the world where individuals and institutions that lend money are not ruthlessly sucking the blood of the poorer segments of society, like peasants, farmers, labourers and other low income groups. Due to the unbearable burden of interest, they are often incapable of repaying their loans. They are too often forced to take fresh loans in order to pay back earlier ones, while the principal sum remains hanging over their heads like the Sword of Damocles even after they have cleared interest and compound interest. A major portion of the hard labour of the working classes is thus eaten up by money barons, and they are left with too little to satisfy even their basic needs. This gradually leads them to lose interest in their work as they see the fruits of their labour being gobbled up by others, leaving nothing for them but misery. The unbearable burden of accursed interest also takes its toll on their physical and mental health. Because of poverty, these people are unable to feed themselves and their families properly or to meet the expenses of their treatment and health care. It is due to the interest-based system of economy that a selected few continue to grow filthy rich by sucking the life-blood of millions of people; yet the community as a whole goes on getting leaner and leaner because of a sharp decline in the production of wealth from the desired level. The situation eventually adversely affects the money barons themselves. The seething anger of the poor masses against the misery and hardship inflicted on them by this heartless class often results in a volcanic eruption that takes away in its flow their lives, property and all the manifestations of their names and their fame.

There are many adverse effects of the second category of loans as well. The following explains the few most pronounced of these:

- An enterprise, however useful and essential for the country and nation, if it is not profitable enough to cover the prevailing rate of interest, fails to attract investors. The country's entire financial resources flow towards the market's more lucrative ventures that offer better rates of interest, regardless of their overall utility and advantage for the country and the community.
- No commercial, industrial, or agricultural enterprise that is capable of attracting capital on interest can guarantee a definite rate of interest for all times and under all circumstances. There can never be any security against a fall compared to the predetermined rate of five, six or even ten percent. Putting aside a guarantee and security against a decline in the rate of interest, nobody can even provide any guarantee that a certain venture will always be profitable, with absolutely no chance for any loss. This automatically brings us to the conclusion that the capital invested in an enterprise, for which the lender might have been offered a guaranteed rate of interest, can never be free from the risk of loss and default.
- Because the investor is not a partner in the venture's profit and loss and his sole concern is interest, which he is sure to get at the predetermined rate, he is naturally unconcerned about its losses or gains. He selfishly keeps in view the dividends that he is going to earn. Whenever he senses a threat of a recessionary trend taking over market, the first thing that he does is to withdraw his capital. This is how investors are often instrumental in actually causing recession through their self-motivated speculations, or at least further aggravating the recessionary trend by their hasty moves.

These are three major disadvantages of an interest-based system which no student of Economics can ever deny. One must therefore admit that, according to the law of nature devised by the Almighty, interest is instrumental not in the growth but in the decay of the national economy.

Let us now look at the economic impact and advantages of *Ṣadaqāt*. If the affluent members of society get used to following the prescribed path of generosity and spend their income according to their economic status on themselves and their families, they can then leave the balance after fulfilling their requirements to help those in need and extend any surplus they are left with as interest-free loans to an entrepreneur, with whom they could participate as partners in an enterprise on a profit and loss sharing basis, or they could even lend it to the government for use in public welfare schemes. In this situation, one can very well imagine then how healthy the mindset and lifestyle would be for the all-round progress and prosperity of the country and the community.

The overall national economic growth of a society like this will be much higher compared to that of a society that survives on an interest-based system.

There is yet another aspect of this matter which must also be borne in mind. One needs to have a share of the national wealth in excess of his requirements in order to lend money to others. This additional part of the income that one earns and which is in excess of one's actual needs is, according to the Holy Qur'ān, a blessing from the Lord (*Faḍl Allāh*). The right way to be thankful to the Lord, the Beneficent, the Merciful, for His Benevolence is that, as His bondsmen, we must also be kind and generous to our fellow humans, just as the Almighty has been so Kind and Gracious to us. Is it then justifiable for a believer to misuse his blessings from the Lord in exploiting others through the accursed system of interest, rather than letting them share in the benefits of his affluence?

8.6. Economic growth without interest

Let us now turn to the crucial question: 'Is it possible to discard interest totally and replace it with a financial system that can serve the fiscal needs of a developing society and state in the modern day world?'

Before discussing this subject, let us first try to remove some misunderstandings that boggle the mind, not only in context of the subject under discussion, but in many other cases as well.

8.6.1. *Some misunderstood facts*

One may notice that the first misunderstood fact is the main one responsible for the question above. Rationally speaking, interest is definitely bad. It has been strictly prohibited by the Holy Qur'ān and the *Sunnah* as well. Because of this, when one asks questions such as '*Can we do without interest?*' or '*Is it feasible to run the economy without interest?*', he is guilty of questioning the Divine Wisdom by believing that something intrinsically bad can be 'inevitable' and that something absolutely correct rationally can be 'impracticable'. This attitude is actually tantamount to 'casting a vote of no-confidence' against nature and its Divine Law. In other words, this simply means that we are living in a corrupt cosmic system, in which some of even our most basic needs have been linked with something that is wrong and unhealthy and the doors to what is good and blissful have been deliberately shut to us. Further, this will lead us to presume that nature itself is so crooked that the very thing that the law declares is wrong becomes useful, essential and practicable; and that which is right according to the law turns out to be useless and impracticable.

Can we, using our sane judgment and in light of our physical and natural sciences and the age-old experience of our history and civilization, ever prove such a slander against nature? Is it true that nature is pro-chaos and anti-harmony? If this is the case, we will be left with no option but to give up any debate concerning right and wrong, good and evil, and leave all hope of healthy living because we will have no ray of hope in this world. But neither human nature nor the nature of our cosmic order can approve this misperception for a moment. Therefore, we cannot afford to foster the notion that a certain idea, though intrinsically bad and harmful for individuals and society, is a 'necessary evil' and must be adopted; and that another idea, which is logically, rationally and intrinsically good and beneficial, can be 'impracticable' and hence avoided. The right is always right and reason demands that it must be followed, while the wrong is always wrong and, according to the dictates of reason and ethics, must necessarily be discarded.

Factually speaking, when something gets accepted in the world, every society and state finds it easier to follow the others, and gradually they find it difficult to change their track onto the right direction. This is true about everything in practice, whether good or bad. The difficulty lies in changing, and the actual reason for convenience is only current usage and prevalence. It will therefore be an act of sheer ignorance to misconstrue a wrong practice as the only viable option that cannot be changed, even by something which is much better and more beneficial for the nation and state.

The second misconception in this context is that the people often tend to dismiss attempts at change as being unfeasible without actually realizing the amount of hard work involved in this. One miserably fails to assess correctly the immense potential of human endeavour to make a necessary change from the beaten track if one summarily dismisses as impracticable anything different from current practice. In a world that has recently witnessed the introduction and implementation of the rationally and intrinsically wrong system of absolute collectivism, and a total ban on individual ownership in the so-called '*Dictatorship of the Proletariat*', it is absurd to pontificate and presume that the scourge of interest cannot be removed and replaced by a social order based on *Zakāh* and *Ṣadaqāt* (mandatory and normal charities) as the anchor-sheets of a state's economic policy. However, what is true is that this task cannot be accomplished by any Tom, Dick or Harry. A revolutionary change like this can only be brought about by those who are duly qualified and have the following qualities:

- They must have personally discarded the interest-based system and have a firm faith in the dynamics of the new order, according to which they are seeking to bring about the desired change.

- They must also be well-versed in the field and duly motivated to follow the path of *Ijtihād* (scholarly re-interpretation of juridical issues), instead of blindly following the beaten track (*Taqlīd*). For this, they must have the required level of *Taqwā* (love and fear of God) and *Tafaqquh* (insight into the juridical issues of *Sharīʿah*). They must be capable of direct access to the Qur'ān and the *Sunnah* and able to translate precepts into practice.

The qualities needed to challenge the old and exert one's best faculties in a planned transition to a new order are the same traits that enabled the champions of extremist ideologies like Communism, Nazism and Fascism to reach their goals. Unless one has these basic qualities, he cannot introduce even the most balanced, benign and scientific changes that Islam recommends.

There is yet another minor misunderstanding which needs to be removed. In response to the healthy criticism and demand for reform, supporters of an interest-based system often ask for an action plan and a roadmap for change. Perhaps they believe that paper is the right domain for action. Practically speaking, you need grounds to act. What can be done on paper is to explain and expose logically the failings and harmful effects of the system in practice and establish the plausibility of the proposed reforms. As for the problems involved in putting these proposals into practice, nothing more can be achieved on paper beyond creating a general awareness about how to set right the wrongs of the old system and how best to implement the new system. As far as a complete picture of the proposed shake-up is concerned, the relevant details and solutions for resolving issues likely to emerge at different stages can neither be pre-determined nor answered beforehand. If you are convinced that the present system is essentially wrong and damaging to the social fabric and that the proposed reform is definitely correct, then take the first step forward and entrust the task of reform to those equipped with the prerequisites of *Īmān* (Faith), Ijtihād and a professional expertise for translating the injunctions and guidance available in the Book of God and the Tradition of the Holy Prophet (*pbuh*) into practice. The day will then naturally dawn when practical issues get resolved as soon as they emerge. Otherwise, how can you expect the fieldwork to be completed simply on paper?

Following this clarification, I need not stress that I am not going to offer a detailed plan for an interest-free economy in this context. Instead, a general outline has been offered of the practical steps necessary for removing the cancer of interest from our national economy and to resolve the apparently major problems which seem to challenge the very thought of discarding the old system.

8.6.2. *First step towards reform*

Most of the problems which have adversely affected our national economy are mainly the result of our having legitimized interest. Obviously, if the doors of interest are open, why would one choose to lend his neighbour *al-qarḍ al-ḥasan*? Why would he participate with an entrepreneur on a profit and loss sharing basis? Why would he lend a helping hand of cooperation for the cause of national development rather than hand over his capital to the money baron who is willing to offer him a certain, predetermined profit on his principal sum? After encouraging the unhealthy traits of human nature and giving them a free hand, how can one expect to check their adverse effects merely by sermonizing and moral exhortations? In fact, you have not just given a free hand to these negative traits but also provided them legal support and further boost by officially adopting the interest-based system. Under such circumstances how can you check the unhealthy impact of this system through partial amendments or inconsequential reforms? The scourge of interest can be checked effectively only by closing its floodgates first.

Those who think that, once an interest-free system is in place, any interest-based system would automatically cease to exist or may eventually be banned as illegal, are trying to put the cart before the horse. As long as interest remains legal, the courts will continue to enforce it through their decrees, and as long as there is no check on the capitalists piling up wealth by enticing every household to join hands in their interest-based transactions, it will not be possible for any interest-free system to take off the ground and flourish. The only way to accomplish this is to ban all interest at the very outset. This small initial step will automatically lead to the rise of an interest-free economic system of economy and find a way of growing and developing – as the dictum goes, 'Necessity is the mother of invention'.

The roots of the unhealthy traits of human nature, of which interest is one manifestation, are so deep that no half-hearted measures or goody-goody plans can eliminate such a scourge from a society. It is essential to achieve our purpose to press into service all those measures proposed by Islam and combat it as earnestly as desired by the Religion of Truth. Islam does not simply condemn interest on moral grounds, it helps us to realize how despicable interest is by proclaiming it *Ḥarām* from religious viewpoint and simultaneously declaring it legally prohibited within its political and administrative jurisdiction wherever Islam holds sway as a government and state. It declares that all interest-based deals are against the law. The act of taking and giving interest, writing the documents for these deals and serving as a witness to a deal have all been pronounced as offences liable for penal action. Due to the gravity of the unhealthy social impact of interest, Islam imposes a severe punishment and the confiscation of property for those found wilfully violating the law. Furthermore, by prescribing *Zakāh* as mandatory for Muslims and entrusting the state with the responsibility for its collection and distribution, the foundations are laid for an entirely different system of economy and finance. Side by side with these practical measures, there is an effective program of public reform through the popular means of education, training, motivation and missionary zeal in order to curb people's inclination for easy money through interest and promote healthier trends and tendencies in them for the successful growth of magnanimity and sympathetic cooperation in society.

8.6.3. *End result of a ban on interest*

Anyone who is sincerely and honestly keen to eliminate interest can follow the steps mentioned above. Steps like the banning of interest and the establishment of a state mechanism for the collection and disbursement of *Zakāh* will lead to the following developments of a revolutionary nature from both the financial and economic points of view:

- The first outcome will be a reversal of the current unhealthy trend of capital formation. The way that capital formation currently takes place inspires our social structure to promote the traits of miserliness and wealth-worship to unimaginable levels, qualities that are already there in varying degrees in every human being. This compels everyone, by way of both fear and greed, to spend as little of his income as possible and save as much as he can. Economic pressure frightens a person into saving for his own future and the future of his family because there is nobody to come to his rescue in harder times. He is tempted to put his savings into attractive schemes to get better dividends. Due to this double stimulant, even those members of society who are only just above the poverty line are tempted to avoid spending and attempt saving instead. Consequently, the market gets flooded with consumer goods and the consumption level declines. As the level of earning goes down, the prospects for industrial and commercial growth correspondingly become more and more bleak. This is how a rise in the level of a few persons' savings becomes instrumental in the decline of the national economy, resulting in thousands being incapable even of earning a living, let alone being able to save.

  On the other hand, when interest is declared illegal and the system of *Zakāh* is in place in an organized, institutional manner, with the state standing as surety for the economic support of each and every member of society, the unnatural factors that promote miserliness and wealth-worship are bound to die a natural death. The people will then spend heartily to meet their day-to-day requirements, and the 'have-nots' will continue to receive financial support through *Zakāh* to sustain their purchasing power and satisfy their needs. In such an atmosphere, the profits of trade and the industrial sectors are both bound to rise to a level at which they are self-reliant and less dependent on external financial assistance, as is the case today. Moreover, these sectors will get the desired capital for progress much more easily when compared with the situation prevailing now. This is because the process of saving will not come to a halt absolutely, as is generally feared. Even people with a normal income will continue to save because of an inherent urge, while others will do so because of the general level of prosperity and growth of income. The circumstances will change so that savings will be motivated not by the elements of fear or greed, but by the people's affluence, earning more than they need and, even after generously spending according to the Islamic teachings, being left with surplus money with no needy or indigent persons around to share this with. These very savings will thus get pooled and passed, on much better terms, to the government, the country's trade and industry and even the neighbouring states.

- The second most welcome result of the abolition of interest will be the urge of the accumulated capital to flow rather than to stagnate. The national economy will continue to receive its lifeblood, the capital, according to its needs and at opportune moments. Under the current system, what makes the capital flow towards trade and commerce is the lure of interest. But the same factor is often also a cause for the stoppage of that flow when capital is hesitant and looking for a better rate of interest. Because of this, the mood of business and commerce and that of the capital are often at variance. When business is eager to attract capital, the capital stubbornly goes on hardening its terms and conditions; and when the situation changes, the capital starts running after the entrepreneur and is ready for investment in any good or bad venture, even on easy terms. When interest is declared unlawful and *Zakāh* is levied at the rate of two and a half percent per annum on all accumulated wealth, capital will then automatically cease to be as wayward as it is today under an interest-based dispensation. In fact, it will relish being invested as soon as possible in different ventures on reasonable terms and conditions, and will keep on circulating instead of lying idle.

- Thirdly, as a natural corollary of the abolition of interest, the loans sector will be totally separated from the trade and commerce sector. Under the present system, the availability of capital is mostly, or rather wholly, in the shape of a loan. If a person or business concern seeks a loan for a profitable venture or a profitless job, for an emergent need or for a long-term project, the loan is offered on only one condition, that the borrower will have to repay it at a predetermined rate of interest. The moment that interest is abolished, the operation of loans will become restricted entirely to the emergent needs only, which carry no profit, and will be managed on the principles of *al-qarḍ al-ḥasan* (benign loans), offered without any 'mark-up' and with no stipulated date for its return. As for any other requirements, whether relating to business, trade, industry and agriculture or public and private sector organizations, investment will be made in these fields exclusively on the principles of profit and loss sharing.

8.7. Availability of loans in an interest-free system

Now, let me explain in greater detail how these two areas of *al-qarḍ al-ḥasan* and investment loans operate in an interest-free economic system.

Let us first take up the general misperception that, with the abolition of interest, the loans' chapter will also stand closed. It may thus be pertinent to discuss first how the end of the accursed system of interest will result in the facilitation of loans, not in the end of their availability. In an interest-free economic order, the loans will not only be easier to obtain, but will be in a much better shape and on very benign terms and conditions.

8.7.1. *For personal needs*

Under the present system, the only way for a poor man to obtain a loan is to knock at the door of the moneylender, and for the well-to-do to approach the Bank, and receive it on interest on the lenders' terms and conditions. In both cases, the borrower does get the loan, provided that he can satisfy the lender or the Bank about timely payment of a fixed rate of interest. The party offering credit is unconcerned whether the loan is being taken for morally good or bad objectives, for extravaganza or for satisfying real needs. The borrower, however, does not get a penny unless he is in a position to satisfy the lending party about payment of interest on schedule, even if his needs are as pressing as arrangements for burying the dead. In the current situation, the pressing needs of the poor and the waywardness of a prince are equally attractive as opportunities for the moneylender to earn more money. Together with his selfishness, the whole system is so heartless that it allows no relaxation or remission to anybody trapped in the tangle, neither for payment of interest nor for repayment of the principal amount of a loan. Nobody has the heart or time to notice the predicament of the poor borrower. These are the 'facilities' to people for obtaining a loan to meet their personal needs.

Now, let us analyse what Islam has to offer by way of interest-free loans through its institution of *Ṣadaqāt*.

To begin with, the Islamic system shuts the doors to extravagance and over-spending because there can be nobody and no institution around to lend money for unlawful or anti-social activities. Consequently, the entire system of lending and borrowing is automatically restricted to genuine demands, and the amounts of loans obtained and extended will naturally be reduced to a level that is reasonable in different individual cases.

Secondly, it will be unlawful for the lender to take any personal or institutional advantage from the borrower and, therefore, the return of the loan will become much easier. Even those with little income will be in a position to arrange repayment in easy instalments and so be relieved of the burden of their debt. If someone has mortgaged his land, house or any other property, the income from this will be deducted towards repayment of loan, thus accelerating the speed of its settlement, rather than being consumed in the payment of interest.

If a loan remains unsettled despite these facilities, the Public Treasury (*Bayt al-Māl*) will come to the poor man's rescue and help him to repay his loan. If the borrower expires without leaving the money to settle his loan, even then it is the Public Treasury's responsibility to arrange for its repayment. Under such an environment of compassion and cooperation, it is also not difficult or hard for a well-to-do person to lend his needy neighbour to redress his hardship, as it is today under an interest-based system, because he will feel secure then about the return of his loan.

If a person is unable to get a loan from anywhere, the doors of *Bayt al-Māl* will be open for him as a last resort. From the Islamic point of view, it is incumbent on individuals to take care of each other's needs and extend a loan if a person in need seeks one. This is actually the barometer for judging the level of the Muslim community's moral strength. In case someone fails to get such assistance from those around him and has to knock on the doors of *Bayt al-Māl*, this would indicate the poor state of a society's moral health. *The one in need is thus assured of getting the amount needed as loan, and the Islamic State's department of moral health and hygiene will intervene to check why the people of a particular area have been so callous as to refuse help to their neighbour in distress.* An incident like this will create the same amount of commotion in a morally upright milieu as is caused today in our materialistic environment by the report of an outbreak of plague in a certain area.

The Islamic system of economy also takes care of personal loans in another way. It is legally binding on commercial concerns and business groups to include, as part of their charter of obligations towards their employees, the provision for offering them a loan under extraordinary circumstances. In addition, the government is required to be generous in the discharge of its duties towards its employees. The charter of their rights and duties includes the facility of loans in their times of need. In fact, this is something that is very important not just from a moral point of view, but also economically and politically. By offering your employees, wage-earners and staff members the facility of an interest-free loan, you are not simply performing an act of virtue, but are actually instrumental in removing the causes of their mental distress, economic problems and physical and material hardships. Protect people from these trials and tribulations and you will notice how quickly their mental and physical satisfaction helps boost their work potential, energizing their minds and bodies and safeguarding them from harmful and negative thoughts and ideologies. Materially, the dividends of this magnanimity may not be as much as one might have expected, but anyone with a small amount of insight can very well imagine how far-reaching the advantages of such an approach are not just for society as a whole, but also for every investor and factory owner, as well as for each and every economic and political institution. The dividends reaped will be much higher in value and more precious in real terms than the 'gains' from interest gathered today by our materialistic world.

8.7.2. *For commercial purposes*

Now let us take up the question of loans that entrepreneurs take for their trade and business. For this purpose, either short-term loans are obtained from commercial banks or transactions are made through 'Bills of Exchange'.[4] In both of these cases, banks levy a negligible rate of interest as their surcharge. No commercial transaction is possible these days without this surcharge.

[4] The 'Bills of Exchange', which are known in Urdu as *Hundī*, or *Ḥawālah,* are what Islamic Jurisprudence (*Fiqh*) calls *Safātij*. According to this kind of transaction, businessmen, who frequently deal with each other and have a common Banker, exchange on credit a large quantity of goods among themselves without paying any cash. In return they give to the other party an undertaking or *Hundi* for the settlement of a loan within a stipulated period of time. If the party concerned is willing to wait, all is well and good; but in the event of their being in need of money during that period, they submit the *Hundi* or Bill of Exchange to their Bank and get the required amount. – Author.

Entrepreneurs therefore become alarmed by the very thought of the denial of a loan by their banks once an interest-system is declared illegal. They rightly ask how the banks can offer a loan or cash our *Hundīs* (Bills of Exchange) once there is no lure of interest?

However, the following question arises: How can the Bank, which holds in its custody the entire deposits and millions of rupees of these entrepreneurs free of interest, refuse to extend them interest-free loans or cash their Bills of Exchange? In the case of its refusal, the Islamic state's merchantile law can take action and the Bank can be forced to extend this service to its clients. A provision to this effect can also be included in the charter of duties of commercial banks.

In fact, millions contributed in deposits by entrepreneurs should themselves serve as an incentive for commercial and investment banks to extend them interest-free loans. In emergencies, the banks can also draw from their reserve funds for this purpose. As a matter of principle, if somebody is not getting any extra amount from these banks in interest, why should he pay them a penny as interest? From a national economic point of view, it is of immense value that traders and businessmen should continue getting loans free of interest and other encumbrances.

As for the management of interest-free loans, the banks can do this safely through interest-free deposits in their Current Accounts. They can meet the nominal expenses incurred on maintaining a ledger, stationery charges, etc. from those deposits. In fact, the cost thus payable will be far below the amount of profit earned by the banks. If this is found to be cumbersome or unfeasible, they can levy normal service charges on their deposit-holders on a monthly or quarterly basis. This will be less expensive for the clients than the amount of interest they would otherwise have paid, and they will therefore accept this most willingly.

8.7.3. *For non-productive public sector needs*

The third important category of loans contains those obtained by the government to meet national emergencies, such as natural calamities and wars, or for non-productive public needs. Under the present economic system, the requirement for all such exigencies is met entirely through interest-based loans. Under the Islamic economic system, however, it will be possible for individuals and institutions to respond generously to a government call for funds because the abolition of interest and the state-management of *Zakāh* should have made them self-reliant and affluent enough to inspire them to hand over their savings to their government voluntarily. In case of a shortfall, the government can seek a loan and the public will willingly extend to it *al-qarḍ al-ḥasan*. If the shortfall persists, the government can then take the following measures:

- use the revenue generated through *Zakāh* and *Khums*;
- invite banks to extend compulsory loans to the government out of their reserves deposited with the Central Bank; or
- as a last resort, bridge the gap by printing the required amount of currency notes, which will be yet another form of public loan.

8.7.4. *International lending*

Now, let us observe how we should deal with loans extended by or obtained from international donor agencies. It is quite clear that, in today's interest/usury-hungry world, we cannot expect to get even a penny as an interest-free development loan for our national needs. The best course left to us is therefore to avoid foreign loans as much as possible, at least until such time as we are ready to rise as a role model and practically demonstrate to other developing nations how a state can help itself and also come to help other nations by extending them a loan without interest in their times of need. As for giving loans to other countries, it may not be difficult for anyone with vision and insight to agree, in light of the discussions above, that once we have the courage to establish a healthy monetary system in our country by abolishing interest and introducing the system of *Zakāh*, our fiscal health will become so strong that we will not only be relieved of the ignominy of going around with a begging bowl in our hand, but will also be in a position to extend help to poorer nations, particularly those in our neighbourhood, and offer them interest-free loans. The day when we are in a position to do this will mark the dawn of a new revolutionary era in modern history, not only from a socio-economic point of view, but also from political, civilizational and moral perspectives. The moment that we create such an epoch-making economic model, we will create a new paradigm for the world, which it may find inspiring enough to emulate. It may then be possible for us to enter into economic and commercial deals with other nations on interest-free basis, and others might start following our lead and engage themselves in deals and MoUs without recourse to the interest-based system. It is possible that the day may dawn when the world's public opinion might unify against the age-old scourge of interest in a wave of anger and hatred, as witnessed against Bretton Woods in Britain in 1945.

This is not wishful thinking. In fact, many perceptive brains across the globe have actually started thinking in these terms and are alarmed by the highly negative impact caused by interest on foreign loans on the world's politics and economy. If the developed world gives up this exploitative system and sincerely and genuinely starts helping the developing and poverty-stricken under-developed countries to stand on their own feet, they will receive double dividends. From the political and sociological perspectives, the gesture is bound to promote an air of friendly cooperation and understanding, rather than mutual tension and hatred; while from the economic viewpoint it will prove to be advantageous. It is worth paying this price in order to deal with a prosperous and affluent economy, instead of sucking the blood from an economy that is already emaciated and bankrupt. These are words of wisdom, which thinking minds are already contemplating, and those who are capable of expressing them are doing so loud and clear. The only thing that is needed is a wise and dynamic nation rising up and eliminating the evil of interest, first from its own home, and then moving forward to pave the way practically for ousting it from the world arena.

8.7.5. *Capital needs of profit-making projects*

Having looked at financing loans, let us now see how we perceive business-financing taking shape in the system we have in view. In this context, as discussed earlier, the abolition of interest will totally eliminate the avenues of guaranteed profit from people's investment, unless it involves their labour and risk. Similarly, the enforcement of *Zakāh* will make it impossible for them to hold back their capital and sit tight on it, like the proverbial cobra guarding a treasure chest. Moreover, under an Islamic government and its benign socio-economic structure, there will be no door left open for the filthy rich to indulge in unwarranted luxuries and extravaganza from their surplus income that has been boosted through the interest channel. Consequently, those with surplus capital will have to avail themselves of any of the following three options:

- If they are not interested in any additional income, they may spend their surplus capital on welfare projects, whether by directly contributing to a charitable work or through gifts and donations to national institutions. They may even hand it over voluntarily and with a sincere motive to the government for use in public welfare schemes and developmental projects. This is how a considerable fund is generated that will always be freely available to the government and other institutions of public welfare, on which they have to pay no interest; in addition, the people will be saved from paying tax to the government in order to finance these schemes.
- If the moneyed people are not keen to earn more, but want to retain their surplus wealth for personal use, they can deposit it in banks. The banks,

instead of keeping it in a fixed deposit, can take the money as a loan payable to them on demand or on a stipulated date. The banks will also be entitled to invest this amount in a business and earn profit. They will, however, guarantee its return to the deposit holder according to agreed terms, although they will not share any profit with their clients, as this will then be entirely the bank's earnings. Imām al-Aʿẓam Abū Ḥanīfah conducted his business largely according to this Islamic concept. Due to the extraordinary level of his honesty and public standing, the people used to deposit their money in his safe custody. Imām al-Aʿẓam accepted this money not as *Amānah* (trust), but as a loan that he invested in his business. According to his biographers, at the time of his death, the total investment in his business through interest-free loans amounted to 50 million Dirhams. According to the *Sharīʿah* rule, the money deposited with someone as trust (*Amānah*) cannot be used by the trustee (*Amīn*). However, in case of its loss due to some unforeseen mishap, like robbery or a natural calamity, the trustee cannot be held responsible for returning the money. Conversely, if the same money is taken as a loan, the borrower is allowed to put it to use to his best advantage, but only on the condition that the principal amount is returned to the lender on the stipulated date and time. Commercial banks can follow the same rule even today.

- Those keen to invest their savings into some profitable business can avail themselves of the option of *Mushārakah*, or equity participation on a profit and loss sharing basis, which has been sanctioned by the Islamic *Sharīʿah*. This partnership can be arranged through government channels or banks. If they want to start a business themselves on a *Mushārakah* basis, they will have to specify the terms and conditions of this partnership and will be bound by the law to determine the profit and loss ratio between the parties concerned. Participation in joint stock companies can similarly be arranged by purchasing these shares. There will then be no market for bonds and debentures, in which the purchaser earns just the predetermined amount.

If the investment is done on a *Mushārakah* basis with the government, the investor will have to buy shares in any profitable government scheme. For example, when the government desires to mobilize resources for a hydro-electric project, it will have to advertise its terms and conditions for public participation and invite them to invest in its shares. Whoever invests in such schemes, whether an individual, an institution or a bank, will become a shareholder with the government and will be eligible for any profit as per the agreed terms. The liability of loss will also be shared in the same proportion by the government and all shareholders. The government is authorized also to gradually start buying back public shares, until eventually the entire profit reverts to its ownership and the venture becomes one hundred percent state property.

As in the case of an interest-based system, the most practicable and profitable form of investment in an interest-free dispensation will also be through banks. I would therefore like to discuss this in greater detail to examine how the banking system can run effectively without interest, and what dividends the profit-seeking clients can earn from this?

8.8. Islamic modes of banking

Our discourse on banking in the book *Sūd* makes it clear that there is nothing wrong or unlawful in the institution of banking itself as such. Actually, it is among the highly important and beneficial legacies of modern times, debased unfortunately by the induction of a single Satanic element. This institution performs so many lawful functions, which are not only useful but also unavoidable given today's socio-economic needs. These include, for example, the transfer of money from one place to another, salary disbursement, remittances from abroad, transactions in foreign currencies, safe custody of valuables, letters of credit, travellers cheques, sale of company shares and agency services that allow a busy person today to be relieved of so many burdens in return for a nominal commission fee paid to his bank. These are the functions which will go on and a permanent institution is indispensable for carrying them out. The bank in itself is highly beneficial for trade, industry, agriculture and for all the sectors of a civil society and economy. Under the present circumstances, it is also desirable that surplus capital, instead of lying scattered around, should have a reservoir from which it can easily be made available to whoever needs it. It is also of immense benefit to the common man, who is saved the trouble of finding out proper avenues for the gainful use of his savings and can safely deposit them in a central pool for better utilization, thus being assured of a certain amount of profit.

Bankers get professionally trained in the fields of money and finance and acquire the insight and expertise not normally available to traders, industrialists and the social sector's other manpower. This insight and expertise are highly valuable assets and can be extremely useful, provided that they are not turned into tools of exploitation in the hands of money barons and are used instead for cooperation with businessmen and entrepreneurs.

Unfortunately, however, the element of interest has demeaned all these good features, and banking benefits and advantages have become very harmful for society. Another damaging aspect of the interest-based system is the virtual conversion of the capital accumulated in banks into the personal property of a few self-seeking capitalists, which they generally use in an extremely anti-social manner. Once these two drawbacks are removed, banking itself emerges as a highly dignified job, much more useful for human civilization than it is in its present form. In fact, it is quite likely that under the Islamic economic system the institution may become even more profitable, and in a more dignified manner for the moneylenders than it is today.

Those who think that the abolition of interest may cause an end to the flow of capital to banks are absolutely wrong and their apprehensions are totally unfounded. According to this misperception, people with no hope of earning a profit can hardly be expected to deposit their surplus money in banks. The factual position is that they will then be denied only the amount of interest, while the prospects for more profits will multiply to an unprecedented level. In the present system of interest-based banking, the rate of profit is predetermined arbitrarily, with clients having no say either in the fixation of the rate of interest or in the manner in which the banks handle their deposits to make money. In interest-free banking the chances of a loss will be minimal, but the opportunities for gain are manifold. The banks will continue simultaneously performing their normal duties for which clients now opt for their services. It is, therefore, a foregone conclusion that the amount of money that flowing today into banks will rise greatly after switching over to an interest-free system. With the growth of trade and business, an increase in job opportunities a and rise in people's income under an interest-free economic dispensation, the rate of capital flow to national banks will naturally rise by leaps and bounds, and the people's additional income will continue to find its way to the safer and more lucrative interest-free accounts.

The capital reserve available in Current Accounts, or 'On-Demand' deposits, will not bring a profit, as is the case with Current Accounts today. This reserve will be used by banks either for day-to-day cash transactions, or for short-term lending to entrepreneurs on an interest-free basis or cashing the Bills of Exchange.

As for the long-term Fixed Deposits, these will essentially consist of the following two categories: (i) deposits of clients desirous of preserving their savings in secure bank accounts – such deposits will be available to banks as loans for investment in profitable ventures, as mentioned earlier; (ii) the second category of fixed-term deposits will include those maintained by account holders keen to invest in trade and business through their banks. Instead of keeping these deposits as *Amānah* (trust), the banks will have to sign a participatory agreement with these clients and then reinvest their capital, along with other similar deposits, on the principle of *Muḍārabah* (trustee-financing) in commercial ventures, industrial projects, agricultural development and in other profitable public sector schemes.

Financing on *Muḍārabah* terms will produce two grand results: (i) the concern of the capitalist and of the business and commerce sectors will become one and the same, with each supporting the other, thereby eliminating once and for all the factors responsible for recessionary trends in today's *Riba*-ridden world; (ii) both capital and enterprise will become cooperators and not competitors, as they are today. The financial wizardry of the capitalist and the commercial insight of the entrepreneur, which remain in opposition now, will start supporting and cooperating with each other to their mutual advantage. The dividends thus earned by banks will in turn pass on in a proportionate manner to their accounts and to shareholders, after deducting necessary administrative expenses. The big difference in this setup will be that the dividends, which are now being pocketed by the shareholders of banks while account-holders are given a paltry amount of interest, will then be equitably distributed between both groups. There will be no fixed rate of interest, but the entire amount of profit, big or small, will be distributed in due proportion among all stakeholders – the clients as well as the shareholders. The corresponding risk of loss and bankruptcy will also be present. However, the major difference will be that the risk of loss and the unlimited prospects for gains, which are now exclusively for shareholders, will then be shared equally by both account holders and the shareholders of commercial banks.

As for monitoring the banking sector's loss due to the accumulation of capital in the hands of a limited number of moneyed people who are capable of manipulating the money market as they please, the *Bayt al-Māl* or State Bank (Central Bank of Pakistan) can be authorized to retain central banking power in its hands and, through its regulatory laws, make it incumbent upon private banks to conduct their business in a manner that leaves no room for capitalists to misuse their financial muscle.

Let us hope that the brief outline of *Ribā*-free banking and finance presented in these paragraphs will effectively serve to dispel all misgivings about the practicability of the abolition of interest.

8.9. Economic and industrial loans from non-Muslim countries[5]

[One of the readers of the monthly *Tarjumān al-Qur'ān* sought Sayyid Mawdūdī's views regarding the following questions:

> 'Can an Islamic government, in an age of inter-dependence, achieve any progress by declaring as totally *Ḥarām* all economic, military and technical assistance or development loans from World Bank on the given rate of interest? How can we then bridge the big gulf of material, industrial, agricultural and scientific advancement that divides the developed West and the under-developed Muslim World between the *Haves* there and the *Have-nots* here? Can we afford to wind up all our domestic interest-based institutions of banking, insurance and finance? Is there a way out from the deeply rooted local practices of usury, *Paghrī* (advance money), goodwill and commission money, brokerage, etc? Can the Muslim countries follow an interest-free lending system in their dealings among themselves?'

Sayyid Mawdūdī's response to these queries is summed up as follows:]

> At no point in time has any Islamic government followed a policy of severing ties with non-Muslim countries, nor can it do so today. But the need for loans does not involve going around with a begging bowl seeking loans, and this at the lender's terms. This kind of relationship with 'donor' countries has been promoted in today's world only by those who lack courage and foresight. Whenever an Islamic government is established, its first priority will be the moral rejuvenation of its people prior to their material advancement. Moral reform of the people involves building their character; ensuring that everyone, from an ordinary member of society to the rulers and administrative cadres, is honest and God-fearing and cares more about their obligations and duties than their rights; and holds onto a nobler objective in life, for which they may even be ready to scarify their life, property, time and all their potential. This means that both ruler and ruled have full confidence in each other, and the people should feel genuinely convinced that they are being governed by those who keep their people's welfare close to their hearts. When a situation like this evolves, no nation will ever face the eventuality of knocking on other doors for loans in order to sustain itself. Under such a healthy dispensation, the people will willingly pay their taxes. The collection rate of taxes levied will be one hundred percent, and the rate of their proper utilization on people's welfare and development will also be one hundred percent. If the need then arises for loans, the people will come out themselves voluntarily with generous

[5] Adapted from *Tarjumān al-Qur'ān* of November, 1961.

> donations, while a major part of the sum may be collected as an interest-free loan and some of it on a profit and loss sharing basis. I sincerely believe that if Pakistan can set the pace in Islamic economics, it may not be long before we emerge as a donor country, instead of remaining dependent on foreign loans. Our ability to experiment successfully with the Islamic principles of banking and finance may soon turn us into a model state for the developing world, offering loans to others rather than being on the receiving end ourselves.

If a situation were to arise in which we are compelled to seek foreign loans for some pressing national needs and for which funds are difficult to generate locally, we may do this as a last resort. Even in such an eventuality, there will be no justification for retaining the system of interest-based loans within the country. Interest can be abolished and the country's entire financial system can very well function on a *Ribā*-free basis. I have established in greater detail in my book *Sūd* (*Interest*) how the banking system can be effectively run on the principles of profit sharing, instead of interest. Similarly, the insurance system can be so remodelled as to conform to the Islamic concept of *Takāful.* As for brokerage, rates of profit, advance money, commission and goodwill, each has a different position according to the *Sharīʿah*. An Islamic state, once established, can review the situation and make amendments wherever necessary. This will obviously have to be done jointly by a scholar of *Sharīʿah* and professional experts in banking and finance.

9 *Zakāh* in Theory and Practice*

9.1. Essence of *Zakāh*

The third of the five pillars of Islam, after *Īmān* (Faith) and *Ṣalāh*, is Mandatory Charity or *Zakāh*. *Ṣawm* or Fast of the holy month of Ramaḍān and *Ḥajj* or Pilgrimage to Holy Ka'bah are the fourth and fifth. This is why *Zakāh* follows *Ṣalāh* immediately in the Holy Qur'ān wherever the attributes of a worthy believer are described.

9.1.1. *Meaning*

The word *Zakāh* in Arabic means 'purity' and 'cleansing'. The act of apportioning a certain amount of money from one's personal assets is termed as *Zakāh* by the Islamic *Sharī'ah*, because it helps in purifying his purse as well as cleansing his self. The person who fails to pay to the subjects of the Lord what is their due out of the resources placed at his disposal makes his wealth and his own self impure. This means that he is ungrateful to the Lord and is so selfish, miserly and given to the love of money and greed that he has no heart even to discharge his duty towards his Benefactor, Who blessed him with resources surplus to his needs. It is hard to expect any worthwhile act of goodness from such a person for his Lord's sake, or that he will offer any sacrifice in the way of his faith and religion. The heart of such a person will, therefore, be anything but pure and his riches nothing but profanity.

9.1.2. *Apostolic tradition*

Since time immemorial, it has been mandatory for all followers of the Prophets of God to observe Prayer and perform *Zakāh*. Exemplified by the teachings of every Apostle, Allah's Religion 'Islam' has never been without these two basic tenets. While mentioning *Sayyidinā* Ibrāhīm and the Prophets that followed him (may Allah's peace be upon all of them), the Holy Qur'ān says:

وَجَعَلۡنَٰهُمۡ أَيِمَّةٗ يَهۡدُونَ بِأَمۡرِنَا وَأَوۡحَيۡنَآ إِلَيۡهِمۡ فِعۡلَ ٱلۡخَيۡرَٰتِ وَإِقَامَ ٱلصَّلَوٰةِ وَإِيتَآءَ ٱلزَّكَوٰةِۖ وَكَانُواْ لَنَا عَٰبِدِينَ ٧٣

* Adapted from Sayyid Mawdūdī's other masterpiece: '*Khuṭubāt*'.

> ('And We made them into leaders to guide people in accordance with Our Command, and We inspired them to do good works, and to establish Prayers, and to give *Zakāh*. They worshipped Us alone.')
>
> (*al-Anbiyā'*, 21: 73)

The following has been said about Prophet Ismā'īl (*pbuh*):

وَكَانَ يَأْمُرُ أَهْلَهُۥ بِٱلصَّلَوٰةِ وَٱلزَّكَوٰةِ وَكَانَ عِندَ رَبِّهِۦ مَرْضِيًّا ﴿٥٥﴾

> ('He enjoined his household to observe Prayer and to give *Zakāh*, and his Lord was well pleased with him.')
>
> (*Maryam*, 19: 55)

Prophet Moses (*pbuh*) prayed to the Lord for his nation that He may grant them the best of both worlds. In response to his prayer, what the Lord pronounced was highly significant:

...قَالَ عَذَابِىٓ أُصِيبُ بِهِۦ مَنْ أَشَآءُ ۖ وَرَحْمَتِى وَسِعَتْ كُلَّ شَىْءٍ ۚ فَسَأَكْتُبُهَا لِلَّذِينَ يَتَّقُونَ وَيُؤْتُونَ ٱلزَّكَوٰةَ وَٱلَّذِينَ هُم بِـَٔايَـٰتِنَا يُؤْمِنُونَ ﴿١٥٦﴾

> ('I afflict whomsoever I wish with my chastisement. As for My Mercy, it encompasses everything. I will show Mercy to those who abstain from evil, pay *Zakāh* and have faith in Our signs.')
>
> (*al-A'rāf*, 7: 156)

Jesus Christ preceded the Last of the Prophets of God, *Sayyidinā* Rasūl Allāh (*pbuh*). The Qur'ān says that Christ was also enjoined to observe *Ṣalāh* and *Zakāh*:

وَجَعَلَنِى مُبَارَكًا أَيْنَ مَا كُنتُ وَأَوْصَـٰنِى بِٱلصَّلَوٰةِ وَٱلزَّكَوٰةِ مَا دُمْتُ حَيًّا ﴿٣١﴾

> ('And has blessed me wherever I might be and has enjoined upon me Prayer and *Zakāh* as long as I live.')
>
> (*Maryam*, 19: 31)

This reaffirms that Islam, as the eternal religion of mankind, was preached and practised by all the Prophets of God since the very beginning, and the Apostolic tradition has established the Religion of Truth on the two grand pillars of *Ṣalāh* and *Zakāh*; no community in the world has ever been exempted from these obligations.

Turning to the Islamic *Sharī'ah*, we can see how closely interlinked both *Ṣalāh* and *Zakāh are* as mandatory duties for all Believers:

ذَٰلِكَ ٱلْكِتَـٰبُ لَا رَيْبَ ۛ فِيهِ ۛ هُدًى لِّلْمُتَّقِينَ ۝٢ ٱلَّذِينَ يُؤْمِنُونَ بِٱلْغَيْبِ وَيُقِيمُونَ ٱلصَّلَوٰةَ وَمِمَّا رَزَقْنَـٰهُمْ يُنفِقُونَ ۝٣

('This is the Book of Allah, there is no doubt in it; it is a guidance for the pious, for those who believe in the existence of that which is beyond the reach of perception, who establish Prayer and spend out of what We have provided them.')

(*al-Baqarah*, 2: 2-3)

The Lord then declared:

أُو۟لَـٰٓئِكَ عَلَىٰ هُدًى مِّن رَّبِّهِمْ ۖ وَأُو۟لَـٰٓئِكَ هُمُ ٱلْمُفْلِحُونَ ۝٥

('Such are on true guidance from their Lord; such are the truly successful.')

(*al-Baqarah*, 2: 5)

This means that those who do not have faith and do not observe *Ṣalāh* and *Zakāh* are neither on the path of Guidance, nor will they ever achieve real prosperity in this world or the Hereafter.

As we proceed further in the same *Sūrah*, we have the following Command from the Lord:

وَأَقِيمُوا۟ ٱلصَّلَوٰةَ وَءَاتُوا۟ ٱلزَّكَوٰةَ وَٱرْكَعُوا۟ مَعَ ٱلرَّٰكِعِينَ ۝٤٣

('Establish Prayer and dispense *Zakāh* (the Purifying Alms) and bow in worship with those who bow.')

(*al-Baqarah*, 2: 43)

The believers are exhorted in a series of *Āyāt* in *Sūrah al-Tawbah* to remain steadfast against the hostilities of anti-Islamic forces and wage against them a relentless struggle for the supremacy of Islam until the enemies of Islam give up their stance and repent; as a clear proof of this change of heart, they will start observing the Islamic code of conduct, of which *Ṣalāh* and *Zakāh* are the dominant symbols:

فَإِن تَابُوا۟ وَأَقَامُوا۟ ٱلصَّلَوٰةَ وَءَاتَوُا۟ ٱلزَّكَوٰةَ فَإِخْوَٰنُكُمْ فِى ٱلدِّينِ ۗ ... ۝١١

('But if they repent and establish Prayer and give *Zakāh* they are your brothers in faith.')

(*al-Tawbah*, 9: 11)

9.2. *Zakāh*'s place in social life

The Book of God frequently uses the term *Infāq fī Sabīlillāh* for *Zakāh* and *Ṣadaqāt* (Mandatory and normal charities), meaning *Spending in the Way of Allah*. It is also proclaimed that whatever one spends in the Way of Allah is *al-qarḍ al-ḥasan*, or a benign loan in the name of Allah *subḥānahū wa taʿālā*, the repayment of which He has made incumbent upon Himself. In addition, it is declared that whatever one gives by way of charity is rewarded with many times more in return and the dividends are guaranteed by the Lord. Let us reflect for a while over this teaching! Is the Lord of the heavens and the earth in need of our alms? Does He require a loan from us to manage His affairs? Is the King of Kings and the Sovereign of all the treasures of the universe demanding a 'loan' for Himself? May Allah forgive us for even a fleeting thought like this! We exist because we are being sustained by Him. Our survival depends on His Beneficence. Whatever the rich or the poor amongst us has is all a gift from Him. From the beggar to the billionaire, everyone is dependent on His Benevolence. He definitely needs no lending for Himself. It is in fact part of the benignness of His Sublime Munificence that He tells us to spend for our own good, in our own cause and to our own advantage, declaring this as a spending in the Way of the Lord and a loan in His Name, the return of which is binding upon Him and for which He also expresses His Gratefulness. The Most Glorified and All Praiseworthy is our Lord! In His infinite Mercy He tells us to give generously to the poor and the indigent, and because the poor cannot repay this, He will pay people back on their behalf. He exhorts us to help our relatives in need and He will be indebted to us for this, not them. We are told that, whatever we do to redress the miseries of orphans, widows, the handicapped, wayfarers and the grief-stricken of our community, will not be an act of generosity towards them as such, but it will be recorded as a loan in His account. We have to demand nothing from them in return, but He has taken upon Himself to reward us for our good deed.

Our duty is to extend a loan to one in need, but we cannot ask him to pay us interest, harass him for the return of our principal amount or, in case of his inability to pay us back, bring him to book in a court of law to get his property confiscated and his family dishonoured. Allah *subḥānahū wa taʿālā* tells us that the return of the loan is His responsibility. If the debtor returns the loan, The Lord will pay us 'interest' on his behalf. But if he is unable to return even the principal sum, He Himself will return to us both the amount of loan as well as the interest. We are similarly told that whatever we invest for the welfare of our fellow human beings, although its benefit is eventually going to return to us, the

Lord will take that investment as an act of kindness to Himself and it will never be allowed to go to waste unsolicited; we should rest assured of its repayment together with many dividends.

We are aware that man by nature is ظَلُوم وَجَهُول, i.e. *given to ignorance and ingratitude.* He lacks foresight; lofty thoughts seldom strike his brain; he is selfish and is unable even to have a clear perception of what is good for him and what is bad. *He is always in hurry* (خُلِقَ ٱلْإِنسَـٰنُ مِنْ عَجَلٍ) and likes to reap the dividends of whatever he does as quickly as possible. He is oblivious to the benefits that may accrue to him in future on a much larger scale. These are his inherent weaknesses, due to which he is always on the look out for personal gains, especially those which are quick, easy to get and tangible, though they may be short-lived. He believes that whatever he has earned or inherited from his ancestors belongs entirely to him, which none has a right to share, and that he can make use of it in the way he likes to satisfy his needs, fulfil his desires and provide himself with comforts and luxuries for life or invest it in ventures that may gain him greater dividends. He spends money because he expects a better return in terms of cash or a raise in his living comforts, or at least a rise in his name, fame and worldly status. If no such benefits are in sight, he does not feel inspired to part with even a little bit of what he has in his purse. He is hardly bothered to lend a helping hand to an orphan or someone dying of hunger or wandering as vagabond, as he feels convinced that it is the responsibility of that orphan's father or the relatives of the indigent to provide a better income or an insurance policy for their near and dear ones to take care of them in their hours of need. He is unconcerned if a widow is passing her life in distress next door, because he considers her late husband responsible for her plight and believes he failed to leave behind a better fortune for her. If a wayfarer is in need of assistance, he is not moved to come to his help and will, instead, blame him for making no proper arrangements for his needs in advance. He feels constrained even to extend a loan to someone, and if he does so, he will do it on the basis of interest; otherwise, what is he going to get out of the money he has so 'wasted', and why should he not invest it in some profit-making concern or interest-bearing venture!

With such a self-seeking mindset, a man with money is either niggardly and prone to wealth-worship, or if he is moved to spend will do so only to his own advantage. He will be loath to part with even a penny unless his personal interest is involved. He may apparently be helping a man in need, but actually he has got a selfish motive. Whatever he gives, he will try to get more in return. When he provides something to an indigent person, he does so at the cost of the poor man's self-respect. If he decides to participate in a project of national importance, he first assesses the dividends this will fetch him. Unless he is assured of a hefty return, not a penny trickles out of his purse.

Where does such a mindset lead? The consequences of such a self-centered approach are diabolical not just for the society, but eventually for the individual himself, who tends to consider it as worthwhile and advantageous for himself due to his short-sightedness and ignorance. When this kind of mentality is at work among the people, national wealth starts accumulating in a few hands and the majority of people go on sliding downwards into the dismal abyss of want and misery. The rich grow richer and the poor become poorer and society succumbs to moral and material degeneration. Its physical health deteriorates and diseases prevail, adversely affecting its potential and ability to produce wealth. The rate of literacy declines; moral values crumble; crimes flourish as the means to gratify one's ambitions; lawlessness prevails; and a situation emerges when riots become rife and the wealthy people get killed and their assets are looted and destroyed until finally everything associated with this class is totally decimated.

One should never be oblivious to the universal truth that the happiness of an individual depends on the happiness of the society to which he belongs. If you have the heart to spend your money on your fellow humans who are in need, this money will circulate like life-blood, keeping the society healthy and eventually returning to you with added benefits. But if you choose to hold it tightly in your purse, spending it only in your personal interest, it will gradually diminish. For example, if you become the guardian of an orphaned child, help him get an education and grow to become a healthy man, you have thus actually contributed to the overall wealth of the society by adding one more person to its qualified manpower reserve. The more that the society benefits from his output, the richer you will grow as its member, although you are not often directly aware of being the source of this benefit. On the contrary, if you follow a different course and, in a show of self-conceit and apathy, leave the orphan at the mercy of the vagaries of time, his inborn capabilities will gradually deteriorate and he may become a vagabond and an unproductive person, incapable of doing any good either for himself or for the society to which he belongs. It is quite possible that the same innocent, orphaned child of yesteryear may grow up to be a criminal breaking into your own house as burglar one day. This simply means that, through your apathy and lust for money, you have turned an otherwise normal person into a vagabond and a worthless member of society, and by making him criminal you have not harmed him alone, but yourself as well. Through just this one example, you may very well imagine, from a broader perspective, how the money that a person selflessly spends for the good of society, which obviously comes out of his pocket, goes on growing and multiplying with more and more benefits until it ultimately returns to the pocket from whence it came with greater dividends than it may have earned had it not been spent in a good cause. A person who holds back his money and does not contribute to the welfare needs of society apparently saves it, or allows it to grow on interest. Practically speaking, however, he devalues his wealth and provides for his self-destruction through his folly. It is this secret that the Lord so succinctly reveals in the Holy Qur'ān:

يَمْحَقُ ٱللَّهُ ٱلرِّبَوٰا۟ وَيُرْبِى ٱلصَّدَقَـٰتِ ۗ ... ﴿٢٧٦﴾

('Allah deprives interest of all blessing, whereas He blesses charity with growth.')

(*al-Baqarah*, 2: 276)

وَمَآ ءَاتَيْتُم مِّن رِّبًا لِّيَرْبُوَا۟ فِىٓ أَمْوَٰلِ ٱلنَّاسِ فَلَا يَرْبُوا۟ عِندَ ٱللَّهِ ۖ وَمَآ ءَاتَيْتُم مِّن زَكَوٰةٍ تُرِيدُونَ وَجْهَ ٱللَّهِ فَأُو۟لَـٰٓئِكَ هُمُ ٱلْمُضْعِفُونَ ﴿٣٩﴾

('Whatever you pay as interest so that it may increase the wealth of people does not increase in the sight of Allah. As for the *Zakāh* that you give, seeking with it Allah's good pleasure, that is multiplied manifold.')

(*al-Rūm*, 30: 39)

Human short-sightedness and ignorance are, nevertheless, obstacles that do not let us properly understand and be motivated by this secret. Man is a slave of his sensory organs: he can see the rupee in his pocket; he knows how it is growing in his accounts; but he is unable to visualize the rupee that leaves his pocket. He does not know whether it is growing and growing where or at what rate, and when it may return to him with added dividends and benefits. He only regrets that a certain amount of money has gone out of his purse, and seems to be gone for good.

Man has not been able to rip this curtain of ignorance from his mind. It is virtually the same the world over. On the one side, there is the capitalist world where every deal is being managed on the basis of *Ribā* and, in spite of their stockpiles of wealth, the graph of problems and miseries is ever on the rise. On the other side are the growing multitudes seething with anger. They are waiting for an opportune moment to pounce on the capitalists' treasure houses and turn the entire spectrum of human civilization and culture upside down.

This greatest enigma of modern times has so far defied a solution. But the All-Knowing and All-Wise Lord has already resolved the problem in His Book, once for all. The key to the successful resolution of man's socio-economic problem lies in *'Īmān billāhi wa bi'l-yawm al-Ākhir'* (faith in Allah *subḥānahū wa ta'ālā* and in the Last Day). One needs to have complete faith in the Almighty and be cognizant of the fact that He alone is the Lord Master of all the treasures of the heavens and the earth; whatever humans may do, they are accountable to Him and will eventually get their reward or punishment on the Day of Reckoning for the good or bad they did here. With such a firm faith, it becomes easier for man to trust in God and spend his wealth in the light of His Guidance, leaving the aspect of profit and loss to Him. Whatever a person spends with this spirit, he will actually be giving to the Lord and it will be entered into His Register. Whether anyone knows of his good deeds in this world or not, nothing can escape the notice of the All-Knowing Lord; and whether someone expresses gratitude or not for the magnanimity done for him, it will be duly acknowledged by the Ever Grateful Lord and there will be a reward in this world, in the Hereafter, or in both.

The normal rule of the Islamic *Sharī'ah* is first to give general instructions enjoining us to do good and refrain from wrong, thereby helping us to adopt the good for our lives and shun the evil. The specifics of the good acts are then elaborated to facilitate their observance in a prescribed manner.

In the case of *Zakāh*, there is also a general order followed by guidance in its specifics. We have been commanded to shun stinginess and greed, as these are the root causes of all ills; to take on صِبْغَةَ ٱللَّهِ or 'Allah's Colour', in all our conduct; to spend in the way of the Lord and to save as much as we can for this to help others to meet their essential needs; and to go to the extent of sacrificing our life and property for the cause of Religion and to make the Writ of God supreme. If we are true in our love of God, we must sacrifice the love of money for His love. This is the general command, which is then supported by the specifics. For example, we have been asked to part with at least a definite amount of money in His Way out of our wealth, and to contribute a certain proportion of our agricultural produce towards the welfare of the indigent and the needy. The injunctions about Prayers, similarly, do not mean that we have to observe only the limited number of *Raka'āt* of the regular Prayers and can spend the rest of the day without remembering the Lord. Those with less than the prescribed amount of money to be eligible for *Zakāh* have not been prevented from spending in the Way of the Lord, and the *Zakāh* payer is not prevented from exceeding the prescribed minimum amount and denying the society the benefit of his affluence and generosity.

9.3. Divine Command about *Zakāh*

There are three separate injunctions about *Zakāh* at three different places in the Holy Qur'ān:

In *Sūrah al-Baqarah*, the believers have been commanded:

يَـٰٓأَيُّهَا ٱلَّذِينَ ءَامَنُوٓا۟ أَنفِقُوا۟ مِن طَيِّبَـٰتِ مَا كَسَبْتُمْ وَمِمَّآ أَخْرَجْنَا لَكُم مِّنَ ٱلْأَرْضِ ... ﴿٢٦٧﴾

('Believers! Spend (in the Way of Allah) out of the good things you have earned and out of what We have produced for you from the earth ...')

(*al-Baqarah*, 2: 267)

In *Sūrah al-An'ām*, the Lord reminds us that it is "He Who has brought into being gardens" and all kinds of crops and fruit-bearing trees. We have, therefore, been ordered to:

... كُلُوا۟ مِن ثَمَرِهِۦٓ إِذَآ أَثْمَرَ وَءَاتُوا۟ حَقَّهُۥ يَوْمَ حَصَادِهِۦ ... ﴿١٤١﴾

('Eat of their fruits when they come to fruition and pay His due on the day of harvesting.')

(*al-An'ām*, 6: 141)

Both of these *Āyāt* relate to the produce obtained from the land. According to the jurists of the Ḥanafī School of Jurisprudence, *Zakāh* is leviable on everything that is reaped from the land, including food grains, vegetables, fruit, etc., but excluding self-grown products, such as wood, grass, bamboos, etc. According to the Prophetic Tradition, a tenth part of the produce will be deducted as *Zakāh* from the rain-fed (arid) land and a twentieth part from the land irrigated by rivers, streams and man-made sources. Specified shares of the produce become mandatory the moment that the crop is harvested.

The following is pronounced, then, in *Sūrah al-Tawbah*:

...وَٱلَّذِينَ يَكْنِزُونَ ٱلذَّهَبَ وَٱلْفِضَّةَ وَلَا يُنفِقُونَهَا فِى سَبِيلِ ٱللَّهِ فَبَشِّرْهُم بِعَذَابٍ أَلِيمٍ ﴿٣٤﴾ يَوْمَ يُحْمَىٰ عَلَيْهَا فِى نَارِ
جَهَنَّمَ فَتُكْوَىٰ بِهَا جِبَاهُهُمْ وَجُنُوبُهُمْ وَظُهُورُهُمْ ۖ هَـٰذَا مَا كَنَزْتُمْ لِأَنفُسِكُمْ فَذُوقُوا۟ مَا كُنتُمْ تَكْنِزُونَ ﴿٣٥﴾

('And there are those who amass gold and silver and do not spend it in the Way of Allah. Announce to them the tidings of a painful chastisement, On a day when they shall be heated up in the Fire of Hell, and their foreheads and their sides and their backs shall be branded with it, (and they shall be told): "This is the treasure which you hoarded for yourselves. Taste, then, the punishment for what you have hoarded".')

(*al-Tawbah*, 9: 34-35)

Details of those eligible to receive *Zakāh* follow next:

إِنَّمَا ٱلصَّدَقَـٰتُ لِلْفُقَرَآءِ وَٱلْمَسَـٰكِينِ وَٱلْعَـٰمِلِينَ عَلَيْهَا وَٱلْمُؤَلَّفَةِ قُلُوبُهُمْ وَفِى ٱلرِّقَابِ وَٱلْغَـٰرِمِينَ وَفِى سَبِيلِ ٱللَّهِ وَٱبْنِ ٱلسَّبِيلِ ... ﴿٦٠﴾

('The alms are meant only for the poor, and the needy, and those who are in charge thereof, those whose hearts are to be reconciled, and to free those in bondage, and to help those burdened with debt, and for expenditure in the Way of Allah, and for the wayfarer.')

(*al-Tawbah*, 9: 60)

The real objective of alms is then explained:

خُذْ مِنْ أَمْوَٰلِهِمْ صَدَقَةً تُطَهِّرُهُمْ وَتُزَكِّيهِم بِهَا ... ﴿١٠٣﴾

('Take alms out of their riches and thereby cleanse them and bring about their growth in righeousness...')

(*al-Tawbah*, 9: 103)

According to these *Āyāt*, the wealth gathered without paying *Zakāh* remains impure. The only way to purify it is to take from it what is due to the Lord and give it to the deserving among His subjects. The Holy Prophet (*pbuh*) warned those amassing gold and silver of severe punishment in the Hereafter. Because of this, the Companions of the Holy Prophet were so worried that they feared even a Dirham saved might cause the Almighty's displeasure. The very thought of this fear was so overpowering that Ḥaḍrat 'Umar finally approached the Prophet of God, who allayed his apprehensions and said that the All-Merciful has made *Zakāh* compulsory for the *Ummah* simply to purify every legitimate penny that one earns. In a similar Tradition, narrated by Abū Sa'īd Khuḍrī, the Prophet of Islam said: 'As you pay *Zakāh* from your property, you discharge what has been due unto you.' In these *Āyāt*, the believers have been enjoined to pay *Zakāh* on agricultural produce and gold and silver ornaments. According to the Prophetic Traditions, we are also required to pay *Zakāh* on merchandise and livestock, like cows, camels and goats.

The minimum prescribed limit (*Niṣāb*) of items liable for *Zakāh* is as follows: (i) 200 Dirhams = 52½ *Tola*s (612.360 grams) of silver; (ii) 20 Dinars = 7½ *Tola*s (87.48 grams) of gold; (iii) a minimum of 5 camels, 40 goats or 30 cows of the livestock; and (iv) merchandise worth 52½ *Tola*s (612.360 grams) of silver. A person in possession of goods of this value for the year will have to pay one-fortieth part of it as *Zakāh*.

Ḥaḍrat ʿUmar and ʿAbd Allāh ibn Masʿūd were of the view, one also held by Imām Abū Ḥanīfah, that *Zakāh* is payable on gold and silver ornaments as well. According to a Prophetic Tradition, when the Holy Prophet (*pbuh*) saw two ladies wearing gold bangles, he enquired if they had paid *Zakāh*. Their reply was negative. To this, the Holy Prophet (*pbuh*) said: 'Would you like to wear bangles of fire in their place on the Day of Judgment?' Mother of the Faithfuls, Ḥaḍrat Umm Salamah (may Allah be pleased with her), narrated that she had a pair of gold anklets and enquired of the Prophet of God whether these also came under the category of *Kanz* (a treasure or hoarded wealth). *Sayyidinā* Rasūl Allāh replied: 'If the element of gold in these was up to the prescribed limit and *Zakāh* has been paid, then it will not be *Kanz*. These Traditions thus confirm that *Zakāh* should be paid on gold and silver ornaments. There is, however, no *Zakāh* on gems and precious stones for personal use.

9.4. Various categories of *Zakāh* distribution

The Holy Qur'ān specifies the following eight categories of those eligible for support from funds generated through *Zakāh*:

إِنَّمَا ٱلصَّدَقَـٰتُ لِلْفُقَرَآءِ وَٱلْمَسَـٰكِينِ وَٱلْعَـٰمِلِينَ عَلَيْهَا وَٱلْمُؤَلَّفَةِ قُلُوبُهُمْ وَفِى ٱلرِّقَابِ وَٱلْغَـٰرِمِينَ وَفِى سَبِيلِ
ٱللَّهِ وَٱبْنِ ٱلسَّبِيلِ ۖ فَرِيضَةً مِّنَ ٱللَّهِ ۗ وَٱللَّهُ عَلِيمٌ حَكِيمٌ ۝٦٠

('The alms are meant only for the poor and the needy, and those who are in charge thereof, those whose hearts are to be reconciled, and to free those in bondage, and to help those burdened with debt, and for expenditure in the Way of Allah, and for the wayfarer. This is an obligation from Allah. Allah is All-Knowing, All-Wise.')

(*al-Tawbah*, 9: 60)

The above *Āyah* of *Sūrah al-Tawbah* specifies the heads prescribed for the disbursement of *Zakāh*. It explains who from among the society members deserves to be helped and what the noble causes are that should be supported from the *Zakāh* funds. The *Āyah* thus throws light on the objectives of the economic reform policy of an Islamic state. The eight categories of the beneficiaries of the *Zakāh* system, mentioned in the *Āyah*, may be briefly explained as follows:

9.4.1. *Al-Fuqarā'* (sing. *Faqīr*)

According to the *Sharīʿah*, a person dependent on others for his subsistence is a *Faqīr*. This category includes everyone who may be in need of help, whether they are permanently disabled due to some physical handicap or old age; or are temporarily in need of assistance but capable of standing on their own feet if provided with timely support, such as orphaned children, widows, the unemployed or those afflicted by disease or accidents.

9.4.2. *Al-Masākīn* (sing. *Miskīn*)

A *Miskīn* is one who is suffering from *Maskanah* or distress more than the ordinary poor. The basic quality of this category of the deserving is described by the Holy Prophet (*pbuh*) as self-esteem, which prevents them from begging in spite of their needs and a lack of resources to sustain themselves and their family. The wordings of the *Ḥadīth* (Prophetic Tradition) are:

اَلمِسكِينُ الَّذِى لَايَجِدُ غِنًى يُغنِيهِ وَلَايُفطَنُ لَهُ فَيُتَصَدَّقُ عَلَيهِ وَلَا يَقُومُ فَيَسْأَلُ النَّاس

('*Miskīn* is he who does not find enough to sustain him. Nor his appearance is so revealing as to move others to help him. Nor does he approach the people begging.')

(Bukhārī)

Such a person occupies a better position in other people's esteem. The affluent members of society are therefore required to be on the look out for such self-respecting persons and provide them with timely assistance.

9.4.3. *Al-'Āmilīn* (sing. *'Āmil*)

These are people employed to collect and distribute *Zakāh* and *Ṣadaqāt* (regular and normal charities) and maintain a record of accounts. This means that those serving in the government department responsible for *Zakāh* administration, although not essentially poor and needy, will be paid from the *Zakāh* funds. It is evident from the mention of this category here, and also from *Āyah* 103 of *Sūrah al-Tawbah* (خُذْ مِنْ أَمْوَالِهِمْ صَدَقَةً Take alms out of their riches), that collection and distribution of *Zakāh* are included in the charter of duties of an Islamic State.

It may be of interest to note in the context of *Zakāh* that the Holy Prophet (*pbuh*) prohibited *Zakāh* items for himself and for members of his illustrious family. He administered *Zakāh* collection and distribution free of charge and made it a rule for *Banī Hāshim* to render this service free as well. On the other hand, every member of his family and *Banī Hāshim* had to pay *Zakāh* if he had the specified amount of valuables on which *Zakāh* was to be calculated. However, it was not lawful for them to accept *Zakāh*, even if they were in need. As for *Banī Hāshim* paying *Zakāh* to a deserving member from their own clans, Imām Abū Yūsuf considers this to be lawful, but the majority of jurists do not permit this.

9.4.4. *Mu'allafat al-Qulūb* or 'those whose hearts are to be reconciled'
This expression is derived from the infinitive *Ta'līf al-qalb*, which means to win the hearts of the people. The rule embodied for this category is that *Zakāh* funds may be used to win the hearts of those engaged in hostile activities against Islam, or to win over the support of those who are in the hostile camp of unbelievers. The category also includes converts to Islam about whom it may legitimately be feared that, if no consideration is shown to them and their loyalty is not fully secured, they may revert to unbelief or become tools in the hands of anti-Islamic forces. Whether rich or poor, they may be paid a lump sum or stipends on a regular or temporary basis in order to secure their support and backing for Islam.

9.4.5. *Fī'l-Riqāb* or 'to free those in bondage'
Zakāh funds can also be used for the freedom and emancipation of slaves, and to redeem and help the prisoners of war and their beleaguered families.

9.4.6. *Al-Ghārimīn* or 'those burdened with debt'
This category includes those who find themselves unable to repay a loan with their available means. They can be helped to restore their economic freedom and dignity. Some jurists are of the view that those who may have incurred a burden of debt due to their wayward lifestyle and extravagance can be extended help only if they categorically renounce their waywardness and repent before the Lord.

9.4.7. *Fī-Sabīlillāh* or 'in the Way of Allah'
This includes those who are engaged in a concerted struggle for the sake of Allah's Cause. The term especially stands for *Jihād* or an organized struggle against the forces of evil. It includes every genuine movement launched to overthrow ungodly systems and replace them by the benign Islamic order. All those engaged in such a struggle may be given assistance from *Zakāh* funds, whether to cover the expenses of their journey, to provide them with the means of transport or for the procurement of arms and equipment and related support. Such assistance may be provided even to those who are otherwise well off and need no financial assistance personally for themselves. The term is comprehensive enough to include every organized struggle waged for the supremacy of the Word of God and to establish the writ of Religion (*Dīn*) as a way of life, whether through missionary means or by armed struggle.

9.4.8. *Ibn al-Sabīl* or 'the Wayfarer'
A traveller, even if he is otherwise rich, is entitled to receive help out of *Zakāh* funds if he is in need of such help during his journey.

Now let us see under what circumstances those in the above eight categories are eligible under the law to receive *Zakāh,* and when are they not.

Nobody is allowed to pay *Zakāh* to his own father or son. Similarly, neither a husband can give *Zakāh* to his wife, nor a wife to her husband. Some jurists are of the view that one cannot give *Zakāh* also to those close relatives whose maintenance and care are obligatory according to the *Sharī'ah,* or to his legal heirs. However, distant relatives, if they are deserving, have a better claim over *Zakāh* than others.

Zakāh is payable only to the deserving people of the Islamic community. The Prophetic Tradition says:

تُؤخَذُ مِن أَغنِيَاءِكُم وَ تُرَدُّ فِى فُقَرَاءِكُم

('It is to be collected from the rich among you and distributed to your poor.')

As for non-Muslims, they can be paid from the funds of normal charity (*Ṣadaqāt*). In fact, Islam does not allow any distinction between Muslim and Non-Muslim when it comes to helping the needy. As *Zakāh* is exclusive to the Muslim community, an act of worship and is collected only from the Muslims, it cannot be disbursed outside this community.

According to Imām Abū Ḥanīfah and his disciples Imām Abū Yūsuf and Imām Muḥammad al-Shaybānī, *Zakāh* funds collected from a certain locality should be distributed only in that particular locality; its use elsewhere is not desirable, provided there is no eligible person in the area of collection. The *Zakāh* funds can also be utilized in emergencies or disasters, like floods, droughts or earthquakes, events that require assistance from far and near to help the affected people of a certain area. Imām Mālik and Sufyān al-Thawrī are of the same view. There is, however, nothing unlawful as such in spending these funds in a place outside the place of its origin.

One section of '*Ulamā'* is of the view that a person with the means to afford two meals a day should not receive *Zakāh.* Imām Abū Ḥanīfah and those belonging to his School of Thought say that anybody in possession of less than Rs.50 or the equivalent is eligible for help from *Zakāh* funds. This amount does not include the value of his household effects, beasts of burden and his attendant. This means that, even if he has all of these in addition to an amount of money less than fifty rupees, he is eligible to receive *Zakāh.* However, it should be borne in mind that there is the observance of the rule on the one hand, and the moral aspect on the other. The quality of moral excellence demands that we must not lose sight of what the Holy Prophet (*pbuh*) has said in this context: (i) 'He who has the means enough for his morning and evening meals but stretches out his hands for alms, gathers fire for himself'; (ii) 'I prefer that a person should gather fire-wood for sale and feed himself than resort to begging'; (iii) 'He who has things to eat or is capable to earn, has no reason to seek *Zakāh*'. These are certainly the qualities of resolve and moral strength.

As for the law, it defines the minimum limit of eligibility for *Zakāh*, which we also find in other Prophetic Traditions: (i) 'A person came to the Holy Prophet (*pbuh*) and submitted: "I have just ten Dirhams. Do I belong to the category of *Miskīn*?" The Holy Prophet replied: "yes".' (ii) Once, two persons approached the Holy Prophet asking for *Zakāh*. The Holy Prophet (*pbuh*) looked at them carefully and then said: 'If you so desire, I may give you *Zakāh*. But the rich and the able-abodied persons fit to earn a living have no share in *Zakāh* funds'. According to these *Aḥādīth*, those having less than the specified amount of *Niṣāb* (minimum limit of *Zakātable* assets) belong to the category of *Fuqarā'* and are eligible under the law to get *Zakāh*. From the moral standpoint, however, only those in need are genuinely eligible for payment out of *Zakāh* funds.

These are the basic rules of *Zakāh*. However, I may add that Islam lays a greater emphasis on the disciplined and systematic manner of doing things. It does not like 'adhocism' or an individualistic style in matters of religion. You can offer *Ṣalāh* away from the mosque, but the *Sharīʿah* demands that it should be performed in the congregation. In the same way, *Zakāh* can be distributed individually if there is no organized system or government mechanism for its collection and distribution; but efforts should be made by the community to have a proper organizational structure for this purpose. To this effect, the Holy Qur'ān has enjoined. (خُذۡ مِنۡ أَمۡوَٰلِهِمۡ صَدَقَةٗ تُطَهِّرُهُمۡ وَتُزَكِّيهِم بِهَا) ('Take alms out of their riches and thereby cleanse them and bring about their growth (in righteousness).') (*al-Tawbah*, 9: 103). In this *Āyah*, Allah *subḥānahū wa taʿālā* tells the Holy Prophet (*pbuh*) to collect *Zakāh* in an institutional form, instead of commanding the Muslims to discharge this duty as an individual act. The appointment of a cadre of *ʿĀmilīn*, or officials responsible for collecting *Zakāh*, similarly reaffirms an institutionalized system for the collection and distribution of *Zakāh*. The Holy Prophet (*pbuh*) has also said: أُمِرتُ أَن آخُذَ الصَّدَقَةَ مِن أَغنِيَاءِكُم وَأَرُدَّهَا فِى فُقَرَاءِكُم ('I have been enjoined to collect alms from the rich among you and distribute it to the poor of the community') (Bukhārī and Muslim). *Zakāh* was therefore collected and distributed by the state during the days of the Holy Prophet (*pbuh*) and *al-Khulafā' al-Rāshidūn*. In fact, this practice was followed by all successive

Islamic governments. In the absence of any state mechanism, this can be done individually; but it is obligatory for the Muslim community to have a proper set-up for the collective management of *Zakāh* because the real dividends of this revolutionary system can be reaped only if it is done in an organized manner.

9.5. Basic rules of *Zakāh*

In response to a comprehensive questionnaire on *Zakāh* from a distinguished reader of *Tarjumān al-Qur'ān*, Sayyid Mawdūdī provided some extremely useful information on the subject. The write-up that follows is based on those Qs and As[1]:

Q 1: How would you define *Zakāh*?

A: *Zakāh's* dictionary meaning is purity and growth. With these attributes inherent in its meaning, *Zakāh* can be defined as a financial act of worship, made mandatory for every *Ṣāḥib al-Niṣāb* Muslim, (who has at the closing of his financial year a balance of the minimum amount of property worth 612.360 grams of silver or 87.48 grams of gold, excluding his household effects, place of residence and items of personal use, other than gold or silver jewellery). It has been made mandatory in order to enable the believer to purify his property by discharging his duty towards the Lord and His subjects, and so that both he and the society of which he is a member may be cleansed of ills like miserliness, selfishness and malice, while the qualities of love, generosity, magnanimity, cooperation and fellow-feeling may flourish and prosper.

Jurists have defined *Zakāh* variously:

حَقٌّ يَجِبُ فِى الـمَـال

(It is a duty made obligatory in one's fortune.)

(*Al-Mughnī* by Ibn Qudāmah, vol.2, p.433)

إِعطَاءُ جُزءٍ مِنَ النِّصَابِ إِلَى فَقِيرٍ وَ نَحوَهُ غَيرُ مُتَّصَفٍ بِمَـانِـعٍ شَرعِيٍّ يُمنَعُ مِن الصَّرفِ إِلَيه

(*Zakāh* is to pay something from *Niṣāb* to the poor and needy, who may be duly qualified by the *Sharī'ah* to get it.)

(*Nayl al-Awṭār*, vol. 4, p.98)

---

[1] Adapted from *Tarjumān Al-Qur'ān*, November, 1950.

تَـمليكُ مَالٍ مَخْصُوصٍ لِـمُستَحِقِّه بِشَرَائِط مَـخْصُوصَةٍ

('To transfer to the deserving the ownership of a certain amount of money according to certain conditions.')

(*Al-Fiqh ʿalā al-Madhāhib al-Arbaʿah*, vol. 1, p.590)

Q 2: For whom is *Zakāh* obligatory? Also, please elaborate in this context the status of women, minor children, prisoners, travellers, insane persons and expatriates.

A. *Zakāh* is mandatory for every sane, adult Muslim man and woman if he or she is *Ṣāḥib al-Niṣāb* and is responsible for its payment himself or herself.

There is more than one view about minor children. Some jurists are of the view that *Zakāh* is not mandatory for an orphan. According to others, when the guardian hands over property to the orphan at the time he qualifies for its management on attaining the age of puberty, he should brief the orphan on the amount of *Zakāh* due to be paid by him for the intervening period. It will then be the responsibility of the adult orphan to pay the arrears of *Zakāh*. A third opinion in this regard is that, if the orphan's assets have been invested in a profitable venture, his guardian will have to pay *Zakāh* on his behalf; otherwise there is no *Zakāh* on his property. According to yet another viewpoint, *Zakāh* will be paid from the orphan's property if he is *Ṣāḥib al-Niṣāb* and his guardian is responsible to do this. I support this last line of thought, which is also corroborated by the following *Ḥadīth*:

اَلَا، مَن وُلِّيَ يَتِيمـاً لَهُ مَالٌ فَلْيَتَّجِر لَهُ فِيهِ وَلَا يَترُكهُ فَتَاكُلُهُ الصَّدَقَة

('Look! Anyone assuming the guardianship of an orphan, who has a fortune, ought to invest it in business instead of keeping it idle to be consumed in payment of *Zakāh*.')

(Tirmidhī, Dāraquṭnī, Bayhaqī, *Kitāb al-Amwāl* of Abū 'Ubayd)

There is a difference of opinion about whether *Zakāh* is obligatory for those suffering from insanity. Personally speaking, I hold the same view in this case as well, that *Zakāh* has to be deducted from the assets of an insane person if he is *Ṣāḥib al-Niṣāb*. This view has been supported by Imām Mālik and Ibn Shihāb al-Zuhrī.

Zakāh will also be paid from the assets of a prisoner. The person responsible for managing the assets in his absence will be required to discharge this duty on the prisoner's behalf, like his other duties. Similarly, a wayfarer, although he himself is included in the category of those eligible for receiving *Zakāh*, cannot be absolved of the responsibility if he is in possession of assets liable for *Zakāh*. Being a traveller entitles him to *Zakāh*, and being rich makes it obligatory for him to pay what is due for him by religion.

A Muslim expatriate from Pakistan residing abroad will pay *Zakāh* if he holds *Niṣāb*-worthy assets within his country. *Zakāh* will also be deducted from the assets of a *Ṣāḥib al-Niṣāb* Muslim citizen of another Muslim country residing in Pakistan; but a Muslim citizen of a non-Muslim country who is living in Pakistan is free either to pay or not to pay *Zakāh* because his constitutional position makes him equal with non-Muslim subjects of the country of his origin:

...وَٱلَّذِينَ ءَامَنُواْ وَلَمْ يُهَاجِرُواْ مَا لَكُم مِّن وَلَـٰيَتِهِم مِّن شَيْءٍ حَتَّىٰ يُهَاجِرُواْ ... ﴿٧٢﴾

('And those who believed but did not migrate (to *Dār al-Islām*), you are under no obligation of alliance unless they migrate.')

(*al-Anfāl*, 8: 72)

Q 3: What should be treated as the age of adulthood that makes a person eligible to pay *Zakāh*?

A: To be eligible to pay *Zakāh*, the requirement is that of *Niṣāb* and not of age. In case of an under-age *Ṣāḥib al-Niṣāb*, his *Walī* (Guardian) is responsible for ensuring its timely payment. On attaining the age of puberty, this will be the responsibility of the person himself.

Q 4: What is the status of gold and silver ornaments of personal use? Is *Zakāh* payable on them as well?

A: There is more than one opinion in this respect. According to one school of thought, no *Zakāh* is payable on jewellery items for a woman's personal use. Those who subscribe to this view include Anas bin Mālik, Sa'īd bin Musayyab, Qatādah and al-Sha'bī. According to another school of Islamic Jurisprudence, *Zakāh* will be deducted from jewellery items for personal use only once in a lifetime. The third viewpoint in this respect is that no *Zakāh* is chargeable on jewellery items that are in regular use, but those that are worn only occasionally and are lying unused most of the time are liable for *Zakāh*. The fourth and most largely upheld opinion is that *Zakāh* is payable on all items of jewellery. This last opinion sounds more logical and correct to me (the author), because the instructions contained in the Prophetic Traditions lay down the *Niṣāb* of gold and silver ornaments, but give no conditions concerning them. Secondly, there are *Aḥādīth* that clearly state the mandatory nature of *Zakāh* on jewellery. According to a well-known *Ḥadīth*, narrated by Tirmidhī, Abū Dāwūd and Nasā'ī, a woman came to the Holy Prophet (*pbuh*) accompanied by her daughter wearing gold bangles. The Prophet asked the woman if she had paid *Zakāh* on the bangles. She said: 'No', on which he remarked:

أَيَسُرُّكَ اَن يُسَوِّرَكَ اللهُ بِهِمَا يَومَ القِيٰمَةِ سِوَارَينِ مِنَ النَّار

('Would you like Allah *subḥānahū wa taʿālā* to put round your arms two bangles of fire in its place on the Day of Judgment?')

In yet another Tradition narrated by Imām Mālik in his *Muwaṭṭa'*, and by Abū Dāwūd and Dāraquṭnī, it has been declared:

مَا اُدِّيَت زَكوٰتُه فَلَيسَ بِكَنزٍ

('The jewellery on which you have paid *Zakāh* is not *Kanz* (a hoarded treasure)'.)

According to Ibn Ḥazm, Ḥaḍrat ʿUmar advised his Governor Abū Mūsā Ashʿarī: 'Ask Muslim ladies to pay *Zakāh* on their jewellery'. Eminent Companions of the Holy Prophet (*pbuh*) and leading jurists, including Sufyān al-Thawrī and Imām al-Aʿẓam Abū Ḥanīfah, are of the same view.

Q 5: In the case of a joint stock company, is it the responsibility of the company to pay *Zakāh* collectively or should the shareholders do this individually?

A: In my opinion, the companies should be made responsible for calculating and arranging payment of *Zakāh* for all their shareholders, excluding those holding shares of less than the *Niṣāb* value or those owning shares for less than a year. Administratively, such an arrangement may be more convenient to handle, while this has nothing repugnant in it concerning the *Sharīʿah* as well. This view also conforms to the stand taken in the matter by Imām Mālik, Imām Shāfiʿī and other jurists (*Bidāyat al-Mujtahid*, vol. 1, p.225).

Q 6: Please let us have your views on the admissibility of *Zakāh* for factories and other commercial establishments.

A: There is no *Zakāh* on machinery and factory equipment. This is leviable on the cost-value of material in stock, whether it is in its raw or finished form, and also on the cash available in a factory's accounts at the closing of the year. There is similarly no *Zakāh* on furniture, stationery items, shops or houses and similar items of personal use that are owned by businessmen and traders. They are required to pay *Zakāh* on goods meant for sale and on cash available at the close of the year in their accounts. The basic principle in this context is that the factors of production, which an entrepreneur employs to make his product, are exempt from *Zakāh*. There is a *Ḥadīth* to this effect:

لَيسَ فِى الإبِلِ العَوَامِلِ صَدَقه

('There is no *Zakāh* on camels harnessed for job (as means of irrigation or transport).')

(*Kitāb al-Amwāl*)

The reason for this exemption is that *Zakāh* is deducted from the produce obtained through these means. In this analogy, the jurists have unanimously declared tools, equipment, machinery and all means of production exempt from *Zakāh*.

Q 7: In the case of transferable shares, who is responsible for paying *Zakāh*, the one who purchased the share or the person who sold it?

A: There is no *Zakāh* on shares sold during the course of one *Zakāh*-year, either for seller or for the buyer, because neither of them have owned these shares for one full year.

Q 8: On what type of assets and items is *Zakāh* to be deducted under the present social scenario, especially with reference to the following:

(a) Cash, silver, gold, jewellery and gems?
(b) Coins of gold, silver or metal and currency notes?
(c) Bank deposits, assets in lockers, money taken in loans, mortgaged property, disputed property or property under litigation?
(d) Gifts?
(e) Insurance Policies and the sum of money received from a Provident Fund?
(f) Livestock, dairy products and agricultural produce, including food grains, vegetables, fruit and flowers?
(g) Minerals?

(h) Buried treasure when discovered?
(i) Antiques?
(j) Honey from the wild and the bee-farms?
(k) Fish, pearls and other marine items?
(l) Oil?
(m) Imports and exports?

A: The Islamic *Sharīʿah* has specified the following items for *Zakāh*: farm products after harvesting has been done; gold and silver upto the prescribed limit (*Niṣāb*), or more when in hand from the beginning until the end of the year; cash as a substitute for gold and silver; livestock when kept for breeding and in continued possession at the beginning and end of the year; minerals; and treasures. Let me now furnish replies item by item:

(a) *Zakāh* is levied on cash, gold, silver and jewellery items. As for jewellery, the gold and silver are weighed for their value, minus the impurities (alloy) contained in it. Gems, whether studded in ornaments or in any other form, are exempt from *Zakāh.* A person dealing in gems and precious stones will, however, pay *Zakāh* just as traders dealing in other goods, i.e. 2.5 percent of their cost-value: 'There is no *Zakāh* on pearls, rubies and gems of all categories, provided these are not for sale. There is a consensus on this of all the Schools of Jurisprudence.' (*Al-Fiqh ʿalā al-Madhāhib al-Arbaʿah*, vol. 1, p.599.)
(b) Metallic coins and currency notes are substitutes for gold and silver because of their value and the purchasing power they carry. These are therefore subject to *Zakāh* like gold and silver. Three out of the four leading jurists, namely Imām al-Aʿẓam Abū Ḥanīfah, Imām Mālik and Imām Shāfiʿī, share the same view. (*Al-Fiqh ʿalā al-Madhāhib al-Arbaʿah*, vol. 1, p.605.)
(c) All bank deposits are subject to *Zakāh* deduction. The same is the case for deposits in government-registered and audited institutions. As for deposits in institutions not registered and audited under any government act, the account-holder himself is responsible to calculate his *Zakāh* and arrange for disbursement.

There is no *Zakāh* on loans drawn and spent on personal needs. But the money obtained in a loan which remains unspent after one full year and conforms to *Niṣāb* is subject to *Zakāh* deduction. A loan invested in business is treated as trading capital and will be included in the total amount for *Zakāh* for the entrepreneur.

Zakāh is also due on the sum extended on loan, the timely return of which is guaranteed to the lender. According to some jurists, the lender will have to pay yearly *Zakāh* on his capital extended as a loan. However, others are of the view that the lender will pay *Zakāh* for the entire period as and when he gets back the amount he lent. This view is held by Ḥaḍrat ʿAlī, Sufyān al-Thawrī and the scholars of the Ḥanafī School of Thought. In case the return of loan is not guaranteed, *Zakāh* will be paid when the lender receives his money back. He will then pay only for the year in which his money is returned.

In the case of a mortgaged property, *Zakāh* will be collected from the person holding that property in his custody. The mortgagee will have to pay *ʿUshr* (one-tenth of the value of property in his possession).

Zakāh on a disputed property will be charged from the person currently occupying it. On the resolution of a dispute, it will be paid by the owner in whose favour its possession is decreed.

(a) If a gift is up to *Niṣāb*, its recipient will pay *Zakāh* on completion of one year of his ownership.
(b) In the case of deductions being compulsory on account of an Insurance Policy or Provident Fund, *Zakāh* will be paid only once after a year from the receipt of the amount. If these are optional then, in my view, the concerned person will have to pay *Zakāh* yearly on the sum of money available in his Insurance or Provident Fund account. This is because it has been his option to save money in this fashion and, though not payable before the stipulated time, he is guaranteed its return with profit.
(c) The livestock of a dairy farm comes under the definition of the factors of production, and hence there is no *Zakāh* on these animals. *Zakāh* will, however, be payable on dairy products in the same way it is due on other factory products.

Of the agricultural produce, that fit for storage is liable for *ʿUshr* or *Khums* (one-tenth or one-fifth of its total value). The same rule is applicable to fruit that can be stored. *ʿUshr* is payable on the produce of arid lands which depend on rains for cultivation, and *Khums* is charged on the produce gathered from irrigated lands. There is no *ʿUshr* on perishable items, like vegetables, flowers and fresh fruit. But if these are sold in a market by the grower, *Zakāh* will be charged on them as in the case of other commercial goods.

(a) Regarding minerals, I believe that the *Ḥanbalīs* (followers of Imām Aḥmad bin Ḥanbal) have the best approach, i.e. everything mined, whether in the shape of minerals or liquids, including oil, gas, mercury, etc., is subject to a 2.5 percent *Zakāh* deduction, if it is a private property and its value is up to the *Niṣāb* level. The same principle was followed during the reign of the Caliph ʿUmar bin ʿAbd al-ʿAzīz. (*Al-Mughnī* by Ibn Qudāmah, vol. 2. p.581.)

(b) In the case of discovered treasure (*Rikāz*), the *Ḥadīth* says that *Khums* is to be charged as *Zakāh.*

(c) There is no *Zakāh* on antiques and precious relics kept at home as souvenirs, but *Zakāh* will be levied on commercial items for sale.

(d) Regarding honey, *Ḥanafiyah* (followers of Imām Abū Ḥanīfah) are of the view that this is subject to *Zakāh.* This viewpoint is shared by ʿAbd Allāh bin ʿUmar, ʿAbd Allāh bin ʿAbbās, Imām Aḥmad, Isḥāq bin Rāhwayh and ʿUmar bin ʿAbd al-ʿAzīz. According to Imām Mālik and Sufyān al-Thawrī, there is no *Zakāh* on honey. Imām Shāfiʿī is of the same view. I also subscribe to the views of the *Ḥanafiyah,* that if it is intended for sale, honey should be subject to *Zakāh* like other commercial commodities.

(e) There is no *Zakāh* on fish, if it is for personal consumption; but when for sale it will be subject to *Zakāh* like other commercial goods.

As for pearls, ambergris and other marine items, I take them to belong to the category of minerals, and hence liable for *Zakāh.* Imām Mālik was of the same view, which was in practice during the reign of the Caliph ʿUmar bin ʿAbd al-ʿAzīz.

(f) Oil also belongs to the category of minerals and is, therefore, subject to *Zakāh.*

(g) There is no *Zakāh* on exports. The duty charged on imports during the period of the second Caliph Ḥaḍrat ʿUmar was also not on account of *Zakāh* but in response to the tax imposed by the neighbouring states on goods imported from the Islamic Caliphate.

Q 9: Did the Rightly-Guided Caliphs make any addition to the list of items for *Zakāh* from the days of the Holy Prophet (*pbuh*)? What rules were observed for such additions or amendments, if any?

A: During *al-Khilāfah al-Rāshidah,* no additions were made to the list of items approved for *Zakāh* by the Holy Prophet (*pbuh*). On comparisons to those items, some additions were made subsequently, as for example the Umayyad Caliph ʿUmar bin ʿAbd al-ʿAzīz imposed *Zakāh* on buffaloes at the rate of *Zakāh* levied on cows by the Holy Prophet (*pbuh*).

Q 10: Is *Zakāh* leviable on metal coins other than those of gold and silver? Is it also to be paid on coins out of use, those withdrawn by the government or coins of other countries held by a person in his custody?

A: *Zakāh* is to be paid on coins of all categories as explained in 8(b). Coins out of use, mutilated or withdrawn by the government will be subject to *Zakāh* if these are made of gold or silver. Their value will be determined according to the ratio of gold and silver contained in them. Foreign currencies, if easily interchangeable locally, are treated as cash. If these are non-convertible, their value will be assessed according to their gold and silver content.

Q 11: How do you define *al-Amwāl al-Ẓāhirah* (open assets) and *al-Amwāl al-Bāṭinah* (hidden assets)? Under what category do you place bank deposits?

A: *Al-Amwāl al-Ẓāhirah* are assets that may be open to government functionaries to assess, while *al-Amwāl al-Bāṭinah* are assets not accessible to state operatives. The money deposited in a bank belongs to the first category.

Q 12: How will you define *al-Māl al-Nāmī* (growing asset) and is *Zakāh* leviable on property of this category alone?

A: *Al-Māl al-Nāmī* is an asset intrinsically amenable to growth or that which can be increased through efforts and struggle. According to this definition, *Zakāh* is levied only on assets of this category. It is charged on accumulated wealth mainly due to the fact that its owner has prevented it from further growth.

Q 13: What rules should apply to *Zakāh* on immovable property, jewellery and items extended on rent, like Taxis, cars, etc.

A: The market value of things offered on rent will be assessed on the basis of the profit earned from them by the owner. 2.5 percent of this profit will be deducted as *Zakāh*. According to Layth bin Saʿd, *Zakāh* was levied on income earned from camels put on rent in Madinah al-Munawwarah. (*Kitāb al-Amwāl*, p.376.)

Q 14: What is the rule of *Zakāh* on domesticated animals like buffalos, chickens and pets? Is *Zakāh* payable on these in cash or kind, or both? What number of these animals makes them worthy of *Zakāh* and under what circumstances?

A: Livestock, including camels, cows, buffalos, sheep, goats and the like, when reared for breeding and up to the *Niṣāb* value, are liable for *Zakāh. Sīrat al-Nabī* by Maulānā Sayyid Sulaymān Nadwī, (vol. 5, pp.165-167), may be referred to for details. If these are for commercial purposes, *Zakāh* will be charged at the prescribed rate of 2.5 percent if their value is up to *Niṣāb*. Animals kept as pets are exempt from *Zakāh*, regardless of their number.

As for poultry, chickens for domestic use are similarly free from *Zakāh*, regardless of their number, but those bred for commercial purposes are subject to *Zakāh*. The poultry farm of layers set up for the sale of eggs also come under the same category.

Zakāh on livestock can be collected both in cash and in kind. There is a ruling of Ḥaḍrat ʿAlī regarding this (*Kitāb al-Amwāl*, p.368).

Q 15: Please let us know the different rates of *Zakāh* charged on various goods and items?

A: The following are the prescribed rates of *Zakāh* on different items.

– Agricultural produce:	@ 10 percent from rain-fed arid lands.
	@ 5 percent from irrigated lands.
– Cash, gold and silver:	@ 2½ percent.
– Commercial goods:	@ 2½ percent.
– Livestock:	as explained above.
– Minerals:	@ 2½ percent.
– *Rikāz* (Discovered Treasure):	@ 2½ percent.
– Factory goods:	@ 2½ percent.

Q 16: Has there been any amendment in the rates of *Zakāh* deduction during the days of *al-Khulafā' al-Rāshidūn* on cash, coins, livestock, commercial goods and agricultural products? If so, please give us reasons for these amendments.

A: There has never been any modification in *Niṣāb* and the rate of *Zakāh*, either during the days of *al-Khulafā' al-Rāshidūn* or ever after them. In fact, nobody is authorized to introduce any change. Whatever was prescribed by the Holy Prophet (*pbuh*) as a matter of rule is sacrosanct and no Muslim can think of making any wilful changes, not even an assembly elected through a popular Muslim vote. Man-made laws are always subject to change, but not the Divine Law. This is why we notice the cases of people evading government taxes and governments amending and modifying their rules and regulations, as demanded by a certain situation.

Q 17: In the case of cash, what are the equivalents in Pakistani currency of 200 silver *Dirhams* and 20 golden *Mithqāls* and, in terms of Pakistan's standard weights and measures how can we equate the *Ṣāʿ* and *Wasaq* for *Zakāh* on food grains?

A: The approved *Niṣāb* for cash, silver, commercial goods, minerals, *Rikāz* and factory goods is their being worth 200 Dirhams in value. The established equivalent of 200 Dirhams is 52½ *Tola*s (= 612.360 grams) of silver and 20 *Mithqāl*s is equal to 7½ *Tola*s (= 87.48 grams) of gold.[2]

Q 18: Is there a fixed term on the expiry of which *Zakāh* is payable on different items?

A: On all items, except for minerals, treasures and agricultural produce, the standard period is the completion of one calendar year, with the proviso of the asset being up to *Niṣāb*. There is no term limit of one year for minerals and treasures, while *Zakāh* is payable on agricultural produce immediately after harvesting is completed, which can even be twice or more within one calendar year. The Holy Qur'ān says: وَءَاتُوا۟ حَقَّهُۥ يَوْمَ حَصَادِهِۦ ('And pay what is due to Him on the day of the crop's harvesting') (*al-Anʿām*, 6: 141).

Q 19: Is *Zakāh* calculated according to the lunar or solar calendar? Is there a particular month for its collection?

A: Since the government in Pakistan is following the solar calendar, there is no harm if *Zakāh* is collected accordingly. No particular calendar has been made obligatory by the *Sharīʿah* for this purpose. Similarly, no particular month has

[2] No details are given here concerning *Ṣāʿ* and *Wasaq* most likely because these measures have long since been out of use and hence no need to equate them with their corresponding modern counterparts in weights and measures. The general principles of *Zakāh* on foodgrains are the same as on agricultural produce, already explained. – Translator.

been earmarked for its collection. An Islamic government can fix any particular month and calendar for the collection and calculation of *Zakāh.*

Q 20: What are the main categories for the disbursement of *Zakāh*? Also, please indicate the meaning and import of the term '*Fī Sabīlillāh*'.

A: The Book of God specifies eight categories for the distribution of funds raised through *Zakāh.* These are as follows: *Fuqarā'* (Poor), *Masākīn* (the Needy), '*Āmilīn* (those employed by the Islamic government for collection of *Zakāh*), *Mu'allafat al-Qulūb* (those whose hearts are to be reconciled), *al-Riqāb* (those in bondage), *Ghārimīn* (those burdened with debt), *fī Sabīlillāh* (in the Way of Allah) and *Ibn al-Sabīl* (the Wayfarer). (For a detailed explanation of these terms, please see Section 9.4 above, pp 199-204).

Q 21: Is it necessary to distribute *Zakāh* to the deserving under each of the eight prescribed categories, or can it be given to the needy according to one's own discretion?

A: It is not essential for the government or an individual to distribute *Zakāh* under each and every category of account. The *Zakāh* funds can be disbursed according to the demands of the situation under various heads, or even under a single category.

Q 22: Under what circumstances is a person from any of the eight eligible categories permitted to receive *Zakāh*? Also, please indicate if the members of Banī Hāshim family and Sayyids are entitled to receive *Zakāh*, especially considering the circumstances prevailing in Pakistan?

A: From among the categories of '*Fuqarā'*' and '*Masākīn*', only those who are not *Ṣāḥib al-Niṣāb* can get *Zakāh.* '*Āmilīn* and *Mu'allafat al-Qulūb*, though *Ṣāḥib al-Niṣāb*, are eligible to be paid from *Zakāh* funds. The slave is entitled to *Zakāh* to win his freedom. One overburdened with a loan can be paid *Zakāh* if he does not have enough resources to relieve him of his debt. Those engaged in *Jihād* in the Way of Allah can get paid out of *Zakāh* funds, even if they are *Ṣāḥib al-Niṣāb. Ibn al-Sabīl* can receive *Zakāh* if he is in need during his journey.

Zakāh is prohibited for Banī Hāshim. However, it is difficult in Pakistan today to ascertain who actually belongs to that noble family, and hence the government can offer *Zakāh* to anyone genuinely in need. It is up to the recipient to avoid *Zakāh* if he is sure of his Hāshimī lineage.

Q 23: Is *Zakāh* payable to individuals, or can it be given to institutions also, like orphanages, destitute homes, educational institutions, etc.?

A: When collected by the government, *Zakāh* can be disbursed to individuals as well as institutions.[3] The government can also set up establishments related to the different heads of *Zakāh*.

Q 24: Can the funds of *Zakāh* be used to provide life-long monthly maintenance allowances to the poor, the needy, widows, the handicapped or those incapable of earning their livelihood due to old age or incapacitation?

A: Yes, *Zakāh* can be given in the form of stipends or allowances to those in need due to temporary or permanent incapacitation, disease, old age, etc.

Q 25: Can the *Zakāh* funds be used for public welfare schemes, like the building of mosques, hospitals, roads, bridges, wells and ponds?

A: The category of *fī Sabīlillāh* is not so loose as to include such works of public welfare.[4]

Q 26: Can a person be offered *al-qarḍ al-ḥasan*, or an interest-free loan, from *Zakāh* funds?

A: There is no harm in extending *al-qarḍ al-ḥasan* from the funds available with the *Zakāh* Administration. In fact, under the prevailing circumstances, it is desirable for the *Bayt-Al-Māl* to have an exclusive allocation of funds for this purpose.

Q 27: Is it necessary for *Zakāh* to be spent in the area where it has been collected from, or can it also be sent outside to help in the emergency needs of disaster relief, or to win hearts (*Ta'līf al-Qulūb*)?

A: It is desirable under normal circumstances to spend the amount in *Zakāh* in the area where it has been collected. During the reign of the Caliph ʿUmar bin

[3] In case there is no official mechanism for the collection and distribution of *Zakāh*, one can give his *Zakāh* both to individuals whom he knows to be deserving and also to institutions genuinely engaged in laudable works of charity. – Translator.

[4] Tax collected by the government is meant to take care of such needs in the public welfare sector. – Translator.

ʿAbd al-ʿAzīz, when the funds of *Zakāh* were transferred from Rayy to Kufah, he ordered the money be returned to its place of origin (*Kitāb al-Amwāl*, p.590). In the case of an emergency, the balance of *Zakāh* funds that are available in any particular area can, however, be transferred to that place to supplement its resources. *Zakāh* collected from an area with lesser needs for its distribution can also be utilized in a place of greater need. It can also be utilized to meet the relief requirements of an area in distress abroad, but not at the cost of *Mustaḥiqqīn* or the deserving or those in greater need at home.

The area of collection means the administrative unit, and it can apply equally to the district, division and province. In Pakistan's context, the province will be the area; within the province, the division; and within division, the district.

Q 28: What is the way of deducting *Zakāh* from the property left behind by one who is deceased?

A: The settlement of the deceased's loan, if any, heads the list of priorities so far as his assets are concerned, followed by the deduction of *Zakāh* and the execution of his will. The remaining part of his assets will then be distributed among his heirs, according to the Islamic Law of Inheritance. Death does not absolve the deceased from the deduction of *Zakāh* from his property. This is the view held by Imām Mālik, Imām Shāfiʿī, Imām Muḥammad, ʿAṭāʾ, Zuhrī, Qatādah, Ishāq bin Rāhwayh and Abū Thawr. Some jurists are of the view that *Zakāh* will be charged only when the deceased has desired this in his will. In my opinion, this is true only about *al-Amwāl al-Bāṭinah* (hidden assets) (like jewellery, etc.), because the deceased is likely to have already paid their *Zakāh* before his death without others knowing this. As for *al-Amwāl al-Ẓāhira* (open assets), for which an Islamic government is in charge of collecting *Zakāh*, there is no such possibility and hence *Zakāh* will remain due until such time as it has been paid.

Q 29: Can you suggest measures to prevent people avoiding payment of *Zakāh*?

A: These measures may include the appointment of honest officials to forestall the possibilities of bribery and irregularities in *Zakāh* Administration, or favouritism in its distribution and the squandering away of *Zakāh* funds on staff salaries and allowances. Secondly, the government should take care in building the society's edifice on moral values and on the love and fear of God. Instead of restricting its role to civil administration and the country's defence, it should also be geared up to fulfil its responsibility of character-building and moral rejuvenation for the people. Thirdly, necessary legislation should be enacted to check the use of unlawful means to avoid any embezzlement of *Zakāh* funds. For example, a person found guilty of transferring assets liable for *Zakāh* in the name of his relative before the close of the year should be brought to the court of law to establish if he did this to avoid payment of *Zakāh*.

Q 30: Should the administration of *Zakāh* be the responsibility of the centre, or of the provinces? If the subject falls under the centre's jurisdiction, what steps need to be taken to determine the shares of the provinces and other areas from the main pool?

A: In my view, the responsibility for the collection and distribution of *Zakāh* should rest with the provinces, with the centre enjoying the powers to divert the surplus of one province to a *Zakāh*-deficient province or area. The centre should also have the power to draw upon the resources of provincial *Zakāh* administration to launch institutions and schemes designed to perform charitable work in the Way of Allah (*Fī-Sabīlillāh*) and to mobilize emergency relief operations within the country and abroad.

Q 31: In your opinion, what is the best way to manage the collection and disbursement of *Zakāh*? Should there be a separate set-up for this purpose, or may the government do this job through its existing departments?

A: I do not think that the government needs to establish a separate department for this purpose. The task of collecting and distributing the different kinds of *Zakāh* may as well be entrusted to the departments engaged in collecting taxes of similar kinds. For example, the job relating to the collection of *Zakāh* on agriculture, livestock, poultry and dairy products can be assigned to the Revenue Department; *Zakāh* on commercial goods may be collected by the Income Tax Department; *Zakāh* on factory products by the Excise Department, and so on. The government treasury should be responsible for its safe custody, while its accounts should be maintained by the office of the Accountant General. If the administration of *Zakāh* is entrusted to the provinces, as earlier proposed, and the job of collecting *Zakāh* is assigned to a department under the central government, the expenses incurred on its collection may be met by the province concerned according to a mutually agreed formula.

As for the distribution and disbursement of *Zakāh* under the different specified heads, a separate set-up is required for this, which should be placed under the supervision of the Minister in charge of *Awqāf* and other religious institutions.

Q 32: Has *Zakāh* ever been treated as a government tax, or is it a tax for the collection and administration of which the government alone is responsible?

A: It must be noted that *Zakāh* is not a Tax, but an act of 'financial worship'. There is a vast difference between these two from the standpoint of the basic concepts and the moral background of each. If government officials and *Zakāh* payers start treating *Zakāh* as a state tax, rather than as *'Ibādah* (an act of worship), this will totally destroy its moral and spiritual value and benefits, which remain the sole objective of this august institution. It will also greatly damage its social impact. To vest the government with the responsibility for its collection and distribution does not mean that it is a government tax. The government of an Islamic State has been made responsible for having a proper mechanism to administer *Zakāh* in order to streamline the arrangements and ensure proper discharge of this act of worship. The collection and disbursement of *Zakāh*, therefore, are as much the responsibility of the Islamic government as is the establishment of the system of regular Prayer and *Ḥajj* arrangements.

Q 33: Was there any tax other than *Zakāh* for public welfare purposes during the days of the Holy Prophet (*pbuh*) and his illustrious Caliphs?

A: The principle laid down in the Prophetic Tradition is that:
إنَّ فِى المَالِ حَقاً سِوَى الزَّكوٰة ('There are obligations in one's property other than *Zakāh*') (Tirmidhī). In light of this rule, nobody can question the right of an Islamic government to levy taxes in addition to administering the *Zakāh* system effectively. Moreover, the disbursement heads of *Zakāh* have been specified by the Book of God. Hence, all other sectors falling under the Islamic State's jurisdiction that need funds to manage them make it incumbent on the government to levy taxes. The Holy Qur'ān also provides us with the general guideline: وَيَسْـَٔلُونَكَ مَاذَا يُنفِقُونَ قُلِ ٱلْعَفْوَ ('They ask: "What should we spend in the Way of Allah?" Say: "Whatever you can spare."') (*al-Baqarah*, 2: 219). The word '*Al-'Afw*' in this *Āyah* is a synonym of 'Economic Surplus' and guides us to the right area for taxation. Moreover, there are precedents for the levying of taxes, in addition to the state's management of *Zakāh*, during the days of *al-Khulafā' al-Rāshidūn*. During the reign of the Second Caliph, an import duty was imposed and the revenue thus generated was not taken as *Zakāh*, but as *Fay'* or as a 'public fund'.

Q 34: What system of *Zakāh* collection and disbursement was followed by Muslim countries in the past and is in practice now?

A: In the earlier days of Islam, collectors were appointed by the government who physically went to inspect *al-Amwāl al-Ẓāhirah* at their place and collect *Zakāh.* The funds generated were deposited in the public treasury (*Bayt al-Māl*), but accounts were maintained separately from the other revenue of the government. Its distribution was carried out by state officials responsible for other duties as well, and no exclusive department or staff was maintained exclusively for this work. Such administrative matters are, however, subject to change according to the changing circumstances. As for the present-day governments of the Muslim world, I am not aware how they are administering *Zakāh* and its distribution.

Q 35: Should the collection and distribution of *Zakāh* be the exclusive responsibility of the government, or can it be managed by a Board of Trustees under joint public-private control?

A: I think that the system for the collection and distribution of *Zakāh* should remain under the administrative control of an Islamic government.

Q 36: What should be the terms of employment, viz. pay and allowances, pension, provident fund, etc., for the staff employed to collect and distribute *Zakāh*?

A: There is no need for anything exclusive in the terms of service, and these should conform to those of similar employees in other government departments. The government on its own should, however, bring about revolutionary changes in pay scales, allowances, etc. of its low-paid staff to remove the yawning gap between the salaries of the lower and higher categories of employees, making them more judicious and equitable.

9.6. Is any change possible in *Niṣāb* and the rate of *Zakāh*'s deduction?[5]

Q 1: One gentleman with religious credentials is firmly of the view that the rate of *Zakāh* deduction may be revised according to the circumstances and needs of the day. He believes that the Holy Prophet (*pbuh*) fixed the rate at 2.5 percent as this was required then, but an Islamic state can now revise this upward or downward as the situation may demand. He argues that the Holy

[5] Adapted from '*Rasā'il-wa-Masā'il*', vol. 4.

Qur'ān speaks of *Zakāh* in so many places, but nowhere does it mention any particular rate for its deduction, which it would definitely have done had that been obligatory. I have tried to impress upon him that the injunctions of the Holy Prophet (*pbuh*) are for all times to come and subject to no amendments or change. To accept his line of argument would mean that the number of *Rakaʿāt* in *Ṣalāh* (the act of bending the body to the knees, followed by two prostrations) would similarly become liable to change according to the demands of the time. Every ruling of the Holy Prophet (*pbuh*) will thus be virtually reduced to a plaything. I pointed out to him that the Holy Prophet has said: فِى الْمَالِ حَقًّا سِوَى الزَّكٰوةِ ('In (your) property there is an obligation other than the Divine obligation of *Zakāh* as well.') (Tirmidhī). Hence, an Islamic state can collect revenue other than *Zakāh*. Had a change in the rate of *Zakāh* collection been admissible, there would have been no need for this injunction. My arguments have, however, failed to impress the gentleman. Will you please enlighten us with your views in this respect!

A: I fully endorse your line of argument. We are not entitled to modify or make amendments in the parameters and lines drawn by the Law-Giver. The Islamic Law (*Sharīʿah*), as it has come down to us from the Book of God and the Prophetic Traditions, is sacrosanct in every respect. Once we allow an attempt to change, whether it is major or minor, this will open up the floodgates for wilful modifications, sparing no Islamic injunction whether they concern *ʿIbādah* (Worship rituals), like *Ṣalāh*, *Ṣawm*, *Zakāh* and *Ḥajj*, or *Muʿāmalāt* (public matters), like *Nikāḥ* (Marriage), *Ṭalāq* (Divorce), *Wirāthah* (Inheritance), etc. To allow such an anarchic situation in matters concerning Religion would also disrupt the balance and harmony established by the Law-Giver for maintaining a just order between the individual and society. Once this order is disturbed, a tug of war is bound to ensue between the two. The individuals may like to change the minimum limit and rate of deduction to suit their interests and the state or those in authority may prefer that it conforms to their interests. The matter may even get politicized and become an issue in general elections. The legislators may thus step in to make laws suited to the rulers' whims. Even in the case of a consensus on such amendments, there can be no spirit of sanctity about them. A sanctimonious act of worship will thus be reduced to a piece of government legislation. As people now evade taxes, they will start attempting to avoid *Zakāh*. Once parliament is allowed to meddle with the *Sharīʿah* laws, the very spirit of their sanctity would evaporate in thin air, and nothing would remain sacrosanct for the people as it is today.

9.7. Company shares and *Zakāh*[6]

Q 1: The issue of determining *Zakāh* on joint stock companies and their shares has been mind-boggling. The share itself is no more than a piece of paper.[7] Through his share, a shareholder becomes the owner or partner of a part of the joint holding or common asset. Now, the question arises about the extent and value of the company's assets. In the case of a construction company or enterprise dealing with real estate or machine tools, the shareholder will naturally be a partner in that enterprise, which your explanation of the rules show to be exempt from *Zakāh.* The cash-value of shares held by a shareholder, though intact, will be part of the total value of assets on the ground in the form of the joint stock company. Why then must an individual shareholder pay *Zakāh* on the value of his share?

A: The shareholder of a joint stock company, having shares up to the value of *Niṣāb*, will be treated as *Ṣāḥib al-Niṣāb.* However, as he has invested his money in a joint stock venture, he will not be required to pay his *Zakāh* individually. It will be for the company to pay *Zakāh* collectively. Every shareholder having assets worth *Niṣāb* is to be handled jointly for the calculation of *Zakāh.* While assessing the total value of assets subject to *Zakāh*, the factors of production like machinery, real estate, furniture and fixtures, etc. will be excluded. Assets consisting of business goods and the money in hand at the end of the assessment year will be included to determine the amount payable. If the company's business is of a different nature, its financial status will be determined in light of its income per annum.

Q 2: Your answer to the queries concerning *Zakāh* on business shares presupposes the existence of an Islamic government and a central mechanism for the collection of *Zakāh.* The real issue is how to arrange collection and payment of *Zakāh* on business assets where there is no such mechanism? I try to calculate *Zakāh* at 2.5 percent, equating the worth of my shares with the currency in circulation; however, the net profit received after the deduction of annual income tax is consumed entirely by *Zakāh.* The dividends received from some shares are too little even to pay *Zakāh*, which I have to do out of my pocket. This is not a plausible proposition in the least.

---

6 Adaptation from *Tarjumān al-Qur'ān*, January, 1951.

7 The share is not just 'a piece of paper', as stated here. In fact it is in itself a precious item. It is the document on the basis of which one is entitled to claim his partnership in a particular enterprise and draw dividends and other benefits. – Translator.

A: *Zakāh* on business shares are not to be calculated as you do for normal assets in your possession. The basic rule regarding *Zakāh* on business shares is that, after a year from the date of starting an enterprise, you should take stock of the business assets at your disposal, calculate its value and then see how much money in cash you have in your accounts. Then, on the basis of the sum total of the two, you may calculate *Zakāh* at 2.5 percent. You may apply the same rule to shares you hold in one or more joint stock companies. You will have to look at the market value of those shares at the end of the year when your *Zakāh* is due. It does not matter how many times a share has been sold and a new one purchased during one year. Your *Zakāh*-year will be calculated from the day you purchased the first share of a certain company and you will be required to pay it on the basis of the market value of your shares at the appointed time of your *Zakāh*-year. Additionally, you will have to see how much you hold in cash, and then you should calculate your *Zakāh* on the total of the two at the rate of one in forty (2.5 percent).

As for government taxes eating up a chunk of your profit, leaving little room for the payment of *Zakāh*, I have no solution for this except to advise you to join those striving for the establishment of an Islamic order in a Muslim state, because this malaise will continue to plague our economy and polity until such time as we have a government that is as considerate about *Zakāh* as it is about income tax.

Q 3: Justice demands that capital invested as shares in a joint stock venture should be liable for *Zakāh* only once. According to the rule you explained in this context, an individual shareholder is exempt from *Zakāh* once it has been deducted on a collective basis by the company. That *Zakāh* should be collected from the company, after excluding those shareholders who are not *Ṣāḥib al-Niṣāb* and those who purchased their shares in the middle of the year, is in itself a difficult proposition. It is not easy to ascertain if a shareholder with a value of assets less than *Niṣāb* in the company does not own assets elsewhere that would make him *Ṣāḥib al-Niṣāb*.

There is yet another aspect that merits attention. The economic fallout from collecting *Zakāh* from individuals based on their personal holdings and shares will be entirely different from that caused by collective deductions. In the latter case, the management of a joint venture is likely to take annual *Zakāh* deductions as part of the company's total outlay, and will accordingly raise the price of its product to cover that amount because it may not always be possible for it to pay the full amount of *Zakāh* from the company's profits alone; alternatively, it may not leave enough in the balance to pay dividends to its shareholders. If individual shareholders pay their *Zakāh* themselves, this will certainly not affect the product's price level causing unnecessary suffering to general consumers.

You also say that items which are rented are also eligible for *Zakāh*. If this is the case, then there should also be *Zakāh* on the value of cabs, trucks, buses and vehicles used for rental. Similarly, a person owning houses and shops who lets them on rent should be required to pay *Zakāh* on their value. But I doubt if this is the case, as I am not aware, first of all, of any such precedent in the past. Secondly, the reference you quote of a Tradition narrated by Layth bin Saʿd in *Kitāb al-Amwāl* (p.376) to support your viewpoint does not appear to be convincing to me. The use of hired camels for rental is not the cause of the levy of *Zakāh* on them, but rather their being a beast of burden. I shall be grateful if you would throw more light on this to remove my confusion.

A: My submissions in the November issue of *Tarjumān al-Qur'ān* (1950) were in response to a government Questionnaire on *Zakāh*, and the line of arguments followed in that piece was based on the hypothesis that the government would set up a mechanism to collect *Zakāh* from private sector companies. The reply to the query given in the July 1962 issue of *Tarjumān* was in a different context, i.e. the requirement for an individual shareholder to pay *Zakāh* in a private sector enterprise that has no arrangement for collective payment. Please keep this backdrop in mind in order to understand the differences. When *Zakāh* is paid by a private firm collectively, the individual shareholder will not be required to calculate and pay *Zakāh* separately on his personal share. It may undoubtedly be difficult for the firm to investigate on its own which of its shareholder is *Ṣāḥib al-Niṣāb* and which is not. It is therefore incumbent on the shareholders themselves to convey this information to their company.

In the case of the state collecting *Zakāh*, the government collectors cannot be expected to remain unaware of a joint-stock company's attempt to include *Zakāh* outlay in its total expenditure, increasing the cost of its products to cover this amount as well. The government can take effective measures to monitor such acts of public fraud. In the absence of any government mechanism for *Zakāh* collection, no Muslim company in a state could be expected to indulge in such a fraudulent practice, which has no moral scruples or religious sensibility. Generally speaking, no enterprise run by Muslims can be so unscrupulous as to pay *Zakāh* with one hand and take it back with the other. Let us just suppose that some companies do indulge in such illegal practice. They will then be required to spend more in their *Zakāh* outlay next year, with a resultant raise in prices of their products, which in turn would lead to further increase in the rate of *Zakāh*; consequently their goods would quickly become too costly to be of much economic worth.

As for *Zakāh* on items let on rent, this matter needs further elaboration. For those entrepreneurs who deal in rentals, the value of their business will be assessed on the basis of the profits earned by their ventures. This does not mean that their *Zakāh* will be calculated on the worth of their vehicles or the furniture items which they rent out because these are the tools and implements which they work with and earn their income, and there is no *Zakāh* levied on tools however costly they may be. In other words, this means that the assessment of a profitable venture will be done on the basis of the value of its profitability. As for houses let on rent, I also have doubts regarding these because I find no precedence of *Zakāh* having been charged on them.

Al-Ibil al-ʿAwāmil or camels harnessed as 'cabs' are exempt from *Zakāh* for the reason explained earlier: i.e. tools, whether they are animate or inanimate, that are used for earning a living require no *Zakāh*. For example, there is no *Zakāh* on bullocks ploughing the field or horses driving a cart. The same is the case for other beasts of burden. On the same terms, the cattle-herds in dairy farms are exempt from *Zakāh*. Their *Zakāh* is, in fact, covered by the *Zakāh* paid on the produce they generate. The camels let on rent are, like cabs, the means of production and hence ought to carry no *Zakāh*. *Zakāh* should indeed be paid on the calculated value of the business that uses these public 'cabs'.[8]

9.8. *Zakāh*'s applicability in *Mushārakah* and *Muḍārabah*[9]

Q 1: Two persons start a business, with one partner investing both his capital and labour and the other participating only through his labour. They decide to divide the profit in three equal parts: one for the capital invested, and the remaining two to be equally distributed among each of the two partners for the labour they put in. I seek your views regarding the following two aspects of *Zakāh* for this joint venture:

(a) If *Zakāh* is assessed collectively on the total value of business, Partner Number Two raises the objection that the sole owner of the venture's capital is Partner Number One, for which he also earns profit and is therefore is solely responsible for the payment of *Zakāh*. Do you think this objection is valid?

(b) There is an element of profit as well as loss in every business venture. *Zakāh*, however, is not concerned with the element of risk, but with

[8] *Tarjumān al-Qur'ān*, February, 1963.

[9] Adapted from *Tarjumān al-Qur'ān*, January, 1953. – Editor.

the value of the capital. Even in the case of a loss, *Zakāh* is charged on the capital in hand. If the above-mentioned joint venture suffers a loss, one-third of the amount of *Zakāh* payable on the share of Partner Number Two will be deducted from his next year's profit, while he will also have to pay one-third of the amount of his *Zakāh* in the next year. It will thus no longer be *Zakāh* for Partner Number Two, but will become a tax on Partner Number One's capital. Do you not think that such a proposition is contrary to the very objectives of *Zakāh*?

A: The replies to both your queries are as follows:

(a) The objection of Partner Number Two is incorrect. *Zakāh* is not only charged on the original capital invested, but on the total value of the venture. The correct method is firstly to deduct *Zakāh* on the basis of the total value, and then to divide the profits between the two partners with the same proportion as was mutually agreed.

(b) The rule observed for *Zakāh* for the business commodity is that it is to be deducted from the value of goods in excess of the minimum prescribed limit (*Niṣāb*). A person participating in a venture through his labour has definitely contributed to the profitability of that venture. This profitability is not due entirely to the capital invested by Partner Number One. Two-thirds of the total amount of *Zakāh* will, therefore, be payable by the Partner who has invested his capital, and one-third by Partner Number Two for the labour he has invested.

9.9. Prescribed minimum limit for *Kunūz* (gold and silver)[10]

Q 1: According to the books of Islamic Jurisprudence, the *Niṣāb* prescribed for silver is 200 Dirhams or 52½ *Tola*s (612.360 grams), and for gold is 20 Dinars or 7½ *Tola*s (87.48 grams). In addition, some religious scholars are of the view that a person in possession of gold and silver of less quantity than the minimum prescribed limit for *Niṣāb* should assess the worth of his gold together with his silver, or silver with his gold, and whichever is found to add up jointly to the *Niṣāb* value should form the basis of his calculation of *Zakāh*. This sounds quite reasonable. But a plea to take silver as the basic metal for calculating *Zakāh* for those in possession of silver only, and gold for those who own only gold, is questionable. This is because, according to this formula, a person having Rs.60 (the worth of 52½ *Tola*s of silver) will be required to pay *Zakāh*, while one

[10] Adapted from *Tarjumān al-Qur'ān*, June, 1946 – Editor.

having Rs.600 (less than the value of 7½ *Tola*s of gold) will be exempt from *Zakāh*, although the latter is richer than the former.

I think that there was not as much difference between the value of gold and that of silver in the past as there is now. During the days of the Holy Prophet (*pbuh*), the difference was 1=7, while today it is 1=75 or 1=80. 140 *Mithqāl* of silver was then the basic *Niṣāb* for *Kunūz* (for both gold and silver).

The Holy Qur'ān has determined the *Niṣāb* of *Kunūz* with silver as the basic metal (140 *Mithqāl* = 52½ *Tola*s), the value of which in terms of gold was then equal to 20 *Mithqāl* (7½ *Tolas*/87.48 grams) of gold. I do not think that 7½ *Tola*s of gold can forever be taken as corresponding to the value of 52½ *Tola*s of silver for calculating *Zakāh*. In fact, the amount of gold that will have to be considered as *Niṣāb* is that which is equal in value to the basic measure of 140 *Mithqāl* of silver. Whoever owns gold should, therefore, assess its value in terms of its equivalent to 52½ *Tola*s of silver and pay *Zakāh* accordingly.

I would be grateful for your considered opinion, because the traditional approach of our books of jurisprudence does not appear to support my standpoint.

A: The views you expressed are correct insofar as the proportionate value of gold and silver is concerned during the golden days of the Holy Prophet (*pbuh*). The *Niṣāb* determined by him was 52½ *Tola*s of silver, which equalled 7½ *Tola*s of gold. I do not, however, see eye to eye with you on the proposition that, because of the large difference in their proportionate value now, silver should be regarded as the basic metal for *Niṣāb* in respect of *Kunūz* (gold and silver). I have the following reasons for differing from your viewpoint:

- It is difficult to decide unilaterally about gold or silver as the basic metal for the *Niṣāb* of *Kunūz*, or whether to reduce the value of gold to correspond to the value of silver or raise the value of silver to come up to the value of gold. Any such action taken by a religious scholar or jurist will be contrary to the dictates of the *Sharīʿah*. The Law-Giver has given separate injunctions regarding both of these precious metals and there is nothing in his decree to suggest overtly or covertly that either silver or gold should be the standard metal for the other.
- The reason that something is apparently more beneficial for the poor also does not provide firm ground on which an amendment could be sought to a confirmed decree.
- The values of both gold and silver are subject to change, which happens frequently. To ignore their fixed specific quantities for *Niṣāb* in favour of

these metals' ever-changing values and the market rates will harm the permanence of the *Sharīʿah* injunction and also cause many practical problems for the people.

- The problem you have mentioned with reference to gold and silver may also arise in the cases of livestock and beasts of burden. There has been a big fluctuation in the proportionate value of their market rates throughout the ages, and there again one may face the question about the value of which of these animals, at what point in time, should be regarded as the standard *Niṣāb* for their *Zakāh.*

In view of the foregoing, the best course open to us is to avoid unnecessary hair-splitting and strictly follow, in letter and spirit, the *Niṣāb* determined by the Law-Giver himself for the different items and observe the weights, measures and quantity which he himself fixed for each of these.

9.10. Difference between *Zakāh* and tax[11]

Q 1: Is it correct in today's socially advanced free world to extract funds forcefully in the name of *Zakāh* to help the poor and the indigent from those well-off members of society who already pay so much in taxes, including income tax?

A: To begin with, it must be borne in mind that *Zakāh* is not a tax, but an act of worship (*ʿIbādah*) and one of the five pillars of Islam. It is as important and indispensable as *Ṣalāh*, *Ṣawm* and *Ḥajj.* Time and again you find in the Holy Qur'ān mentions of *Ṣalāh*, and *Zakāh*, because they are dominant features of a Muslim society, which the Apostles of the Almighty have always enjoined their followers to follow since time immemorial. The basic flaw in your approach is, therefore, to treat *Zakāh* as a tax. Just as an Islamic government is not authorized to exempt its functionaries from offering regular Prayer on the plea that they are already performing duties for the state, in exactly the same manner it cannot absolve the rich from paying *Zakāh* on their wealth because they have contributed to the national exchequer what they ought by way of tax. An Islamic government is duty bound by the Lord to prepare its working schedule in such a way as to allow its staff enough time for offering *Ṣalāh.* Similarly, it is required to provide enough space in its taxation system for the well-off to pay, in addition to the government taxes, what is mandatory for them by way of *Zakāh* in the interests of the poor and the less privileged in the society. They should do

[11] Adapted from *Tarjumān al-Qur'ān*, December, 1961.

this to help their government achieve the goal of a welfare state where the rich do not get richer and the poor poorer.

It may further be noted that the taxation system in practice everywhere in the world follows neither the objectives nor the means specific to *Zakāh*. The way these have been specified in the Book of God make it the most remarkable and exclusively benign system for social uplift and moral rejuvenation. Hence, it would be wrong to confuse *Zakāh* with tax.

9.11. Is it permissible to levy income tax over and above *Zakāh*?[12]

Q 1: Is it permitted by the *Sharīʿah* to levy income tax on people over and above *Zakāh*?

A: Yes. An Islamic State is entitled to generate its revenue through income tax and other taxes, in addition to keeping in place a proper mechanism for the collection and distribution of *Zakāh*. The various heads for the collection and disbursement of *Zakāh* have been notified in *Sūrah al-Tawbah* 9: 60. The Prophet of God (*pbuh*) has similarly laid down the minimum limit of *Niṣāb* and the rate of its deduction, and these are all sacrosanct and subject to no modification or change. The state is obviously free, therefore, to levy taxes as required by the imperatives of national progress and development. What it levies in this way is a form of assistance sought from its citizens to help manage its affairs. In the case of a compulsory collection, this is called tax; when it is voluntary, it is a donation; and when the funds are collected from the public with the proviso of return, they are loans. *Zakāh* and all other types of state collections are neither interchangeable, nor can anything else take the place of *Zakāh* or remit it. This is in principle the reply to your query.

I may, however, go further to assure you that, once a truly Islamic government is established in our country and its affairs are run honestly and sincerely according to the principles of the *Sharīʿah*, there will remain no need for so many taxes as we have now. The world today from East to West, as you may be well aware, is witnessing an ever-increasing number of the cases of tax evasion and fraud. On the one hand, hardly ten percent of the funds generated through taxes are spent on the purpose for which they are collected. On the other hand, there is a general tendency to avoid and evade tax. If the system of governance is reformed, even one-quarter of the current taxes may suffice to fulfil national needs and their efficacy is bound to improve greatly.

---

[12] Adapted from *Tarjumān al-Qur'ān*, September, 1954 – Editor.

10 Islam and Social Justice*

10.1. Falsehood in the garb of truth

Among the miracles of *Aḥsan al-Taqwīm*, or the best mould in which Allah *subḥānahū wa taʿālā* has created man, is the fact that he is seldom attracted by naked falsehood and open temptation. This is why the Devil (Satan) is often compelled to camouflage falsehood and temptation for man in the garb of goodness and virtue. He would have never succeeded in tempting the Father of mankind, *Sayyidinā* Ādam, may Allah's peace be upon him and upon the last of His Prophets, had he told him the truth plainly that he wanted him to disobey the Lord so that he could get out of the Garden of Eden. Instead, he slyly took the course of deceit and seduced him:

...يَـٰٓـَٔادَمُ هَلۡ أَدُلُّكَ عَلَىٰ شَجَرَةِ ٱلۡخُلۡدِ وَمُلۡكٍ لَّا يَبۡلَىٰ ۝

('Adam! Shall I direct you to a tree of eternal life and an abiding kingdom?')
(*Ṭā Hā*, 20: 120)

This is the eternal truth about man's instinct.[1] Every act of folly and blunder that he is encouraged to commit is mainly due either to misleading slogans or a deceitful garb, in which temptations are presented to him by the Devil and its disciples.

10.1.1. *Deception one: capitalism and secular democracy*

The biggest deception of our modern times, to which humanity is being subjected today, is that being inflicted in the name of 'social justice'. The Devil has

---

* Based on the paper read by Sayyid Mawdūdī at the special session of World Muslim Congress, held at Makkah al-Mukarramah during *Ḥajj*, 1962. – Editor.

[1] Man is born innocent. He is true to his nature and free from all blemishes of character. This eternal truth has been so beautifully explained by the Holy Prophet (*pbuh*) in a well known *Ḥadīth*: كُلُّ مَوْلُودٍ يُولَدُ عَلَى الْفِطْرَةِ، فَأَبَوَاهُ يُهَوِّدَانِهِ وَيُنَصِّرَانِهِ وَيُمَجِّسَانِهِ ('Every child is born on his natural instinct [of submission to the Will of the Lord – Islam]') (Bukhārī). It is then his parents who make him a Jew, a Christian or a fire-worshipper.'). There is no room in Islam for the doctrine invented by St. Paul that the sin of *Sayyidinā* Ādam (*pbuh*) passed on to his progeny and that God had to crucify His One and Only Son to redeem humanity from that. – Translator.

earlier deceived humanity for a very long time under the names of 'liberty' and 'liberalism'. On that basis, he succeeded in raising the systems of capitalism and secular democracy during the eighteenth century. These were then the dominant trends and regarded as the last word in the socio-political advancement of mankind. Everybody who was keen to pass as a progressive had no option but to sing for liberty and liberalism. The people then believed that, if there was any panacea for the ills facing humanity anywhere in the world, it was to be found in the systems of capitalism and secular democracy as they flourished in the West. However, things soon took a different turn and the people started realizing that Western capitalism, as it was enshrined in its model of secular democracy, was actually responsible for inundating the earth with so much imbalance, tyranny and oppression. It was thus no longer possible for the accursed Devil to deceive humanity any further by what was once the most tempting slogan.

10.1.2. *Deception two: social justice and communism*

However, the Devil soon hoisted the banner of yet another fraud under the names of 'social justice' and 'communism'. In the garb of these deceptions, efforts are being made today to establish yet another system of tyranny and exploitation. The new system has succeeded in taking a number of countries into its stranglehold and is perpetrating in these places brutality and repression to an extent never known before in human history. Due to the successful trickery of the perpetrators of this deception, many countries in the world have been duped into believing that the system is a panacea for all their socio-political and economic ills. Nevertheless, the day is not far off when the truth of this deception will also be exposed and the whole fabric of the system torn into shreds.[2]

10.1.3. *Modern Muslims' intellectual servility*

The Muslims are blessed to have in the Book of God and the Tradition of the Holy Prophet (*pbuh*) a priceless and everlasting treasure of Eternal Guidance for mankind. This is a Guidance that is available to them for all eternity to put them on the right path in all spheres of life and protect them from falling into the Devil's traps. Unfortunately, however, they are generally ignorant of the riches that rest secure with them. They remain dazed under colonialism's

[2] The statement made so authoritatively in such an august gathering in 1962 might have sounded then to some as mere political sloganeering or wishful thinking. History now bears witness to its veracity and the deep insight and sagacity of that great visionary of our times. – Translator.

tight grip and are part of its intellectual and civilizational servitude. This is why we are regularly faced here with the echo of slogans raised from time to time by the camp followers of the dominant world powers. When the West was reverberating with the ideas floated by the French Revolution, every educated person in the Muslim world took upon himself to gloat over those and tried to get himself tailored to suit their new mould. He felt that, unless he subscribed to these concepts, he might be treated as backward and labeled as reactionary. As this phase of history was over, our educated groups began shifting their *Qiblah* (focus of attention) until they discovered a new ideal in the forms of socialism and communism. Such intellectual servility and somersaults could be condoned to some extent, but the most atrocious part was that these serfs of the West's intellectual colonialism tried every time to have Islam also to change its *Qiblah* toward the direction to which they moved. They gave the impression that, as Muslims, they could not live without Islam and it must therefore follow their whims. Their desire has been that Islam should invariably toe the '*ism*', which they thought was essential for their progress and development, so that Islam should not be equated with obscurantism. This is why efforts made earlier to establish liberalism, capitalism and secular democracy as being very much Islamic are now being diverted to prove that the concept of social justice in Islam is exactly the same as that found in socialism and communism. This pathetic ignorance of our educated elite is in fact the most abysmal point in their intellectual servitude.

10.2. Social justice in theory and practice

In this brief resume, let me try to explain the exact meaning of social justice and the right way to establish it as a system. Those bent upon projecting socialism as the best form of social justice are unlikely to realize their mistake and retract their steps because the ignorant can only be reformed as long as he is just ignorant; but when he becomes a ruler as well, he presumes to be 'omniscient', and hence becomes incorrigible. This phenomenon has been best explained by the Qur'ānic dictum: مَا عَلِمْتُ لَكُم مِّنْ إِلَٰهٍ غَيْرِي ('I have known no deity for you other than myself') (*al-Qaṣaṣ*, 28: 38). However by the Grace of God, the common man always remains capable of understanding the truth, if properly groomed. It is the ordinary man who is being misled by the misguided leaders, who are out today to promote their fallacy through him. This exposé is therefore addressed primarily to the people in general, to whom I would like to communicate the correct position.

Let us see what social justice stands for, and how it can best be established.

10.2.1. *Islam alone guarantees social justice*

Let me begin by stating categorically that those who often raise the slogan 'Islam is also a torch-bearer of social justice' are wrong. The factually correct statement is: 'Islam alone guarantees social justice!' Islam is the religion Allah *subḥānahū wa taʿālā* has revealed for the guidance of mankind. As its Creator and Sustainer, He is the sole Authority to determine what justice stands for and how can it be established among the people. No one else is qualified to determine the parameters of justice and tyranny. Neither is anybody capable of establishing a system of real justice on his own. A human being is not the master of his own destiny, neither is he a self-governed entity. He is therefore least qualified to determine for himself the standards of right and wrong. His position in the universe is that of God's bondsman and subject, and it is thus not for him, but for his Master and the Supreme Lord, to set the standards of right and wrong, justice and tyranny. Furthermore, it is not possible for a human brain to remain uninfluenced by its inherent biases, likes and dislikes. Hence, not even an assembly of scholars and intellectuals can ever determine fairly what is right and what is wrong for man in life. This is because of the limitations of human sciences and the handicaps of human wisdom. It is not possible for any person or group of people to evolve on their own a system that is truly based on justice. Many man-made systems, which have initially appeared to be based on the principles of justice, have had their hollowness eventually exposed by practical experience. History has thus recorded the failure of many systems in the past, and man's folly has been shown in his move from one pitfall to another in an attempt to test yet one more model of his brain's creation. Humanity can therefore have no perfect model of governance, except the system created and revealed by the All-Knowing and All-Wise Lord, the Most Compassionate, the Most Merciful.

10.2.2. *Social justice: the goal before Islam*

The second thing that must be borne in mind at the very outset is that justice is not merely an attribute that Islam has cherished. In fact, this is the objective that the Religion of Peace has kept before itself to promote and inspire mankind to achieve in individual and collective lives. The Lord has revealed Islam to establish the writ of justice in human society:

لَقَدْ أَرْسَلْنَا رُسُلَنَا بِٱلْبَيِّنَـٰتِ وَأَنزَلْنَا مَعَهُمُ ٱلْكِتَـٰبَ وَٱلْمِيزَانَ لِيَقُومَ ٱلنَّاسُ بِٱلْقِسْطِ ۖ وَأَنزَلْنَا ٱلْحَدِيدَ فِيهِ بَأْسٌ
شَدِيدٌ وَمَنَـٰفِعُ لِلنَّاسِ وَلِيَعْلَمَ ٱللَّهُ مَن يَنصُرُهُۥ وَرُسُلَهُۥ بِٱلْغَيْبِ ۚ إِنَّ ٱللَّهَ قَوِىٌّ عَزِيزٌ ﴿٢٥﴾

> ('Indeed We sent Our Messengers with Clear Signs, and sent down with them the Book and the Balance that people may uphold justice. And We sent down iron, wherein there is awesome power and many benefits for people, so that Allah may know who, without even having seen Him, helps Him and His Messengers. Surely Allah is Most Strong, Most Mighty.'[3])
>
> (*al-Ḥadīd*, 57: 25)

These are the two things which, if they are kept in mind, mean that no Muslim can ever deviate in his search for social justice to any fountainhead other than that of Allah *subḥānahū wa taʿālā* and His Holy Prophet (*pbuh*). The moment he feels the need for justice, he will realize that it is only found with the Lord and His Apostle. He will also come to know that he need do nothing to establish justice other than establishing the writ of the Religion of Truth in the land. Once Islam is established in both letter and spirit, and in its entirety, God's earth will start blooming with the blessings of justice. Justice is nothing apart from Islam. In fact, Islam in itself is justice incarnate, and to establish Islam means to establish the Writ of Justice.

10.2.3. *Growth and development of human personality*

Every human society is made up of a multitude of individuals. Each and every component of this enormous machine is itself full of life, wisdom and vitality. Every individual has a personality of his own, for the growth and development of which he needs proper opportunity. He has a taste and temperament of his own. He has his own leanings and aspirations. He has a body and soul that have their own demands. He is not a lifeless tool that is of no importance other than to be a part of the machine, with the real purpose and value and its tools being merely pegs designed to fit in the place each is designed for. Tools only exist to

---

[3] Here we find a succinct statement describing the essence of the missions of all the Prophets. Every Messenger of God brought with him three things: (i) *bayyināt*: Clear Signs, strong and persuasive arguments and lucid directives; (ii) a Book embodying the teachings needed for mankind's guidance so that people could turn to it for enlightenment; and (iii) *mīzān*, which is the criteria for right and wrong that can precisely indicate, as does a balance, the golden mean of justice that eschews extremes in thought, moral conduct and inter-human relationships.

The statement that God 'sent down iron' immediately after stating the mission of the Prophets clearly indicates that the word 'iron' is not used here in its literal sense; instead, it is used figuratively to signify political and military power. The purpose of the verse, therefore, is to stress that God did not raise His Messengers simply to put forward a scheme to establish justice. It was also a part of the Messengers' missions to strive to put that scheme into effect. Likewise, it was a part of their mission to acquire the power needed to establish justice and to render powerless all those who would try to disrupt or resist that scheme. (*Towards Understanding the Qur'ān*, Abridged version of *Tafhīm al-Qur'ān*, fnn. 16 and 17, p.1132.)

fill well-defined slots for a particular purpose, and have no individuality of their own. On the contrary, human society is a group of individuals; it is a bouquet of flowers of multiple hues and fragrances, with each flower having its own unique identity and place in life. Individuals are not designed for the group, but the group is to serve its individual members. It is they who form the complex whole of human society. They therefore need opportunities to fulfil their needs and satisfy the demands of their bodies and souls.

10.2.4. *Personal accountability*

Each and every individual is accountable before his Lord, the Creator and Sustainer. Everyone has to face the Day of Reckoning after spending the specified period of his trial on earth. He will then answer before the Lord for the opportunities, capabilities and resources granted to him and the use to which he has put these to in order to build his character within the prescribed parameters. Every person is accountable to the Lord in an individual capacity, and not as a group. The families, tribes and communities will not stand up to be held accountable collectively. Each and every individual will be separated from his near and dear ones and will stand in the dock alone to account for his deeds before the Almighty.

10.2.5. *Individual freedom*

Both of these aspects – the growth and development of the human personality in this world and his accountability in the Hereafter – demand that the individual must have complete freedom of action here. A social order that does not allow the individual his freedom is instrumental in distorting and throttling his personality. The stifling suffocation of such a system prevents the free flow of his inborn talents and potential, and he finds himself a captive of the system, deprived of vigour, merely stale and stagnant. The ultimate responsibility for putting free souls into this situation, and also for the lapses they commit in their state of captivity, will therefore fall in the Hereafter on the shoulders of those in charge of initiating and running such a repressive system. They will be held to account not only for their own misdeeds, but also for the crime of forcing multitudes of their fellow humans, without their consent and in pursuance of the rulers' own interests, into subjugation to a system that led to the distortion of their personalities. Obviously, no person believing in the Hereafter can think of facing his Lord with such an awful and back-breaking burden on his shoulders. If he has fear of the Lord and of the Day of Reckoning, he will definitely be compelled to allow his fellow beings to enjoy more freedom in order to let the responsibility for the deeds of others shift from his shoulders to the shoulders of the individuals themselves, to let them face the consequences of whatever good or bad they may do in this world.

10.2.6. *Social institutions and their writ*

So far we have dealt with personal freedom. As for society, this is composed of families, clans, tribes, communities and nations. Its basic unit consists of a man, his spouse and their offspring, which thus blossoms into a family. A group of families then make '*Birādarīs*' or 'Brotherhoods', clans and tribes, and from them emerge communities or nations, and a nation then forms a state to enforce its collective will in a certain area. In their different forms, all of these social institutions are needed to provide an individual with the opportunity to grow and develop his personality with their help and support and under their protection. This creates an opportunity which it is impossible for him to gain on his own. However, a prime objective like this cannot be achieved unless each of these institutions enjoys a measure of control over individuals, with bigger institutions having influence over the smaller ones. This is essential in order to prevent individuals from an unbridled freedom and from encroaching on each other's personal freedom and rights; it is also right for harnessing their potential for the common weal of the society as a whole.

From this emerges the enigmatic question of the role that social institutions are expected to play in order to streamline the opposing demands of individuals and the collective whole. On the one hand, the imperatives of human advancement demand that an individual should have free play for his personality in the society of which he is a member, which will help him build his character according to his aptitude and potential. Similarly, families, clans, tribes and various other groups should also have the opportunity to enjoy the freedom essential to their respective fields of action in their larger spheres. On the other hand, the dictates of human progress and development also demand that families should have control over individuals, tribes and clans over families, and the community over tribes and clans; over and above all, the state should have full sway over every individual and institution, whether big or small, in order to keep them all in check and let none transgress its limits. We are faced with the same issue on a global level, where it is essential for each nation and state to enjoy complete freedom and self-rule, while it is also imperative to have a supreme body to keep these independent states and nations in check and ensure that none of them transgresses its limits and harms another.

Social justice thus involves a happy blend of checks and freedoms. Each individual, family, clan, tribe and nation must have a desired level of freedom in their respective spheres, while simultaneously there must be a system of control to keep each of these in check. While enjoying the freedom they need in their respective spheres, each of these may thus also render the services required of them for the collective well-being of society and humanity as a whole.

10.3. Failings of capitalism and communism

Viewed in this context, it should be distinctly clear that, just as the system based on fallacious theories of personal freedom, which emerged in the aftermath of the French Revolution, was contrary to the norms of social justice, in the same way or rather even worse than this is the ideology of communism that is now being introduced in pursuance of the misleading thoughts of Marx and Engels, which is in total violation of the dictates of social justice. The drawback of the old system was that it left the individual's unbridled freedom to transgress his limits and encroach upon the rights of families, clans, brotherhoods, tribes, communities and nations, and society's regulatory authority was allowed to erode in the name of the public interest. The error made by the new system is that it has endowed the state with extraordinary powers, almost totally denying individuals, families, clans, brotherhoods and every social institution their respective freedom. It reduces them to the position of inanimate tools under the coercive power of a repressive state. The claim that communism can lead to the establishment of social justice in the land is nothing but a complete lie.

10.4. Communism: the worst form of social repression

Communism is in fact 'social repression' in its worst form. It is a coercive system of state tyranny worse than any experienced by humanity in its recorded history, not even during the darkest days of the repressive rules of Genghis Khan, the Pharaohs or Nimrod. No sane person can call it 'social justice' to let one or a gang of upstarts coin a set of ideas and then forcibly grab power, exploiting the unchecked authority of the state and government to impose their writ on the millions of people inhabiting the land. How can any civilized society permit a small group of self-seeking autocrats to grab the people's property, dislodge them from their lands, occupy their factories in the name of 'nationalization' and virtually turn the entire country into a jail? How can one justify an act that reduces a country into a police state, where no one is free to raise a voice of dissent, make an appeal, complain or seek redressal of his grievances, one where everyone finds the doors of justice totally shut? What can be the most appropriate name for a place where there is no party other than one imposed on the people through the state's repressive power, where there is no public organization or platform to raise one's voice, where there is no free press to let the people express their views and no free court for the oppressed to seek justice? How can the civilized world condone a system that draws sustenance from the brute force of state spies and paid intelligence hounds of the one and only 'Party' in power, a system where every citizen is apprehensive of every other, where the intelligence network is so widespread and powerful that everyone feels afraid to open his mouth, even within the four walls of his own home? Can this system be called a democracy, when the charade it periodically arranges under the name of elections has no place for any opposition to participate? The system has chosen for itself the nomenclature of the '*Dictatorship of the Proletariat*', or the rule of the working classes. But is this truly so? Isn't this actually the most repressive rule of a few top members of the 'Party' and its elitist 'Polit Bureau'?

Hypothetically, let us suppose that communism could facilitate the equitable distribution of wealth – though it has been unable to do this so far – even then, social justice does not simply mean economic equality. Let us not question whether the top autocrat in a communist system and the common peasant living under its stranglehold both enjoy the same economic status! Let us instead ask: can a perfect economic equality, if the system manages to succeed in introducing this for all segments of society, be called real social justice? Is it justice to allow the Dictator at the top and the coterie of his chosen few absolute freedom to impose their thoughts on the entire nation with the help of the state's police, intelligence and repressive armed might, denying everyone else the right to open their lips even to utter a word of dissent? Is it justice to allow the ruler control of all avenues of the state media and its propaganda machinery to build his image, perpetuate his rule and project the 'blessings' of communism, while everybody else is denied the opportunity to express his views or approach the press, and no two persons can join together to form a party or organization in the public interest? Can it be called justice to eliminate all private ownership of farms and factories and to allow only one landlord and mill-owner to dominate the land in the form of the ruling party and its government, while the government itself comprises a handful of despots whose sole concern is not to ameliorate the people's lot, but to subjugate them? Is man all stomach and human life simply confined to the economic needs of the belly? Can we take economic parity – and that in name only – as justice in its true sense? Every effort to establish economic parity, howsoever genuine and sincere it may be, can only be justified if it is not made at the cost of the individual's liberty and his personal freedom, or involve a denial of the basic human rights of the people. A system that floods every walk of life with tyranny and oppression, although it may temporarily succeed – if at all – in an equitable distribution of wealth, cannot be called a system of social justice, but is one of social repression. Communism unfortunately enjoys the dubious distinction of being the worst form of social exploitation and brutality that human history has ever known.

10.5. Justice in Islam

Now let me briefly explain what Islam calls *ʿAdl*, or justice. There is no room in Islam for any individual or group of persons to sit together and invent their own concept of justice for the society, and then impose it on the people through brute force without allowing anybody to say a word against their self-conceived notions. The glorious history of Islam is a witness to the fact that not even the Righteous Caliphs enjoyed this position. Even the Holy Prophet (*pbuh*) did not claim to have such an exclusive status. It is only the Divine Prerogative of Allah *subḥānahū wa taʿālā* to dictate His Will to His bondsmen. *Sayyidinā* Rasūl Allāh, may Allah's peace be upon him, his family and all his Companions also followed His Dictates both in letter and spirit. It is binding upon Muslims to follow the injunctions of the Holy Prophet (*pbuh*) not because these are his orders, but because they are from the Lord, conveyed to humanity through the Last of His Apostles. The Holy Prophet was himself duty-bound to obey the injunctions he asked the Nation of Islam to follow. This is the reason why the Divine Law of Islamic *Sharīʿah* is sacrosanct and inviolable. Beyond this, however, there is no restriction on anyone expressing their views. Islam guarantees people's fundamental human rights, and in an Islamic polity there is no room for a despot or self-willed dictator.

10.5.1. *Parameters of personal freedom*

Allah *subḥānahu wa taʿālā* has Himself defined the limits of one's freedom in Islam. *Sharīʿah* has clearly determined the parameters that a Muslim must observe. A man is expected to know what is permissible and lawful (*Ḥalāl*) for him, and what is prohibited (*Ḥarām*) that he cannot indulge in; what is obligatory that he must do; what rights others owe to him, and what he owes to others; how the ownership of an asset can lawfully be transferred to him; what society is required to do in order to improve the individual's lot; and what restrictions have been imposed on individuals, families, brotherhoods, clans and the community in the interests of society's well-being. All of these have been permanently codified in the sacrosanct Constitution of the Qur'ān and the *Sunnah*. It is a Constitution that none can abrogate or amend. According to the law of personal freedom, which is guaranteed by this Constitution, no one has the right to transgress the limits set for his freedom; at the same time, nobody is permitted to deny a person the freedom guaranteed to him by the Law. No person is allowed to transgress the limits of *Ḥarām* while seeking his fortune and earning money, or in spending what he has earned. On the other hand, the right to own through lawful means is fully protected by the Law and no authority, however powerful, can take this right away. Similarly, everyone is duty-bound to abide by the rules and contribute the best he can for society's moral and economic uplift. Nobody is authorized, however, to force him into doing more than his duty, unless he is willing to do this voluntarily. The same is true of the society and the state. It is as binding on them to discharge their obligations towards individuals and give them their due as it is obligatory for individuals to observe the rights of the society and the state. If this Constitution is enforced in its true spirit, it is bound to lead to the establishment of a just social order and a model welfare state. So long as this Constitution is there, nobody can hoodwink the Muslims to believe in the misleading slogans of "Islamic Socialism" or "Socialist Islam" because Islam is *Dīn*, meaning a complete code of conduct and the Qur'ān, the *Sunnah* represent the perfect Constitution and they need no appendage to make them complete.

The Islamic Constitution strikes such a balance between the rights and obligations of individuals, the society and the state that each complements the others. The individual has not been allowed the freedom to harm the interests of the society, nor is the society authorized to deny the individual his rights that assist in the proper growth and development of his personality.

10.5.2. *Preconditions for transfer of wealth*

Islam has approved only three ways for the transfer of wealth to an individual: (i) *Wirāthah*, or inheritance; (ii) *Hibah*, or gift; and (iii) *Kasb*, or earning. The only inheritance that is lawful is when the legal heir of the deceased receives from the latter's lawful legacy according to the *Sharīʿah* rules. Similarly, a gift is lawful if it has been offered by a lawful owner to somebody within the parameters of the *Sharīʿah*. If the gift has been conferred by the government, it will only be lawful if it is granted in recognition of a person's meritorious services in the interests of the nation and the state. Moreover, the only government that is competent to offer gifts from public treasury is one that is run through a representative *Shūrā* Council, which is accountable to the people. As for *Kasb*, Islam permits earning through *Ḥalāl* means only, and even a penny earned through unlawful means is *Ḥarām*. Everything that is earned through burglary, extortion, pilfering weights and measures, deception and perfidy, bribery, fraud, betting, gambling, withholding the stock to raise prices of goods in the market, prostitution, drug trade, interest-based transactions and trading in vulgarity is *Ḥarām*. By strictly observing these parameters, whatever one earns is legitimate. No individual or institution is authorized to impose any restriction on this income, either to increase it through fair means or foul or to curtail it forcibly if the volume is huge. As for wealth gathered by transcending the limits set by the *Sharīʿah*, every Muslim citizen of the state has the right to raise the question: مِن اَينَ لَكَ هٰذا (How did you get this?). The source of any dubious income will have to be scrutinized by the law and, if it is proved that it has been earned through unlawful means, the Islamic government has the right to confiscate it in the national interest.

10.5.3. *Restrictions on the use of wealth*

No individual has been given unlicensed freedom, even to spend the money he has earned lawfully. Some legal restrictions have been imposed by the *Sharīʿah* in this respect to ensure that nobody misuses his wealth for the detriment of society or spends it in a way that is unhealthy and harmful for his own self morally or economically. No one is permitted to spend his wealth on things that show disobedience to the Lord or for things harmful for the society's moral and economic health. This is why we see that drinking and gambling are disallowed; there is no room for adultery and fornication; no place for bonded labour, serfs and slaves; no trading as slaves of those born free, whether male or female, so that they are forced to work and generate income for their 'masters'. Islam similarly puts strict curbs on overspending, living beyond one's means and extravaganza. No member of a Muslim society is permitted to revel in his riches while his neighbour is hungry for want of food. Islam allows the individual to use his surplus money to generate more, provided that he follows fair means for this. He is not authorized to exceed the limits imposed by the *Sharīʿah* in this respect.

10.5.4. *In service of the society*

Islam has made *Zakāh* mandatory so that those with surplus money in excess of the prescribed limit (*Niṣāb*) use this in the service of society. It levies *Zakāh* on business goods, agricultural products, livestock and other assets as well. The benevolent system of *Zakāh* is so revolutionary that, if it were to be introduced anywhere in the world today and the funds generated were spent judiciously in the light of the Qur'ānic injunctions, no person could remain deprived of the basic necessities of life there. The system eliminates the curse of the stratification of society into the privileged and the under-privileged.

The wealth one may gather, even after regular payment of *Zakāh*, is distributed among his heirs when he dies because Islam does not like to let accumulation perpetuate to become a cartel in a few hands.

10.5.5. *Eradication of injustice*

Islam promotes mutual goodwill and understanding between landlord and farm-worker, mill-owner and labour, in order to enable them to run their affairs amicably and to sort out matters by taking each other into their confidence, without allowing the law to intervene. But wherever there is injustice and high-handedness, the Islamic government is legally bound to intervene and let the law take its course to provide justice to the aggrieved.

10.5.6. *Nationalization and public interest*
The Islamic *Sharīʿah* does not prohibit the government taking control of any commercial or industrial enterprise. In the absence of a suitable private management to run an industry or trade, the government can assume charge in the public interest. Similarly, if the government is of the view that allowing a certain venture in the private sector is against the national interest, it can turn it into a public sector enterprise. A private sector enterprise that is run on lines detrimental to the national interest can be handled similarly. The government is then authorized to intervene and take charge of it and, after giving compensation to its owners, arrange a suitable restructuring of its management according to the dictates of the national interest.

However, Islam does not permit nationalization as a state policy. It does not allow the means of production to be monopolized by the government and the state to become the sole landlord, trader and industrialist of the land.

10.5.7. *Use of the public treasury* (Bayt al-Māl)
According to the decree of the Islamic *Sharīʿah, Bayt al-Māl* is the Divine-cum-Public Property, with nobody enjoying an ownership right. As with other matters of public interest, the affairs of *Bayt al-Māl* are to be looked after in consultation with public representatives. All receipts and issues of the Public Treasury are a sacred national trust and are subject to public scrutiny and accountability.

10.5.8. *The basic issue!*
To conclude, let me ask every thinking mind: 'If social justice is taken to mean only economic justice, then what about the economic justice that Islam seeks to establish? Can this not suffice us to meet our needs? Why must we opt for a system that denies the people their freedom, violates basic human rights, grabs private lands and properties and reduces a whole nation to the level of serfs and bondsmen of a chosen few, and all this in the name of social justice?'

Let us seriously ponder over the basic issue: What is the obstacle that prevents us as Muslims from establishing the rule of *Sharīʿah*? Why can we not base our polity on the Islamic Constitution that guarantees the people their basic rights, freedom, social justice and economic welfare? Why can we not rise to provide the world with a model of governance which is free from the extremes of capitalism and communism? Instead of becoming the harbingers of joy for others, why are we hell-bent on acting like the lackeys of others? The time has come for us to rise up to the occasion, grab the challenge and show the world how Islam can bring happiness to humanity if it is practised individually and collectively in letter and spirit in all walks of life, including statecraft, economics, politics, etc.

11 Issues of Labour, Insurance and Price Control

11.1. Labour-related issues and their solutions[1]

Our defective economic system remains the main cause of the problems that face industrial and farm labour and the issues they are struggling hard to cope with today. The principal factor responsible for the failings of this system is the corrupt social order of which our economic system is just a small component. As long as there is no change in this corrupt order as a whole, and economic disorder is consequently not set right, no tangible or worthwhile improvement can be expected in the lives of the working class.

11.1.1. *What has caused the damage?*

The current economic system of our country is not simply the legacy of the British imperialism, but it embodies the drawbacks of the pre-*Rāj* period as well. As is evident from the writings of Shāh Walīullāh Muḥaddith Dihlawī, the people were groaning even then under an inhospitable and repressive economic dispensation. When the British established their colonial rule, they added more ills and imposed an even worse system in the land. The reason for this deterioration was that: (i) the new rulers were the flag-bearers of a purely materialistic culture; (ii) it was the heyday of Western capitalism and there was no authority to keep a check on the all-powerful capitalists; and (iii) the colonial nature of British rule and the objectives they had set themselves were to grab more and more benefits from the natives and to serve their national interest by hook or by crook. Due to these three factors, the system they imposed on the people became an embodiment of repression and tyranny.

Fortunately, we were able to rid ourselves of the imperialist rule, but, even after their departure, we have sadly failed to make any significant headway to introduce a change in the colonial economic structure. The prime factor responsible for the prolongation of colonial policies in every area has been the absence of any ideological basis for the political changeover. Even a day before independence,

---

[1] Adapted from Sayyid Mawdūdī's address delivered at Pakistan Labour Welfare Committee Convention, 13 May, 1957. – Editor.

nobody had the faintest idea of a roadmap for the system to be followed in the post-colonial days of our political independence. There was no programme or plan of action before the nation and its leaders to steer the ship through political chaos and economic backwardness safely to its ultimate destination of an *Islamic Welfare State.* This is the reason why we have not witnessed any respite in our troubles since we gained independence from the British. In fact, it is just the opposite. Our problems have gone on multiplying with each passing day. The system introduced by the colonial regime, which was based on its capitalistic, materialistic and imperialistic approach, remains in force even today. Instead of bringing about a change, the system is being further strengthened. The Islamic Republic has not cared to introduce any amendment or modification to the pre-independence laws, which the *Rāj* had promulgated to safeguard its own interests. The rules and regulations enforced by the colonial masters to maintain their stranglehold remain intact. Our administrative policy continues to be the same, and the education system is treading on the dotted lines.

Had our independence been the natural consequence of a well-planned ideological and moral struggle, there would have been a well-defined roadmap before us since the start, on the basis of which the country could have marched forward after gaining independence. Such a roadmap ought to have been prepared long ago to help the nation move forward on a well-charted course without wasting a day after independence. However, this did not happen, and hence the problems of our colonial days continue multiplying with each passing day, instead of getting reduced and redressed.

11.1.2. *The real need*

Our real need today is for a total overhaul of the entire system inherited from the British. As long as we do not do this, no improvement is possible and no redressal of our grievances or betterment of our lot can be expected. The cure for all of our socio-economic malaise lies in pulling out the existing system from its very roots and re-establishing it on new moral and ideological foundations which can guarantee social justice to the people – the real beneficiaries. Such a healthy change is bound to usher in a new era of social emancipation for the poor and an improvement of the lot of the common man.

As per my conviction, it is only Islam that provides the basis for a way of life that guarantees social justice to man. What we are striving for is to establish this system and way of life. There can be a difference of opinion concerning its details, but the exact blueprint of that system is available to the world in the Qur'ān and the *Sunnah* of the Holy Prophet (*pbuh*), which are the fountainhead of our Religion. Only an interpretation of the Islamic system that conforms to this blueprint will therefore be naturally acceptable. A public consensus in a Muslim society will eventually be the arbiter for accepting or rejecting a particular interpretation, and hence there is no cause for anxiety on the diversity of views in this process. Any democratic set-up established according to the guidelines of the Qur'ān and the *Sunnah* can definitely be a guarantor of justice and social uplift for the people.

11.1.3. *Resolution of problems*

As long as there is no such basic and all-embracing change in the system, the first objective before us should be the establishment of the writ of justice as far as possible. Secondly, no stone should be left unturned in redressing the grievances and removing the difficulties of the working class; and thirdly, no agents of white or red imperialism should be allowed to exploit these problems and use our labour folk as tools for any system other than Islam.

The last of the three objectives mentioned above needs some elaboration. Different people in the world have different mindsets. Let me cite the example of a patient groaning with pain. Some may be tempted to seize the 'opportunity' offered by his pain to rob him of his valuables. Another person may think differently and try to get first aid for him so that his pain is reduced at least before proper treatment comes to him. Both of these mindsets are presently at work in the context of the working classes. The modern capitalist system has multiplied the problems of these people. A group of their so-called 'well-wishers' is out simply to exploit their problems for political ends. Their objective is not to redress these problems or to remove grievances, but to complicate them further. Instead of providing a remedy, the group wants to agitate them so much that they may be compelled to turn violent and use their anger to create a law and order situation. They can thus successfully exploit the resulting 'violent revolution' to impose a communist system on the people. The paradise for the workers that this group promises under this system is in fact no better than hell. The real ordeal for farm labour, industrial workers and the downtrodden will begin the moment that the communist system takes charge, God forbid, of the land. The plight of workers and peasants is certainly alarming today; but what they may face under a communist set-up is unthinkable. Today you can at least raise your voice and submit your demands, stage rallies and demonstrations if these demands are not accepted, raise a hue and cry and have the choice to leave one place of work for another. In the *workers' paradise* of communism, all the doors to dissent will be totally shut because every factory, every inch of land, the press and media and all means of subsistence will be concentrated within the hands of one sole authority in the land, which holds the reins of power and controls everything from the resources of the land to the police, CID, military, judiciary and jails. No worker can even think of raising a finger of disapproval under such a system, never mind staging protest rallies, processions or strikes from work.

No door will thus remain open for anybody to try his luck. The whole country will just have one single landlord, and the peasants will have no option but to till their land, and even that on his terms and conditions. There will be just one mill-owner in the land, and the workers will have to work for him and will get in return what he may be pleased to dole out, rather than what may help them satisfy their needs. It is for this system of repression and tyranny that this particular group is trying to use the working classes as a tool. The group's interest in their problems and issues is not to achieve a resolution, but to exploit them for a socialist revolution. In order to deceive the innocent workers and peasants, it keeps them fed on false hopes that the revolution will take over all the factories and lands from the feudalists and capitalists to hand them over to industrial workers and farm labour, making them the owners. In fact, if the system is in place, everything will pass into the ownership of the state and all workers will be reduced to the level of serfs and bonded labour for the communist state. The group that is vocal everywhere in the world today for workers' rights will be silent in a communist set-up. One may very well ask these self-styled 'champions' of the rights of the working classes: Why don't they raise their voices for the sake of the oppressed workers and farmers of communist states, who have been forced to toil under the most trying conditions, much worse than they had experienced prior to the communist 'revolution' in their land? My considered opinion, therefore, is that communism is not a panacea at all for the ills created by the capitalist system. Rather, it is worse than capitalism in many ways, especially in its treatment of the working classes, in whose name the communist 'revolution' was staged, and who are now being used as fodder for the unscrupulous and ruthless *Dictatorship of the Proletariat*!

11.1.4. *Agenda for reform*

I am of the firm view that, for as long as our land remains deprived of the blessings of Islamic rule, some interim measures may be taken to remove the grievances of the oppressed working classes to improve their lot. They should not be left at the mercy of the slogan-mongers and political exploiters, who merely want to use them for their own ulterior motives.

I do not believe in any form of class-conflict. In fact Islam seeks to eliminate completely all class distinctions and the feudalist structure of local polity. Classes emerge in a society as a result of the dominance of a wrong system.

The erosion of ethical and moral values gives rise to class distinctions, and the prevalence of injustice creates biases and hatred among various segments of society. Communism aims at boosting class biases further and, by playing upon the feelings of hate and anger against the high-handedness of the privileged classes, making the under-privileged rise in rebellion against the existing order. Instead of trying to improve the situation systematically and wage a concerted struggle to replace the prevailing feudal and capitalist structure of economy and polity eventually with a benign system of socio-economic justice, their sole objective is to disrupt everything and, in the resulting void, impose the worst ever dictatorship that is the communist system.

As harbingers of Islamic revolution, on the other hand, our struggle is not aimed at fomenting class-conflict and exploiting the poverty and deprivation of the under-privileged. Nor do we believe in any short cut to the introduction of the benign Islamic social order, or using the crutches and patronage of any dictator in the land to bring about our much-coveted Islamic revolution. We take human society as one single body with various segments as its limbs. Each limb of the body has its own place and function in that organic whole, and nobody can think of the hand fighting the leg or the head revolting against the heart because the survival of the body and all its parts depends on their interdependence and support for each other. Similarly we would like all segments of society to contribute what they can to the best of their ability and potential for its well-being. To achieve this, each segment is expected to be supportive of the others. Instead of class-conflict, we would therefore like to see each class being compassionate, considerate and sympathetic to the others. Their interrelationship should be one of cooperation, with each person complementing the others, and not that of conflict and antagonistic competition.

We would like everyone, whether employer or employee, to know well what his rights and his duties are, and then try to discharge them faithfully. The more the individuals are particular about their obligations, and the more their sense of responsibility increases, the less chance there will be of conflict. This will start a cycle of resolution of all problems, minor or major.

We would like to reawaken the people's moral sense and release their moral being from the clutches of the animal within him, which has overpowered people for too long. If this moral being within becomes free from the crippling dominance of the animal that is there and starts doing things in the natural way, as should be expected of him, the fountainhead of all ills will begin to run dry.

I am firmly of the view that those engaged in reforming society should try to reform the economic system at the same time. They should show workers the right course of action, as well as those taking the work from them.

I also take this opportunity to categorically tell employers that, if they do not wish to drag themselves into the pitfalls of destruction, they must not become blinded by their passion to earn more. They must give up unlawful practices, including profiteering; they must give to those whom they employ as labour what is their due; and they must not aim to monopolize every benefit of national progress and prosperity. They should be willing and even keen to let these benefits also reach the common man, because it is through their combined and concerted efforts and human resources that this progress in their ventures has been possible. Wealth is not only produced through capital. Capital alone is of no value unless it is linked to enterprise, organization, technical skill and physical labour. It is with this value-addition that capital produces the dividends called wealth, and to earn this successfully, the society's entire socio-political edifice, called the state, contributes the best that it can. If these dividends are judiciously distributed among all the elements of production, avoiding ways and means disapproved by Islam, the dictates of social justice are bound to prevail and there will be no room left for any subversive movement to raise its ugly head that may lead eventually to the destruction of employers themselves.

As for the workers, I have to tell them the following. They should realize themselves what are the rights due to them judiciously and lawfully, and what is the rightful share of those investing their capital, organizational and entrepreneurial abilities and technical skills, which together with their hard work go to produce the results! Any movement that people intend to launch for their rights must essentially be based on justice. They must not be lead away by fantastic notions of their rights, which the elements bent upon starting a class war in the land are trying their best to hammer into their heads. The struggle of the workers for their lawful rights must also be made through lawful means. It will then become naturally binding for all the seekers of truth to stand by their side.

The measures that we intend to introduce to reform the country's economic system may be summed up as follows:

- To legally ban interest, betting, gambling and all unethical means declared *Ḥarām* by the *Sharī'ah*, and keep open to the people only the doors of *Ḥalāl* sources of income. Also, to block totally all avenues of spending wealth unlawfully (through *Ḥarām* means and on unlawful activities). The capitalist system can be uprooted completely with these measures, while a free economy will continue to thrive, as is essential for democracy.
- To carry out strict accountability of the rich in light of Islamic principles and to retrieve from them everything that they may have amassed through

unlawful means to be deposited in the Public Treasury. This is how it will be possible to do away with the unjust accumulation of wealth, which has been made possible due to the prevalence of illegal means and the ill-gotten opulence of a corrupt system.

- To remove the economic imbalance created by the feudal system of landholding that has given rise to so many problems. For this, action needs to be taken in light of the following *Sharīʿah* rule: 'Extraordinary reform measures can be taken under extraordinary circumstances provided these are not in conflict with Islamic principles'. Keeping this precept in view, we can take following steps:

  - Abolish those feudal landholdings, old and new, which may have emerged due to the misuse of state authority by any regime, past or present.
  - Reduce the ownership right of land to a certain limit (e.g. 100-200 acres), with the government purchasing the surplus. This should be an emergency measure to redress the old wrongs, but not a permanent one because such restrictions, if enforced on a permanent basis, will stand in conflict with the Law of Inheritance and other *Sharīʿah* laws.
  - As a general rule to be followed strictly in respect of land, whether it is public property, acquired through means mentioned above or reclaimed through irrigation schemes, it will be offered for sale in easy instalments to landless farmers or to those in possession of less than an economically-viable amount of land. Farmers of adjoining areas will rightly be given preference in this regard. The unhealthy practice of doling out such lands as gifts to government officials or to the influential will be stopped forthwith, and all such previous gifts retrieved from those concerned. There will also be no more selling of government land by auction.
  - Islamic injunctions relating to *Muzāraʿah* (a crop-sharing contract) are to be strictly followed and all un-Islamic practices stopped and made unlawful to foreclose the possibility of the revival of feudal tyranny.
  - The existing gap of over one to 100 in the remuneration ratio should be reduced for the time being to one to 20, and then gradually brought down to a level of one to 10. It should also be decided once for all that no remuneration will be less than the minimum level of wages necessary to satisfy the basic needs of an average family, according to

the inflationary trend of that period. Thus, a continuous process of review will have to be followed to maintain the desired level of wages and remunerations.

- Low-paid employees should be provided with necessary facilities relating to their housing, treatment and children's education.
- Workers of all industrial units may be offered a bonus in cash, in addition to the minimum desirable wages mentioned above. They may also be made partners through bonus shares in the ownership of the industrial units to which they belong. This will go a long way to boost their interest further in those units, and will also make them shareholders in the profits of the wealth they contribute to produce through their labour.
- The existing labour laws should be changed and replaced by a more judicious set of laws aimed at transforming the present state of conflict between capital and labour into a faithful relationship of cooperation, allowing the workers to have their due and, in case of a dispute, facilitating a just and honourable resolution.
- The country's existing rules, regulations and administrative policies should be amended and reformed so as to remove control by a selected few over the national sectors of trade and industry, and allow more and more members of society to participate as partners in progress. The loopholes in the existing laws and policies may also be removed that have resulted in flourishing of profiteering and prices soaring, which have made the people's lives miserable and have denied the common man the benefits of national economic growth.
- Key industries of basic importance, which cannot be left in private hands in the supreme national interest, may be managed as national enterprises. The decision to determine which of our industrial units must necessarily be managed as state enterprises should rest with the popularly elected Assembly. While taking such a decision, the Assembly and the people's representatives must ensure that state control will not lead to the well-known drawbacks of bureaucratic high-handedness that cause immense damage to nationalized units, rather than making them more productive and beneficial for the state and the people.
- Our entire banking and insurance system, which is in fact the brainchild of capitalists and we have borrowed and put in place without bothering to check its inherent defects at all, will have to be changed drastically and rebuilt on the Islamic foundations of *Mushārakah*

(equity participation), *Muḍārabah* (trustee financing) and *Takāful* (cooperative insurance). Unless these basic amendments are introduced, the act of nationalization alone will do no good and redress none of the wrongs from which they have suffered for so long.

- By properly organizing the system of collecting and distributing *Zakāh*, the state can effectively introduce the programme of *Kifālah ʿĀmmah* (general security), a scheme that has no better counterpart in the realm of social security in the world so far. This is how we can guarantee the provision of food, clothing, shelter, treatment and education to all segments of the society, especially the downtrodden.

Finally, let us carefully note that the economy is not the sole problem facing human life. It is in fact inter-related very deeply with other problems. As long as far-reaching reforms are not introduced in all walks of life, namely social conduct, lifestyle, education, politics, law and public administration, no programme of economic reform, however revolutionary, can bring about the desired results, be fruitful and meet the people's expectations.

11.2. Insurance and measures for reform[2]

Q 1: I am not quite sure about the permissibility or otherwise of the insurance business according to the *Sharīʿah*. If the existing insurance business is not permitted, what measures can be taken for this in accord with the Islamic *Sharīʿah*? If it is banned, millions of people will lose the benefits they now get through this worldwide business that every nation has reorganized on an extensive level and is getting dividends from. It is unfortunate that we are not yet quite clear about this. Will you please guide us to the right course?

A: There are three major objections due to which the insurance business cannot be termed lawful according to the *Sharīʿah*.

The first objection is that a major portion of the amount the premium insurance companies receive is reinvested by them in interest-based business, and as such those who are insured automatically become part of an unlawful process.

Secondly, the handsome amount that life insurance companies promise to pay to their policyholders in the case of death, accident, fire or other eventualities, has an element of gambling in it.

Thirdly, the amount paid following the demise of the policyholder ought to be distributed among his heirs, according to the Islamic Law of Inheritance.

---

[2] Based on Sayyid Mawdūdī's replies to questions on the subject during the 1957 convention of 'Labour Welfare Committee Pakistan'. – Editor.

However, this is not the case, and the amount is handed over to the person or persons whom the deceased nominated in his policy document. From the *Sharīʿah* point of view, no Will is valid in the case of legal heirs and they have to get their share as determined by the Law.

As for the second part of question regarding measures which can make the insurance business Islamic, the answer is not so simple that it can be discussed summarily. It needs a committee of experts who are also well-versed in Islamic law, while being fully aware of insurance matters as well, to review the whole issue and recommend viable reforms to help the business commercially on the one hand, and bring it in conformity to the *Sharīʿah* on the other. As long as this is not done, let us accept in principle that we are guilty of a wrongdoing. Once we lose even our sense of guilt, there will remain no chance of rectifying our mistakes.

The insurance industry is, without doubt, of great importance today around the world. However, this plea cannot make a *Ḥarām* thing *Ḥalāl*, nor can it serve as an argument for justifying the continuation of anything in a state that claims to be Islamic. As Muslims, it is obligatory for us to treat *Ḥarām* as *Ḥarām*, and to continue trying to find a way out for reform.

Q 2: You are correct in saying that the insurance business needs basic changes to make it Islamic. But you may also be aware that this needs a long and time-consuming process. I have so far avoided the life insurance business in our insurance company. But on careful study, I have come to the conclusion that the existing drawbacks of the life insurance business can be removed by the following measures:

(a) While depositing security money with the government, the company can advise it against investing this amount in any interest-based venture, but in a state enterprise or in purchasing shares of public sector organizations such as PIDC (Pakistan Industrial Development Corporation). We hope that the government will accede to this request and we can thus avoid being a partner in an interest-based business.

(b) The company under law can cancel the insurance policy of a policy-holder, or even refuse to accept it at the very outset. We can provide in the rules that a person desirous of getting his policy money distributed to his heirs, according to the law of inheritance, can do so and the company will facilitate that process. The company may refuse to accept an insurance policy of those declining to agree to this term. This may also serve as an incentive to those who seek a *Sharīʿah*-based insurance policy.

(c) As a safeguard against the possibility of gambling, those getting insured may be advised and inspired to agree to receive themselves or through their legal heirs the actual policy money they contributed, and not the additional amount which the insurance companies generally promise to pay.

Some time back, I decided to sell my insurance company. Subsequently, however, I realized that this may not be the right step, and I should rather try to find a way to run it on Islamic lines, which others may also follow. I shall be grateful for your guidance.

A: The measures you propose may help in reforming the insurance business and removing the causes of its impermissibility. In my view, the least that can be done to Islamize the insurance industry may be summed up as follows:

(a) The government should be agreeable to the provision of investing an insurance company's security deposit in a state enterprise or semi-governmental industrial or commercial venture on the principle of partnership, and the company should not be given a fixed amount of dividend but only that which is its due on a proportionate basis.

(b) The company may also invest its capital in profitable, non-interest bearing ventures, which may bring it dividends on a proportionate basis, but without any interest.

(c) Insurance Policies should be approved for those clients who agree: (i) to the provision that, after their death, their heirs will receive in claim only the actual amount they contributed; and (ii) that the said amount will be distributed among their legal heirs according to the Islamic Law of Inheritance.

(d) Policyholders keen to receive dividends on their policy money may be required to agree to the investment of their amount in non-interest bearing ventures on a profit and loss sharing basis, as mentioned above.

If you succeed in introducing these four terms and conditions in reforming your business, it may help to make your insurance company not only Islamically-oriented, but may also serve as a trendsetter and a guide for others who wish to follow your lead in this field.

11.3. The question of price control[3]

Q 1: These are the days of market control, but nothing is available to shopkeepers on a controlled rate and this is why they are compelled to buy essential items at higher rates from the 'black market'. They obviously cannot sell these goods at the government's control rates, and invariably have to charge more to avoid a loss. However, some people describe such dealings as fraudulent and dishonest. The police are also there to apprehend shopkeepers for charging more than the rates fixed by the government. What has the *Sharī'ah* to say about this?

A: Morally speaking, the government has no right to enforce '*Tas'īr*' (price control) until and unless it ensures a supply of goods to the people at these control rates. Without making such an arrangement, the mere act of price fixing will definitely imply that it wants to encourage hoarders to hide the goods they have piled up, and then either withhold them from the market fearing government action or start selling them on the black market at higher rates. The government is aware of all this, but is still bent upon introducing price controls. It has no right morally, therefore, to demand that consumers or retailers strictly follow its price-list.

Everybody is aware today that the common man, petty shopkeepers and retailers cannot get anything from the big traders, wholesalers and hoarders at the rate fixed by the government. When they get things at a higher price from the black market, they obviously cannot be expected to sell these on the open market at government rates. Under these circumstances, whoever purchases something from that black market or at the black market rates does not commit a moral offence. Similarly, a shopkeeper selling things he purchased from the black market at rates higher than those fixed by government is not guilty of a moral offence. If the government apprehends and arrests him under its Price Control Act, it will be guilty of yet another offence over and above its crime of failing to maintain a regular supply of essential commodities in an open market at its own approved rates.

Let us now look at price control from the Islamic perspective and see how it views '*Tas'īr*'. During a spell of drought in Madinah Munawwarah, the people requested that the Holy Prophet (*pbuh*) introduce price control. His response was:

اِنَّ السِّعرَ غَلَاؤُه وَ رُخصُه بِيَدِ الله وَ اِنِّى اُرِيدُ اَنْ اَلقَىٰ اللهَ وَلَيسَ لِاَحدٍ عِندِى مَظْلِمَةٌ يَطْلُبُنِى بِهَا

[3] Based on Sayyid Mawdūdī's write-up in *Tarjumān al-Qur'ān*, July-October, 1944.

('The matter concerning the rise and fall of prices is in the hands of God and I would wish to meet the Almighty without having to answer to Him about any injustice done to anyone for which he may have a case against me.')

(Abū Dawūd and Tirmidhī)

The Holy Prophet then impressed upon the people in his addresses, meetings and conversations the virtue of maintaining a regular supply and keeping prices steady, and the dire consequences of hoarding and taking advantage of a natural calamity to one's own benefit. He declared:

اَلجَالِبُ مَرزُوقٌ وَالـمُحتَكِرُ مَلعُونٌ

('He who maintains regular market supply is blessed by better earning and the one who indulges in hoarding is accursed.')

(Ibn Māja)

The following *Aḥādīth* are recorded from Mishkāt, *Kitāb al-Buyū*ʿ, *Bāb fī al-Iḥtikār*)

مَنِ احتَكَرَ طَعَاماً اَربَعِينَ يوماً يُرِيدُ بِه الغَلَاءَ فَقَد بَرِئَ مَنَ اللهِ وَ بَرِئَ اللهُ مِنه

('He who keeps foodgrains hoarded for forty days with the intention to let prices soar, he has no concern with the Almighty, nor is the Almighty in the least concerned about him.')

بِئسَ العَبدُ المُحتَكِرُ، إن اَرخَصَ اللهُ الاَسعَارَ حَزِنَ وَإِنَ اَغلَاهَا فَرِحَ

('How bad is he who is given to hoarding. When the rates are down due to Allah's blessing, he is sad and when prices soar he is glad.')

مَنِ احتَكَرَ طَعَاماً اَربَعِينَ يوماً ثُمَّ تَصَدَّقَ بِه لَم يَكُن لَهُ كَفَّارَة

('He who kept foodgrains hoarded for forty days and then donated them even as charity, this will not be a reparation for his sin.')

These warnings and exhortations from *Sayyidinā* Rasūl Allāh did wonders for the trading community of the time, which was so reformed that the Islamic State did not have to take legal measures in this respect.

This was the extraordinary position of a ruler whose government was based on solid moral foundations. The real strength of such a ruler lies not in his police force, judiciary, controlling authority or ordinances. His respect, love, awe and control emanate from the inner core of his people's hearts and souls. They draw sustenance from him as a role model. He reforms not just the conduct, but also the intents, thoughts, mindsets and value-systems, and the people voluntarily abide by his rulings, injunctions and orders, which in themselves are exemplary and just. On the contrary, the rulers who wield authority in the world generally suffer from their own shortcomings and corrupt moral conduct. They have no *locus standi* for their governance other than their repressive state power. When faced with eventualities such as we find today, they invariably take recourse to the use of force, instead of morally reforming themselves first and then their people. This is how they further corrupt those who are already in need of a moral face-lift due to their own misconduct.

12 Recodification of the Economic Laws of Islam*

The global scenario today is definitely not the same as it was in the past. There has been a dramatic change in the world's civilizational and economic scenes, due to which the format of financial and commercial deals has also changed drastically. Consequently, the juridical laws framed during the early days of Islam against the backdrop of the socio-economic situation of Hijāz, the Levant and Egypt fall short of meeting the Muslim world's current needs. Our illustrious legists and religious scholars did a pioneering job in interpreting the injunctions of the Islamic *Sharī'ah*, but this was done according to the situation prevailing at the time. The change that has taken place today in the socio-economic realm therefore calls for a thorough review and updating of the laws and precepts available in our books of jurisprudence concerning sale and purchase, finance and economy. There cannot be any other opinion regarding the need for fresh codification of the economic and fiscal laws of Islam, although one may differ about how we should proceed with this onerous and challenging task.

12.1. The constant and the variables

The way that a group of modernists[1] amongst us would like to recodify the laws, guided and goaded by their own whims, actually amounts not to a recodification of the *Sharī'ah* Laws, but a daring attempt to distort them willfully. In simple terms, this may be seen as an attempt to commit apostasy in the economic domain of our lives. The measures they would like us to follow in this respect are totally at odds with Islam in their objectives, principles, rules and regulations. Their sole objective is to earn wealth, while Islam impresses upon a Muslim the need to earn through *Ḥalāl* means, and altogether shun anything *Ḥarām*. Their aspiration in life is to become millionnaires overnight by fair means or

* Taken from Sayyid Mawdūdī's book *Sūd* (*Interest*).

[1] The group of modernists to which the author refers here is the followers of global capitalism. They were vociferous at that time in projecting the capitalist system of economy as being in conformity with Islam. As for the socialist system, the author has already discussed in detail its inherent flaws and anti-Islamic character. – Translator.

foul. Islam, on the other hand, forbids its followers from encroaching on the rights of others, or recoursing to unhealthy means. According to these people, a successful entrepreneur is one who can amass wealth, control more and more economic resources and thus acquire all the comforts and luxuries of life, respect and authority irrespective of the means he may have used to achieve this status. They seem to have no regard for the moral and ethical aspects of their pursuit and do not care if their self-interest drags the world into a dungeon of chaos, corruption, immorality, lawlessness and material and spiritual ruin. They believe that it is the end that matters, and not the means.

On the contrary, a person is only successful according to Islam if he has earned his living through honesty and uprightness and by keeping the interests and obligations of others in sight as well. If such an entrepreneur succeeds in becoming a millionnaire, this would mean that Allah *subḥānahū wa taʿālā* has blessed his efforts and the wealth he has earned through correct means is a reward for his integrity. But if he continues toiling for the rest of his life and fails to get even the bare minimum for his survival, is dressed in tatters and lives in a ramshackle abode, he is not a failure in life because he did not barter away his lofty principles for temporary gains.[2] It is this divergence of approach that leads these modernists away to the capitalist route, a path diametrically opposed to Islam. The ease, license and permissiveness they need to traverse this path cannot be available to them in Islam. If somebody is keen to follow the capitalist track, he should stop deceiving himself by performing lip service to Islam, and should instead devote himself wholeheartedly to following the US and Western model of economy and finance.

As for those who are committed Muslims and would like to follow Islam in all areas of their individual and collective lives, they need a set of new rules and regulations in the realms of business and finance. They need this not to draw the maximum benefits from capitalist institutions or to find a way out within Islamic law to become wealthy business tycoons, billionaires and the owners of factories and mills, but for the sole purpose of following the dictates of the Qur'ān and the *Sunnah* as they tackle the problems of modern day business, economics and finance. They need these rules and regulations to avoid falling into the capitalist trap and to escape the Almighty's displeasure; then, when they are faced with challenges in their dealings with other nations, they will benefit from the concessions available in these rules within the parameters of

---

[2] In fact, it is obligatory for an Islamic state to ensure that life is made comfortable for every citizen and the dependent members of his family by satisfying their basic needs through its infallible social security apparatus of the system of *Zakāh*. – Editor.

the Islamic *Sharīʿah.* It is therefore essential to recodify the economic laws of Islam, for which our religious scholars must feel duty-bound to do the required spadework.

12.2. The need to modernize

Like all legal codes, the Islamic law is also not static. It can face future challenges and provide guidance and legal cover under changing circumstances at all times and everywhere. The injunctions of the Holy Qur'ān and the *Sunnah* are irrevocable and everlasting for all times and places. The laws based on these injunctions, which were codified around twelve centuries ago by eminent jurists of the world of Islam, can be modified, amended and reframed whenever the need arises. Intellectual integrity, sagacity and a balance in approach and outlook are the hallmarks of the legislation done so far by our great jurists. The principal objective of this legislation has been to organize social conduct and the interrelationship of people in a manner that promotes among them a spirit of cooperation, compassion and sympathetic coordination, instead of conflict and antagonistic competition.

These laws have always aimed at facilitating mutual trust and a sense of interdependence by defining in clear terms and a judicious manner the people's rights and obligations. Allah *subḥānahū wa taʿālā,* in His infinite Mercy and the Knowledge He has of the best of His Creatures – the humans, with their strong and weak points – has provided the Guidance necessary for all walks of life. His Prophet (*pbuh*) through his glorious example, on the other hand, stands out to us as a practical model of how this Divine Guidance should be put into practice. The steps he took to implement this Guidance and his personal example in this regard helped by offering to humanity the guiding principles which are most comprehensive, universally beneficial and thoroughly practicable for successfully conducting human affairs everywhere and at all times. These are principles which are eternal and irrevocable. Now it is up to our religious scholars and legislators to continue drawing upon these guiding principles of the Islamic *Sharīʿah* to frame within their broad perspective new laws, rules and regulations to meet the demands of the changed situation and to settle various issues in a manner that fulfills the basic purpose and objective of the Law-Giver (*pbuh*). The *Sharīʿah* principles are unchangeable, but the legal measures which the jurists and religious scholars formulate on the basis of these principles are not. The principles are fundamental in nature and are for all times and places, while the measures are for a given situation and especially directed at the set of problems and issues for which they were originally framed.

12.3. Essential prerequisites for the modernization of statutes and by-laws

The Islamic *Sharīʿah* thus offers a comprehensive, solid, tried and tested and universal framework according to which fresh legislation can be formed, new laws framed and old ones amended to meet the demands of a particular situation. In this context, religious scholars and jurists that are duly qualified are fully entitled in each context to frame statutes and by-laws, and to explain subsidiary issues within the context of the *Sharīʿah*. However, this does not mean that anybody claiming religious expertise has the liberty to willfully re-interpret Islamic injunctions and distort them to suit his own personal agenda in utter disregard of the real objectives of the Law-giver.

Let me now explain the necessary prerequisites, rules and regulations for this onerous task of recodification of the economic laws of Islam.

12.3.1. *First prerequisite*

The first essential prerequisite for the recodification and framing of by-laws is a perfect understanding of the *Sharīʿah* and a complete grooming in its essence and spirit. This is something which can only be achieved through knowledge of the Holy Qur'ān and insight into the *Sīrah* (life record) of the Holy Prophet (*pbuh*).[3] A scholar with a comprehensive knowledge and a deeper insight into these two can rightly be expected to understand correctly the tone and tenor of the Islamic *Sharīʿah*. His insight will always tell him which of the various methods is in conformity with the dictates of the *Sharīʿah*, and which is not. With such an insight and discerning capability, any effort that is sincerely made to frame a by-law or to modify one will be blessed with success and serve to further the cause of *Sharīʿah* in that particular realm. Ḥaḍrat ʿUmar's ruling against the enforcement of *Ḥadd* punishment on a Muslim soldier during a war, the step taken by Saʿd bin Abī Waqqāṣ who was the Islamic legion's Commander at the battle of Qādisiyah, his decision to pardon Abū Mihjan al-Thaqafī for drinking wine and the Second Caliph's ruling against chopping off the burglar's hand may all be cited as examples of the right approach of *Ijtihād* in light of

[3] It is not amiss to point out here that the end of the culture of *Ijtihād* in the Muslim world today is mainly due to the expulsion from our religious curricula of serious studies of the Qur'ān and the *Sīrah* of the Holy Prophet. These studies have been replaced by a superficial knowledge of various Schools of Islamic *Fiqh* (jurisprudence). Our religious education is thus imparted in such a manner that, from the very outset, the student is not allowed to keep in view the basic difference between the irrevocable injunctions of the Qur'ān and the *Sunnah* and the variable nature of the statutes and by-laws framed by the *Fuqahā'* (jurists). Nobody can claim to be fit for *Ijtihād* unless he has developed a deeper insight into the teachings of the Holy Qur'ān and thoughtfully studied the *Sunnah* of the Holy Prophet, a quality that cannot be achieved even by devoting one's lifetime to studying books of *Fiqh*. – Author.

the true spirit of the *Sharīʿah*. Apparently, these decisions seem to be contrary to the injunctions of the *Sharīʿah*. But those with a deeper insight into its true essence and spirit realize that such exceptional and extraordinary situations demand exceptional and extraordinary approaches, which is actually in total harmony with the objectives of the Law-giver.

The incident relating to the salves of Ḥāṭib bin Abī Baltaʿah belongs to the same category. A man from the Muzaynah tribe lodged a complaint with the Second Caliph about Ḥāṭib's slaves stealing his camels. The immediate response was in favour of enforcing the *Ḥadd* punishment of chopping off their hands from the wrist. However, after he pondered for a while over their plight, he called for Ḥāṭib and strongly reprimanded him for putting them in that situation by denying them even their basic needs. The Second Caliph decreed that these poor men were so miserable that, for them, even to eat carrion to save their lives would have been permissible. He therefore pardoned them and ordered Ḥāṭib to compensate the owner of the camels by paying him a penalty. Similarly, Ḥaḍrat ʿUmar's ruling concerning three divorces at a time was apparently at variance with the practice followed during the Holy Prophet's time. Since his rulings were not in fact a deviation but a follow-up to the Holy Prophet's tradition of balance, sagacity and the maximum allowance of justice, no one from amongst the eminent Companions of *Sayyidinā* Rasūl Allāh, of whom there were many in Madinah al-Munawwarah in those days, objected to these decisions.

This goes to establish that the first prerequisite for the recodification of laws is a perfect knowledge of the *Sharīʿah* and a deep insight into its essence and spirit. Any attempt at modifying or modernizing the law without these is bound to lead to nothing but chaos, confusion and a deviation from the hallowed traditions of the Divine Law.

12.3.2. *Second prerequisite*

After a thorough understanding of the *Sharīʿah*'s mood and temperament, the next essential requirement is for an overview of the injunctions pertaining to a particular field in which legislation is required, followed by a careful study of these injunctions to understand the real objectives of the Law-giver and the strategy He would have adopted for reorganizing that particular area within the overall scheme of a Muslim's life. Without a deep insight into this perspective, no legislation or amendment to the law can be in accord with the aims and objectives of the Law-giver. In the realm of Islamic Law, the external format of injunctions is not as important as their intent and purpose. The real significance of a jurist's work lies in his ability to focus on the objective of the Law-giver, as well as the wisdom and sagacity behind a particular law. At times it may happen that acting according to the apparent meaning of a certain ruling (issued in a particular context) may mean losing the very purpose for which that particular ruling was initially given. We all know the emphasis that the Holy Qur'ān has laid on *Amr bi'l maʿrūf wa'l-nahy ʿani'l-munkar* (to enjoin good and forbid evil). The Prophet of God (*pbuh*) also declared this to be a prime duty of the faithful. In spite of this, he did not approve of armed revolt (*Khurūj*) against oppressive and autocratic rulers. The reason for this is that the principal objective before the Law-giver is to replace the bad with the good, but not to create more chaos and confusion in the land. It is therefore not desirable to launch into any misadventure when the chances of its success may be slim and the risk of failure great.

The biographers of *ʿAllamah* Ibn Taymīyah narrate that, during the time of the Tartar onslaught, he came across a group of boozers masquerading in a tavern. Those accompanying Ibn Taymīyah tried to dissuade them from drinking wine. The great Islamic scholar and reformist stopped his companions from doing this. The reason he gave is valid for all times and imbibes the very spirit of the Islamic Law. Ibn Taymīyah said:

> 'Leave them alone. Allah *subḥānahū wa taʿālā* has forbidden wine to prevent social and moral corruption and disorder, and in this particular case alcohol has at least prevented these miscreants from a greater disorder, i.e. loot and plunder. To stop them from their pastime now would mean a deviation from the very objective before the Law-giver in declaring wine *Ḥarām*.'

This goes to show that the application of a rule may vary from situation to situation. This variation must, however, be dictated by the actual aims and objectives of the Law-giver, and not by any personal agenda of the jurist or legislator.

Similarly, there are certain terms used by the *Sharīʿah* in the context of a certain law in a particular situation. In this case, it is for the legist to interpret that term or phrase correctly in the present context in order to implement the law properly in its true perspective or to frame by-laws in keeping with the aims and objectives of the Law-giver. For example, the Holy Prophet (*pbuh*) prescribed one *Ṣāʿ* of dates, barley or raisin as *Ṣadaqat al-Fiṭr*. This does not mean that exactly this measure of those very commodities, which were then the staple diet and in common use, are to be given in charity at the conclusion of the month of fasting. This is because the Law-giver did not mean to restrict charity to a particular item of foodgrain or a particular measurement. His objective, rather, was to involve the whole community in the noble act of charity before it enjoyed the blessings of *ʿĪd al-Fiṭr*, and to let those without the means to share in the happiness of the occasion also. Today, therefore, any measure equal to *Ṣāʿ* and any food items of common use will serve the objective of *Ṣadaqat al-Fiṭr*, while the standard measure and quantity will always remain the same as that fixed by the Law-giver.

12.3.3. *Third prerequisite*

The legist must also have a thorough knowledge of the principles of legislation and the style followed by the Law-giver in order to carefully observe these in his legislation. This is a quality that can be achieved only when one has thoroughly studied the essentials of the Islamic *Sharīʿah* and looked deeply into each and every injunction in it. How did the Law-giver establish balance and harmony among the rules he gave to humanity? What measures did he take to prevent wrong and secure right? How did he take due care of human nature? On what lines did he reorganize human affairs and how did he subject them to discipline? How did he encourage humans towards their lofty ideals, take into consideration their inherent weaknesses and at the same time create the necessary facilities for them? All of these aspects need careful study and serious reflection, for which the literal meaning and full import of the Qur'ānic text and the wisdom and sagacity of the Holy Prophet's actions and sayings definitely have to be kept in view.

Anybody endowed with such knowledge, scholarship, legal acumen and insight, and above all integrity of character, can reframe the rules according to the demands of a particular situation or deduce and formulate new by-laws for matters about which there are no clear-cut instructions or precedents available. A scholar of this calibre is rightly not expected to deviate from the Islamic principles of legislation while undertaking the task of *Ijtihād*. To quote an example, according to an injunction of the Holy Qur'ān, *Jizyāh* (capital tax) was levied on the 'People of the Book' (Jews and Christians). Following the principles of *Ijtihād*, the Companions of the Holy Prophet extended this law also to the Zoroastrians of Persia, the idolaters of India and the Berbers of North Africa. During the glorious reign of the four Caliphs, the swift expansion of the Islamic Caliphate brought to the fore many similar matters about which there were no definite rulings in the Qur'ān and the *Sunnah*. The illustrious Companions of the Holy Prophet then codified various by-laws and rules to cope with these emerging issues in conformity with the true spirit and fundamentals of the Islamic *Sharīʿah*.

12.3.4. *Fourth prerequisite*

The changing circumstances and situations that call for modifications or reframing of by-laws need to be examined in the following two ways. Firstly, we should take note of the exact nature of any change that may have taken place, its essential characteristics and the factors responsible for it. Secondly, we should see these changes from the *Sharīʿah* perspective, and frame the necessary amendments in the by-laws to suit the new situation. For example, let us take the issue of interest. In order to recodify the economic laws, we have to look first at the economic scenario of the modern world and carefully study the modern methods of economic and financial transactions. We have to understand the underlying forces governing economic activities, learn about the various concepts and principles at work and the practical shapes that they are taking. We then have to see how to categorize the changes that have taken place in the field of economy and finance from the Islamic legal perspective, and how to frame rules that can be applicable to these categories; all this time, we must also be in accord with the dictates of the *Sharīʿah*, its legal vision and its objectives.

Putting aside the peripherals, in principle we can classify these changes into the following two broad categories.

- In category one we may place those changes that take place due to a change in the socio-cultural environment. These are, in fact, the natural outcome of the evolutionary process of man's intellectual and scientific advancement, new discoveries of Divine Bounties, developments in the realms of material resources, transport and communication and the means of production and rapid expansion in the field of international relations. From the point of view of the Islamic Law, these are natural changes which cannot be reversed, nor it is desirable to do so. We are required instead to formulate, according to the *Sharīʿah*'s principles of legislation, fresh by-laws, rules and regulations to cater for such changes taking place in the realms of trade, economy and finance. This is incumbent upon us in order to facilitate the world of Islam to face the new challenges Islamically, instead of lagging behind or following un-Islamic practices for which there are better alternatives available in the *Sharīʿah* itself.
- Under the second category come those changes which are not the natural outcome of the civilizational process of change, but result from the hegemonic control of the capitalist neo-colonialism on the world's trade,

economy and finance. This is the type of the ruthless capitalism[4] that held sway during the pre-Islamic days of *Jāhilīyah*, and which was kept subdued by Islam for centuries. This has now re-surfaced to dominate the global economic scene. Today's capitalism is a re-incarnation of that old tradition of capital worship,[5] and this has now taken over the reins of the world's economic realm, with its new-fanged countenance and deadly features. The changes that have taken place as a result of the dominance of the capitalist trend are not natural or real transformations in the eyes of the Islamic Law. These are actually sham transformations, which can be effectively wiped out; and this is in fact what is badly needed for humanity's salvation and welfare.

As Muslims we are duty-bound to use all of our intellectual, moral and material resources to remove this repressive system from the world's economic scene and replace it with the benign system of economy and finance bequeathed to us by Islam. The obligation to fight world capitalism falls more on the shoulders of Muslims than on the communists. The communist is simply motivated by the issue of bread and butter; while for a Muslim, it is a question of his Religion and social conduct. The communist is all out to fight for the sake of the Proletariat alone; the Muslim's fight, however, is for the good of mankind, and this includes the capitalists as well. The communist's conflict is for his own selfish ends; but the Muslim's is for the sake of Allah's Pleasure and to enforce His Law. No Muslim can ever compromise, therefore, with the ruthless capitalist system. If one really is a Muslim and cares to make the writ of God supreme in all walks of life, including economy and finance, he is under a constant obligation from the Lord to try his best to change this devilish system and gracefully bear with any material loss which he is likely to suffer in the process. Whatever legislation Muslim jurists and economic experts pass for this purpose will naturally not be aimed at facilitating the world of Islam getting absorbed in the capitalist system and achieving material progress under its tutelage. Instead, the sole purpose of this legislation will be to rescue the Muslims

[4] We are not using the term here in its narrow, textbook sense, but with a much wider connotation that is inherent in its very essence. Textbook capitalism is the product of Europe's Industrial Revolution, but in its real sense it has been present since ancient times. It has always played havoc with the social fabric of human society in one way or another, especially in times when man has allowed his socio-economic matters to slip into the hands of the devil and deviated from the Divine Guidance in conducting the affairs of his life. – Author.

[5] We may recall to our minds in this context the mythical Greek god of wealth 'Mammon' and the Hindu goddess 'Luxumi Devi'. – Translator.

in particular, and the world at large, from the stranglehold of capitalism, to shut all the doors of economic exploitation, to prevent further growth of this oppressive system and to usher in a new economic order of genuine progress and prosperity for the world.

12.4. General rules of exception

The Islamic *Sharī'ah* offers sufficient room for relief in exceptional cases and exigencies. One of the principles of Islamic Jurisprudence is:

اَلضَّرُوراَتُ تُبِيحُ المَحظُورَات

('Exigencies relax the rules.')

and

اَلمَشَقَّةُ تَجلِبُ االتَّيسِير

('Hardship earns relaxation and lets the impermissible become permissible.')

The same principles have been reiterated on different occasions by the Holy Qur'ān and the *Sunnah* as well:

لَا يُكَلِّفُ ٱللَّهُ نَفْسًا إِلَّا وُسْعَهَا ... ﴿٢٨٦﴾

('Allah does not lay a responsibility on anyone beyond his capacity.')
(*al-Baqarah*, 2: 286)

...يُرِيدُ ٱللَّهُ بِكُمُ ٱلْيُسْرَ وَلَا يُرِيدُ بِكُمُ ٱلْعُسْرَ... ﴿١٨٥﴾

(Allah wants ease and not hardship for you ...)
(*al-Baqarah*, 2: 185)

...وَمَا جَعَلَ عَلَيْكُمْ فِى ٱلدِّينِ مِنْ حَرَجٍ... ﴿٧٨﴾

('He has not laid upon you any hardship in religion.')
(*al-Ḥajj*, 22: 78)

اَحَبُّ الدِّينِ اِلَى الله تَعَالٰى اَلحَنِيفِيَهُ السَّمحَه

('The best way in Religion is that which is straightforward, easy and tolerant.')
(Ibn Ḥajar, *Fatḥ al-Bārī* and Aḥmad ibn Ḥanbal)

لَاضَرَرَ وَلَا ضِرَارَ فِى الاسلام

('There is nothing injurious and harmful in Islam.')

(Ibn Māja and al-Dāraquṭnī)

This is thus an established rule in the Islamic *Sharī'ah*. Islam is for ease and relaxation where there is a hardship. However, this does not mean that it can be made into a routine practice, so that anybody anywhere could stand up and say that he is hard-pressed and cannot perform a certain duty the way it has been prescribed by the Qur'ān and the *Sunnah* and would like to have a relaxation. There are definite rules and regulations for this relaxation, which can be understood when one looks carefully at the exceptions approved by the *Sharī'ah*.

Among the rules to be observed for exceptions, the following may particularly be borne in mind to avoid any willful deviation from the established norms of the Islamic Law:

- The first step is to note the nature of any hardship. Each and every situation that may appear difficult does not justify a relaxation, otherwise no law can remain practicable at all. For example, the difficulty of *Wuḍū'* (ablution) in winter, the hardship of *Ṣawm* (Fast) in summer, the fatigue of travel for the *Ḥajj* and the risks involved in *Jihād* are definitely hard options for a Muslim. Nevertheless, these are not the type of hardships which call for any relaxation of the normal law. *Hardships justifying relaxations are only those which are likely to cause harm* (ضَرَرَ). To cite a few examples, a journey full of trials and tribulations, a state of illness, the coercion and repression of a tyrant, financial problems, a physical handicap, the extraordinary situation of riot, unrest and persecution or a natural calamity are such exceptional circumstances for which the *Sharī'ah* has magnanimously allowed relaxations.
- Relaxation must necessarily correspond to the level of hardship. For example, a person who can perform his Prayer seated is not allowed to discharge this duty lying in bed; and one who is so sick that he cannot even leave his bed can perform it reclining, but is not permitted to do it by gesticulation like the one who, God forbid, is paralyzed. Similarly, an ailment that needs a ten-day relaxation and *Qaḍā'* (subsequent completion) of *Ṣawm* cannot justify the postponement of Fasting for the whole month of Ramaḍān. A person in distress who has no option to save his life except by eating carrion or drinking a little alcohol cannot take this as a license to exceed his dire need. Similarly, no physician is

allowed to bare his patient's body beyond the affected parts that need to be examined for treatment. The second rule in this context is, therefore, that *the quantum of all relaxations is to be determined strictly by the quantum of hardship and need.*

- Thirdly, to prevent harm, no alternative course is permissible that may be either equally or more harmful. The only measures that are permitted are those which are relatively less harmful or absolutely harmless. This rule is one of the principle of Islamic Jurisprudence:

  إِذَا ابْتُلِيْتَ بِبَلِيَّتَيْنِ فَاخْتَرْ اَهْوَنَهُمَا

  ('When caught between two evils, choose the lesser one.')

It is therefore not lawful to succumb to a greater evil or hardship while trying to escape a lesser one.

- The fourth rule is to *give priority to repelling the wrong over securing the right.* According to the Islamic *Sharīʿah*, it is more important, in order of priority, first to remove the evil, avoid the *forbidden* (*Ḥarām*) and prevent the wrong, and then to seek good and observe the 'do's'. This is why the same level of magnanimity that the Islamic Law displays in granting relaxations of 'do's in times of hardships is not allowed for relaxing the restrictions on 'don'ts'. This is evident in the difference between the extent of exceptions permitted for *Ṣalāh*, *Ṣawm* and *Ḥajj* and those allowed for the use of *Ḥarām* things.
- According to the fifth rule, *permission for relaxation ceases to apply once the cause is not there.* For example, *Tayammum* (symbolic purification with dust when water is not available) is not permitted once water becomes available for *Wuḍū'*.

12.5. Relaxation in the case of interest

Let us now see, in light of the foregoing, how far the *Sharīʿah* rules can be relaxed in the case of interest and bank loans.

One thing is certain: lending money on loan and taking loans on interest are not one and the same thing. Circumstances may compel one to take a loan even on interest, but there can be no compulsion for extending a loan on interest. Earning profit through interest is like eating carrion. There are, however, situations when carrion eating may be permissible to save life, as discussed above. However, can there be any such compulsion for relaxing the rule for interest?

Every necessity cannot be so compelling and unavoidable as to justify taking out interest-based loans. For example, lavish spending on weddings or funerals is not a necessity. To build a house or own a car similarly are not real urgencies. Nothing can justify the extravaganza of luxurious living or the passion to multiply one's riches by promoting his business and trade through fair means or foul. There are plenty of matters which are generally taken as emergency cases, and for which thousands of rupees are borrowed from *Mahājans* (traditional Hindu moneylenders) and commercial banks. Such 'exigencies' have no worth so far as the *Sharīʿah* is concerned. People commit a grave sin who borrow money on interest for such matters.[6] As for those who lend to earn interest, they are the worst losers because they are not only indulging in something that is *Ḥarām*, but they are also serving as the conduit for *Ḥarām* means and encouraging others to partake in a forbidden deal.

Exceptional cases in the realm of finance for which the *Sharīʿah* may consider relaxing its rules are very few. For example, in eventualities like a natural calamity, a situation where someone's life and honour are at stake or where there is a real risk of unbearable loss or irreparable damage, the affected person can obtain a loan on interest if there are none to stand by his side and extend him financial help or give him an interest-free loan. In such eventualities, well-off Muslims will be the real sinners who fail to lend a helping hand to their brother in need. It is their callousness that actually compels him to take recourse to forbidden means. I will go a step further and say that the burden of a sin like this actually falls on the shoulders of the entire community because of its failure to establish the Islamic institutions of social security and public welfare, like *Zakāh*, *Ṣadaqāt* and *Awqāf* (mandatory charity, normal charity and endowments). In the case of an Islamic state and government, this will be taken as being due to their sinful negligence, for which they will be accountable before the Lord, as well as to their people.[7]

A loan taken on interest should have to be: (i) only as much as is essentially needed for a certain exigency; and (ii) the borrower has to pool whatever resources he can to get rid of it as quickly as possible. It is up to his good sense

---

[6] Borrowing money, even interest-free, to satisfy one's urge for luxuries, as also all unchecked spendings are undesirable in themselves. According to the well-known Prophetic Tradition, on the Day of Reckoning each one of us will have to account compulsorily for the following: (i) How did he utilize the life-span granted to him? (ii) To what use did he put the energies and potential of his youth? (iii) How did he earn his living and how did he spend what he earned? and (iv) how did he best utilize the knowledge he acquired? – Translator.

[7] Islam's is the middle road. It asks individuals and the society never to deviate from the path of moderation and balance. It does not approve of those who revel in riches while teeming millions around them are left to live in want and suffering, even below subsistence level.

and discretion to determine the nature of the exigency and the amount of money he needs to borrow. The more God-fearing and strong in his faith he is, the more cautious he would naturally be in this regard.

Those who have bank deposits, insurance policies or stakes in a Provident Fund must consider their principal capital alone as their rightful money. They are also required to pay *Zakāh* on the principal amount at a rate of 2.5 percent per annum because, unless they do this, their deposits will remain impure – something that as Muslims they would definitely like to avoid.

The second most important thing I may stress in this context is that I do not consider it lawful to leave the amount of interest with banks, insurance companies and the Provident Fund Administration, because this will serve to add strength to their interest-based deals. The best use for this money is to withdraw it from those places and spend it on the needy and indigent of the community, because in our society today they are no better than the hapless souls who are permitted to eat carrion to save their souls.[8]

An economic imbalance like this is not expected from a society claiming to be Islamic. *Sūrah al-Balad* (90) condemns those who boastfully talk of their social status and capability to spend as much as they can to satisfy their personal ego. The All-Merciful reminds such people to make the best use of the faculties granted to them to discern the truth and differentiate the right from the wrong, because if they did not, it would lead them to their own destruction:

يَقُولُ أَهْلَكْتُ مَالًا لُّبَدًا ﴿٦﴾ أَيَحْسَبُ أَن لَّمْ يَرَهُۥٓ أَحَدٌ ﴿٧﴾ أَلَمْ نَجْعَل لَّهُۥ عَيْنَيْنِ ﴿٨﴾ وَلِسَانًا وَشَفَتَيْنِ ﴿٩﴾ وَهَدَيْنَٰهُ
ٱلنَّجْدَيْنِ ﴿١٠﴾ فَلَا ٱقْتَحَمَ ٱلْعَقَبَةَ ﴿١١﴾ وَمَآ أَدْرَىٰكَ مَا ٱلْعَقَبَةُ ﴿١٢﴾ فَكُّ رَقَبَةٍ ﴿١٣﴾ أَوْ إِطْعَٰمٌ فِى يَوْمٍ ذِى مَسْغَبَةٍ ﴿١٤﴾
يَتِيمًا ذَا مَقْرَبَةٍ ﴿١٥﴾ أَوْ مِسْكِينًا ذَا مَتْرَبَةٍ ﴿١٦﴾ ثُمَّ كَانَ مِنَ ٱلَّذِينَ ءَامَنُوا۟ وَتَوَاصَوْا۟ بِٱلصَّبْرِ وَتَوَاصَوْا۟ بِٱلْمَرْحَمَةِ ﴿١٧﴾
أُو۟لَٰٓئِكَ أَصْحَٰبُ ٱلْمَيْمَنَةِ ﴿١٨﴾ وَٱلَّذِينَ كَفَرُوا۟ بِـَٔايَٰتِنَا هُمْ أَصْحَٰبُ ٱلْمَشْـَٔمَةِ ﴿١٩﴾ عَلَيْهِمْ نَارٌ مُّؤْصَدَةٌۢ ﴿٢٠﴾

('He says: 'I have squandered enormous wealth.' Does he believe that none has seen him? Did We not grant him two eyes. And a tongue and two lips? And did We not show him the two highroads (of good and evil)? But he did not venture to scale the difficult steep. And what do you know what that difficult steep is? It is freeing somone's neck from slavery; or giving food on a day of hunger to an orphan near of kin; or to a destitute lying in dust; and, then besides this, he be one of those who believed, and enjoined upon one another steadfastness and enjoined upon one another compassion. These are the People of the Right Hand. As for those who rejected Our Signs, they are the People of the Left Hand. Upon them shall be a Fire that will hem them in.').

(*al-Balad*, 90: 6-20). – Translator.

[8] To my mind, this is the correct approach because the money paid as interest to the policy or account-holders comes out of the pockets of the poor themselves. The interest, whether it is paid from the government treasury, banks or insurance companies, actually originates from the revenue gathered from the earnings of the common man, the majority of whom are poor. – Author.

My third point relates to exercising the maximum possible care in order to avoid any profit accruing in financial transactions and business deals which have even a semblance of interest. If it is not possible to escape such 'profits' completely, the amount thus gathered may be disposed of in the manner recommended in the preceding paragraph. For a sincere Muslim, the most cherished principle should always be to repel the wrong instead of running after material benefits. The greatest asset of a believer is the Pleasure of his Lord the Creator and the reward of the Hereafter, and not temporary gains which are often so transitory that one has to lament later on why one lost the everlasting for something so superfluous and transient.

These relaxations are essentially intended for individuals and can eventually be extended only to those Muslim communities who are under foreign domination, and hence incapable of independently framing their own economic and fiscal policies. No Muslim nation that is independent and free, however, is permitted to avail themselves of such exceptions, unless it is established that there are no viable alternatives available and hence it cannot manage its banking and finance sectors, or its trade and industry, without recourse to an interest-based system. However, the very premise is wrong, as has been reaffirmed academically, theoretically and practically, because all these sectors can be run effectively and efficiently on an interest-free basis. To insist on continuing with the accursed system of interest is, therefore, nothing short of an open revolt against Allah *subḥānahū wa taʿālā* and the benign injunctions of the Holy Qur'ān and the *Sunnah*, which have banned all forms of usury and interest.

Glossary

al-ʿAdl: 'Justice', in its substantive sense; 'just and well-balanced' in its adjectival sense.

al-ʿAfw: Lexically it has the meanings of 'pardon, forgiveness, effacement, and amnesty'; in juridical terms it means 'surplus'.

Aḥādīth (Sing. *Ḥadīth*): In juridical terms, it means 'Prophetic Tradition', i.e. a report that relates the spoken words, deeds and approval of the Holy Prophet (*pbuh*); lexically it means 'modern, novel, recent, speech and chatter'.

Ahl al-Dhimmah: *Al-Dhimmah* lexically means 'protection, care, and custody'. As a legal term it means 'the covenant of protection'. *Ahl al-Dhimmah* are thus the non-Muslim subjects of an Islamic state who enjoy state protection of their lives and properties in return for living as peaceful citizens within rather than as combatants of the state, and also by paying a small token annual capital tax, the *Jizyah*.

Amīr al-Mu'minīn: 'Leader of the Faithful'; historically, the title was used by the caliphs.

al-Amr bil maʿrūf wa al-nahy ʿan al-munkar: 'To enjoin good and forbid evil. This is an individual obligation on every Muslim; collectively, it is also a primary duty of an Islamic state to spread goodness and to prevent vice.

al-Amwāl al-Bāṭinah: 'Hidden assets', i.e. those funds that no government functionary can have access to unless they are declared by the concerned person.

Amwāl al-Fay': Funds raised chiefly through *Jizyah*, the capital tax, and *Kharāj*, the land tax, which are levied on the non-Muslim subjects of the Islamic State (*Ahl al-Dhimmah*/*Dhimmī*s), which historically have been less than *Zakāh*, *Khums*, and *ʿUshr*, the mandatory levies placed on Muslims. *Jizyah and Kharāj* are discretionary taxes that can be waived for *Dhimmī*s.

Amwāl al-Ghanīmah: War gains, including the revenue generated from conquered land.

al-Amwāl al-Ẓāhirah: 'Assets that are open and accessible to state officials', such as bank deposits, property, etc.

Anṣār: Derived from the infinitive *naṣr* meaning 'to help and assist, to become victorious and to triumph', *Anṣār* is the plural of *nāṣir* and means in an historical sense the helpers of the emigrants from Makkah to the Islamic State of Madīnah. These were local Muslims who helped their uprooted brethren-in-faith to settle and start new lives.

Āyāt (Sing. *Āyah*): Lecixically, the word *Āyah* means 'sign, mark, marvel, wonder'. With reference to the Holy Qur'ān, an *Āyah* is a verse, phrase, or line which is rich in meaning and miraculous in expression.

al-ʿĀmilīn (Sing. *al-ʿĀmil*): Those who are charged with the collection of *Zakāh* and *Ṣadaqah*; they may be paid for their services out of *Zakāh* funds.

Bayt al-Māl: The public or national treasury.

al-Buyūʿ (Sing. *Bayʿ*): 'Trade and commerce'; its singular form means 'sale' or 'to sell'.

Ḍāmin: The guarantor, or a person in authority who is answerable for the responsibility that he or she is asked to discharge.

Dār al-Islām: The homeland of Islam and Muslims, which is not defined on an ethnic or racial basis. *Dār* means 'home or habitation'; *al-Islām* means the religion of peace, security, and well-being. Its opposite *Dār al-Ḥarb* means the 'Land of War' or the enemy territory, the territory of forces at war with Islam and Muslims.

Dhimmī: A free non-Muslim subject of an Islamic state.

Dīn: Lexically it means religion, faith, or belief. As an Islamic term it stands for a way of life and a complete code of conduct.

al-Duyūn: 'Debt and credit'; in the singular form *Dayn* it means debt.

Faḥsh: Indecency, obscenity, monstrosity, obscene language.

Faḥshā': Lewdness, abomination, vile deed, criminal act.

Fay' see ***Amwāl al-Fay'***

Fī Sabīlillāh: Lexically it means 'in the way of Allah'; as a Qur'ānic term it denotes every good cause and expenditure in the way of Allah or the means to further the cause of good.

Fuqahā' (Sing. *Faqīh*): Jurists, experts in Islamic jurisprudence.

al-Fuqarā' (Sing. *Faqīr*): The needy and deserving.

al-Furqān: A name and attribute of the Qur'ān. From the root *al-farq*, which means to differentiate, distinguish, and separate, *al-Furqān* means the touchstone by which to differentiate and distinguish right from wrong, good from bad, and virtue from vice.

al-Ghārimīn: Those burdened with debt, from the root *gharm* meaning loss or damage.

Ḥadd (Pl. *Ḥudūd*): lexically it means 'limit, borderline or terminal point'. As a term in Islamic *Sharīʿah*, *Ḥadd* is the fixed punishment stipulated in the Qur'ān for major crimes such as fornication, adultery, theft, robbery, and use of alcoholic drinks and other intoxicants.

Ḥanābilah or ***Ḥanbalīs***: The followers of the Legal School founded by Imām Aḥmad bin Ḥanbal.

Ḥanafiyah or ***al-Aḥnāf***: the followers of the Legal School founded by Imām Abū Ḥanīfah.

Ḥuqūq Allāh: In the singular form, *Ḥaqq* means right or truth. As a legal term, *Ḥuqūq Allāh* are the rights of God which humans as His subjects owe towards Him and for which they are answerable and are liable for either reward or punishment in respect of them.

Ḥuqūq al-ʿIbād: The rights owed by Allah's subjects to each other; these rights are not only moral obligations but may also take on a legal form, which renders a failure to observe them a matter of legal penalty.

ʿIbādah (Pl. *ʿIbādāt*): Lexically it means 'worship'; in Islam, *ʿibādah* is the obligation to turn one's entire life in all its facets into an act of worship and to strive to become a true *ʿAbd* (Pl. *ʿIbād*) or bondsman of Allah, so its meaning is not confined to ritual acts of worship alone.

al-Ibil al-ʿAwāmil: Camels harnessed for the purposes of transportation or agricultural work such as irrigation. *Al-Ibil* means 'camels' and *al-ʿAwāmil* the plural form of *al-ʿĀmil* means 'working'.

Ibn al-Sabīl: Lexically this Qur'ānic phrase means 'the son of the one on the way'; legally, it means the wayfarer or traveller, who is entitled to financial assistance if genuinely in need during his journey, regardless of his general financial status.

Iḥsān: This Qur'ānic term stands for extreme beneficence and doing good to others without expectation of return, appreciation or reward.

Iḥtikār: Lexically, this means 'hoarding'; in Islamic economics, it means purposefully to hold back consumer goods in order to create scarcity of supply to engineer a rise in market prices.

Ijārah: 'Leasing, to let on lease or to rent', from the root *a-j-r* meaning wage, recompense, and fare.

Ijtihād: A legal term that denotes the scholarly re-interpretation of juridical issues according to certain principles laid down by the *Sharīʿah*. The root word *jahd* means effort, attempt, and struggle.

Infāq: 'To spend or disburse', from the root *n-f-q* meaning to sell out or exhaust. The *Sharīʿah* term *Infāq fī Sabīlillāh* means voluntary spending in the Way of Allah, or charity for a good cause.

Isrāf: Intemperance in spending, extravagance.

Jāhilī: The ways of the Days of Ignorance (*Jāhilīyah*), or the pre-Islamic customs and manners of Arabia.

Jihād: A concerted collective struggle for a noble cause.

Jizyah: An annual token capital tax paid by the *Ahl al-Dhimmah* to the state in return for protection; it is charged at a nominal rate which is normally less than the rate of *Zakāh*.

Kafālah: Guaranty, security, surety. *Kafālah Māliyah* means collateral surety.

Kanz: (Pl. *Kunūz*): Lexically it means 'treasure'; as a legal term *kanz* denotes hoarded wealth of gold and silver, etc.

Khāliṣah: Certain kinds of land that have been declared as state property.

Kharāj: Land tax. *Kharājī* is the land on which *Kharāj* is paid.

al-Khilāfah al-Rāshidah: The system of the Caliphate declared by law as being rightly-guided. The term is used as the nomenclature for the system of governance followed by the first four Caliphs of Islam.

Al-Khulafā' al-Rāshidūn (Sing. *al-Khalīfah al-Rāshid*): The Rightly-Guided Caliphs of Islam: Ḥaḍrat Abū Bakr, Ḥaḍrat 'Umar, Ḥaḍrat 'Uthmān, and Ḥaḍrat 'Alī.

Khums: 'One-fifth'; as a legal term it means the mandatory levy on war gains that has to be deposited in the public treasury.

Kunūz see ***Kanz***

al-Māl al-Nāmī: Lexically, it means wealth that is growing; as a legal term, it stands for the asset that is intrinsically amenable to growth or that which can be increased through effort.

al-Masākīn (Sing. *Miskīn*): Those who are afflicted with distress more than the ordinary poor are, but whose self-esteem prevents them from asking for help.

Mawāt: A legal term used to denote wasteland with no owner or whose owner has died and the land has been left unused. It also stands for the flooded land or land that has put out of use by having reverted to wilderness.

Mithqāl: The Arab measure to weigh gold and silver. The Caliph 'Abd al-Malik used it for the first time in 77/696 as the basic measurement by which to standardise his coinage: one *Dīnār* equalled one *Mithqāl*, which was equivalent to 65.5 grains or 4.25 grams; *Mithqāl* thus became synonymous with *Dīnār*. The silver *Dirham* was equal to 7/10 *Mithqāl*. In Egypt, one *Mithqāl* equalled 24 *Qīrāṭ*, from which comes 'carat', the basic modern unit for measuring the weight of gold, silver, and previous stones the world over today. Also from the root *thiql* which means weight or burden.

Mu'allafat al-Qulūb: *Mu'allafat* means to be familiar, intimate and acquainted, and *Qulūb* is the plural of *Qalb* meaning 'heart'. The term thus means 'those whose hearts are to be won over'.

Muḍārabah: A legal term meaning trustee-financing or partnership.

al-Muhājirūn (Sing. *Muhājir*): Emigrants; historically they were the Muslims who left their homes in Makkah to emigrate to Madīnah.

Mujāhid: One who struggles for a noble cause.

Mushārakah: Equity participation on a profit-and-loss-sharing basis, from the root: *sh-r-k* meaning 'to participate, to join'.

Muzāra'ah: Sharecropping contract according to which the landlord and the farmer share the produce equitably between themselves, from the root word *z-r-'* meaning 'to plough, to raise and to grow'.

Niṣāb: Lexically, 'to plant firmly in the ground'; legally it means the minimum amount of valuables (savings, gold, silver, agricultural produce, livestock, etc.) on which *Zakāh* is annually deducted according to the rate prescribed for each category.

al-Qarḍ al-Ḥasan: Lexically a 'benign or goodly loan'; in legal terms, it is an interest-free loan with no stipulated due date. If a person to whom such a loan is extended to fulfil his genuine need is unable to return the amount, then the person or the institution extending the loan is expected to treat it as a charitable donation.

al-Rahn: Mortgage.

Rikāz (Pl. *Arkizah*): Precious minerals or treasure buried in the earth. The infinitive *rakz* means 'to plant or ram into the ground'.

Ṣā': An ancient measure to weigh food grains.

Ṣāḥib al-Niṣāb: A Muslim in possession of the *Zakātable* limit of wealth or assets who is obliged to pay *Zakāh*.

Sīrah: Lexically, the word means 'conduct, demeanour, and way of life'; as an Islamic discipline it stands for the rigorously verified history of the life, times, and achievements of *Sayyidinā Rasūl Allāh (pbuh)*.

Ta'līf al-Qalb: 'To win the hearts of the people'.

Tafaqquh: 'To develop capability and insight into the legal system of Islam'; the infinitive *fiqh* lexically means 'to understand or to comprehend'.

Takāful: The Islamic system of insurance.

Taqlīd: Lexically it means 'to blindly follow and imitate'; in legal terminology, it stands for judicial conformism or the unquestioning adoption of a particular legal school (*madhhab*). Its opposite is *Ijtihād* or nonconformism in legal matters or pursuing the scholarly quest for the correct ruling on any matter in light of the injunctions of the Qur'ān and the *Sunnah*.

Taqwā: Lexically it stands for 'protection of the self from the temptations of vice'; as a Qur'ānic term it means the quality of immense uprightness informed by both love and fear of one's Lord. *Waqi* and *Wiqāyah*, both nouns from the same root, mean protection, safeguard and prevention.

Tasʿir: Price control.

ʿUshr/ʿUshrī: 'One-tenth'; as a legal term it means the mandatory levy on agricultural produce to be deposited in the public treasury.

Wasaq: An ancient measure to weigh food grains.

Wirāthah: Inheritance.

Short Biographies

Abū Bakr al-Jaṣṣāṣ (305/917-370/981)*: Aḥmad bin ʿAlī Abū Bakr al-Rāzī, better known as al-Jaṣṣāṣ, was an eminent scholar of Ḥanafī School of Islamic Jurisprudence. His best known books are *Aḥkām al-Qur'ān*; *Kitāb al-Uṣūl*, a commentary on Imām Muḥammad al-Shaybānī's *Al-Jāmiʿ Al-Kabīr*; and a commentary on Imām al-Ṭaḥāwī's *al-Mukhtaṣar fī al-Fiqh*.

Abū Dāwūd (202/817-275/889): Abū Dāwūd Sulayman bin al-Ashʿath al-Sijistānī was a leading Traditionist (*Muḥaddith*) acknowledged for his *Kitāb al-Sunan*, one of the six cannonical books of Prophetic Traditions. As a collection of *Ṣaḥīḥ* (Trustworthy) *Aḥādīth* (Traditions), its generic title *Sunan* signifies those Traditions that deal with matters ordained, allowed, or forbidden by Islamic Law.

Abū Ḥanīfah al-Nuʿmān bin Thābit, al-Imām al-Aʿẓam, (80/699-150/767): a pioneering theologian, jurist, and founder of the most widely-followed School of Islamic Jurisprudence. His legal thought was marked by a high degree of reasoning and juridical insight. He taught and trained many luminaries of Islamic Law such as Imām Abū Yūsuf, Imām Muḥammad al-Shaybānī, Dāwūd al-Ṭā'ī, and Ḥasan bin Ziyād al-Lu'lū'ī; among Traditionists, his students included ʿAbd Allāh bin al-Mubārak and Imām al-Ṭaḥāwī.

Abū ʿUbayd al-Qāsim bin Sallām (154/770-224/838): Grammarian, jurist and Qur'ān scholar. His *Kitāb al-Amwāl* is the best known of his books dealing with the sources of revenue and areas of public expenditure.

Abū Yūsuf, Imām, (113/731-182/798): Trained by Abū Ḥanīfah, Abū Yūsuf rose to eminence as a scholar, jurist and a pioneer of the Ḥanafī School. He also studied under other eminent jurists such as Imām Mālik bin Anas and Imām al-Layth bin Saʿd. He was appointed the *Qāḍī* (Judge) of Kūfah by the ʿAbbāsid Caliph Hārūn al-Rashīd and was the first *Qāḍī al-Quḍāt* (Chief Justice). *Kitāb al-Kharāj*, among his best known works, deals with important economic and legal subjects, such as public finance, taxation and criminal justice.

Abul Aʿlā Mawdūdī see **Mawdūdī**

---

* Dates are listed as Hijrī/Gregorian.

Abul Ḥasan ʿAlī al-Marghinānī (530/1135-593/1197): Among the greatest jurists of the Ḥanafī School. His much acclaimed *al-Hidāyah* represents the corpus of Ḥanafī Law and forges an organic link with other Schools of Law.

Aḥmad bin Ḥanbal, Imām, (164/780-241/855): Aḥmad bin Muḥammd bin Ḥanbal was a highly regarded religious scholar, Jurist, and Traditionist of Islam, and founder of the Ḥanbalī School of Jurisprudence. He was imprisoned and persecuted during the reign of the ʿAbbāsid Caliphs al-Ma'mūn and al-Muʿtaṣim for his refusal to accept the Muʿtazilah doctrine of the creation of the Qur'ān. His most celebrated work is the *Musnad*, a vast collection of Traditions, classified according to the narrator rather than by subject.

ʿAlī Muttaqī (888/1477-975/1567): ʿAlī bin Ḥusāmuddīn bin Qāḍī Khān of Jaunpur, India. His acclaimed works include *Kanz al-ʿUmmāl fī Sunan al-Aqwāl wa al-Afʿāl,* an edited adaption of *Jāmiʿ al-Kabīr* of al-Suyūṭī, *Manhaj al-ʿUmmāl*, an abridgement of al-Suyūṭī's *al-Jāmiʿ al-Ṣaghīr*, and *al-Fuṣūl,* an annotated commentary of al-Jazarī's *Jāmiʿ al-Uṣūl.*

al-Ālūsī (1217/1802-1270/1854): Abul Thanā' Maḥmūd Shihāb al-Dīn, a descendant of Imāms Ḥasan and Ḥusayn, was Muftī of Baghdad and an outstanding scholar and thinker. His most celebrated work is *Rūḥ al-Maʿānī,* a highly regarded Qur'ān commentary in nine volumes.

Banū al-ʿAbbās: Descendants of the Holy Prophet's uncle ʿAbbās bin ʿAbd al-Muṭṭalib. His descendant Abul ʿAbbās ʿAbd Allāh al-Saffāḥ founded the ʿAbbāsid Dynasty in 132/750 by ousting the Umayyads.

Banū Hāshim: Hāshim was the great-grandfather of the Holy Prophet, and a prominent leader of the tribe of Quraysh whose descendants came to be known as the Banū Hāshim, the tribe of Hāshim, or the Hāshimīs.

Banū al-Naḍīr: a tribe of Jews of Madīnah. For their treachery and their attempted assassination of the Holy Prophet and some of his prominent Companions, a successful campaign was waged to expel them from Madīnah in 4/625.

Banū Umayyah: Descendants of Umayyah, son of ʿAbd al-Shams bin ʿAbd Manāf and a cousin to Hāshim. Muʿāwiyah bin Abī Sufyān, the caliph who succeeded ʿAlī, was his grandson and founder of the Umayyad Dynasty and caliphate.

al-Bayḍāwī (d. c.685/1286): Abul Khayr Nāṣir al-Dīn ʿAbd Allāh bin ʿUmar bin Muḥammad bin ʿAlī was a Shāfiʿī jurist, who rose to the position of *Qāḍī al-Quḍāt* (Chief Justice) of Shīrāz, Persia. He wrote works on law, *ʿilm al-kalām*, Arabic grammar and history. His best known publication is his influential Qur'ān commentary, *Anwār al-Tanzīl wa Asrār al-Ta'wīl*, itself a skilful condensation of al-Zamakhsharī's *Kashshāf*, which corrected the Muʿtazilite views of the original.

al-Bayhaqī (384/994-458/1066): Abū Bakr Aḥmad bin al-Ḥusayn bin ʿAlī bin ʿAbd Allāh al-Bayhaqī was a reputed Traditionist and Shāfiʿī jurist. His best known work is a ten-volume compendium of Traditions, *Kitāb al-Sunan al-Kubrā*; another work *Kitāb al-Mabsuṭ fī Nuṣūṣ al-Shāfiʿī* deals with the principles of jurisprudence (*Uṣūl al-Fiqh*) as enunciated by Imām al-Shāfiʿī.

Bidāyat al-Mujtāhid wa Nihāyat al-Muqtaṣid see **Ibn Rushd**

al-Bukhārī (194/809-256/890): the great Traditionist of the world of Islam, Imām Abū ʿAbd Allāh Muḥammad bin Ismāʿīl bin Ibrāhīm bin al-Mughīrah al-Bukhārī, devoted his life to the sciences of *Ḥadīth* (Tradition). Gifted with an extraordinary memory, he travelled extensively over 16 years to collect *Aḥādīth*, verifying them according to the strictest standards for his collection, *al-Jāmiʿ al-Ṣaḥīḥ*, which has been acknowledged universally as the most authentic book after the Book of Allah.

Dāraquṭnī (306/918-385/995): Abul Ḥasan ʿAlī bin ʿUmar bin Aḥmad bin Mahdī al-Dāraquṭnī was a prominent Traditionist of his day. His *Kitāb al-Sunan* is the best known of his books.

al-Fiqh ʿala al-Madhāhib al-Arbaʿah see **al-Jazīrī**

Ibn ʿAbd al-Barr (368/978-463/1072): Yūsuf bin ʿAbd Allāh bin ʿAbd al-Barr, also known as Abū ʿUmar al-Nawawī al-Qurṭubī, an eminent Traditionist of the Mālikī School. His best-known books include *al-Istīʿāb fī Asmā' al-Aṣḥāb, al-Kāfī fī Madhhab Mālik, al-Maghāzī, al-Tawḥīd limā fī al-Muwaṭṭa' min al-Maʿānī wa al-Asānīd*, and *al-Istidhkār li Madhhab ʿUlamā' al-Amṣār.*

Ibn al-ʿArabī (468/1075-543/1148): Abū Bakr Muḥammad bin ʿAbd Allāh al-Muʿāfirī, an Andalucian judge and jurist of the Mālikī School, who wrote on *Ḥadīth, Fiqh*, Qur'ān sciences, grammar, and history. His well-known works include his *Tafsīr Aḥkām al-Qur'ān, ʿĀriḍat al-Aḥwadī*, a commentary on *Jāmiʿ al-Tirmidhī*; and *al-ʿAwāṣim min al-Qawāṣim*, a heresiographical history of the Shīʿah.

Ibn Ḥazm (384/994-456/1064): Abū Muḥammad ʿAlī bin Aḥmad bin Saʿīd bin Ḥazm was an outstanding Andalucian historian, religious scholar and poet. His well-known works include *Jamharat al-Ansāb* on Arab genealogy, *Kitāb al-Aḥkām fī Uṣūl al-Aḥkām, Ibṭāl al-Qiyās wa al-Ra'y wa al-Istiḥsān wa al-Taqlīd*

Wa al-Ta'līl, Kitāb al-Faṣl fī al-Milal wa al-Ahwā', and *Kitāb al-Nāsikh wa al-Mansūkh.*

Ibn Jarīr (224/838-319/923): Abū Ja'far Muḥammad bin Jarīr al-Ṭabarī was one of the earliest and most prominent Persian historians and commentators of the Holy Qur'ān. His greatest works include his multi-volume *Ta'rīkh al-Rusul wa al-Mulūk,* a universal chronicle up until 302/915 and *Jāmi' al-Bayān fī Ta'wīl al-Qur'ān,* his great Qur'ān exegesis, which noted commentators like Jalāl al-Dīn al-Suyūṭī and al-Baghawī largely relied upon.

Ibn Kathīr (700/1300-774/1373): 'Imād al-Dīn Ismā'īl bin 'Umar bin Kathīr was among the best-known historians and Traditionists of Syria, who was influenced by Ibn Taymīyah. His most important works included his multi-volume history of Islam, *al-Bidāyah wa al-Nihāyah,* his encyclopedia of the first Muslim Traditionists and another of the Companions who had transmitted the Traditions, as well as a vast *Tafsīr.*

Ibn Mājah (209/824-273/887): Abū 'Abd Allāh Muḥammad bin Yazīd bin Mājah al-Raba'ī al-Qazwīnī was a Traditionist whose *Kitāb al-Sunan* is regarded as one of the six canonical collections of Traditions (*al-Ṣiḥāḥ al-Sittah*). His other works include a voluminous *Tafsīr* and a *Ta'rīkh,* that deals with the scholarship of his birthplace Qazwīn.

Ibn Manẓūr (630/1232-711/1311): Abul Faḍl Jamāl al-Dīn Muḥammad bin Mukarram al-Miṣrī al-Khazrajī was a respected literary figure and a prolific writer who is thought to have composed 500 works. His masterpiece, *Lisān al-'Arab,* his Arabic dictionary, established him as a great philologist.

Ibn al-Qayyim Al-Jawzīyah (691/1292-751/1350): Shams al-Dīn Abū Bakr Muḥammad bin Abī Bakr bin Ayyūb al-Zar'ī was the most famous pupil of Ibn Taymīyah. Well versed in the disciplines of his day, he excelled in the Qur'ān exegesis, *Ḥadīth,* and *Uṣūl al-Fiqh.* Among his many famous works are *Zād al-Ma'ād fī Huda Khayr al-'Ibād* and *I'lām al-Muwaqqi'īn.*

Ibn Qudāmah (541/1147-620/1223): Muwaffaq al-Dīn Abū Muḥammad 'Abd Allāh bin Aḥmad bin Muḥammad, al-Ḥanbalī al-Maqdisī, a noted Ḥanbalī jurist, whose *al-Mughnī* is regarded as being among the best books of Islamic jurisprudence, and who was minded to follow the consensus (*Ijmā'*) on issues of legal significance. His other notable works are *al-Muqni'*, *Rawḍat al-Nāẓir*, and *al-'Umdah.*

Ibn Rushd (520/1126-595/1198): Abul Walīd Muḥammad bin Aḥmad bin Muḥammad bin Rushd was an accomplished commentator on Aristotle and Plato, who was well versed in the Qur'ān sciences, jurisprudence, physics, medicine, biology, astronomy, theology and philosophy. He served as the chief court physician in Marrakesh, and later as *Qāḍī* (Judge) of Seville and then of Cordova. His celebrated works include his legal text *Bidāyat al-Mujtahid wa Nihāyat al-Muqtaṣid*, his medical work *al-Kulliyāt* and his reply to Imām Ghazālī's attack on philosophy, *Tahāfut al-Tahāfut.*

Ibn Shihāb al-Zuhrī (c.50/670-124/742): Abū Bakr Muḥammad bin Muslim bin ʿUbayd Allāh bin ʿAbd Allāh bin Shihāb was an early Traditionist during the Umayyad era who was among the pioneers of *ʿIlm al-Ḥadīth* (Science of Prophetic Traditions) and a noted jurist. His collected *Sunan* was copied and sent to different parts of the Caliphate under the orders of the Caliph ʿUmar bin ʿAbd al-ʿAzīz.

Ibn Taymīyah (661/1263-728/1328): Taqī al-Dīn Abul ʿAbbās Aḥmad bin ʿAbd al-Ḥalīm bin ʿAbd al-Salām Ibn Taymiyyah al-Ḥarrānī al-Ḥanbalī was a noted jurist, theologian and logician, who gained noterity for his independence of thought. Yet his celebrated pupils included scholars like Ibn al-Qayyim, Ibn Qudāmah, al-Dhahabī, Ibn Kathīr and many others. He authored some 500 works, the majority of which have survived. Some of his famous works are *Majmūʿ al-Fatāwā al-Kubrā, al-Radd ʿalā al-Manṭiqiyyīn,* and *al-Siyāsah al-Sharʿiyyah.*

al-Istīʿāb see **Ibn ʿAbd Al-Barr**

Jāmiʿ al-Bayān see **Ibn Jarīr**

al-Jāmiʿ al-Ṣaḥīḥ see **al-Bukhārī**

Kanz al-ʿUmmāl see **ʿAlī Muttaqī**

Kitāb al-Kharāj see **Abū Yūsuf**

al-Layth bin Saʿd (94/ 713-175/ 791): Abul Ḥārith Saʿd bin ʿAbd al-Raḥmān al-Fahmī was a great Ṭābiʿī Traditionist of Persian origin. He also is ranked among the leading early authorities in Islamic jurisprudence alongside Imām Abū Ḥanīfah, Sufyān al-Thawrī, Imām Mālik bin Anas and Ibn Abī Laylah, Ibn Jurayḥ, and al-Awzāʿī.

Lisān al-ʿArab see **Ibn Manẓūr**

Mālik bin Anas, al-Imām, (c.93/711-179/796): Abū ʿAbd Allāh Mālik bin Anas bin Mālik bin ʿAlī bin ʿĀmr bin al-Ḥārith al-Aṣbaḥī is counted as being among the first great Traditionists and Jurists, and is seen as the founder of the Mālikī School of Law. His best-known work *al-Muwaṭṭa'* is held to be the earliest surviving major compendium of Islamic jurisprudence, of which two complete recensions survive, one of which is by Imām Muḥammad bin al-Ḥasan al-Shaybānī.

Mawdūdī (1321/1903-1399/1979): Born in Aurangabad, India, Sayyid Abul Aʿlā Mawdūdī is considered as being one of the leading scholars and religious revivalists of the twentieth century. In 1927, his first major work *al-Jihād fī al-Islām* (*War and Peace in Islam*) was published. The book established him at once as a writer of standing at just the age of 27. In 1933, Mawdūdī founded a monthly journal *Tarjumān al-Qur'ān* which was to serve as the main platform for his ideas. In Lahore in 1941 he founded what was to become a major revivalist movement, the Jamāʿat-i-Islāmī, which aimed to challenge the socio-political order of the day and to uphold the cause of Islam, and which he led until 1972. After the creation of Pakistan in 1947, he was a leading figure in getting the 22-Point Objectives Resolution of 1951 to be adopted by the country's religious scholars, which defined the fundamental principles of the Islamic State, and which eventually came to form part of the Constitution of the Islamic Republic of Pakistan. Mawdūdī's struggle often saw him in and out of jail between 1948 and 1964, but this experience left him undetered.

Sayyid Mawdūdī's intellectual and ideological contribution was immense. He wrote some 80 books and tracts which covered a wide variety of subjects, including *Tafsīr, Sīrah*, law, history, politics, economics, and the social sciences. His *magnum opus* is his Qur'ān commentary *Tafhīm al-Qur'ān* (1974-1972) in six volumes. Among his other notable works are *Pardah/Purdah and Status of Women in Islam* (1939/1972); *Islām aur Ḍabṭ-i-Wilādat/Birth Control: Its Social, Political, Economic, Moral and Religious Aspects* (1951/1968); *Islāmī Riyāsat/Islamic Law and Constitution* (1952/1960); *Tajdīd-i-Iḥyā'-i-Dīn/A Short History of the Revivalist Movement in Islam* (1952/1963); *Shahādat-i-Ḥaqq/ Witness Unto Mankind* (1957/1986); *Islam aur ʿAdl-i-Ijtimāʿī* (Islam and Social Justice) (1963); *Khilāfat wa Mulūkiyat* (Caliphate and Monarchy) (1967); and *Qur'ān kī Chār Bunyādī Iṣṭilāhen: Ilāh, Rabb, ʿIbādāt, Dīn/Four Key Concepts of the Qur'ān* (1969/2006). Some of his works on Islamic economics include *Sūd* (Interest) (1948-1952); *Mas'alah-i-Milkīyat-i-Zamīn* (The Question of Land Ownership) (1950); and *Maʿāshīyāt-i-Islām/First Principles of Islamic Economics* (1970/2011). For an overview of his life and thought as well as for a comprehensive bibliography of Mawdūdī's writings, the collection of Khurshid Ahmad and Zafar Ishaq Ansari (eds.) *Islamic Perspectives: Studies in Honour of Sayyid Abul Aʿla Mawdudi* (Leicester, 1980) may be consulted.

al-Mughnī see **Ibn Qudāmah**

Muslim, Imām, (206/821-261/875): Abul Ḥusayn Muslim bin al-Ḥajjāj bin Muslim al-Qushayrī was an emiment Traditionist who compiled *al-Ṣaḥīḥ*, which stands as only second in rank to the work of Imām al-Bukhārī. Many eminent commentaries have been written on his collection, among the most popular of which has been that of Imām al-Nawawī. Among Imām Muslim's other works are *al-Musnad al-Kabīr, al-Jāmiʿ al-Kabīr, Kitāb al-ʿIlal, Kitāb al-Ṭabaqāt, Kitāb Awhām al-Muḥaddithīn.*

Muḥummad al-Shaybānī, Imām, (132/750-189/805): Abū ʿAbd Allāh Muḥummad bin al-Ḥasan bin Farqad was a great jurist of the Ḥanafī School, third in eminence only to Imām Abū Yūsuf and Imām Abū Ḥanīfah. His greatest contribution was to preserve and promote the viewpoints of the Ḥanafī viewpoint in works like *Kitāb al-Aṣl, Kitāb al-Jāmiʿ al-Kabīr*, and *Kitāb al-Jāmiʿ al-Ṣaghīr.*

al-Muwaṭṭa' see **Mālik bin Anas**

al-Nasā'ī (215/830-303/915): He is ʿAbd al-Raḥmān Aḥmad bin ʿAlī bin Shuʿayb bin Baḥr bin Sinān, a highly respected Traditionist and author of *al-Sunan*, one of the six canonical collections of *Aḥādīth.*

Nayl al-Awṭār see **al-Shawkānī**

al-Rāzī, Imām, (543/1149-606/1209): Abū ʿAbd Allāh Muḥmmad Fakhr al-Dīn bin Ḍiyā' al-Dīn Abul Qāsim ʿUmar bin al-Ḥusayn was a highly celebrated religious scholar, Qur'ān exegete and scholastic theologian. His works are huge in number and are encyclopaedic in nature, and address fields such as Qur'ān studies, jurisprudence, history, dogmatics (*Uṣūl al-Dīn*), philosophy and rhetoric. Among his works are his exegesis *Mafātīḥ al-Ghayb*, a treatise on the Divine Names, *Lawāmiʿ al-Bayyināt fī al-Asmā'ī wa al-Ṣifāt*, and *al-Muʿallim fī Uṣūl al-Dīn*, which deals with dogmatics, the methodology of law, jurisprudence, and the rules of controversy and dialectics.

al-Shāfiʿī, Imām, (150/767-204/820): Abū ʿAbd Allāh Muḥammad bin Idrīs, bin al-ʿAbbās bin ʿUthmān bin Shāfiʿī was a major jurist in the history of Islam, and founder of the Shāfiʿī School of Law, the second largest in Sunnī Islam. He is regarded as the central pioneer in the establishment of *Uṣūl al-Fiqh* as an independent discipline, which he sets out in his treatise *al-Risālah.* In his magnum opus *Kitāb al-Umm* al-Shāfiʿī sets out to apply the principles that he had elucidated in *al-Risālah* across a wide range of legal issues, and, on the basis of his rigorous use of textual evidences, he also considered to be a Traditionist.

al-Shawkānī (1173/1760-1255/1839): Muḥammad bin ʿAlī bin Muḥammad bin ʿAbd Allāh al-Shawkānī was a noted Yemeni jurist and reformer, who rejected his *Zaydī Shīʿah* upbrining to adopt a Sunnī reformist position. Some of his well-known works include *Tafsīr Fatḥ al-Qadīr, Nayl al-Awṭār*, and *Irshād al-Fūḥūl*, a book on *Uṣūl al-Fiqh.*

Sufyān al-Thawrī (96/715-161/778): Abū ʿAbd Allāh Sufyān bin Saʿīd bin Masrūq al-Thawrī al-Kūfī was an early Traditionist, Qur'ān exegete, famed ascetic, and jurist and founder of the Thawrīyyah School of Law in Kūfah. Surviving in fragmentary form, his works include *al-Jāmiʿ al-Kabīr* and *al-Jāmiʿ al-Ṣaghīr*, two *Ḥadīth* collections; *Kitāb al-Farā'iḍ* on inheritance law; *Tafsīr al-Qur'ān al-Kabīr*; and *al-Iʿtiqād*, a collection of religious treatises.

al-Ṭabarānī (260/873-360/971): Abul Qāsim Sulaymān bin Ayyūb bin Muṭayyir al-Ṭabarānī was one of the most important Traditionists of his age. He is known especially for his three works on *Ḥadīth*: *al-Muʿjam al-Kabīr ʿalā Asmā' al-Ṣaḥābah*, *al-Muʿjam al-Awsaṭ fī Aḥādīth al-Afrād wa al-Gharā'ib*, and *al-Muʿjam al-Ṣaghīr*.

al-Ṭabarī see **Ibn Jarīr**

Tarjumān al-Qur'ān see **Mawdūdī**

al-Tirmidhī (210/823-297/892): Abū ʿĪsā Muḥammad bin ʿĪsā bin Sawrah was a great Traditionist and author of one of the six canonical books of Tradition, *al-Jāmiʿ al-Ṣaḥīḥ*, and was a prominent pupil of Imām al-Bukhārī. His *al-Jāmiʿ* is commonly ranked third in order of precedence after *al-Ṣaḥīḥayn* of al-Bukhārī and Muslim.

ʿUmar bin ʿAbd ʿAzīz (60/680-101/720): ʿUmar bin ʿAbd ʿAzīz bin Marwān bin al-Ḥakam, fifth Caliph of the Marwānid branch of the Umayyad Dynasty, who reigned briefly between 99/717 and 101/720, and is remembered his nobility and piety, as well as for his accomplishments as the ruler of an expansive and prosperous Caliphate. He is often regarded as the fifth Rightly-Guided Caliph after *al-Khulafā' al-Rāshidūn*.

Zād al-Maʿād see **Ibn al-Qayyim**

al-Zamakhsharī (467/1075-538/1144): Abul Qāsim Muḥammad bin ʿUmar al-Zamakhsharī excelled in the fields of linguistics, philology, lexicography, and exegesis. His most important work is *al-Kashshāf ʿan Ḥaqā'iq al-Tanzīl* (528/1134), an exegesis that highlighted the linguistic excellence of the Qur'ān and its miraculous diction and style. The work has been held in high esteem in Sunnī circles despite his Muʿtazilite leanings. Other works include *Kitāb al-Mufaṣṣal fī al-Naḥw*, *Asās al-Balāghah*, and the bi-lingual Arabic-Persian dictionary *Muqaddimat al-Adab*.

Index

Abū ʿUbayd, 55n, 123-6, 132-3, 135, 141, 205
Abū Bakr, 133-4, 140-1
Abū Bakr al-Jaṣṣāṣ, 146
Abū Ḥanīfah al-Nuʿmān, Imām, 56n, 131, 183, 199, 202, 207, 209, 211
Abū Yūsuf, Imām, 123, 125, 128, 131-6, 143, 200, 202
Abul Aʿlā Mawdūdī *see* Mawdūdī
ʿAdl, 103-4, 239
ʿAfw, 219
Aḥkām al-Qur'ān (of Abū Bakr al-Jaṣṣāṣ), 146
Ahl al-Dhimmah, 54n, 125
Aḥmad bin Ḥanbal, Imām, 131, 211
ʿAlī bin Abī Ṭālib, 127, 210, 213
Amānah, 183, 186
ʿĀmil, 200, 203, 215
Amīn, 183
Amr bi'l maʿrūf wa'l-nahy ʿan al-munkar, 263
Al-Amwāl al-Bāṭinah, 212, 217
Amwāl al-Ghanīmah, 49-50, 56n
Al-Amwāl al-Ẓāhirah, 212, 217

Baksheesh, 134
Banking, 177, 180-1, 183-6, 208-9, 212, 269, 271
Bayʿ, 145-8; also *see* Trade
Bayt al-Māl, 20-2, 49, 76, 150, 178, 186, 216, 220, 242
Bukhl, 108, 112

Capital, 11-13, 22, 27, 37, 54-6nn, 87, 91, 98-100, 119, 139-40, 145-7, 152-3, 155-6, 160-6, 170, 174-7, 182-6, 195, 230-2, 237, 249, 251, 254, 271; and *Zakāh* on, 96, 210, 223, 225-6; worship of, 11-10, 148, 164, 266
Capitalism, 15, 19-21, 61-80, 83, 86, 90, 97, 150, 153-4, 161-3, 165-6, 244-8, 258n, 259, 265-7
Charity *see Infāq, Ṣadaqah, Zakāh*
Communism, 15-17, 97, 106, 119, 150, 173, 231-2, 237-8, 246-8, 266

Dār al-Islām, 206
Ḍāmin, 151
Dhimmah, 54n, 125-8
Dīnār, 198, 226
Dirham, 198, 203, 214, 226

Faḥshā', 105
Fascism, 17, 22
Fay', 54-6nn, 115, 219
Feudalism, 15, 90, 119, 134-6, 140, 247-8, 250
Fi'l-Riqāb, 201, 215
Al-Fiqh ʿalā al-Madhāhib al-Arbaʿah, 205, 209
Fraud, 62-3
Fuqahā', 35, 261
Al-Fuqarā', 199-200, 203, 215

Al-Ghārimūn, 71, 201, 215

Ḥadd, 261-2
Ḥadīth, 35, 132, 140, 200, 203, 205, 207-8, 211, 230n, 269
Ḥajj, 43, 149

Ḥalāl, 26, 33, 239; earnings, 18, 34, 61, 85, 92, 98, 107-8, 240, 258; spending, 109, 111, 249; trade, 148
Ḥanābilah, 56n, 211
Ḥanafiyah, 56n, 197, 210-11
Ḥarām, 26, 85, 239, 253, 258, 263, 269; earnings, 18, 34-8, 61, 92, 98, 107, 240; interest/usury, 100, 148, 174, 249, 270; spending, 107, 109, 111
Hibah, 240
Hundīs, 180
Ḥuqūq al-ʿIbād, 4n, 95

ʿIbādah, 57, 89, 221; *Zakāh* as, 96, 219, 228
Al-Ibil al-ʿAwāmil, 225
Ibn Ḥazm, 207
Ibn Jarīr, 146
Ibn Qudāmah, 204, 211
Ibn al-Sabīl, 202-4, 215
Iḥtikār, 94
Ijtihād, 100-1, 173, 261, 264
Infāq fī Sabīlillāh, 45, 96, 108, 192; *Fī Sabīlillāh*, 67, 74, 201, 215-6, 218
Inheritance *see Wirāthah*
Inṣāf, 103
Insurance, 20-1, 187-8, 210, 251-5
Interest *see Ribā*
Isrāf, 108, 112

Jāhilīyah, 145-6, 266
Jihād, 110, 167, 201, 215, 268
Jizyah, 54n, 56n, 115, 125-6, 264
Justice, 16, 18, 90, 92-3, 97-9, 101, 103-4, 122, 136, 150, 159, 246, 248-9, 262; economic, 57, 59, 64n, 112-15, 141-2; social, 9, 81-2, 85-6, 89, 230-43, 245

Kafālah, 151
Kanz, 199, 207
Kanz al-ʿUmmāl (of ʿAlī Muttaqī), 132-3
Kasb, 240
Kharāj, 54n, 56, 97, 115, 125-6, 128, 133
Khāliṣah, 129, 132-3, 135
Al-Khulafāʾ al-Rāshidūn, 59, 122, 124-6, 132, 136, 203, 211, 213, 219
Khums, 114-15, 181, 210-11
Kitāb al-Amwāl (of Abū ʿUbayd), 123-6, 127-9nn, 132-3, 135, 141, 205, 208, 212-13, 217, 224
Kitāb al-Kharāj (of Abū Yūsuf), 123, 125, 127n, 128, 131-6
Kunūz, 226-8

Land, 119-143; categories of, 122-9; and *Muzāraʿah*, 98-9, 141-2; confiscation/distribution of land by the state, 55n, 132-6, 140-1, 250; ownership of, 8, 30, 91, 119-22, 129-32, 136-40; tax on, 54-7nn, 76-7, 154n, 210; wasteland, 83-4; *Zakāh* on, 48, 197, 213
Layth bin Saʿd, 212, 224

Madīnah, 55n, 123-4, 212, 262
Mahājan, 270
Majlis al-Shūrā, 55n
Makkah, 124, 126, 129n, 149
Al-Māl al-Nāmī, 212
Al-Masākīn, 200, 215
Masʾala-i-Milkīyat-i-Zamīn (by Mawdūdī), 119n, 154n
Mawāt, 128-9, 132, 135
Mawdūdī, 33n, 54n, 81n, 87n, 189n, 230n, 244n, 252n, 255n, 258n
Mithqāl, 214, 227
Miskīn, 200, 203
Money, 18-20, 39, 41-2, 67-73, 78-80
Muʾallafat al-Qulūb, 201, 215
Muʿāmalāt, 221
Muḍārabah, 91, 98, 139-40, 186, 225-6, 252
Al-Mughnī (by Ibn Qudāmah), 204, 211
Muḥārabah, 12
Munkar, 105

Mushārakah, 91, 139-40, 154n, 183, 225-6, 251
Muzāraʿah, 98, 138-41, 154n, 250

Nayl al-Awṭār (by al-Shawkānī), 204
Niṣāb, 48, 198, 203-4, 206-7, 209-11, 213-14, 220-3, 226-9, 241; *Ṣāḥib al-Niṣāb*, 204-6, 215, 222-4

Price controls, 255-7
Profit and loss sharing *see Mushārakah*
Al-Qarḍ al-Ḥasan, 167-8, 177, 181, 192, 216

Qur'ān, 58-9

Rabwah, 144
Al-Rahn, 155
Rasā'il-wa-Masā'il (by Mawdūdī), 144n,
al-Rāzī, Imām Fakhr al-Dīn, 146
Ribā, 144-88, 265; and banking, 184-6; and capitalism, 11, 14, 19, 75; and compensation, 150-8; and distributive justice, 114, 240; and economic growth, 69-73, 93, 100-1, 171-7; and insurance, 252-4; and loans, 177-84, 187-8, 216; and meaning of, 144-6; and prohibition of, 26, 37-8, 54n, 66, 85, 148-50, 249, 269-72; and trade and commerce, 146-8; in pre-Islamic Arabia, 146
Rikāz, 211, 213-14
Rizq, 107

Ṣāʿ, 263
Ṣadaqah, 45, 48, 54n, 70, 77, 96, 99, 120-1, 139, 157, 168, 170, 172, 178, 192, 200, 202, 270
Ṣadaqat al-Fiṭr, 263-4
Ṣāḥib al-Niṣāb see Niṣāb
Sharīʿah, 18, 21-2, 192, 221, 239; and codification of law, 242, 258-72; and distribution of wealth, 92, 240-1, 250; and ethics of spending wealth, 108; and financing, 183; and general accessibility to nature's bounties, 83; and insurance, 252-4; and interest (*Ribā*), 144n, 154n, 269-70; and limits of the free economy, 85, 109, 242; and livelihoods, 35; and rights of kin, 104; and rights of ownership, 83-4, 122-3, 134-6, 138-40, 142, 242, 250; and spirit of competition, 84; and price controls, 255-7; and taxation, 97, 229; and *Zakāh*, 189, 199, 202, 204, 209, 214, 227-8
Shuḥḥa al-Nafs, 108
Sūd (by Mawdūdī), 100, 144n, 184, 188, 258
Sufyān al-Thawrī, 207, 211

Tabdhīr, 108
Tafhīm al-Qur'ān (by Mawdūdī), 33n, 54n, 56-7n, 64-5nn, 68n, 144n, 234n
Takāful, 188, 252
Ta'līf al-Qalb, 201, 216
Tarjumān al-Qur'ān (periodical), 140-1nn, 187, 204, 222n, 224, 225-6nn, 228-9nn, 255n
Tasʿīr, 255
Taxation, 182; capital taxes, 54n, 115, 125-8, 264; land taxes, 54-5n, 97, 115, 124-8; state taxes, 54n, 216n, 219-20, 229; and *Zakāh*, 47, 96, 218-20, 222-3, 228-9; on imports and exports, 22, 211
Tola, 198, 214, 226-7
Trade, 8, 22, 69-70, 85-6, 99, 113, 125, 156, 160, 162, 176-7, 242, 251, 265; and banking, 184-6; difference between *Ribā* and, 145-8, 164-6

ʿUlamā', 202
ʿUmar, 55n, 104, 110-11, 125-9, 131-5, 141, 198-9, 207, 211, 216, 261
ʿUmar bin ʿAbd al-ʿAzīz, 132, 211-12
Umayyads, 212

Usury *see Ribā*
'Uthmān bin 'Affān, 132-3
Al-'Ushr, 85-6, 114-15, 123-4, 126, 128, 210

Walī, 206
Al-Waqf, 76n, 219, 270
Wasaq, 214
Wealth, 19, 26, 145, 249; accumulation of, 14, 19-20, 38-9, 51, 59, 67, 148, 161, 164-5, 175-6, 250, 258-9; circulation of, 20-22, 54n, 78, 114; creation of, 15, 169; desire for, 11; distribution of, 12, 29-30, 52, 76, 79, 92-4, 238, 240-1; spending of, 28, 39-42, 44, 57, 69-73, 107-11, 249; unlawful use of, 38; *Zakāh* on, 48-9, 73-6, 189-229
Wirāthah, 8, 21, 50-2, 54n, 76, 84, 97-8, 114, 123, 128, 136, 138, 140, 217, 221, 240, 250, 252-4

Zād al-Ma'ād (by Ibn al-Qayyim), 124
Zakāh, 73-5; 96-7, 189-229; and social welfare, 99; and tax, 228-9; categories of, 189-203; collection of, 48; distribution of, 50